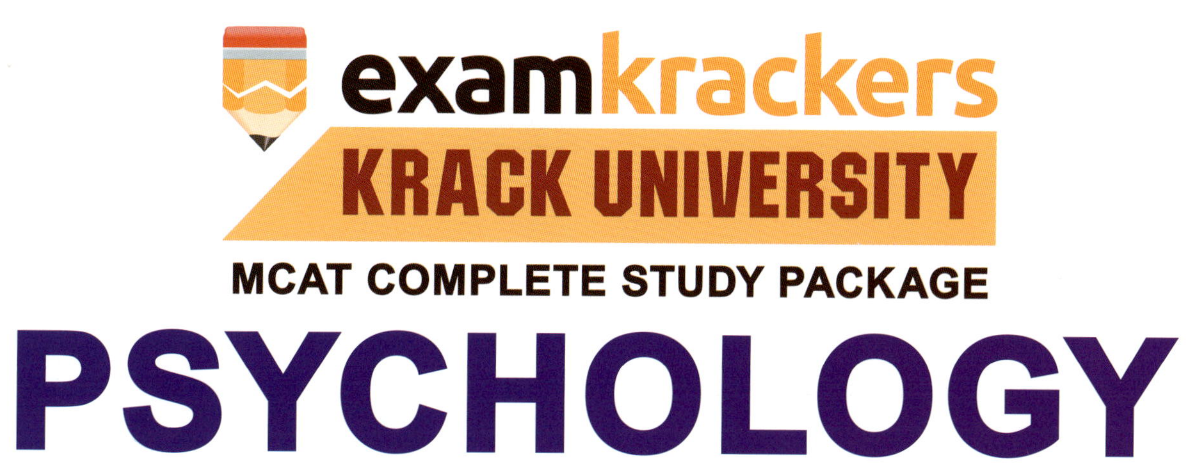

MCAT COMPLETE STUDY PACKAGE

PSYCHOLOGY

KrackU Edition 1

Published in the United States of America by Osote Publishing, New Jersey.

ISBN 978-1-951127-24-4 (Volume 4)
ISBN 978-1-893858-99-2 (7 Volume Set)

Examkrackers KRACKU Edition 1

To purchase additional copies of this book or the rest of the 7 volume set,
call 859-305-6568 or fax orders to 859-305-6458.
examkrackers.com

Printed and bound in China

Acknowledgements

Examkrackers and Jonathan Orsay would like to acknowledge all those who contributed to this book and the Krack University project. In no particular order they include administrators Silvia Orsay and Dustin Suddeth; artists Steve Edwards, Marissa Dehler, Chris Thomas, and Jen Manell; marketers Julianna Orsay, Averie Perez; content developers Cole Niebuhr, Ashleigh Louis, Mike Muzinich, Mike Moore, Zain Chaudry, Anna Haywar d, Ava Lovato, Wanyan Ma, Angela McGaugh, Michael Muzinich, Jay Patel, Teebro Rahman, Ramin Rajaii, Jacob Burton, Elizabeth Osifalujo, Kaitlyn Barkley, Anthony Cardillo, Mayer Chalom, Amit Chaudhari, Saad Chaudry, Steven Chen, Daniel Eichorn, Shelby Faulconer, Jacob Fry, Michael Hollis, Sunmee Huh, Daniel Kim, Riley Larkin, Eunice Lee, Ari Marin, Allison Morris, Victor Pinto, Haroon Riyaz, Christopher Schwartz, Anthony Seitz, Rose Trotta, Rebecca Zeng, Clare Westerman, Taylor Duffy, Kaitlin Shinn, Ritwik Bhatia, Audrey Stephanie Maghiro, Mukti Patel, Arthur Cleroux, Kelly Kirkpatrick, Ari Marine, Emily Wenzel, Nipun Velupally, Tyler Culpepper, Nikola Srnic, Ashleigh Louis, Averie Perez, and Cole Niebuhr.

This Book Includes Online Exams!

Your purchase of this book gives you access to online practice mini-MCAT exams at **examkrackers.com**.

Start your Krack University Free Trial!

This Examkrackers MCAT Complete Study Package book is a powerful self-study tool that becomes even more effective when you pair it with Examkrackers' innovative new software program Krack University.

Try Krack U for free at **examkrackers.com**.

What's in This Book

The Examkrackers MCAT Complete Study Package covers all the science concepts tested by the MCAT and slightly more. It contains slightly more because much of what makes the MCAT difficult is the context in which the basic science is presented. That context is the 'slightly more' part. One reason that Examkrackers books are more effective at raising your MCAT score is because they present the concepts simply at first, so that you may understand them well, and then present background science, so that you may recognize the concepts in the more complicated context in which they are presented on the real MCAT.

Hopefully, you will find the content in these books presented quite differently than it is presented in other prep books. Most of the content of the Examkrackers MCAT Complete Study Package was written by Jonathan Orsay, who has decades of experience teaching and writing about MCAT preparation. Unlike the teams of students that write most prep books, Orsay has taken, not just the AAMC published exams that resemble the MCAT, but many real MCATs. Orsay was devoted to studying specifically MCAT before most contributors to other prep books were even born. It is likely that no one in the entire country, including writers of the real MCAT, has as much experience in MCAT as Jon Orsay.

How to Use This Book

Read each chapter three times:

1. Your first pass through each chapter should be quick, light, and enjoyable.
2. Your second read should be a deep, careful study. After the second read, take the 30-minute online MCAT practice exam at examkrackers.com.
    - If you attend Examkrackers Live-Online class, complete your second reading of each chapter before you attend that chapter's online class meeting. If you attend Krack University, finish your second reading of a chapter before watching that chapter's video.
    - If you attend Examkrackers Live-Online class or if you attend Krack University, review your exam stats with one of our free online tutors.
3. Use your third reading to focus on weak areas and improve your performance.

We recommend that you use this book in conjunction with the AAMC materials at AAMC.org.

Study diligently, trust this book to guide you, and you will reach your MCAT goals.

Table of Contents

PSY

Sensation and Perception 1

1.1 Sensation Versus Perception

Sensory systems collect information from the real world, and the brain translates that information into a perception of reality. **Sensation** is the collection of the information, and **perception** is how the individual organizes and interprets that information. More technically, sensation is the conversion of physical stimuli from the environment into electrochemical signals in the body, while perception is the interpretation of these electrochemical signals into a functional representation of the environment.

Sensation vs. Perception

Perception varies from person to person based upon factors such as memory, emotions, and expectations. The interpretation of perception requires assumptions that are not always accurate. In other words, the brain makes inferences (educated guesses) about reality stitching together current sensations with memories of similar sensations and experiences.

SENSATION is real, while PERCEPTION is an interpretation of reality and is highly individualized.

Psychophysics attempts to quantify the relationship between sensation and perception. A psychophysical experiment has three important elements.

1. Simple responses by the subject
2. Extensive data collection from each subject
3. Precise manipulation of experimental stimuli

Psychophysics is quantitative. Psychophysics attempts to use numbers to scientifically explain the connection between sensation and perception.

1.2 Top-Down/Bottom-Up Processing

Human sensory systems provide too many stimuli to be processed efficiently by the brain. Even if the brain could process the stimuli, the information collected would provide an ambiguous picture of reality. That's because, by itself, a photon striking the retina doesn't contain the information about the distance it has traveled. By itself, an air molecule striking the eardrum does not contain information about the direction from which it came. Together, all the molecules and photons interacting with the body's sensory systems do not contain exact information about the environment. The brain must make inferences about reality.

In **top-down processing**, prior knowledge influences perception — context and experience shape understanding. By using familiar contextual clues to fill gaps in the information, top-down processing allows the environmental stimuli to be filtered. It is a processing shortcut.

Savvy business Salty views the world top-down from high in his penthouse. He relies on his vast business experience to make judgments.

Down below, Hippie, surfer Salty feels the waves in his soul and just rides them to wherever they take him. He is a bottom-up processor.

An example of top-down processing is pattern recognition, such as perceiving shapes where they do not exist, reading words with missing letters, and even relying on how an old mobile phone worked in order to navigate a new mobile phone.

Two Examples of Top-down Processing

Because top-down processing replaces real information with preconceived notions, it is subject to bias and misinterpretation.

In **bottom-up processing,** perception is based on new stimuli from one's current external environment and is not shaped by context or previous experiences. Bottom-up processing is data-driven and happens in real time. If you were to rely upon bottom-up processing to appreciate how a car's steering wheel works, you would have to closely inspect the entire mechanism from the steering wheel down to the tires, or you would have to actually drive the car and feel it turn as you turned the wheel.

Neither type of processing is sufficient on its own. Without top-down processing, it would be difficult to organize the crude information provided by sensation into a useful model—a new identification pathway would be required for each new stimulus. However, without bottom-up processing, top-down processing would operate in a vacuum without moment-to-moment input from one's surroundings.

1.3 Perceptual Organization

Vision

In terms of vision, sensation occurs when electromagnetic waves strike the back of the inner eye. This type of information transfer is neither perfect nor complete, so the brain must make inferences when organizing the information. Certain visual cues guide this process, which is called **perceptual organization**.

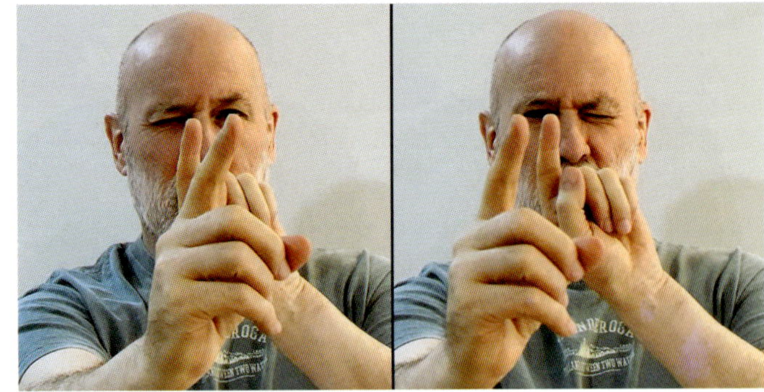

Retinal Disparity–Binocular Method of Depth Perception

A single eye cannot discern the distance traveled by light waves. Thus, a single eye gathers a single flat image. The two eyes in a human head have slightly different vantage points from which to collect light waves. The resulting disparity between the two images is called **retinal disparity**. The brain subconsciously compares these two images using **parallax** to reveal differences between the distance of different objects. Due to parallax, a more distant object will appear further to the right from a rightward vantage point. Try lining up your fingers and closing one eye. The more distant finger will appear more to the right when viewed with just your right eye and more to the left when viewed with just the left eye. Your brain evaluates the distances of the two fingers by comparing the left-eye and right-eye images.

Additionally, in order to focus on a single object in front of a human, the eyes must turn slightly towards each other in a cross-eyed fashion known as **convergence**. The brain's visual cortex associates greater convergence with a nearer object.

Convergence—Binocular Method of Depth Perception

Convergence and retinal disparity are **binocular cues,** where the eyes work together to provide **depth perception**.

There are also visual cues that require only one eye. These are called **monocular cues**. Relative size, relative height, interposition (overlap), shading and contour, and motion parallax are monocular cues.

The first four cues are said to be based upon **form**. Form refers to the visual appearance of elements that the brain combines to create the perception of an object. Those elements include the region of space around an object. The object in this context becomes associated with a region of space, creating the perception of depth or distance.

Monocular cues based upon **form** associate an object with the space around it, creating the perception of distance or depth.

Relative size is a monocular cue based upon form. Relative size makes a larger object appear to be closer when compared to a smaller object at the same distance. The smaller ball in the diagram appears to be farther away than the larger balls for no other reason than it is smaller.

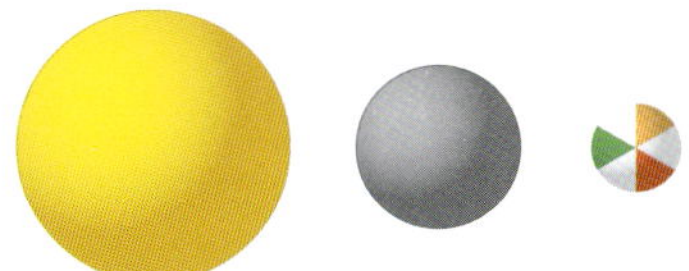

Size—Monocular Cue of Form

The monocular cue of **relative height** makes objects higher in our field of view appear to be more distant.

Height—Monocular Cue of Form

Overlap (or interposition) makes one object appear nearer than another because the nearer object in front of a more distant object will block the light reflecting off the distant object from reaching our eyes. Our brain perceives an object blocking out light from another object as closer.

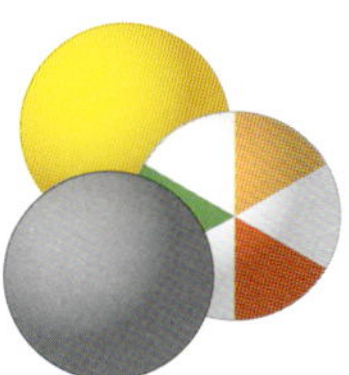

Overlap—Monocular Cue of Form

Shading and contour are monocular cues that create a perception of position and shape. The shading on the top of the circle makes it appear to recede into the screen. The shading on the bottom of the circle makes it appear to extend from the page.

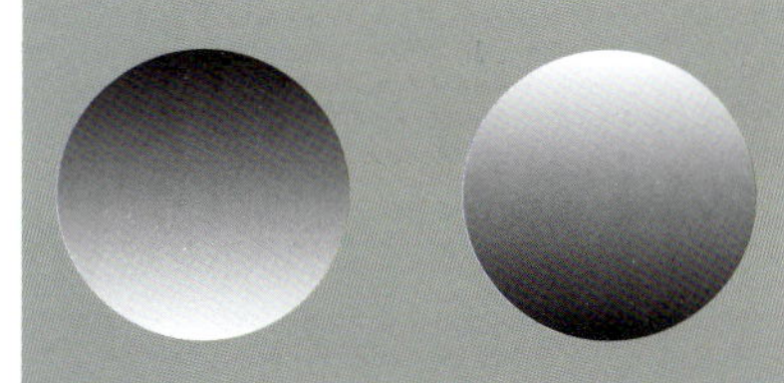

Shading and Contour—Monocular Cue of Form

Motion parallax is a monocular cue based upon motion. Motion parallax reveals distance through relative motion. As we move past objects, more distant objects appear to move more slowly than closer objects. For example, to a passenger in a moving car, the trees along the road will appear to pass by more quickly than the distant mountains. The beach ball below appears to be closer because it is moving faster. To visualize this, ask yourself which ball would pass in front if they were to continue and overlap.

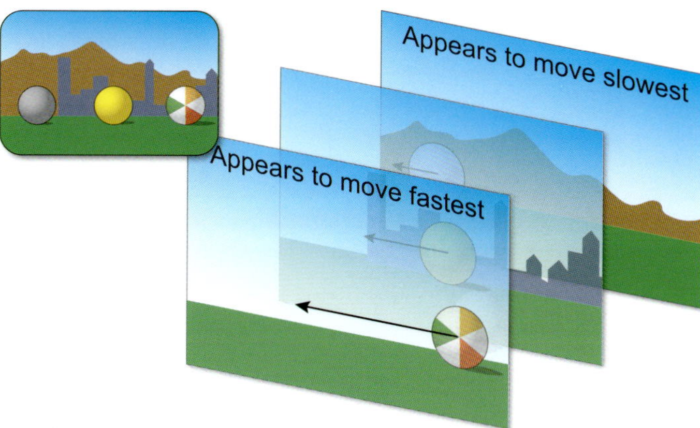

Depth perception requiring **two eyes** (binocular cues) includes:

1. Retinal disparity (a type of parallax)
2. Convergence

Depth perception requiring only **one eye** (monocular cues) includes:

1. Relative size
2. Relative height
3. Overlap (interposition)
4. Shading and contour
5. Motion parallax

Retinal Disparity

Convergence

Perceptual Organization: Binocular Cues

You have probably known since an early age that we have five senses: vision, hearing (audition), smell (olfaction), taste (gustation), and touch (somatosensation). It turns out that this notion of five senses is oversimplified. We also have sensory systems that provide information about balance (the vestibular sense), body position and movement (proprioception and kinesthesia), pain (nociception), and temperature (thermoception).

Relative Size

Overlap (Interposition)

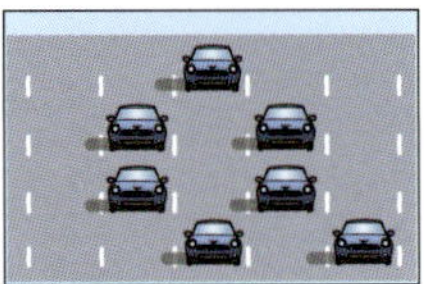
Relative Height

Motion Parallax

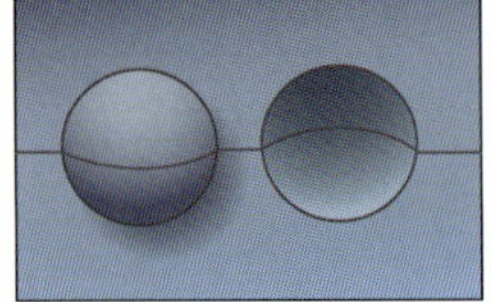
Shading and Contour

Perceptual Organization: Monocular Cues

People tend to assume that the size, color, and shape of things remain constant, so much so that some convincing illusions can result. This phenomenon is called **subjective constancy**.

> **Subjective constancy** means we tend to perceive things the way we are accustomed to thinking about them.

Size constancy is the perception that an object has a fixed size, regardless of the size of its image on the retina. Looking down long straight railroad tracks, the tracks appear to converge. The distance between the tracks far off is smaller in the image on our retina than the distance between the tracks nearby. Nevertheless, our experience tells us that the distance between the tracks remains constant, so we perceive it as such. This is size constancy. Looking at the illusion in the box below, our brain perceives that, like railroad tracks, the lines are parallel and the distance between them remains constant. The monocular cue of relative size makes us perceive the size of the balls as relative to the distance between the lines. Since we perceive the distance between the lines as constant, we perceive the balls as getting larger as the lines get closer together. This creates the illusion as our brain struggles between the conflicting perceptions created by size constancy and relative size. The monocular cue of height is also at work in this illusion.

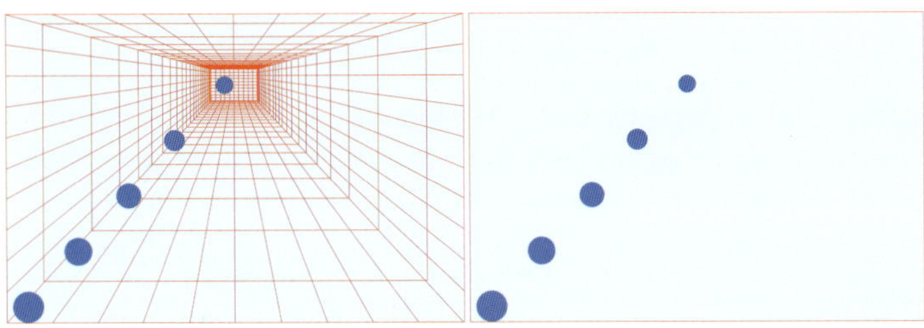

Color constancy is the perception that an object doesn't change color. Even though under various lighting conditions light reflected from the same object will have various wavelengths, the light might be perceived to be the same color. This is due to color constancy—the perception that objects tend to remain the same color.

Color Constancy—Type of Subjective Constancy

Shape constancy is the perception that an object has a fixed shape regardless of the changing shape projected on the retina due to the changing angle from which it is viewed. For instance, a door is perceived as a rectangle even though it never projects a perfectly rectangular image on the retina.

Shape Constancy—Type of Subjective Constancy

1.4 Gestalt Principles

Gestalt principles are grouping principles. A simplification of Gestalt principles is that perception contains more information than sensation. Visually, a picture perceived as one whole entity is considered to contain more information than each part perceived separately. A group of objects visually sensed may be perceived to form figures and events that are not intrinsic to any individual part of the group.

Figure-ground organization is the idea that humans tend to organize their perceptions into figures and backgrounds. Figures tend to be curved outward, symmetrical, relatively small, and enclosed. The Rubin vase is an example of this type of organization where the brain struggles to choose which part of the image is figure and which part is background.

The Rubin Vase

Often figure-ground is included in the Gestalt grouping principles. It is sometimes called law of perception.

The word **pragnanz** means pithiness. If something is pithy, it is concise and meaningful. In Gestalt psychology, pragnanz refers to how the brain interprets images in the simplest manner possible. The **law of Pragnanz** (a.k.a. law of good Gestalt, law of good figure, or law of simplicity) states that stimuli tend to be perceived as simple, orderly, and symmetric. Pragnanz is sometimes the single name for the three Gestalt laws of simplicity, proximity, and continuity, or sometimes it is used to mean the overarching Gestalt grouping principles. Gestalt principles tend to identify methods of simplifying images.

There are many Gestalt principles with many names. Here are some common ones:

1. **Law of Proximity:** Objects close together are perceived as grouped.
2. **Law of Similarity:** Objects that are similar in shape, color, or other qualities tend to be perceived as grouped.
3. **Law of Closure:** Gaps between objects are perceived as closed to form figures. Objects tend to be perceived as complete even when only partially finished.
4. **Law of Continuity:** Aligned objects are perceived to continue behind obstructions. The law of continuity (a.k.a. law of good continuation) states that we tend to see aligned objects as two parts of the same continuing object.
5. **Law of Symmetry:** Objects are perceived in ways that create symmetry, such as geometric shapes. objects tend to be perceived as symmetric around a center point. When two objects are not connected, the mind tends to perceive them as one symmetric shape.
6. **Law of Past Experience:** Objects tend to be perceived based upon past experience. Unlike the other Gestalt grouping principles, the law of past experience depends upon culture and past experience.
7. **Law of Common Fate:** Objects that move or change together are perceived as grouped. Moving objects tend to be perceived as moving along smooth, often straight, paths.
8. **Law of Common Region:** Objects sharing a common region tend to be perceived as grouped.
9. **Law of Parallelism:** Objects that are aligned parallel to one another tend to be perceived as grouped.
10. **Law of Connectedness:** Objects that are connected tend to be perceived as grouped.

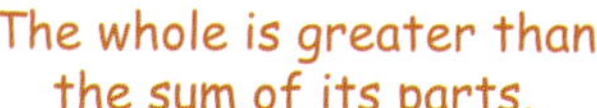

There is no point in trying to memorize every name and variation of the Gestalt principles. There are too many with too many names. Instead, do practice problems. The questions turn out to be fairly simple if you are familiar with the idea of grouping. Just ask yourself, "Why are they grouped?" and choose the best answer.

On the MCAT, if none of the answer choices seem to apply, and Pragnanz is an option, then Pragnanz is the best guess.

Figure-ground
Pragnanz
Proximity
Similarity
Closure
Continuity
Symmetry
Past Experience
Common Fate
Common Region
Parallelism
Connectedness

Gestalt Principles

1.5 Sensory Processing

Absolute Threshold of Sensation

The **absolute threshold** of a sensation is the minimum intensity of a stimulus that can be detected. In psychophysical experiments, an intensity level detected 50% of the time is usually chosen as the standard of detection. The absolute threshold varies with individuals. It also varies with the psychological state of the individual. Biological characteristics generally set the threshold, but psychological characteristics may modify it.

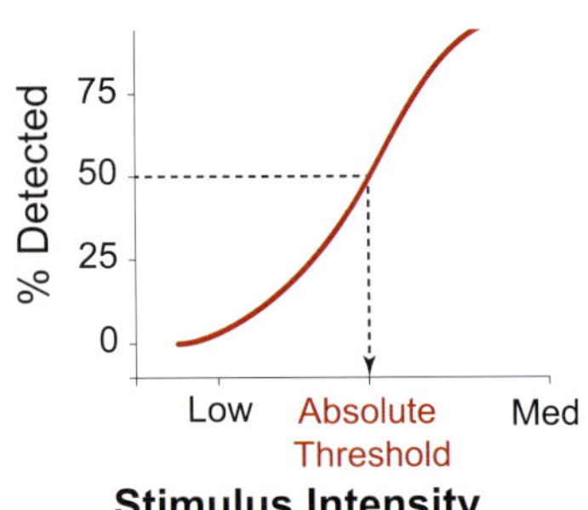

A **subliminal stimulus** is a stimulus below the absolute threshold. Research suggests that a subliminal stimulus has little to no effect on conscious perception but nevertheless can cause robust changes in brain activity.

The threshold intensity can barely be detected; the subliminal stimulus cannot be consciously detected.

Weber's Law

The **just noticeable difference (JND)** in a stimulus is the smallest noticeable difference in the intensity of a stimulus while it is being experienced. Unlike the absolute threshold, which compares the lack of a stimulus to a new stimulus, the JND measures the change in the intensity of a stimulus that is already being applied. As the intensity of a stimulus becomes stronger, the smallest detectable change in intensity becomes greater. In other words, it is more difficult to detect a change in a stronger stimulus. According to **Weber's law**, the intensity of a stimulus and the change in intensity necessary to detect a change in that same stimulus are directly proportional. The louder the music, the more you have to turn it up to notice that it's been turned up.

The noticeable difference in the intensity (ΔI) of a stimulus is directly proportional to the intensity of the stimulus (I).

$$\frac{\Delta I}{I} = K$$

where ΔI *is* the JND.

Weber's law holds reasonably well for most types of sensory perception.

The stronger the stimulus, the larger the JND.

Signal Detection Theory

Signal detection theory (SDT) focuses on how an individual differentiates a **signal** (important stimuli) from **noise** (unimportant stimuli).

Imagine a deer in the forest attempting to drink from a stream. The deer tries to discriminate between the harmless noises of the forest and the footsteps of a stalking tiger. He thinks he hears something in the bushes. Is it a signal that there is a tiger, or is it just background noise?

The distribution frequencies of the signal and the noise can be represented by two histograms compared across some discriminating factor of the stimulus, such as intensity. Standard SDT assumes these histograms form identical bell-shaped curves. The one on the left represents the relative frequency of noises; the one on the right represents the relative frequency of signals. Relative frequencies are used so that the histograms will be the same size, even when there are more noises than signals. The x-axis represents intensity (or some other discriminating factor).

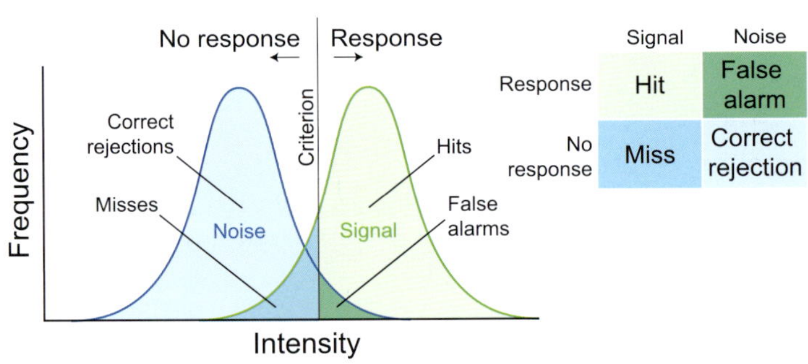

	Signal	Noise
Response	Hit	False alarm
No response	Miss	Correct rejection

Signal Detection Theory Histogram

One important difference between signal detection theory and absolute threshold is the decision-making aspect of signal detection theory. The deer must decide which sounds are only background noise and which might be the signal that a tiger is lurking. A sound from a tiger is a signal, to which the deer wants to respond. Other sounds are noise, to which the deer doesn't want to respond. A brave, thirsty deer will be less discriminating than a frightened, less thirsty deer and will tend to identify fewer sounds as signals.

In signal detection theory, there are four possibilities.

1. Hit (an identification of a signal as a signal)
2. Miss (an identification of a signal as noise)
3. False alarm (an identification of noise as a signal)
4. Correct rejection (an identification of noise as noise)

Hits and correct rejections are desirable, while misses and false alarms are not. All hits and misses are under the right histogram, while all correct rejections and false alarms are under the left histogram. This means that hits and misses must add up to 100% of all signals, while correct rejections and false alarms must add to 100% of all noises.

The subject (the deer) chooses a **criterion** to distinguish a noise from a signal. The criterion is a line separating noise from signals. If intensity is the discriminating factor (the x-axis), then the criterion must be an intensity level above which all sounds will be treated as signals and below which all sounds will be treated as noise. In the case of the deer where intensity is the discriminating factor, if the sound is loud enough, it is treated as a tiger; otherwise, it is ignored.

Bias is any tendency to preferentially identify a sound as either a noise or a signal. Bias is reflected on an SDT graph by the position of the criterion relative to the midpoint between the histograms (the mean average of the two peaks). A **nonbiased criterion** is exactly at the midpoint. A nonbiased criterion produces the same ratio of hits to misses as the ratio of correct rejections to false alarms.

A criterion to the right of the midpoint is called a **conservative bias**. A conservative bias (strict criterion) increases correct rejections and misses while decreasing hits and false alarms. A conservative bias is said to increase **specificity** because a positive identification is more likely to be correct, while a negative identification is more likely to be incorrect. A criterion to the left of the midpoint is called a **liberal bias**. A liberal bias (lax criterion) decreases correct rejections and misses while increasing hits and false alarms. A liberal bias is said to increase **sensitivity** because a negative identification is more likely to be correct, while a positive identification is more likely to be incorrect.

SDT theory may be applied to disease testing where a false alarm is a false positive. A liberal strategy produces more false positives (an uninfected patient testing positive) but fewer false negatives (a sick patient testing negative; a miss). This is desirable during a pandemic because it reduces the number of unidentified infected individuals who might spread the disease. However, the disadvantage of the liberal strategy is the additional financial cost incurred in treating healthy patients and the emotional stress inflicted on healthy patients being misdiagnosed as sick.

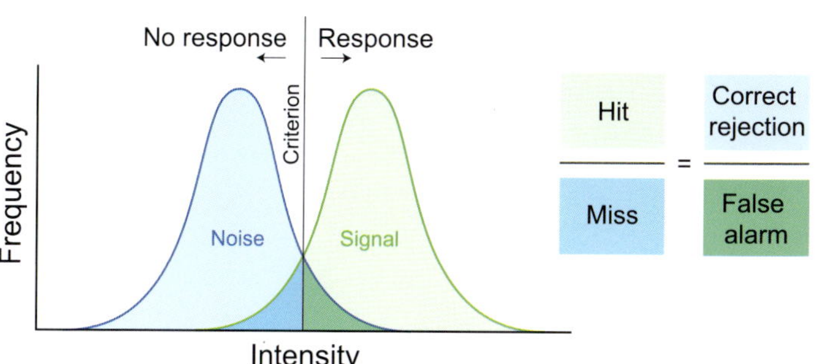

Nonbiased STD Histogram

The tendency to prefer correct rejections over hits is called a **conservative strategy** (represented by positive or high beta). So, a brave, thirsty deer will likely have a positive bias because he is more concerned with getting a drink. The brave deer has decided that he is not running unless he is certain there is a tiger. On the other hand, the tendency to prefer hits over correct rejections is called a **liberal strategy** (represented by negative or low beta). A frightened, less thirsty deer will likely have a negative bias because he is more concerned with not being eaten. The frightened deer wants to flee from nearly every sound. On the histogram graph, the criterion will be to the right of unbiased for a conservative strategy and to the left of unbiased for a liberal strategy.

> If you are familiar with politics then you can remember SDT strategies because they are the same. Conservatives are on the right and liberals are on the left.

In this way, the perceived reward or punishment for decisions affects an individual's decision-making strategy and his bias. Whether an individual should choose a liberal or conservative strategy, his bias depends upon the value he places on hits and correct rejections. If an individual is rewarded for hits, he will be more liberal. If he is rewarded for correct rejections, he will be more conservative.

The whole point of signal detection theory is to provide a method of analysis for discriminability that doesn't rely on hit rate alone. Only by tracking both hit rate and false alarm rate can discriminability be measured. Discriminability is the probability of the hit rate minus the probability of the false alarm rate. That is more than you need to know for the MCAT.

1.6 Sensory Receptors

The process by which a physical stimulus is received and turned into an electrochemical signal is called **sensory transduction**. The body uses **sensory receptors** in the peripheral nervous system (PNS) to detect internal and external stimuli. A sensory receptor is the receptive portion of a sensory neuron or sometimes a separate cell that activates a sensory neuron. The receptor is changed by the physical stimulus. It then translates the physical stimulus into an electrochemical signal. The signal is conveyed to the central nervous system (CNS) along a **sensory neuron** (afferent neuron).

There are three ways to classify receptors: 1) type, 2) location, and 3) function.

Receptor types fall into three categories.

1. Free nerve ending
2. Encapsulated ending
3. Receptor cell

Free nerve ending receptors are simply dendrites embedded in the tissue.

A neuron is a single cell. The action potential travels over a part of the neuron called the axon. A nerve is a bundle of axons. 'Nerve endings' really means 'dendrites' or 'neuron endings'.

Encapsulated ending receptors are dendrites encapsulated by connective tissue that enhances their sensitivity.

Receptor cells are distinct cells (not neurons) that activate neurons. Each kind of receptor cell is designed to receive and transduce a specific type of physical stimulus, e.g. the photoreceptor of the eye is designed to be activated by light.

Receptors can be classified by **location** relative to the stimulus.

1. Exteroceptor
2. Interoceptor
3. Proprioceptor

Exteroceptor	Interoceptor	Proprioceptor
Sounds like 'external'	Sounds like 'internal'	'Pro' sounds like doing a 'procedure' or being a 'pro' athlete.
Skin	Internal organs	Muscle

We find receptors in three locations.

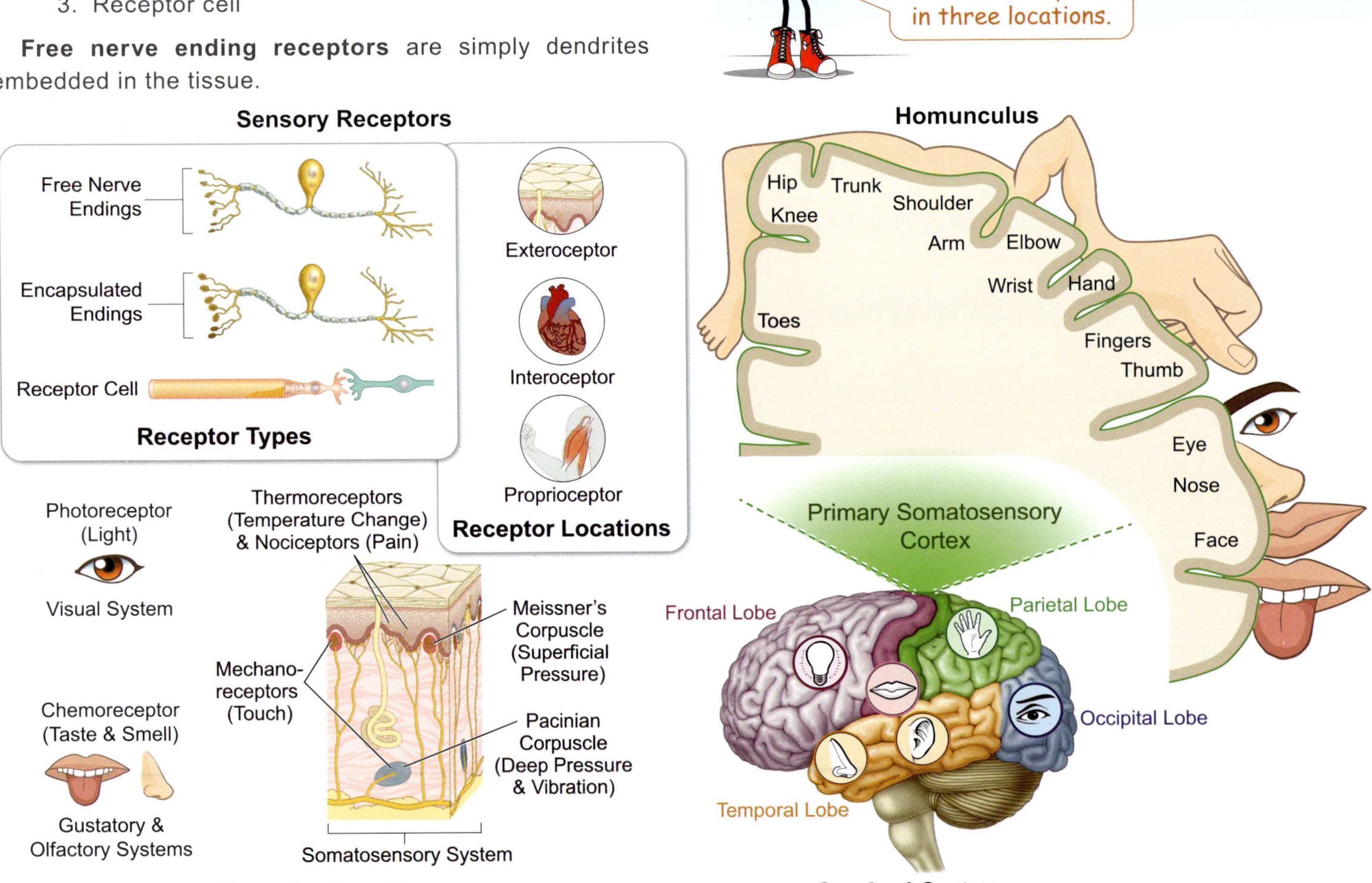

An **exteroceptor** is located near the external environment. The skin has exteroceptors.

An **interoceptor** is located internally. It receives stimulus from the internal organs and tissues monitoring things like blood pressure.

A **proprioceptor** is located in a moving body part. Proprioceptors sense movement.

Some receptor functions are:

1. Mechanoreceptors for touch
2. Thermoreceptors for temperature change
3. Nociceptors for pain
4. Photoreceptors (electromagnetic receptors) for light
5. Chemoreceptors for taste, smell, and blood chemistry

Mechanoreceptors, thermoreceptors, nociceptors, and their sensory neurons make up the **somatosensory system**, which handles most sensation except for vision, smell, and taste.

Mechanoreceptors respond to physical touch, such as pressure, distortion, or vibration. **Pacinian corpuscles**, which respond to vibration and heavy touch, and **Meissner's corpuscles**, which respond to light touch, are mechanoreceptors.

Thermoreceptors respond to changes in temperature but can also be set off by chemical stimuli.

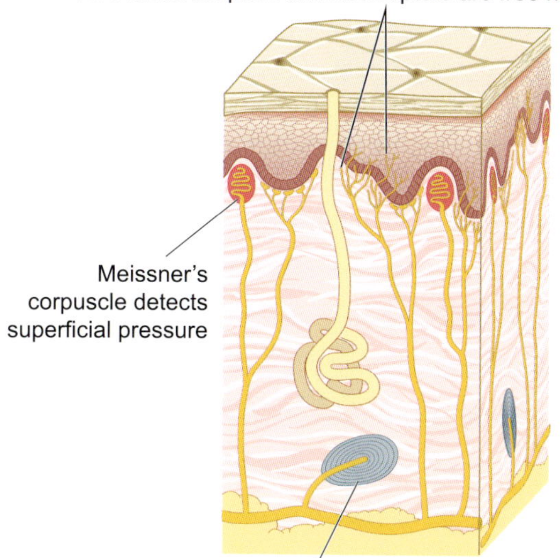

Nociceptors respond to touch, heat, and some specific chemicals, but their main job is to respond to stimuli that will be experienced as pain.

There are many different types of receptors that respond to both pain and to changes in temperature. The most important group of receptors for nociception and thermoreception are called **TRP** (transient receptor potential) **channels**.

TRP channels are located on the surfaces of nociceptors and thermoreceptors. These channels undergo conformational changes when they are exposed to stimuli like heat, hydrogen ions, cold, and chemicals released by cells that have been damaged by a mechanical stimulus. These conformational changes set off a chemical cascade that ultimately creates an action potential.

The signals from nociceptors and thermoreceptors travel along neurons within nerve fibers that connect the receptor to the spinal cord. There are three types of nerve fibers used by these receptors: Aβ, Aδ, and C.

Aβ (A-beta) nerve fibers have a large diameter, are thickly myelinated, and conduct signals faster than the other two types of nerve fiber. **Aδ (A-delta) nerve fibers** are thinner than Aβ fibers, have a thin layer of myelin, and have a slower conduction speed than Aβ fibers. Type **C nerve fibers** are smaller than both Aβ and Aδ fibers, are unmyelinated, and have the slowest conduction speed of the three types.

	Diameter	Myelination	Conduction Speed
Aβ	Thick	Thick	Fast
Aδ	Medium	Light	Medium
C	Thin	None	Slow

Photoreceptors are a type of electromagnetic receptor. They detect the physical stimulus of photons entering the eye.

Chemoreceptors respond to chemicals, acting as biological sensors for various body systems. They are important for maintaining homeostasis and in the systems for gustation and olfaction.

Recall that a photon is an electromagnetic wave. Photoreceptors detect photons. Gustation is taste, while olfaction is smell.

Each sensory receptor is specific, meaning that each responds best to its own types of stimuli. After converting a stimulus into a neural signal, a sensory neuron carries the information to the central nervous system.

The intensity of a stimulus is communicated by the number of receptors activated, the types of receptors activated, and the rate at which the receptors fire. In general, the greater number of signals firing at a given time, the stronger the stimulus.

Some receptors respond slowly to stimuli and fire as long as the stimulus is present – these are called **tonic receptors**. Their main job is to communicate the duration of the stimulus. Other receptors adapt quickly to stimuli and fire when the intensity or rate of the stimulus changes – these are called **phasic receptors**. They stop firing soon after a stimulus occurs and only start firing again when the stimulus changes.

Somatosensory Pathways and Processing

Somatosensory information ends up in a region of the brain called the **primary somatosensory cortex (PSC)**, which is located in the postcentral gyrus of the parietal lobe. (A gyrus is a ridge in the cerebral cortex. A groove between ridges is called a sulcus.) The primary somatosensory cortex contains different areas responsible for processing somatosensory information from different locations of your body. That is, there is an area of the PSC that processes somatosensory information from your arm, while a different part of the PSC deals with information from your lips.

Different parts of the body have different densities of somatosensory receptors. The areas that have more receptors take up more space in the PSC. For example, because there are more receptors per square millimeter on your face than on your back, the space in the PSC devoted to processing sensory information from your face is much greater than that of your back.

A **homunculus** is a representation of how much space different areas of the body take up in the PSC. When presented in two dimensions, each body part is shown next to the region of the PSC that processes sensory information from it (on the contralateral side). The size of each body part reflects the density of sensory receptors on that region of the body. The homunculus runs down the length of the PSC, with the sensory information pertaining to the hip and knee at the top and the sensory information pertaining to the face coming down the side towards the ear.

Keep in mind that the homunculus only refers to the relative representation of the sensory areas, so the large mouth, for example, simply reflects the high density of sensory neurons devoted to that region of the body. Somatic sensations, like touch, are first processed in the PSC, but then sent to the secondary somatosensory cortex for higher-order processing. Other sensory experiences are processed elsewhere, including smell (olfactory cortex), hearing (auditory cortex), taste (gustatory cortex), and vision (visual cortex). Areas of the frontal lobe, including the prefrontal cortex and orbitofrontal cortex, aid in integrating sensory information as well.

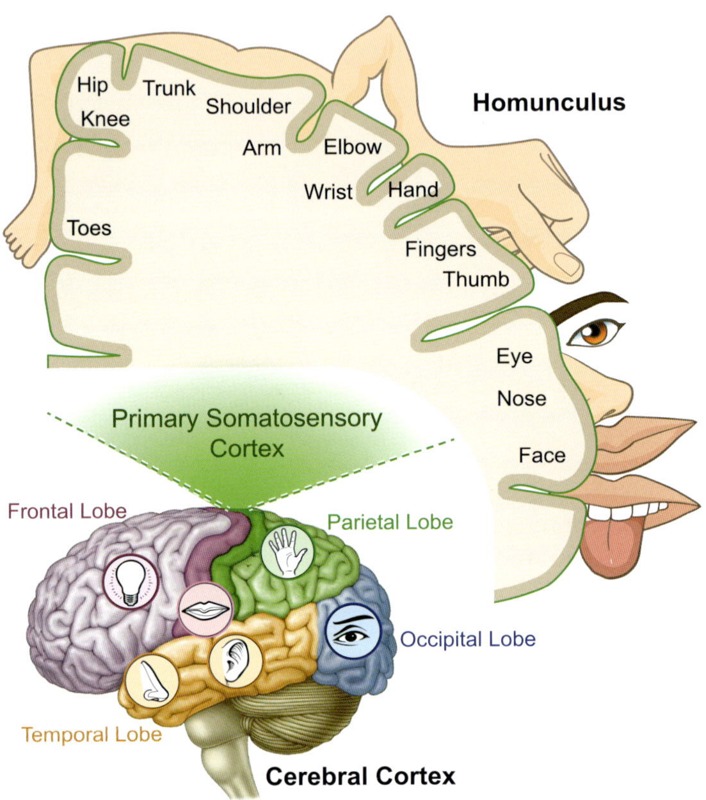

Sensory Adaptation

Sensory systems adapt their sensitivity to their current environment. Such **sensory adaptations** occur in response to short continuous exposure to stimuli. Sensory adaptations are usually temporary, lasting as long as the stimulus. For example, Meissner's corpuscles in the skin fire rapidly in response to light pressure. However, if the pressure remains constant, the firing quickly dies down, resulting in a loss of awareness of the pressure. During exposure to loud noise, the tensor tympani in the middle ear contracts and dampens hearing. In bright light, the pupil constricts while rods and cones become desensitized. In darkness, the pupil dilates while rods and cones become more sensitive. With each sniff of wine, the ability of a sommelier (wine steward) to smell and taste wine is temporarily decreased.

1.7 Vision

Structure and Function of the Eye

The **eye** detects light and converts it into action potentials in neurons. An eye is a biological lens that can adjust to focus on objects of different sizes and distances.

Following the path of a photon heading for a photoreceptor, it reflects off an object in the environment and strikes the **cornea**. The cornea is made mostly of collagen and is nonvascular. From the cornea, light goes to the **anterior chamber**, which is filled with **aqueous humor**. Aqueous humor is formed by the **ciliary bodies** and leaks out of the **canal of Schlemm**.

From the cornea, light enters the **anterior chamber** in front of the **iris** and passes to the **7**

behind the iris. Both chambers are filled with **aqueous humor**, which provides nutrients and helps maintain intraocular pressure. Aqueous humor is formed by the **ciliary bodies** and leaks out of the **canal of Schlemm**.

From the anterior chamber, the photon enters the **lens**. The shape of the lens is regulated by **suspensory ligaments**, which change the focal length of the lens to ensure the image is projected directly onto the retina. The **ciliary muscle**, which encircles the lens, is connected to the suspensory ligaments. When the ciliary muscle contracts, the lens becomes more like a sphere and brings its focal point closer to the lens. When the muscle relaxes, the lens flattens, increasing the focal distance. This process is called **accommodation**.

Accommodation involves contraction of the ciliary muscle, which causes the lens to become more spherical, thereby increasing its focusing power.

After passing through the lens, the photon enters the **vitreous chamber**, which is filled with **vitreous humor**. The vitreous humor helps focus light onto the retina. Since the eye acts as a converging lens and the object is outside the focal distance, the image on the retina is real and inverted.

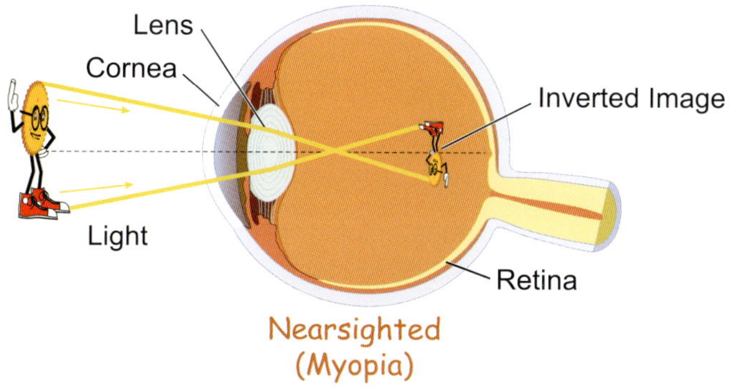

Nearsighted (Myopia)

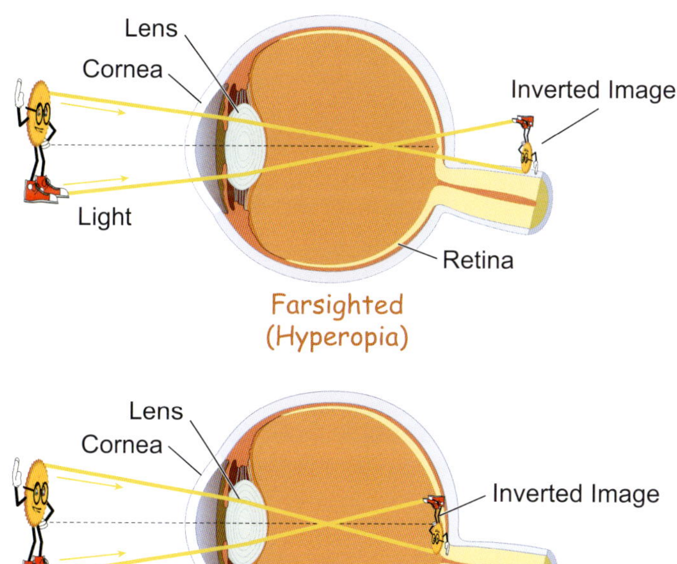

Farsighted (Hyperopia)

Just Right!

The **retina** covers the inside of the back (distal portion) of the eye. It contains photoreceptors called **rods** and **cones.** The tips of these cells contain light sensitive photochemicals called **pigments** that undergo a chemical change when a specific electron is struck by a single photon.

Humans can only see the wavelengths of light to which our pigments respond. The pigment in rod cells is called **rhodopsin**. Rhodopsin is made of a protein bound to a prosthetic group called **retinal**, which is derived from vitamin A. The photon isomerizes the retinal, causing the rod cell membrane to become less permeable to sodium ions, which in turn causes it to hyperpolarize. Rods respond to all photons with wavelengths in the visible spectrum (390 nm to 700 nm), so they cannot distinguish colors.

There are three types of cones, each containing a different pigment that is stimulated by a slightly different spectrum of wavelengths. This is how cones can distinguish colors. Vitamin A is a precursor to all the pigments in both rods and cones.

Remember that rods are used for night vision and peripheral vision, while cones are used for color vision and fine detail.

The **fovea** is a small point on the retina containing mostly cones. This is the point on the retina where vision is most acute.

The **iris** is the colored portion of the eye that creates the opening called the **pupil**. The iris contains both circular and radial muscles. In the dark, the sympathetic nervous system contracts the radial muscles of the iris, dilating the pupil and allowing more light to enter the eye. In bright light, the parasympathetic nervous system contracts the circular muscles of the iris, constricting the pupil and screening out light.

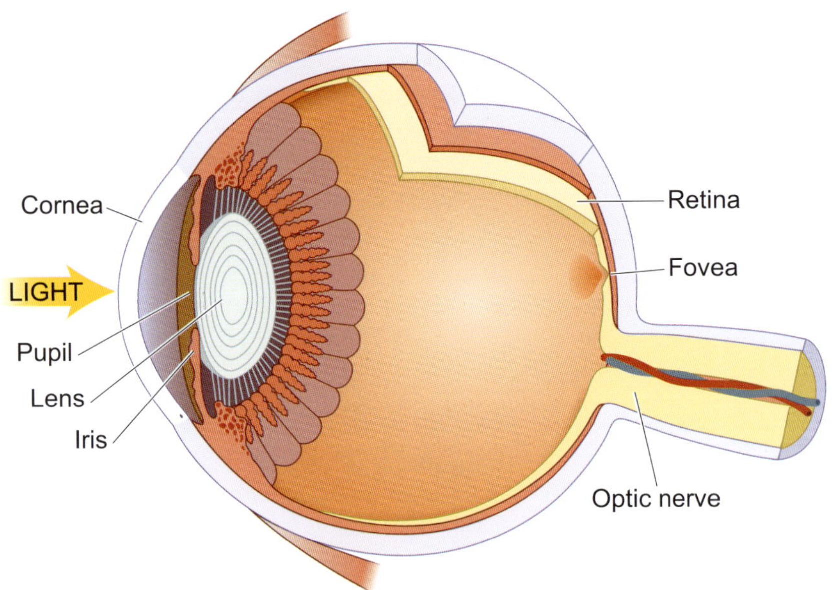

Anatomy of the Eye

> The iris and ciliary muscle work differently. The iris has radial muscles that contract to dilate the pupil and circular muscle that contracts to constrict the pupil. On the other hand, the opening made by the ring of the ciliary muscle enlarges upon contraction, pulling on the ciliary processes and suspensory ligaments connected to the lens and flattening the lens.

The **choroid** is the network of blood vessels that help nourish the eye. The **sclera** is what is commonly called the "white" of the eye and is a thick, tough covering of fibrous tissue that covers most of the eye.

The Phototransduction Cascade

Photoreceptors are a bit different from neurons and other cells that can produce action potentials. Neurons normally fire when they detect a stimulus, like an action potential from a nearby neuron or a neurotransmitter binding to proteins in the cell membrane. Photoreceptors are the opposite - they fire at regular intervals when there's no stimulus and stop firing when a stimulus is detected.

> Photoreceptors are strange because they remain in a state of depolarization, releasing neurotransmitter when they are NOT stimulated. When struck by a photon, they become hyperpolarized and stop releasing neurotransmitter.

Photoreceptors are usually active, releasing a steady stream of the neurotransmitter glutamate. The phototransduction cascade starts by deactivating rods and cones, causing them to release less glutamate, which activates sensory neurons.

Rods and cones have three main parts: an outer section where the structures sensitive to light are located, an inner section, which houses the essential parts of the cell (such as the nucleus, mitochondria, and others), and a synaptic terminal that passes information on to other cells in the retina.

The outer section is full of membranous structures called **discs**, which are stacked atop one another and are about as wide as the outer section of the cell. In rods, these discs are studded with thousands of **rhodopsin** complexes, made up of a G protein coupled receptor bound to **retinal**. Cones use **photopsins** instead of rhodopsin, but they also need retinal to function.

When no photons are hitting the retina, the retinal is bound to its coupled receptor in the **11-*cis*** conformation. After a photon passes through the eye and strikes the retinal in a photoreceptor, the retinal changes its shape from bent to straight and becomes an **11-*trans*-retinal**. Retinal's transformation from a cis to trans conformation marks the beginning of a chemical cascade in the photoreceptor.

R Rod cell; C Cone cell; B Bipolar cell; G Ganglion cell; H Horizontal cell; A Amacrine cell

Optic nerve fibers · Light · Active rhodopsin · Na^+ channels closed · **Light** · Glutamate released · Inactive rhodopsin · Na^+ channels open · **Dark**

11-*cis*-retinal

Photon

11-*trans*-retinal

Several other proteins that participate in the phototransduction cascade are bound to rhodopsin. One of these, called **transducin**, breaks apart into subunits when the retinal is converted from 11-*cis*-retinal to 11-*trans*-retinal. The alpha

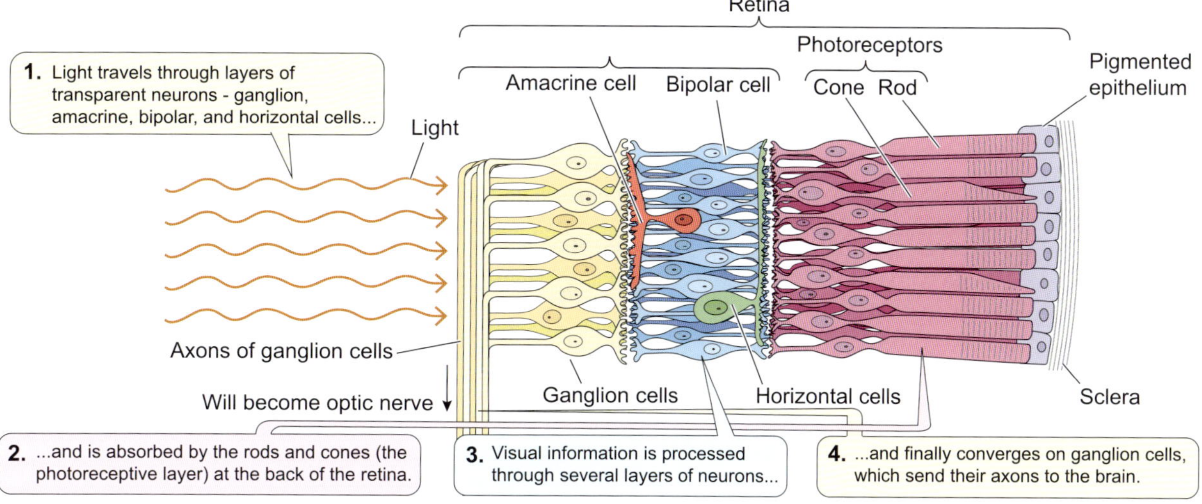

Phototransduction Cascade

subunit of transducin then binds to **phosphodiesterase**, another protein that sits on the surface of the discs in photoreceptors.

Phosphodiesterase hydrolyzes cyclic GMP (cGMP), which then turns into ordinary GMP. In photoreceptors, cGMP is usually bound to sodium channels, keeping them open and allowing sodium ions to enter the cell. When cGMP is converted into GMP, there is less cGMP to bind to the sodium channels, and some of the channels close. Every channel that closes helps **hyperpolarize** the cell membrane. When photoreceptors hyperpolarize, they deactivate, releasing less glutamate into the synaptic cleft.

Two different cell types, **on-center bipolar cells** and **off-center bipolar cells**, use glutamate receptors on their surfaces to detect glutamate released by nearby photoreceptors. When light hits a photoreceptor, leading to a decrease in the amount of glutamate secreted, the different types of bipolar cells respond differently. On-center bipolar cells become active, while off-center bipolar cells become inactive.

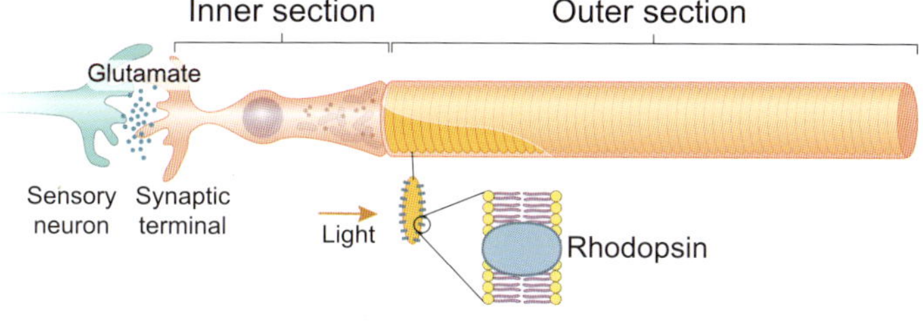

Rod Structure

Bipolar cells communicate with **retinal ganglion cells**. Like bipolar cells, there are both **on-center retinal ganglion cells** and **off-center retinal ganglion cells**. When on-center bipolar cells activate, they cause on-center retinal ganglion cells to become active. Likewise, when off-center bipolar cells deactivate, off-center retinal ganglion cells also become inactive.

The axons of retinal ganglion cells combine with glial cells to form the **optic nerves**, which leave the eyes to convey visual information to the brain. Some of the axons from each eye cross to the opposite side of the brain. They cross over at a point called the **optic chiasm**. Other axons that come from the eye project to the temporal lobe on the same side of the body as their associated eye.

Information from the right side of the visual field is processed in the left side of the brain, while information from the left side of the visual field is processed by the right side of the brain.

Visual Processing

The optic nerves travel to the **lateral geniculate nucleus (LGN)** of the thalamus, which preserves the visual map created by the ganglion cells and projects this information to the **primary visual cortex**, located in the occipital lobe. Groups of neurons within the primary visual cortex are specialized for the detection of specific aspects of visual stimuli, particularly lines and edges of different orientations.

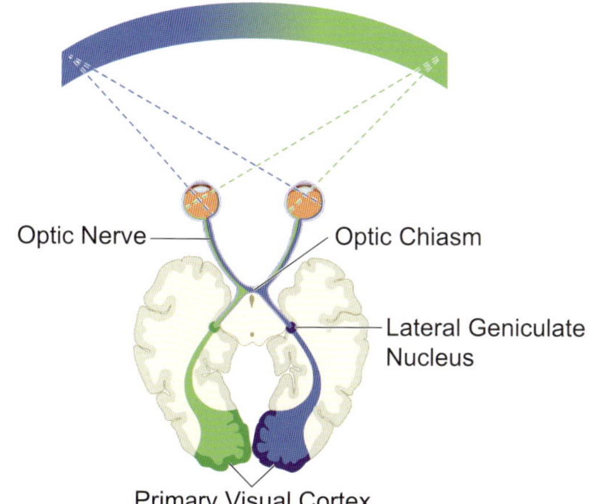

Two main pathways carry signals from the retina to the LGN in the thalamus. The P cells of the **parvocellular pathway** make up the largest pathway with the smallest cells. Small P cells conduct signals slowly. P Cells respond to fine detail, color, size, and shape. The high-speed **magnocellular pathway** contains large M cells, which are colorblind but respond to location, speed, and direction of movement.

In the LGN, information is passed to other neurons that carry it on to the visual cortex.

The simultaneous processing of information about the same stimulus along separate pathways is called **parallel processing**.

> For P cells, think color, shape, and detail. For M cells, think motion. For parallel processing, imagine two ideas about the same subject moving along parallel paths through the brain.

Feature detection describes how the brain perceives the external world by dividing it into specific features. For instance, concerning vision, the brain sorts outside stimuli into features like color, shape, and motion. Each feature is compared to stored memories in order to identify what is being viewed. From this information, the brain creates an image that exists only in the mind.

> Basically, the brain collects information, breaks it down into features, looks for a memory with similar features, and creates an image that is NOT exactly like reality.

1.8 Hearing

Structure and Function of the Ear

The **ear** detects the physical stimulus of sound (fluid pressure waves) and converts it into action potentials in neurons. The ear has three sections: the **outer ear**, the **middle ear**, and the **inner ear**.

From outside the ear looking in, the outer ear starts with the auricle. The auricle or **pinna** is the flap of skin and cartilage that is commonly called the ear. When a sound wave enters the ear, it hits the auricle first. The auricle then directs the sound wave into the **external auditory canal**, which then carries the wave to the **tympanic membrane** or **eardrum**.

The middle ear begins at the eardrum and contains three small bones (ossicles): the **malleus**, the **incus**, and the **stapes**. These three bones act as a lever system, translating the wave into a physical vibration that is conveyed to the **oval window**.

> The malleus, incus, and stapes are also called the hammer, anvil, and stirrup. They are easy to remember because malleus sounds like mallet, so it is the hammer; stapes begins with the letters s and t like stirrup.

The inner ear begins at the oval window, which is connected to the **cochlea**. The wave gets passed from the oval window to the **scala vestibuli** (vestibular duct), where it follows the spiral shape of the cochlea until it reaches the center. At the center, the wave travels through the **scala tympani** (tympanic duct) until it reaches the **round window**. The movement of the wave causes the **organ of Corti** to vibrate. The organ of Corti is the ear's version of a retina, since it is the structure that converts the external stimulus into a neural impulse. The organ of Corti sits on the **basilar membrane**, which separates the scala vestibuli from the scala tympani.

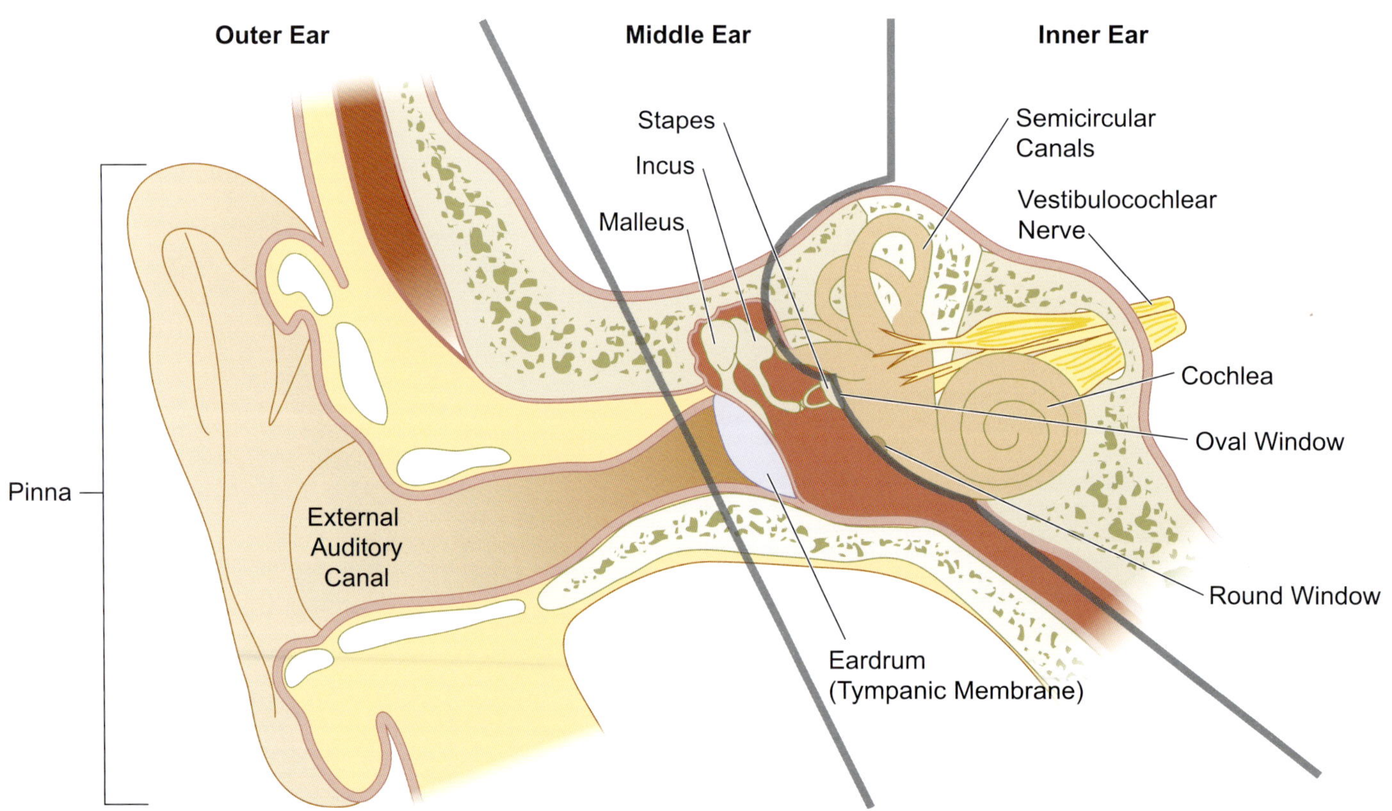

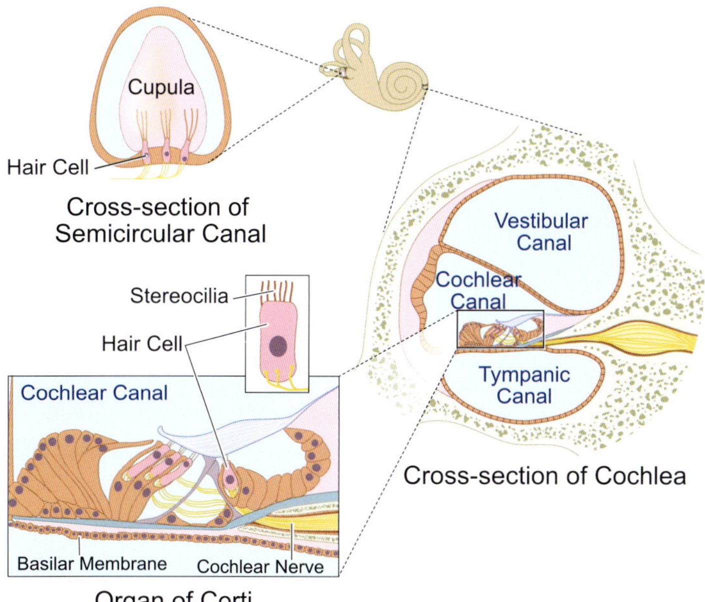

Cross-section of Cochlea

Organ of Corti

The **hair cells** of the organ of Corti contain organelles called **stereocilia**, which cause action potentials to be fired when they move. These action potentials are sent to the brain via the **auditory nerve** for processing.

Aside from the cochlea, the inner ear also contains **semicircular canals** and **otolith organs**, both of which are involved in the vestibular system. Both structures are filled with fluid and hair cells. When the fluid moves, the body detects motion. All three semicircular canals are at right angles to one another, which allows for the detection of movement in all three dimensions. The semicircular canals detect the direction and speed of angular acceleration (twisting of the head), while the otolith organs detect the direction and speed of linear acceleration and positioning of the head relative to gravity (tilt).

Auditory Processing

The hair cells of the organ of Corti are mechanoreceptors. They sense when microvilli bend after the organ of Corti starts vibrating in response to a sound wave.

Depending on the direction in which the microvilli bend, hair cells experience hyperpolarization or depolarization. When they depolarize, hair cells release a neurotransmitter that can cause an electrical signal to be conveyed to the brain.

As auditory information travels through the brain, it undergoes processing and integration. Neural signals encoding sound information primarily travel along a pathway that starts with the auditory nerve and then proceeds to the **cochlear nuclei** within the medulla. Next, axons of the cochlear nuclei synapse with neurons within the **inferior colliculus**.

From there, the electrical signals are passed on to the **medial geniculate nucleus** of the thalamus. Finally, the **auditory cortex** in the temporal lobe receives information from the thalamus.

The auditory cortex is where the detection of complex features of auditory information, such as patterns, takes place.

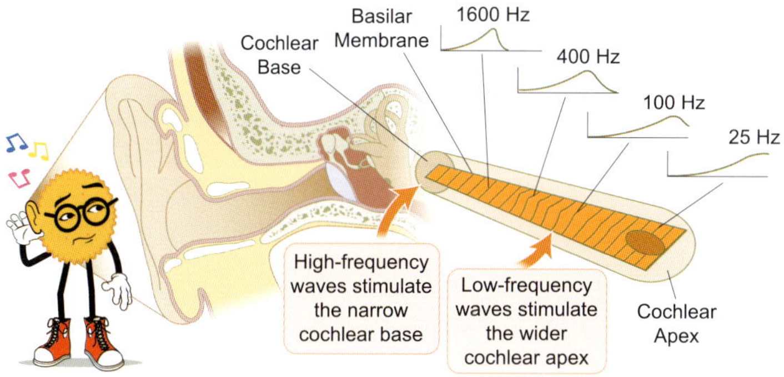

Cochlear Base
Basilar Membrane
1600 Hz
400 Hz
100 Hz
25 Hz
High-frequency waves stimulate the narrow cochlear base
Low-frequency waves stimulate the wider cochlear apex
Cochlear Apex

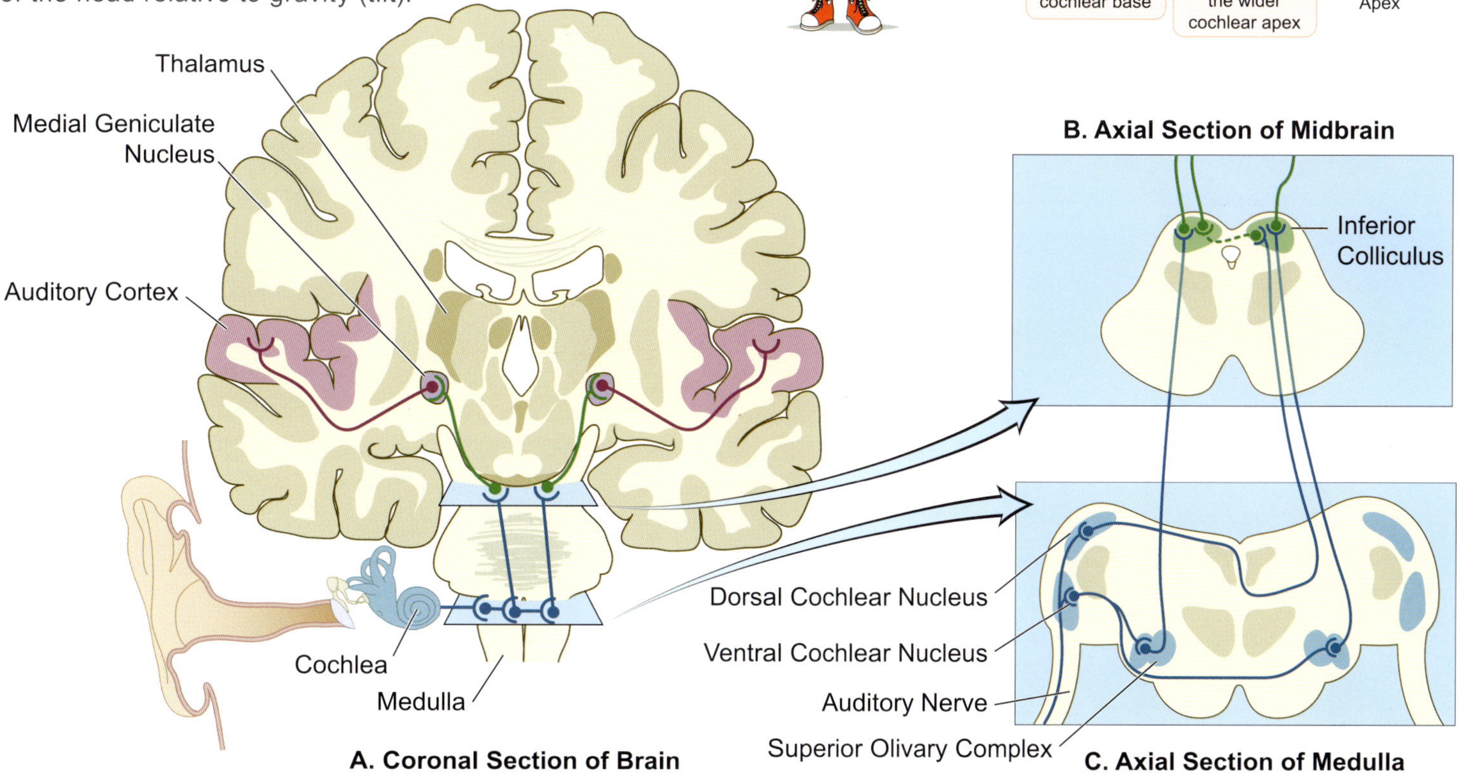

Thalamus
Medial Geniculate Nucleus
Auditory Cortex
Cochlea
Medulla
Dorsal Cochlear Nucleus
Ventral Cochlear Nucleus
Auditory Nerve
Superior Olivary Complex
Inferior Colliculus

B. Axial Section of Midbrain

A. Coronal Section of Brain

C. Axial Section of Medulla

Remember that both visual and auditory information pass through the thalamus for processing.

Humans can hear sounds ranging from 20 Hz to 20,000 Hz. How does the ear distinguish between low-frequency sounds, such as that of a foghorn, and high-frequency sounds, such as that of a mosquito's wingbeats? Imagine that instead of a spiral, the cochlea were uncoiled and laid flat. As a wave enters the cochlea from the oval window, high-frequency waves stimulate the basilar membrane close to the base or the start of the cochlea. In contrast, low-frequency waves stimulate the basilar membrane close to the apex or end of the cochlea. The hair cells in the stimulated area send signals to the brain that encode the frequency of the received wave. This setup is called **basilar tuning**.

1.9 Other Senses

Gustation

Gustation, or the sense of taste, relies heavily on chemoreceptors. The chemoreceptors used in gustation are called **gustatory cells**. Gustatory cells are located in **taste buds**, which are found all over the top of the tongue.

The taste system evolved to help organisms identify harmful and nutritionally beneficial substances. There are five taste sensations.

1. Bitter
2. Sour
3. Salty
4. Sweet
5. Umami (Savory)

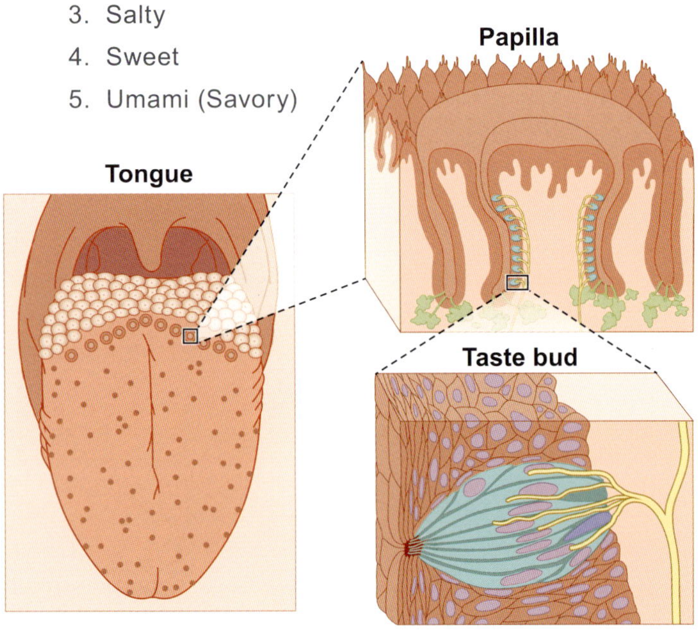

Papilla

Tongue

Taste bud

Each gustatory cell can detect all of the five taste sensations.

Every flavor profile is made up of some combination of the five taste sensations. The binding of chemicals to chemoreceptors in the taste buds causes these sensory receptors to trigger action potentials in associated sensory neurons. Sensory information from the binding of many chemicals to different chemoreceptors is combined in higher-level processing to produce the psychological experience of taste. In the brain, this is primarily accomplished in the gustatory cortex, which is located in the insular cortex, also known as the insula. The insula is not visible on the surface of the brain because it lies within the folds of the cortex that is covered by the frontal, temporal, and parietal lobes.

Olfaction

Olfaction, or the sense of smell, also relies on chemoreceptors. Chemoreceptors concentrated in the nasal cavity bind gaseous chemicals called **odorants**. Each type of olfactory receptor binds to a set of chemicals instead of to only one chemical. There are many more types of olfactory receptors than gustatory receptors.

Unlike gustatory cells, olfactory chemoreceptors are themselves sensory neurons. The axons of the olfactory chemoreceptors form the **olfactory nerve**. The binding of chemicals to G-protein coupled receptors on the chemoreceptors triggers an action potential that is transmitted by the olfactory nerve to neurons of the **olfactory bulb**.

Neural signals in the **olfactory pathways** *do not* pass through the thalamus before reaching higher cortical levels in the brain. The olfactory bulb projects directly to the **piriform (olfactory) cortex** in the temporal lobe. The piriform cortex conveys olfactory information to the **orbitofrontal cortex**, where it is integrated with other sensory information.

The olfactory bulb also projects to the amygdala and hippocampus in the temporal lobe, providing a direct pathway for smell to influence processes of memory and emotional experience.

The olfactory bulb also projects to the amygdala and hippocampus, which helps explain why some smells feel nostalgic, even if we can't remember exactly where or when we smelled the same thing before.

Some species have a related but separate set of sensory receptors that detect a specific type of odorant called **pheromones**. What makes pheromones different from other types of smell stimuli is that they are not perceived consciously. Pheromones are thought to exert a subconscious influence on aggression and sexual behavior. It is unclear whether there are pheromones that affect human behavior, but some olfactory compounds that influence social interaction and sexual attraction may exist.

Pain

The experience of **pain** is inherently subjective. The bottom-up processing involved in the perception of pain is very similar to that of other senses. Nociceptors convert a physical stimulus into action potentials that eventually reach the thalamus and get passed onto higher cortical areas for processing. However, the brain also exerts top-down

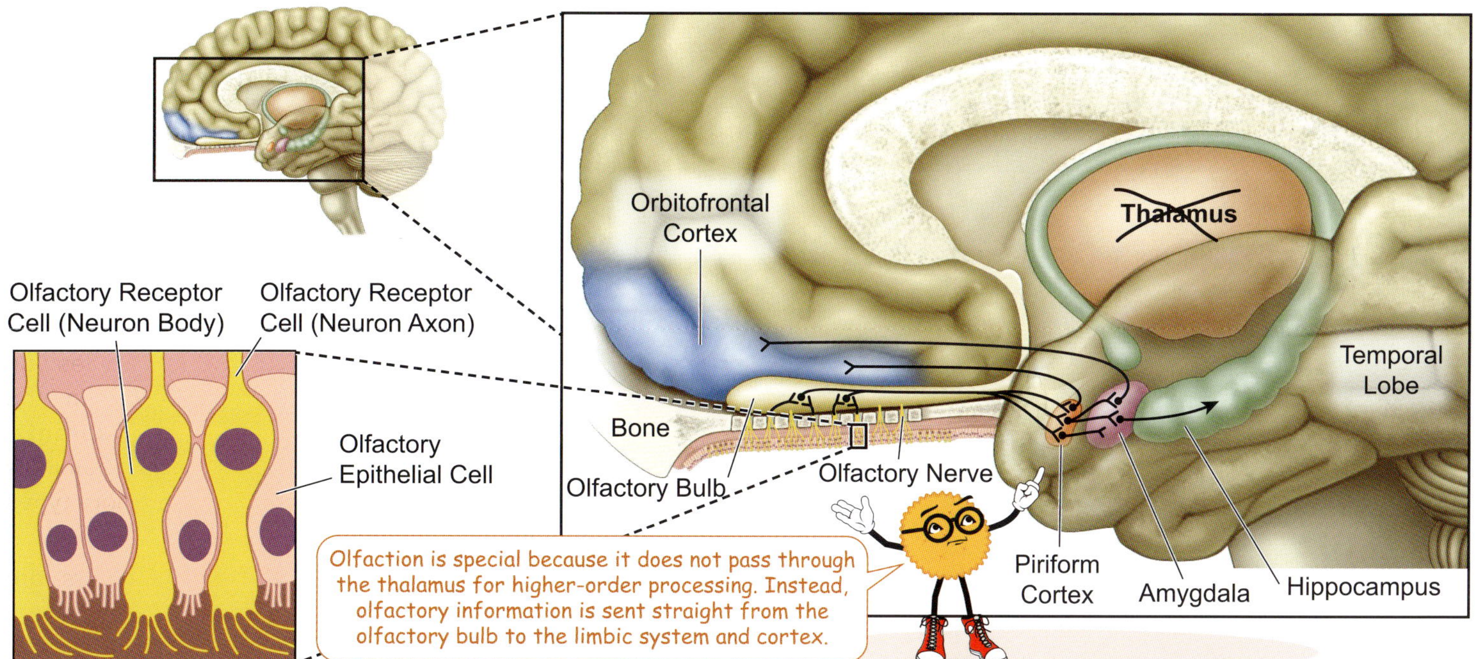

influence that impacts how people experience pain. Both pathways are important—pain is necessary for knowing when a stimulus is dangerous, but too much pain can get in the way of other actions necessary for survival.

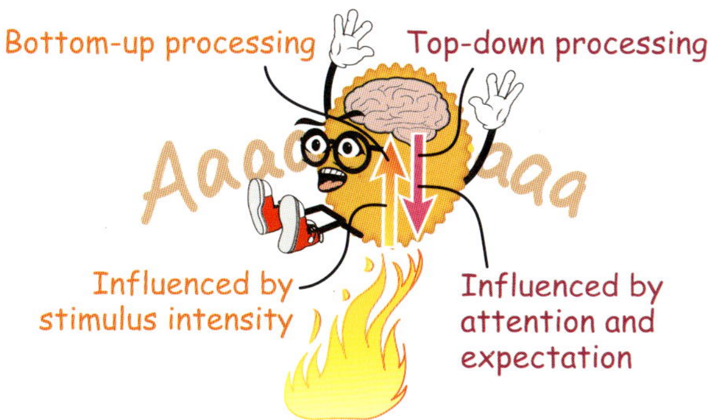

Kinesthetic Sense

Kinesthetic sense is knowing body position and motion. Kinesthesis is the sensory input that relates the position and motion of body parts via muscle spindles and, to a lesser extent, skin stretch receptors during tension and compression of skeletal muscles. Muscle spindles and skin receptors maintain static levels of discharge that increase proportionately with an increase in muscle length. The contribution of joint receptors to kinesthesis is minor or does not exist. During muscle contraction, coordination with the cerebellum and the parietal cortex provides additional cues. The awareness of effort due to activation of voluntary motor functions also plays a role in kinesthesis. Though awareness of position and movement exists, no clearly defined sensation accompanies kinesthesis.

Muscle memory is a kinesthetic concept.

> Kinesthetic sense is knowing where your body parts are and where they are going, even when your eyes are closed.

> Kinesthetic sense is knowing what to do with your arms and legs so you can catch a football while running at the same time.

Vestibular Sense

Vestibular sense is the feeling of balance and spatial orientation. This sense relies on the vestibular system located in the inner ear. When you move your body, the vestibular system detects that movement and signals the body to make adjustments to maintain balance. The vestibular sense works with the kinesthetic system to form an overall sense of the body.

> Vestibular sense is related to motion sickness. It occurs when the vestibular system conflicts with other sensory signals, like those from the visual system.

Attention, Memory, and Cognition 2

2.1 Attention

Attention is the focus on certain stimuli to the exclusion of other stimuli. It selects sensory information for perceptual processing. Attention is limited in capacity—a single individual is able to process a finite amount of information at any moment. The amount of mental resources that you devote to a task is called **cognitive load**. Devoting attention increases cognitive load.

> Attention is controllable, selective, and limited. It is the progression by which external stimuli form internal representations that gain conscious awareness.

> Attention is what your brain chooses to focus on from all the sights, sounds, smells, and feelings striking your body.

One way to think about attention is the **spotlight model**. A spotlight makes a circle of light. At the center of this circle is the focus, where everything is well-lighted. Just around the focus is the fringe, where there is still light, but things are not as clear. Around the fringe is the margin, a line outside of which is dark. Attention can be thought to work like a spotlight. When we focus our attention on an area, we notice the things around that area (in the fringe), but we notice with less detail, and there are some things (outside the margin) that we don't notice at all. In this model of attention, the stuff outside the margin is not processed.

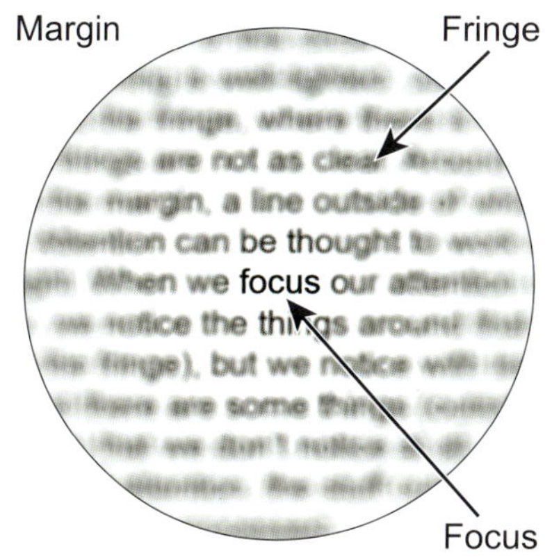

Notice that in the spotlight model, we can select the direction in which to point the light. Like the spotlight, our attention is selective. **Selective attention** is the process of focusing on relevant stimuli while filtering out irrelevant stimuli to the task at hand. Think of an athlete playing on a field with 60,000 screaming fans. How do they focus on the game at hand without being distracted by all the extraneous noise? Competitive and experienced athletes are skilled at selecting the stimuli on which to focus while filtering out the less important stimuli.

Selective attention occurs when we focus on certain stimuli and block out others. The **cocktail party effect** is an example of selective attention. At a noisy party, you can selectively attend to a conversation while blocking out background noise. Additionally, suppose someone having a conversation nearby says your name. In that case, your attention may be drawn suddenly to that conversation, even if you did not notice a word of the conversation before.

Both the "focus" and the "blocking out" aspects of selective attention are important.

A source of confusion may be that the cocktail party effect refers to both the idea that you can block out background noise, and the idea that you notice your name in a noisy room.

Alternating attention is the ability to switch between tasks; to stop one task to perform another and then be able to return to the initial task. This type of attention is common in everyday life such as consulting a recipe, following the directions and then returning to the recipe for next steps in the food preparation process. Another example might be working on a paper, stopping to pick up and comfort a screaming child, and then returning to writing the paper.

Divided attention, also known as **multitasking**, splits perceptual resources between multiple stimuli. In simple English, it means paying attention to more than one thing at a time. Multitasking results in lower productivity because attentional resources are finite. An example of divided attention is listening to a teacher while taking notes.

Three factors influence our ability to multitask.

1. **Task similarity:** Dissimilar tasks are easier to perform simultaneously than similar tasks. For instance, it is more difficult to write a paper while listening to a talk show than to write a paper while listening to music without words.
2. **Task difficulty:** Effectiveness decreases as tasks become more difficult.
3. **Practice:** Cognitive load decreases with practice.

Try patting your head and rubbing your belly and see if you switch your attention back and forth. It's easier to count backwards from 50 while you rub your belly than to pat your head while you rub your belly. That is because it is more difficult to do similar tasks at the same time than dissimilar tasks at the same time.

Because attentional resources are finite, divided attention results in lower cognitive efficiency. When one stimulus makes it difficult to attend to another stimulus, it is called **cognitive interference**. Practice reduces the effect of cognitive interference, making multitasking more efficient.

The **Stroop effect** is a demonstration of cognitive interference during divided attention.

As quickly as you can, say the color that each word is printing in aloud.

Yellow **Purple** **Black** **White**

Green **Blue** **Red** **Orange**

Now do it again with the words below.

Yellow **Purple** **Black** **White**

Green **Blue** **Red** **Orange**

One theory as to why it is more difficult to say the second set of colors is that the task of reading has a cognitive load that is so low that you automatically pay attention to the meaning of the words. Your attention to the meaning of the words provides cognitive interference with your attention to the color and makes the task of saying the colors less efficient.

"Interference" is a word that is used a lot in psychology. Don't confuse "cognitive interference" with "memory interference," where one memory interferes with another, causing forgetfulness in long-term memory. Memory interference is the more important term for MCAT psychology.

Sustained attention is attention to a stimulus over a long period of time. This is different from selective attention because in selective attention there are other stimuli within the task that compete for attention, such as many voices at a party, compared to sustained attention where the competition is a different task entirely, typically a more desirable and/or engaging one, such as wanting to watch

TV while you are studying. Sustained attention imposes a large cognitive load.

Cues draw attention toward a stimulus. There are endogenous and exogenous cues. **Endogenous cues** require processing. A spoken name is an endogenous cue because it requires the name to be processed before attention is drawn. An endogenous cue is an example of top-down processing because its response requires processing. Endogenous cues need to be learned.

Exogenous cues, on the other hand, automatically draw attention to a stimulus without top-down processing. For instance, a loud noise that diverts your attention to it is an exogenous cue because the noise did not need to be processed in order to draw attention. An exogenous cue is an example of bottom-up processing because it creates an immediate response to a stimulus without forethought. Exogenous cues do NOT require learning.

Endogenous: Internal, voluntary, top-down

Exogenous: External, involuntary, bottom-up

> Endogenous cues are internal, learned, and require voluntary top-down processing before attention is drawn to the stimulus. Exogenous cues are innate, external, and involuntarily demand your attention automatically through bottom-up processing.

Exogenous cues result in attentional capture. **Attentional capture** occurs when attention is involuntarily directed towards a stimulus due to some characteristic of the stimulus. A sudden distracting background motion or noise may cause attentional capture.

It is easier to block out non-task-related stimuli when there are a lot of them. If you try to read a book while sitting next to two people having an interesting conversation, you may have difficulty blocking out the conversation. However, if several other people come by and start having separate conversations around you, the noise may become a background murmur that is easily ignored.

Overt orienting is refocusing the body, especially the eyes, onto a new object of attention. **Covert orienting** is a mental shift of attention without moving the body, head, or eyes. Both are forms of selective attention. Covert orienting doesn't change what information is processed, but it instead changes how the information is processed. Overt and covert may apply to other sensory systems as well.

As previously mentioned, most stimuli detected by the sensory system are not processed and do not enter conscious awareness; however, exogenous cues are processed and do enter conscious awareness. **Inattentional blindness** or **perceptual blindness** occurs when an otherwise exogenous cue detected by the sensory system goes unnoticed due to selective attention. For instance, an actor playing Hamlet might forget to remove his watch. The audience is focused on the play—although the actor is aware of the watch, the audience does not notice it. Inattentional blindness occurs most often when a task has a high cognitive load, and the unnoticed stimulus is task-irrelevant.

Inattentional blindness is different from **change blindness**, which is the failure to notice a change in one's immediate environment. In one experiment demonstrating change blindness, a researcher engages a subject in conversation. During a distraction, a new researcher replaces the first researcher and continues the conversation. Only about half the subjects noticed the change. Change blindness is often accompanied by a momentary distraction during the transition. Illusionists may use change blindness to their advantage when performing.

> Change blindness is when something in your environment changes right before your eyes and you do not notice it happening.

There are two categories of stimuli:

1. Distal, and
2. Proximal

A **distal stimulus** is an object in the environment that provides information for the proximal stimulus. The **proximal stimulus** is a bit less well-defined. It may be the physical quantity striking the sensory receptor, or it may be the neural activity caused by the sensory transduction. A phone is the distal stimulus, while the pressure waves striking the eardrum is the proximal stimulus. A painting is a distal stimulus, while the electromagnetic radiation striking the retina is the proximal stimulus.

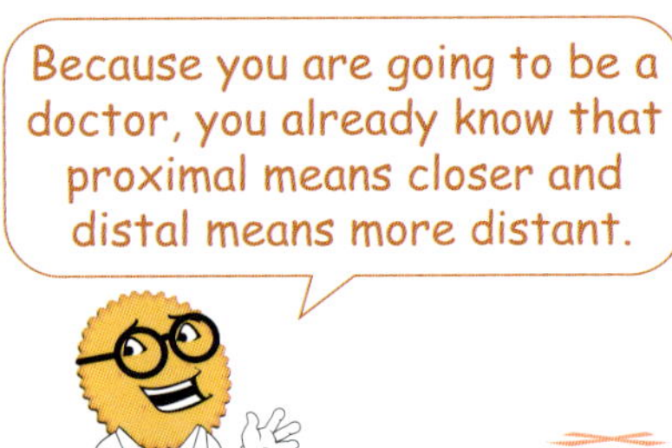

2.2 Attention Processing Theories

Stimuli detected by the sensory system are too numerous for processing. In other words, we can't pay attention to ALL of them. The brain has a finite capacity to process information. Donald Broadbent proposed the **filter model of early selection theory** to explain how preattentive processing works. According to this model, the large number of stimuli received by the sensory receptors temporarily enter a sensory buffer with functionally unlimited capacity. This glut of stimuli creates a bottleneck. The bottleneck acts as a **filter** and allows only stimuli with specific physical characteristics such as (in the case of sound) intensity, direction, and pitch to pass through. The stimuli that get through the filter are further processed before entering working memory. The rest of the stimuli quickly decay.

In Broadbent's theory, rejected stimuli are eliminated early in processing. Also, semantic features are NOT selected for during the filtering process. This means that Broadbent's theory does NOT explain the cocktail party effect, where the semantic feature of a name can draw attention.

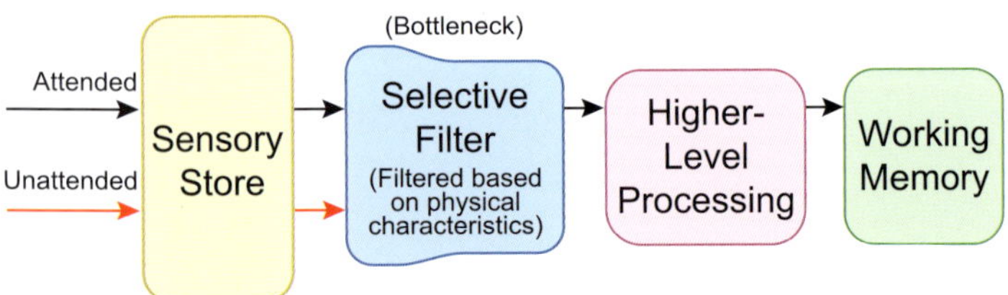

Broadbent's Filter Model of Early Selection

With Broadbent, remember that filtering happens early and for physical features only.

Anne Treisman revised Broadbent's model, suggesting that stimuli are attenuated rather than filtered. In Treisman's **attenuation theory**, all information from the sensory buffer passes through an **attenuator**, "dampening" some of the information coming in without losing it altogether. In the case of auditory information, louder sounds, sounds that fall in the frequency range of human speech, and other elements might be left relatively untouched while quieter sounds or environmental noises are dampened.

The attenuator precedes a bottleneck, after which the information is sorted according to an internal hierarchy of factors—in the case of auditory information, it is thought that features of spoken language, like words and grammatical structures, are identified and assigned meaning in this step. The processed information is then passed into working memory.

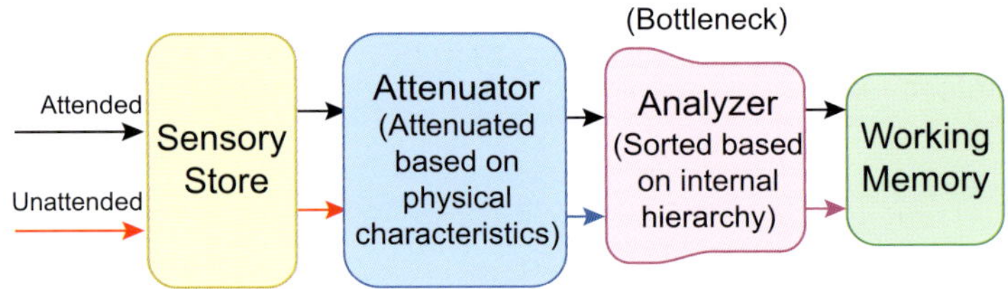

Treisman's Attenuation Model

With Treisman, remember "attenuation," NOT "filtration," so that all information is still available.

Diana Deutsch and her husband, J. Anthony Deutsch, proposed a **late selection model** in which stimuli are analyzed for meaning before selection. They argued that filtering occurs later than in Broadbent's model—just before entry into working memory—and that relevance of information has an important role in the selection process. In the Deutsch and Deutsch model, we perceive everything, though we are not consciously aware of everything we perceive.

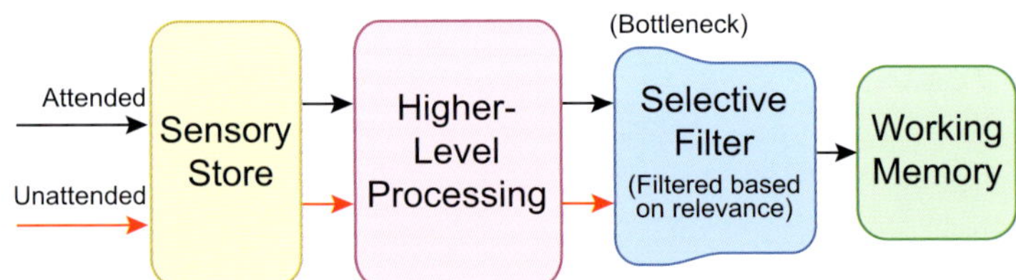

Deutsch and Deutsch's Late Selection Model

Broadbent used a dichotic listening test to develop his theory. A **dichotic listening test** uses **speech shadowing** to test attention. A subject wears headphones that play different stories in each ear. The subject is asked to immediately repeat or shadow only the story played in his right ear. Afterward, he is questioned about what he heard in his left ear. Typically, the subject can identify the gender of the speaker in the left ear but cannot identify what was said.

Treisman also used dichotic listening. In Treisman's experiment, people listened to different nonsensical streams of words from each ear. When asked to repeat what had been said, they used elements of both streams to create a sensical meaning.

The Deutsch and Deutsch model predicts that the subject should be able to repeat the same number of words from either ear in a dichotic listening test.

> Where Broadbent's theory filters out some stimuli early in the first step, Treisman's theory just "turns down the volume" on some stimuli in the first step. The Deutsch and Deutsch model puts the filter late in the process, just before information enters working memory.

2.3 Memory

The **Atkinson-Shiffrin model** proposed three stages of information processing.

1. Sensory memory
2. Short-term memory (later called working memory)
3. Long-term memory

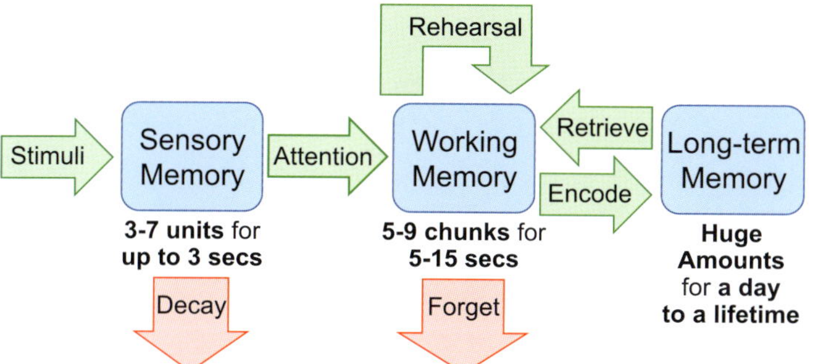

Atkinson-Shiffrin Model

A computer encodes, stores, and uses information to produce an output. According to the Atkinson-Shiffrin model, the brain is like a computer. The brain receives information via sensory stimuli, processes the information, stores it, and eventually uses it. Each processing system systematically alters the information. The information is then stored in memory and used when needed. For instance, when you read, the eye receives sensory info from the page of the book. The information is processed into meaningful units and stored. The output is your behavior in response to what you read, like when you read the words aloud.

Like computers from the 20th century, the Atkinson-Shiffrin model is a **serial processing** model; one piece of information is processed at a time. Contrary to this model, modern evidence indicates that humans are capable of **parallel processing** or running several cognitive processing tasks at one time.

Sensory memory is the first stage of the Atkinson-Shiffrin model. Sensory memory collects all sensory information coming into the brain and sorts it to decide what requires attention. Information not attended to from sensory memory is discarded and lost forever in a process called **decay**.

Two Components of Sensory Memory

Sensory memory is also called the sensory register. Two components of sensory memory are **iconic (visual) memory** and **echoic (auditory) memory**. Iconic memory lasts for a very short time, less than a second, while echoic memory lasts for about 3-4 seconds.

From the sensory memory, attention moves information into **short-term memory**. Short-term memory can hold 5 to 9 chunks of information. The brain has a way of grouping information into memorable chunks. For instance, the sequence of numbers: 2-3-5-9-3-5-2-3-8-7 is easier to remember if you "chunk" it into 235-935-2387. Chunks remain in short-term memory for about 5-15 seconds.

Rehearsal refers to how a person works with the information in working memory. There are two methods of rehearsal: maintenance and elaborative rehearsal.

Maintenance rehearsal is the repetition of a thought over and over in order to keep it in short-term memory and perhaps transfer it to long-term memory.

Elaborative rehearsal is the attaching of meaning to a thought in order to keep it in short-term memory and transfer it into long-term memory. The goal of rehearsal is to move an item from short-term memory to long-term memory. This process is called **encoding**. Elaborative rehearsal is a more efficient encoding mechanism than maintenance rehearsal.

> You should link "attention" with "short-term memory." Attention to information is required in order for that information to enter short-term memory.

Baddeley and Hitch changed and expanded the concept of short-term memory to **working memory**.

In the Baddeley and Hitch model, instead of directing information to a single storage system called short-term memory, attention directs information to a **central executive.** The central executive deals with cognitive tasks such as math and problem solving. It also decides what attended information receives priority. So, if you are taking notes and listening to the professor, the central executive decides your focus. The central executive also decides to which specialized storage system of working memory information should be sent.

Visual-spatial information goes to a **visuospatial sketchpad**. The visuospatial sketchpad is responsible for spatial manipulation of visual images. It reminds us where we are in relation to other objects in the environment. Using information from long-term memory, it also relays and manipulates mental maps of familiar places.

Visuospatial Sketchpad

Spoken and written information goes to the **phonological loop**, where it is further divided and sent to either the phonological store or the articulatory control process. The **phonological store** maintains spoken information for 1-2 seconds. Written information must be converted before entering the phonological store. The **articulatory control process** rehearses verbal information and keeps sending it back to the phonological store. This is how we temporarily remember a phone number. The articulatory control process also decodes written information into speech so the phonological store can receive it.

The fact that it is easier to think about a piece of visual information and a piece of verbal information at the same time than it is to think about two pieces of verbal information or two pieces of visual information is evidence that these two systems are separate, as predicted by the Baddeley and Hitch model. This phenomenon is known as the **dual coding hypothesis**.

Baddeley later added an **episodic buffer** to his model. The episodic buffer acts as a backup system that communicates with long-term memory and the components of working memory.

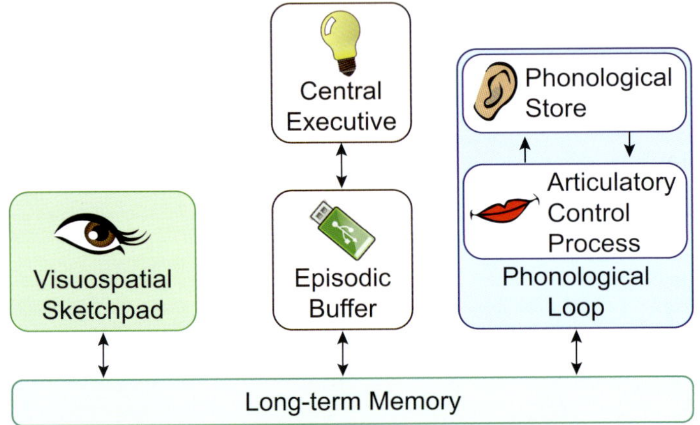

Baddeley and Hitch Model Of Working Memory

Encoding

Encoding involves automatic processing and effortful processing. Like it sounds, **automatic processing** occurs without effort. You can remember what you had for breakfast today, even though while you were eating breakfast, you weren't trying to encode it into your memory—it was encoded into your memory automatically. On the other hand, **effortful processing** refers to encoding that requires effort. When you study for a test, you are engaged in effortful processing.

There are four types of encoding.

1. **Visual encoding** is the encoding of images.
2. **Acoustic encoding** is the coding of sounds, especially words. Memorizing the words in a song is an example of acoustic encoding.
3. **Elaborative encoding** is the associating of new information with already known information.
4. **Semantic encoding** is the encoding of words and their meaning.

Recoding involves converting information into a form that makes sense to us. Recoding always occurs during the encoding process. Recoding can introduce errors into memory by adding information that was not originally there.

Many processes assist in encoding. Some examples are rote rehearsal, chunking, mnemonics, the self-referencing effect, and the spacing effect. The least effective of these is rote rehearsal, which is simply repeating something over and over again.

I will not rely on rote rehearsal.
I will not rely on rote rehearsal.
I will not rely on rote rehearsal.

Chunking is the grouping together of items into one meaningful unit to enhance your memory. Chunking allows you to reduce the number of items in your short term memory without reducing the amount of information.

Mnemonics link knowledge that you already have with new information that you are trying to remember. There are many examples of mnemonics, including, but not limited to song, rhyme, acronym, image, model, **pegword**, and the **method of loci**. Using multiple mnemonics at once is more effective than using just one at a time.

Mnemonic Strategies

When you associate information with something about yourself, you tend to remember it better. This is called the **self-referencing effect**. This is demonstrated when a person is given a list of adjectives to remember and is asked if each word describes himself. He is more likely to remember the words on the list if he has had the opportunity to relate the adjectives to himself.

Encoding specificity refers to the fact that the environment in which you learn information affects your ability to recall it. Specifically, it is easier to recall information when you are in an environment similar to the one where you first learned it. For example, if you study for a test while wearing earplugs, you will be more likely to recall the information you learned while taking the test if you are wearing earplugs. When preparing for the MCAT, it is important to try to keep your environment as consistent as possible, and it is doubly important that you mimic test-taking conditions when taking practice exams.

I'm capitalizing on encoding specificity by taking practice tests in a space that mimics the real test-taking environment!

The **spacing effect** demonstrates that the effectiveness of encoding is improved by separating learning sessions in time. The opposite of the spacing effect is cramming.

Storage

Long-term memory provides nearly permanent storage for information and perhaps infinite storage capacity. Learning occurs when information has entered into long-term memory.

There are implicit and explicit long-term memories. **Explicit memory** is information that you consciously remember. Explicit memories include episodic and semantic memories. **Episodic memories** are memories associated with events in your life. **Semantic memories** have to do with language-based knowledge. They are facts, concepts, and other knowledge that can be called into memory. For instance, when you study for the MCAT, you create semantic memories about the content (the facts you learn) and episodic memories about the process (remembering an episode of studying or of taking the test). Due to semantic memories, bilingual speakers remember more about their childhood when asked about it in their childhood language.

Episodic memories are of episodes of your life—the answers to "what," "where," and "when." Semantic memories come in hand when you're trying to remember concepts for an exam.

Episodic Semantic

Implicit memory is information that you are not necessarily consciously aware of holding. You are unaware they are being formed. Implicit memories are behavioral or procedural memories. They store information on how to do things without the application of conscious thought, such as riding a bike, brushing your teeth, or playing the piano.

Types Of Encoding	Types Of Retrieval
Visual Image processing **Example:** Logos SALTY'S PIZZA	**Free Recall** Accessing memories without reliance on cues I can freely recall the letters of the alphabet without any cues! A B C D...
Acoustic Sound processing, especially words **Example:** Memorizing words to a song O Sole Mio!	**Recollection** Reconstructing memories based upon small cues Wow, this song triggered a recollection of me and my sister going to the beach as teenagers!
Elaborative Associating new information with previously known information **Example:** Pegword mnemonic	**Recognition** Recognizing familiar information using notable cues I couldn't picture his face, but now that I see him, I definitely recognize Bob in the crowd!
Semantic Processing words and their meaning **Example:** Associating the word "cat" with a furry animal "Cat"	**Relearning** Refreshing old information using all information as cues I thought I had forgotten French, but it came right back when I traveled to Paris!

Implicit memories also include **emotional conditioning**, such as being afraid of ghosts due to a scary movie you watched when you were a child.

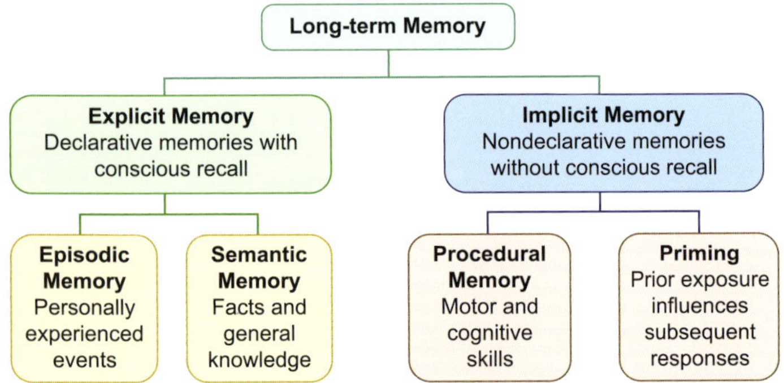

Long-term Memory Classification

An interesting example of explicit vs. implicit memory is the position of the letters on a keyboard. When you type, you implicitly recall where the letters are. But if you were asked to write the letters in order, that would require explicit memory.

A **semantic network** is a schema for encoding concepts. In a semantic network, each concept is represented as a node attached by lines to other nodes. According to this model, when one node is accessed, it triggers other nodes in a chain reaction that spreads across the network. This is called **spreading activation**. This means that you encode concepts by connecting them to other concepts, building a network of attachments that may connect all concepts. For instance, thinking of a circus may trigger other concepts such as elephants, tents, and clowns.

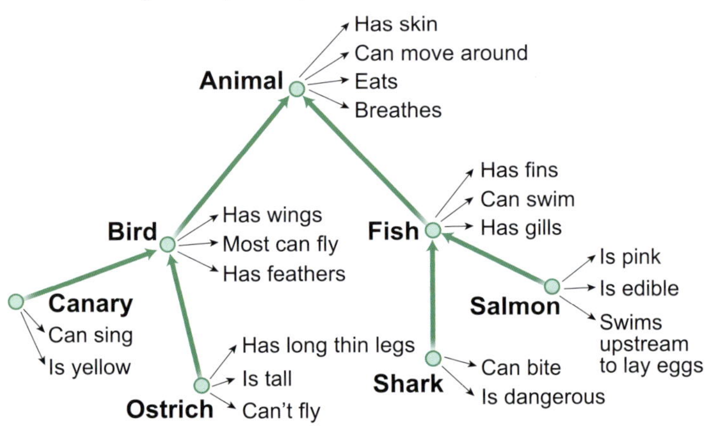

A schema is a cognitive framework or concept that helps organize and interpret information.

2.4 Memory Retrieval

Memory is selective—some information is lost, some information is retained, and some false information is created.

Available information is the entire amount of information in our long-term memory. The portion that we can retrieve is called **accessible information**. Accessible information represents a small fraction of the available information. You may have memorized how many ATPs are produced by glycolysis (that information may be available in your long-term memory), but that does not mean you will be able to access it under stressful test conditions.

Information in long-term memory cannot be accessed directly. To access information in long-term memory, it must be retrieved (or brought back) into working memory. The process of transferring information from long-term memory to working memory is called **retrieval**. There are four methods of retrieval, listed here from least effective to most effective.

1. **(Free) Recall:** Accessing memories without reliance on cues
2. **Recollection:** Reconstructing memories based upon cues
3. **Recognition:** Recognizing familiar information
4. **Relearning:** Relearning previously learned information

(Free) Recall is the attempt to remember without using cues. Recall is the least effective way of accessing memory. The **serial position effect** explains how the recall of listed items is affected by their order. The **primacy effect** says that recall of items mentioned first will be more efficient than recall of items mentioned in the middle of the list. The **recency effect** says that recall of items mentioned most recently or last on the list will be more efficient than recall of items in the middle of the list. If the efficiency of recall is graphed versus list position, a u-shaped curve is formed.

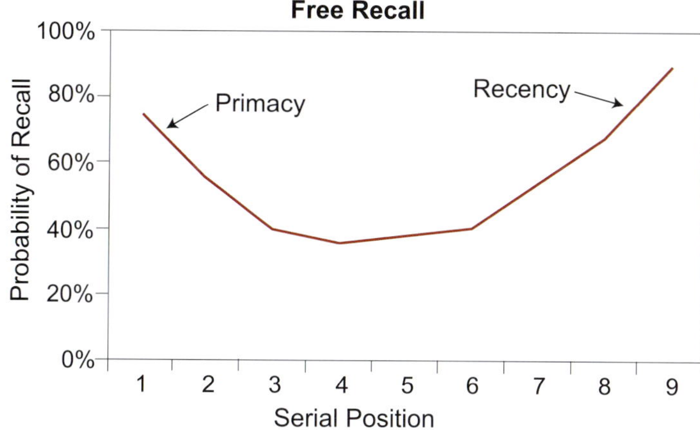

Recollection is the use of retrieval cues to aid in remembering. A **retrieval cue** is anything associated with a memory that initiates its retrieval. A song that reminds you of a childhood memory is a retrieval cue.

In order to work well, a retrieval cue should be distinctive. For instance, let's say your favorite dog breed is a Dalmatian, and you remember the name because both dog and Dalmatian start with a "d". That may work as long as you are only trying to remember the name of one dog breed; however, it won't work if you also want to remember dachshund, Doberman, Dutch shepherd, and many other dog breeds that start with a "d". This effect is referred to as the **cue overload principle**: a cue can only be effective when it is not attached to too many memories.

Complex associations between the memory and the retrieval cue make better cues.

Priming is an example of using retrieval cues. **Priming** is a technique in which earlier exposure to a stimulus facilitates or inhibits a response to the same or similar stimulus. So, if after reading about brick houses you are shown the word "b_ _ck" and asked to fill in the blanks, you are more likely to complete the word as "brick" than as "block."

Priming is most effective when the retrieval cue and the information to be remembered use the same modality. For example, visual priming works best with visual cues, while verbal priming works best with verbal cues. You are more likely to say "apple" when primed with red objects than when primed with the written or spoken word "red," because the apple is the color red, so the retrieval cue should be a color, not a word.

Negative priming occurs when exposure to a stimulus inhibits a future response to the same or similar stimulus. Imagine that you were shown cut-outs of a red dog and blue cat and asked to remember the red object. You might say to yourself, "remember the dog, NOT the cat." Next, you were shown cut-outs of a red cat and a blue horse and asked to name the red object. The cat is red, so it is the correct choice. However, you would be negatively primed against saying "cat," so your response would likely be slowed due to negative priming.

Recognition is the identification of information that you have already learned. It involves comparison. You use recognition on a multiple-choice test. In a recognition test, the correct answer acts as a retrieval cue. You might recognize someone yet not be able to recall how you know the person. Still, sometimes recall may happen before recognition. For instance, here is a recognition test. Which of the following are the last names of famous assassins? Oswald, Booth, Ray, and Evans. The same test may be easier as a recall test where the actual answer is not given. Provide the last names of these three famous assassins: Lee Harvey _________, John Wilkes _________, and James Earl _________. (If you still can't answer these questions, you might need to take a history class.)

The ease of retrieving memories can be affected by how shallow or how deep the processing used to encode them is. **Shallow processing** involves focusing on more superficial aspects of words and ideas, such as whether a word is italicized or if it starts with the letter "b." **Deep processing** involves focusing on the meanings of words and ideas and relating them to similar concepts. If you were to try to remember the word "hat" by conceptualizing it as an object that you can wear on your head, that would be deep processing.

Using deep processing makes memories inherently easier to recall than using shallow processing.

Relearning involves refreshing old information. It is faster to relearn than to learn for the first time. Relearning is the most efficient way to remember information. In relearning, the retrieval cue is the entire amount of information that is stored.

Methods Of Memory Retrieval

You can think of the four methods of retrieval as accessing information using successively more retrieval cues: recall uses no cues, recollection uses small cues, recognition uses nearly all the information as a cue, and relearning uses all the information as a cue.

Each retrieval of a memory makes the memory more likely to be retrieved in the future. This is called the **testing effect**. However, the retrieval of one memory may inhibit the future retrieval of a related memory. This is called **retrieval-induced forgetting**.

When a distant memory is retrieved, some spurious information may be added to fill in the gaps. The more often the memory is retrieved along with the spurious information, the more strongly it is encoded into the memory as actual fact. An especially vivid story can even manufacture an entirely **false memory**. Thus, retrieval will strengthen both accurate and inaccurate memories.

Distortion is when memories are altered with misinformation. There are three types of **distortion**:

1. **Misattribution** is when the source of the memory is confused, like when you tell your partner what a wonderful time you had when you saw that movie together and your partner says, "Nope, wasn't me."
2. **Suggestibility** involves false memories, but the false memory was suggested to you by someone else, like with leading questions during an interview with a police officer after an accident.

3. **Bias** is when memories are distorted by a belief system, like when you mistakenly remember the truck driver was a man because you associate driving a truck with men.

Intrusion is where you can't forget, even if you might want to. There is one type of **intrusion**:

1. **Persistence** is an involuntary recall of undesirable memories, like a jingle from a commercial that you can't get out of your head.

Memory retrieval can be negatively impacted in three ways:

1. Forgetting the information;
2. Retrieving distorted information; and
3. Persistently retrieving unwanted, intrusive information.

Emotion and Memory

Emotion influences long-term memories during learning and retrieval. Emotional events may create longer-lasting, more vivid, and sometimes more accurate memories. **State-dependent memory** refers to the phenomenon that it is easier to remember information when your state of mind or mood during encoding matches the state at retrieval. This is basically the mindset/mood version of encoding specificity. Also, in a phenomenon known as the **mood congruence effect**, you tend to recall memories, or aspects of memories, that align with your current mood.

Methods Of Memory Retrieval

Flashbulb memories are another example of how emotion affects memory. Flashbulb memories are vivid memories related to emotional events, such as the 9/11 attacks or the assassination of JFK. Interestingly, despite the high confidence reported by people who have them, flashbulb memories tend to be inaccurate. Important components of creating flashbulb memories are:

1. Importance of event
2. Consequences
3. Distinction
4. Personal involvement
5. Proximity

Even if the memory is not vivid, memories tied to emotions are easier to recall than neutral memories. However, this effect only seems to occur when the brain has had some time to process the memory and not right after the event occurs.

Memories are not videos.

Remember that memory is not a perfect replication of a past event. It is subject to the influence of misinformation. Each time it is recalled, a memory is modified. Source monitoring, or remembering where the information came from, is a common source of memory error.

2.5 Forgetting, Memory, and Neurocognitive Disorders

Sometimes one memory gets in the way of retrieving a similar memory. This is called **memory interference**. An example of memory interference is when you can't recall what you had for breakfast last Sunday because what you had the other days interferes with your recall.

There are two types of memory interference: proactive and retroactive interference. **Proactive interference** makes it difficult to learn new things, like when you replace your old phone number with a new one. **Retroactive interference** makes it difficult to remember old things because new memories interfere, like trying to remember your old phone number after you just learned your new one.

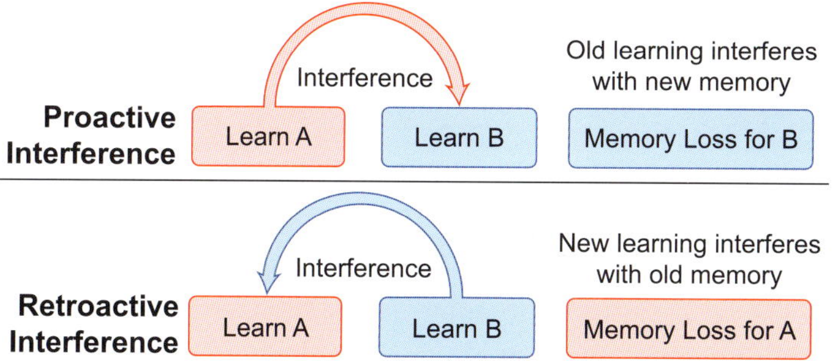

Ironically, forgetting has the advantage of reducing memory interference. There are three ways that memory can fail: forgetting, distortion, and intrusion.

Forgetting is when the memory cannot be retrieved. There are three types of forgetting.

1. **Transience** is when accessibility of memory decreases over time, quickly at first, and then more slowly. The **Ebbinghaus forgetting curve** illustrates how memory decays quickly before leveling off.
2. **Absentmindedness** is caused by a lack of attention.
3. **Blocking** is when accessibility is temporarily blocked, like when the name is on the tip of your tongue.

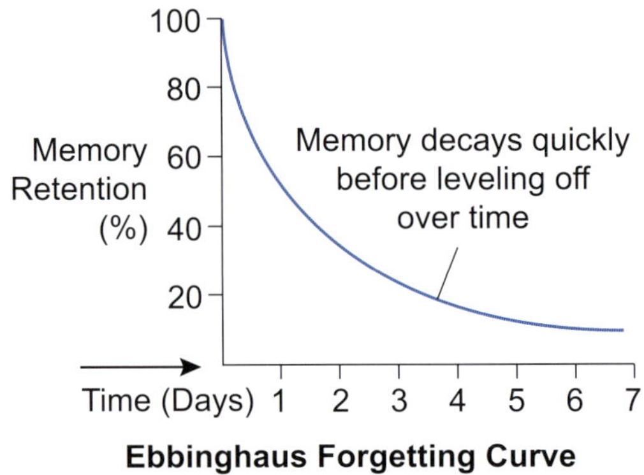

Ebbinghaus Forgetting Curve

Different cognitive functions decline, remain constant, and some even improve with age. All of the senses decline in old age. The size of the brain decreases as it loses neurons. **Age-related memory impairment (AMI)** occurs in several memory types but is especially noticeable in episodic memory. Implicit memory remains relatively constant. Semantic memory typically improves with age. AMI is NOT associated with memory loss due to Alzheimer's disease, Wernicke-Korsakoff syndrome, and other diseases.

Dementia is a general term for a decline in memory, communication, and thinking that is severe enough to affect daily life. Dementia is more severe than the average cognitive loss due to aging. It is caused by damage to brain cells or changes in the brain. Alterations in mood and behavior are common symptoms. Dementia is not a normal part of aging but affects over half of people above the age of 85. As the average age of the global population rises, so does the prevalence of dementia—it is now one of the most common causes of death worldwide.

Alzheimer's disease (AD) accounts for over 60% of dementia cases. It is NOT a normal part of aging. The risk of Alzheimer's increases with age, but fewer than 1 in 5 individuals over 65 develop the disease, rising to 1 in 3 over 85 years old. As Alzheimer's is a specific type of dementia, the symptoms of Alzheimer's include the symptoms of dementia. Early symptoms include memory loss, personality change, and the inability to learn and retain new information, followed by confusion, depression, difficulty recognizing family members, and, only in late stages, loss of coordination. Alzheimer's begins in the temporal lobes and spreads throughout most of the brain.

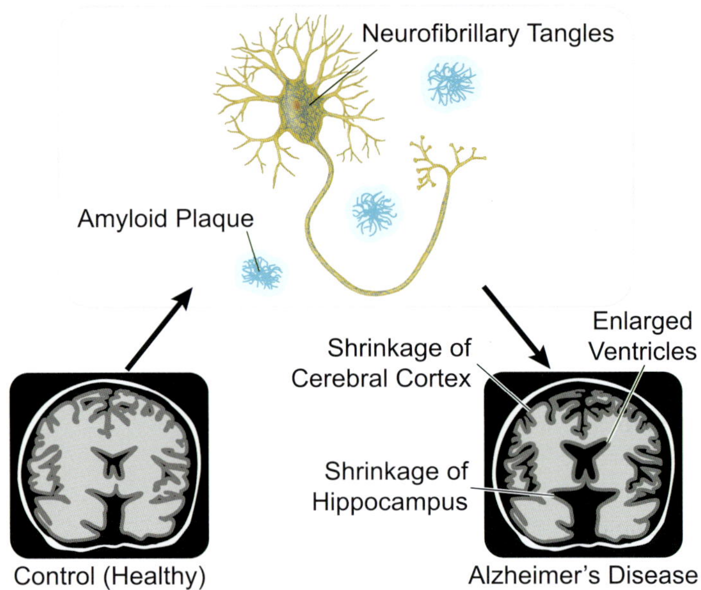

In Alzheimer's patients, neuritic plaques form between dying neurons and neurofibrillary tangles inside the neurons. As neurons die and the brain shrinks, there is also a reduction in the production of proteinaceous neurotransmitters, such as acetylcholine, norepinephrine, serotonin, and somatostatin.

The cause of Alzheimer's is unknown, but suspected agents include genetic predisposition, abnormal protein deposits in the brain, environmental factors, and immune system problems.

Parkinson's disease (PD) is a disease of the central nervous system. Symptoms begin mainly with the motor system, including shaking, rigidity, and slow movement, and progress slowly to non-motor symptoms leading to dementia. The death of cells in the substantia nigra in the midbrain leads to a shortage of the neurotransmitter dopamine, particularly in the basal ganglia. Presently, there is no cure. Treatment is designed to lessen the severity of symptoms. Since dopamine cannot cross the blood-brain barrier, L-dopa or dopamine agonists are used. L-dopa is converted in the brain to dopamine, while dopamine agonists mimic the effects of dopamine. Treatment becomes less effective over time and is accompanied by side effects such as involuntary movements. Risk factors for PD are complex, including genetic and environmental components.

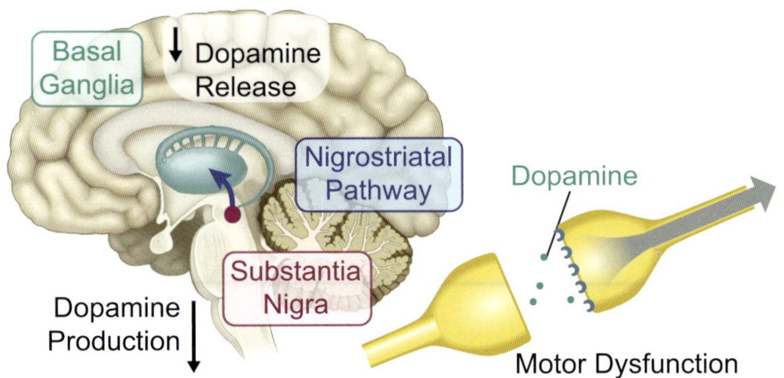

Parkinson's Disease Pre-treatment

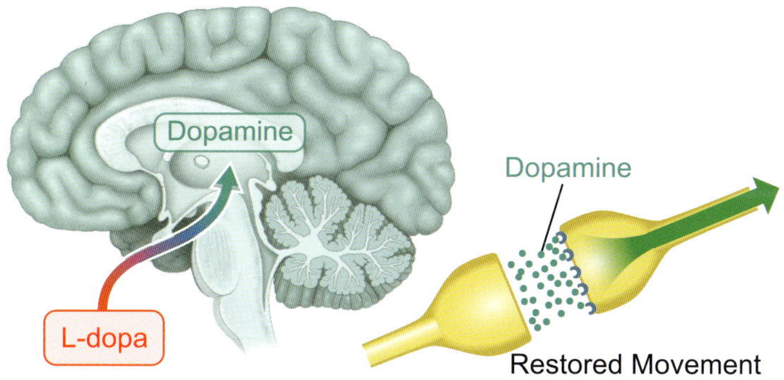

Parkinson's Disease Post-treatment

Huntington's disease is an inherited neurodegenerative disorder that affects motor and cognitive abilities and gradually progresses into dementia. It is more common in people of Western European descent than in those of African or Asian descent. The onset of symptoms typically occurs in middle age. Memory decline begins before motor function impairment and damage to the basal ganglia is particularly pronounced.

Wernicke-Korsakoff syndrome (WKS) is a chronic memory disorder manifesting in an inability to form new memories and learn new tasks, loss of existing memory, and confabulation. An important symptom of WKS is retrograde amnesia that follows a **temporal curve**—newer memories are more affected than older memories. The temporal curve of Korsakoff's syndrome indicates that normal consolidation of memory may continue for as long as two years or more since the age of the memory is the factor that determines whether or not it is preserved. WKS is brought on by a lack of B1 (thiamine), usually created by overconsumption of alcohol, eating disorders, or malnutrition. **Wernicke encephalopathy** is the name for a milder stage of Wernicke-Korsakoff syndrome.

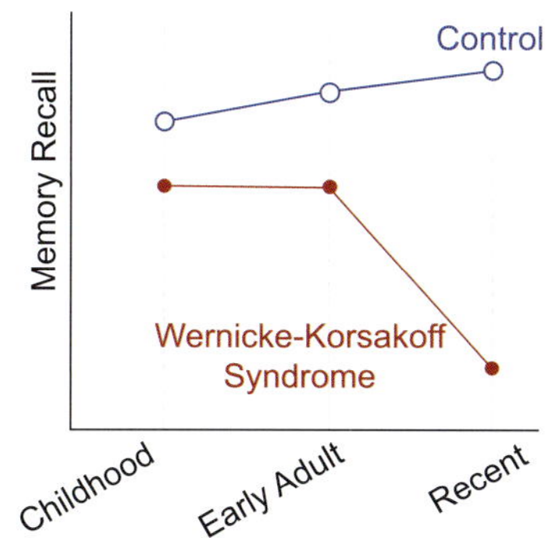

Retrograde Amnesia Temporal Curve

Changes in Synaptic Connections

Rather than being contained in a single spot or pathway, the physical changes in the brain that store a single memory are believed to be scattered around the brain. An **engram** is a group of neurons that physically represent memory. The existence of an engram is somewhat hypothetical. The **equipotentiality hypothesis** states that if a part of an engram is damaged, a replacement part will form in a new area.

Areas of the brain believed to be important to memory are the amygdala, the hippocampus, the cerebellum, and parts of the cortex. The **amygdala** regulates emotions, such as fear and aggression. This may explain why memories connected to emotions are easier to access when the same emotions are experienced. The **hippocampus** connects new information with the cortex, making it necessary to form semantic memories. It plays an important role in the consolidation of long-term explicit memory. Implicit memories require the **cerebellum**, while the **cerebral cortex** is involved with semantic memory.

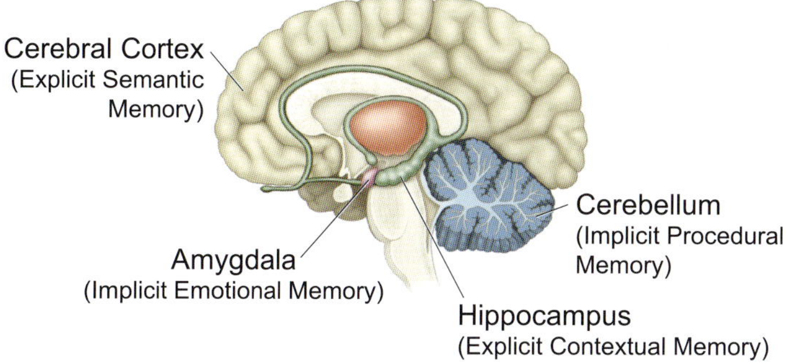

The neurotransmitters that regulate memory are epinephrine, dopamine, serotonin, glutamate, and acetylcholine. Memory consolidation occurs through repeated activity between neurons leading to increased neurotransmitters in the synapses, which, in turn, leads to more synapses and increased synaptic efficiency.

Though encoding and consolidation are often used interchangeably, the term **consolidation** may be used to distinguish the long-term processes of memory formation from the short-term processes of encoding. In addition, consolidation more typically focuses on memory formation at the cellular level. When one neuron fires, it activates the next neuron in the pathway via the connecting synapse. Multiple firing of this pair strengthens the synapse and increases the likelihood that they will fire again. **Long-term potentiation** occurs when the neurons are permanently sensitized to each other. In this manner, a memory network is created.

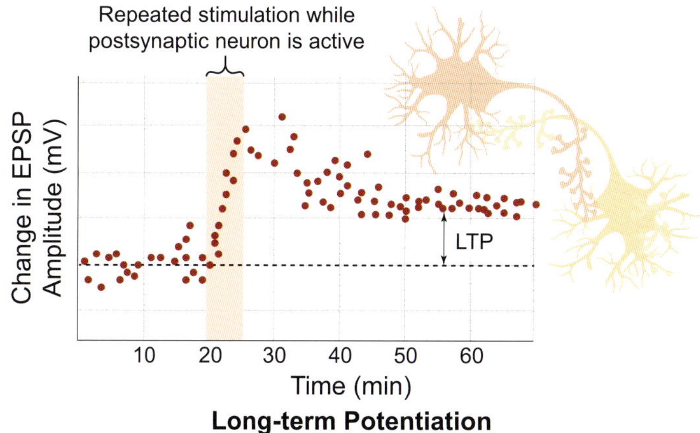

Long-term Potentiation

Over time, the network pathways can change to become more efficient in a phenomenon known as **neural plasticity**.

The changes in the network may introduce inaccuracies into the memory. **Long-term depression** may occur as well when synapses are inhibited. High-frequency impulses potentiate, while low-frequency impulses depress.

Each neuron is connected to thousands of other neurons, and each connection is involved in multiple memories. The pattern of connection distinguishes between memories in a given network.

Neural plasticity allows other parts of my brain to take over for the damaged ones.

2.6 Cognition Development

Cognition is any form of awareness. Among other things, it includes thinking, remembering, reasoning, imagining, and problem solving. Traditionally, it is one of three components of the mind.

1. **Cognition**: a form of knowing or awareness.
2. **Affect**: a feeling, emotion, or mood.
3. **Conation**: an inclination to act with purpose; an instinct, a wish, or a desire to do something.

Cognition is thinking.

Cognitive Development

Jean Piaget was interested in intellectual development. He believed that children were not less intelligent than adults, but that they just thought differently. Children didn't only accumulate knowledge as they grew—the way they processed knowledge changed as well. **Piaget** proposed **four stages of cognitive development**.

1. **Sensorimotor:** up to 18-24 months
2. **Preoperational:** up to 7 years old
3. **Concrete Operational:** up to 12 years old
4. **Formal Operational:** adolescence through adulthood

Stages may overlap, but no stage may be skipped.

During the early **sensorimotor stage,** the child is aware only of his immediate environment. He gathers only simple information through his senses. Nevertheless, it is a period of dramatic intellectual growth. Not until 7 to 9 months does the infant gain **object permanence (or constancy),** where he realizes objects still exist even after he can't see the object. Object permanence is a sign that memory is starting to develop. Language development begins toward the end of the sensorimotor stage.

During the **preoperational stage**, language, symbolic thinking, memory, and imagination develop. Words and pictures are understood as symbols representing more than themselves. The child engages in make-believe. He is egocentric and unable to see the world from someone else's perspective. For instance, he may allow someone else a turn, but it will be so he can have his turn, not because he finds satisfaction in seeing someone else happy.

When the child reaches the **concrete operational stage,** he begins to think about what others might think. He begins to focus on the world around him, using inductive logic, generalizing from his experiences to make inferences about the real world. Still, thinking is rigid in this stage, and the child struggles with abstract concepts.

A test to discover if the child has passed out of the preoperational stage and into the concrete operational stage is to show the child two identical glasses with the same amount of water. Now pour the water from one glass into a short fat glass and the water from the other into a tall thin glass and ask him which has more water. If the child answers correctly, he is using logic to explain the real world, and he is out of the preoperational stage and into the concrete operational stage. This ability is called conservation.

The **formal operational stage** comes with the ability to think abstractly and reason through hypothetical situations. The use of symbols in algebra and science becomes possible. The child begins using deductive logic and thinking about philosophical and moral issues. Hypothetical reasoning and planning for the future are clear indicators of the formal operational stage.

Let's go through a visual mnemonic to help remember Piaget's stages.

Stage 1: Picture yourself as a baby on the floor of a playpen. Inside the playpen are a blindfold and a toy motor. You put on the blindfold so you can no longer see the toy motorboat. However, you know it's there because you sense the motorboat. That's object permanence during the sensorimotor stage.

Stage 2: You crawl out of the crib and into your highchair at two years old as you begin stage 2. Your mother scrubs your hands before feeding you alphabet soup, but you are using your new skill of imagination to pretend she is a nurse preparing you, the doctor, in preop. You tell her, "I am the best doctor in the world." The alphabet soup represents language, which means you can use symbolic thinking. Pretending to be in preop represents "pretend play" in the preoperational stage. And, of course, your statement represents your egocentric viewpoint in the preoperational stage.

Stage 3: Next, you climb on the kitchen counter and stand on seven concrete blocks (for seven years old) so you can get even higher. Imagine how the blocks must be stacked to make seven. You hold a thin glass of water in your hand and pour it into a fat glass and say, "Look, it's the same amount of water!" You realize that if this is true for water in glasses, it must be true for all the rivers dumping into the ocean. That's using inductive logic in the concrete stage.

Stage 4: Finally, since you are a child genius, you become a doctor at 12 years old. You are dressed in a tuxedo (formal wear). You are operating for free in a remote village of poor, starving people because you are thinking about higher principles as you are supposed to in the formal operational stage.

Pretty silly, but it'll help you remember Piaget's stages!

The 4 P's Mnemonic	Stage	Age	Cognitive Development Stage Characteristics
Permanence	Sensorimotor	0-2	Gather information using senses and immediate environment Learn to differentiate self from external objects Recognize object permanence (constancy) Language development begins
Pretend	Preoperational	2-7	Advancement in language and symbolic thinking Egocentric point of view Imaginative play with make-believe elements Classification of objects using single attributes (shape, color, etc.)
Perspective	Concrete Operational	7-12	Perspective widens to include other people Rigid thinking that involves concrete concepts only Inductive logic and inference based on experience Recognize conservation (classification using multiple attributes)
Picasso	Formal Operational	12+	Abstract thinking and reasoning through hypothetical situations Advanced use of symbols and symbolic thinking Deductive logic and inference based on reasoning Consideration of philosophical and moral factors

Piaget's Mental Models

The category into which an object is placed is its **schema**. What is the difference between a house and a hut? The exact difference is difficult to pinpoint, but there are structures that are clearly houses and not huts. Your idea of what makes a house a house is your schema of a house. A flying car is only a car and not a plane because it fits into the observer's schema of a car.

One explanation for inattentional blindness (and all the other mental blindness phenomena) is that your schema creates an expectation of certain stimuli and not others. This influences how you perceive events, and such an expectation is called your **perceptual set**.

Schemas either expand or shift when new information is presented. A child might consider cats as small, furry creatures with long tails until he sees a lion. At that point, he might adjust his schema of cats to include *large*, furry creatures with long tails. The expansion of a schema to incorporate new information is known as **assimilation**. When the same child sees a hairless cat, he might adjust his schema by changing it to include small and large creatures that may or may not be furry but have long tails. This change of information (rather than the incorporation of new information) to his schema is called **accommodation**.

Equilibration is an attempt to find a balance between assimilation and accommodation.

Assimilation is incorporating new information into an existing schema. In this case, the girl has added zebra to her schema of large 4-legged animals. Accommodation is creating a new schema based on new information. In this case, the girl has created a new schema for zebras and can now differentiate between horses and zebras. Equilibrium is the balance between these two.

Cognitive Changes in Late Adulthood

Our cognition changes as we age. We get better at some things, stay stable in others, and some of our mental functions decline. For example, our semantic memory improves until we are about 55, and our vocabulary tends to grow over time as well. Elderly people typically are better at using knowledge and experience to make decisions, enhancing their skill in reading comprehension and analogies. They tend to be able to separate emotions from logical decisions more effectively than younger adults. Many functions, such as our procedural memory, recognition memory, and temporal order memory, stay stable. Others decline, ranging from executive functioning to prospective memory. Loss of contextual information of an episodic memory also becomes more common. Processing speed slows, and multitasking becomes more difficult as the elderly tend to be more easily distracted.

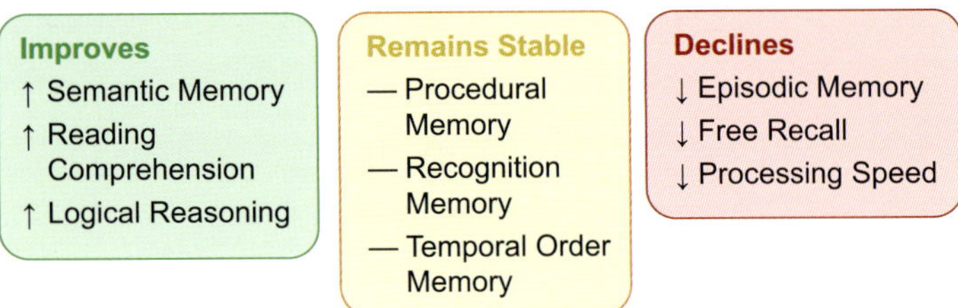

Cognitive Changes in Late Adulthood

Culture and Cognitive Development

The culture a person is raised in may affect his cognitive development and thinking. For example, it has been found that people born and raised in East Asia tend to use a **holistic cognitive style** that focuses more on context and relationships between the objects in a scene. In contrast, people born and raised in America and Europe tend to use an **analytic cognitive style** that focuses more on discrete objects and their properties. In other words, Easterners see the whole, while Westerners see the parts.

Other cultural differences in cognition have been found, including people's preferred logical reasoning patterns, their vulnerability to hindsight bias, and their ability to tolerate contradictions. Keeping this in mind, there is little evidence to suggest that cultural variations in cognition can cause changes in neural structure.

Holistically, I see a fish who lives in a bowl surrounded with water and a decorative plant that is located in the middle of our room.

Analytically, I see a brightly colored goldfish, a glass water bowl, a decorative plant, and various rocks.

Heredity and Environment on Cognitive Development

Both a person's genes and his environment are involved in cognitive development. Current research suggests that about half of the variance in general cognition is attributable to genetic factors. This means that when you look at the general population, about half of the difference in cognitive function between two individuals is likely due to differences in their genes. The other half is attributed to differences in their environments. Much of the research concerning environmental influences on cognitive development is focused on the prenatal period. Environmental factors that can influence cognitive development during this time include parental smoking, alcohol use, and the use of other drugs such as cocaine and heroin. After he is born, his social class, education, nutrition, and other factors correlate with his cognitive development. The extent to which heredity and environment contribute to cognitive development is still extremely controversial, and much remains unknown about what causes differences in cognitive development between individuals.

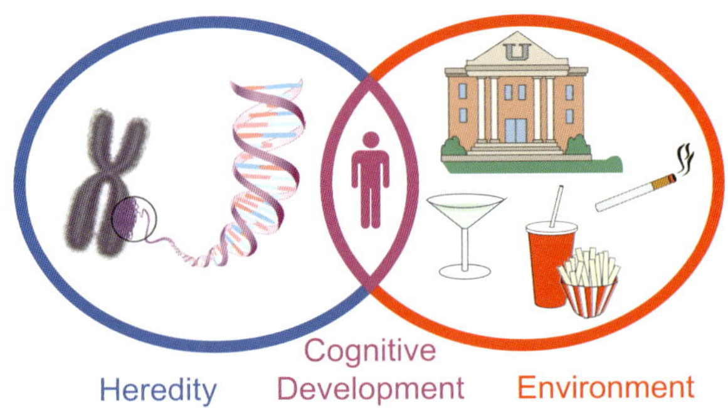

Biological Factors that Affect Cognition

How cognition occurs on a biological level is not yet well understood. There are hundreds, if not thousands, of genes linked to a person's performance on cognitive tests. Some alleles of these genes have been found to increase or decrease performance on specific cognitive tests, while other alleles have been linked to the development of disorders that affect cognition, such as Alzheimer's disease, Huntington's disease, and Parkinson's disease. The individual effects of each gene are usually small, but combinations of these genes have been linked to the early or more severe development of cognitive disorders.

Decisions, Intelligence, and Consciousness 3

3.1 Problem-Solving and Decision-Making

Humans are excellent problem solvers. We have to solve problems ranging from taking care of biological needs, such hunger or tiredness, to making major life decisions, such as choosing who to marry or choosing a career path. There are two main types of problems: **well-defined** and **ill-defined**.

Problem: Unscramble the letters to make a word.

There's a clear goal and solution. I am confident the problem is solved correctly and the goal has been reached.

Well-defined Problem

Problem: Maximize public health.

Educate people
Improve infrastructure
Reduce inequalities
Clean air and water
Teach stress management

There are many ways of getting there and none of them are clearly the optimal solution. I'll never know if/when the goal has been sufficiently reached or whether it could have been done better another way.

Ill-defined Problem

Well-defined problems have a clear starting and ending point, and it is easy to see whether the problem has been solved or not. Needing to take out the garbage is an example of a well-defined problem.

Ill-defined problems lack both a clear starting and ending point. There is no clear goal to be achieved, and if there is, the methods by which it can be achieved are unclear. Figuring out how to live a fulfilling life is an example of an ill-defined problem. Although there are ways to make your life more fulfilling, they vary from person to person. Although ill-defined problems can be solved, they have ambiguous outcomes.

There are several methods our brains use to solve problems. First, there is **trial-and-error**, which involves making random guesses to solve a problem until something works. Imagine you are trying to open your high-school locker but have forgotten the combination. Using trial-and-error would mean picking a random combination, testing it, and forgetting the combination you used right after trying it. This method is highly inefficient: if you tested one combination on a standard combination lock every five seconds, it might take you a little over seven months to get your locker open—and that's assuming you don't repeat combinations.

Let's look at solving strategies in today's lesson at Salty's Academy of Problem Solving.

Problem Types

Well-defined
Calculate the area of this triangle.

Ill-defined
Write a compelling story.

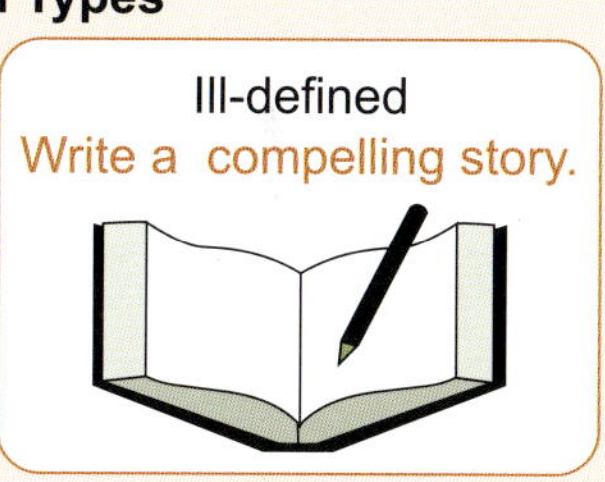

Approaches

Trial-and-error
Solve this cube by randomly turning different parts.

Algorithm
Follow the exact steps needed to solve this cube.

Heuristics

Means-end Analysis
Break down a big problem into manageable sub-problems.

Working Backwards
Start with the endpoint and work backwards to understand the solution.

Answer Key

Fixations (Limitations in Problem-solving)

Mental Set
How can I connect all nine dots with four straight lines?

Functional Fixedness
How do I keep these rolls of paper from unrolling?

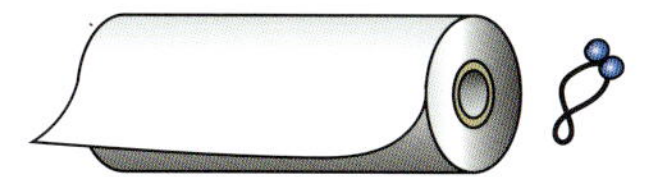

Intuition

Incubation
Let's take time away from the problem.

Insight
Aha! I thought of the answer while I was eating lunch!

Another method is using an **algorithm**. An algorithm is a logical, systematic approach to solving a problem. Think about your locker again. Instead of testing random combinations, an example of an algorithm would be to start at 1-1-1, then try 1-1-2, 1-1-3, and so on. Although this method does not necessarily save time, it is guaranteed that you will get the right combination eventually.

Whether it's random guesses with trial-and-error or a systematic set of attempts with an algorithm, the truth remains that it would be faster to just cut it off!

The most common type of problem-solving method our brains use is a **heuristic**. A heuristic is a mental shortcut used to save time when solving problems. If you remember that you got to choose your locker combination, you might first try testing numbers that mean something to you, like your birthday.

Although heuristics reduce the time needed to solve problems, they do not guarantee correct solutions. It is entirely possible that you chose a random set of numbers for your locker combination and told yourself that you would remember forever—in that instance, you would be better off buying a pair of bolt cutters.

Heuristics can be thought of as rules of thumb—helpful, but not precise nor guaranteed to be accurate.

The brain uses dozens of different heuristics while solving problems. For example, consider **means-end analysis**. Means-end analysis involves breaking up a larger problem into smaller, more manageable subproblems. Then, you attack the biggest subproblem first.

Another common heuristic is **working backward**. Instead of beginning at a starting point and working towards an end goal, working backward involves envisioning the end goal and thinking about ways to get back to the starting point.

Looking at my list of expenses, I can reduce costs in a few areas. These manageable subgoals of spending less money on certain expenses will eventually solve my main problem of needing a new computer.

Means-end Analysis

Now that I know the answer to the problem, it's much easier to work backwards to figure out how to solve it!

Working Backward

The brain uses dozens of heuristics to make problem-solving easier. If we do not want to take up too much time or expend too much effort, we often use **intuition** to make decisions based on instinct. Intuitive decisions almost always rely on heuristics and are ineffective in solving complex problems.

Despite this, sometimes we get stuck on a certain problem—this is called **fixation**. There are many barriers to effective problem-solving, one of which is the unconscious tendency to approach problems in a particular way. One example is known as a **mental set**—the unnecessary constraint that is imposed on problem-solving due to attempting to solve problems based on strategies that were previously successful for other problems, even though it may not work well for the current one. Another example is **functional fixedness**, which refers to the tendency to only consider objects in terms of their usual functions. Many riddles capitalize on this barrier to problem-solving. For example, the solution may require that you use the match box as a candle holder or the stapler as a heavy item to weigh down a string to give it momentum when swung.

Try to solve the nine dot problem yourself! The goal is to connect all of the dots with no more than four straight lines and without lifting the pencil at any point.

Nine Dot Problem

If we take a different approach or keep trying to solve the problem for enough time, insight can occur. **Insight** is that "aha!" moment when the solution finally clicks. Aside from continually working on a problem, insight can occur after you have stopped consciously trying to solve it and switched to doing something else instead. This process is called **incubation**, and it suggests that even though we have stopped consciously focusing on a particular problem, our brains can continue to work on them subconsciously.

If you've ever given up on trying to understand a math problem, only to realize the answer when you're eating dinner later, you've experienced insight through incubation.

Heuristics, Biases, and Decision-Making

To solve problems, we also have to make decisions. **Decision-making** involves making a judgment about the desirability, effectiveness, or probability of a given outcome. For example, you might make a decision about which problem-solving method to use based on how likely you think each method is to work.

Decision-making, like problem-solving, is made faster and easier by heuristics. Without looking it up, which do you think is more common: death by a dog attack or death by heatstroke? To make this decision, you probably used the **availability heuristic**—meaning that you used concrete examples that readily came to mind. For example, you may have thought about news stories you have read about dog attacks or remembered that a family friend passed away due to heatstroke. Although the availability heuristic can be useful, our personal experiences do not always align with the actual state of the world.

Dog attacks and other violent events are more sensationalized than everyday risks like heat-stroke. Therefore, you'll likely encounter more examples of it throughout your life even though it's statistically much less probable.

Since stories about dog attacks are more often publicized than stories about heatstroke, it would not be surprising if people answered that dog attacks are more likely to cause death. However, the risk of dying from heatstroke is much higher than the risk of dying from a dog attack (1 in 7,700 people versus 1 in 118,776 people).

Another common heuristic used in decision-making is the **representativeness heuristic**. When we use the representativeness heuristic, we make decisions based on **prototypes** or a general idea of what we think is normal or expected. For example, if you saw a picture of a middle-aged woman who wears glasses and is reading a book, would you decide that she's more likely to be a librarian or a sales associate? Many people would choose librarian because the description conforms to their prototype. However, it's much more probable that she's a sales associate based simply on the number of people employed in those careers.

I'm never flying again. It's much too dangerous. I'll stick to driving—you don't see nearly as many stories about people dying that way!

Availability Heuristic

Which six-coin flip sequence is more likely?

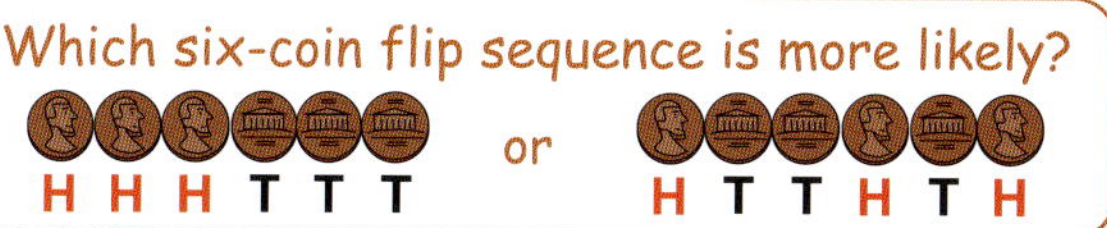

Obviously, the second one looks random and thus is more likely to happen.

Actually, random flips are not self-correcting, so either pattern is equally likely, but the second one looks more like your prototype of random, so you think t's more likely.

Representativeness Heuristic

Make sure that you can tell the difference between availability and representativeness. When using the availability heuristic, we recall specific examples that come to mind, for example new stories, conversations, or our personal experiences that are related to the decision we are trying to make. The representativeness heuristic relies on prototypes, which are general ideas regarding a topic. Prototypes do not have to be recallable memories.

The representativeness heuristic is commonly associated with a **conjunction fallacy**, in which people think that the likelihood of two events occurring together is more likely than one of the two events occurring on its own. Imagine a person named Clyde who has his own garden and belongs to a local organization in his town that replants trees. When people are asked whether he is a college instructor or an environmentalist instructor, they are more likely to choose the second option because it conforms to their prototype of someone who has a garden and participates in environmental projects. However, because not every college instructor is an environmentalist, it must be more likely that Clyde is just an instructor and not both an instructor and an environmentalist, even though it might be tempting to say otherwise based on how he is portrayed.

Probabilities fall somewhere between 0.0–1.0. When you combine two probabilities, you multiply their respective values to ascertain their combined probability. Therefore, the probability of two events is never higher than the probability of one of those events alone.

When making decisions, we often fall prey to **biases**. Biases are patterns of deviation from logical thought or judgment and influence every aspect of problem-solving and decision-making. One bias is called **overconfidence**, which is a tendency to be more confident that a decision is correct than you should be. If you have ever answered a test question that you were 100% sure about, only to find that you got the wrong answer, you have experienced overconfidence.

Another bias is **belief perseverance**, which involves actively rejecting or rationalizing facts contrary to beliefs you hold. Belief perseverance is most obvious when emotionally charged topics such as politics and religion are involved, but it also extends to aspects of daily life.

A third type of bias is **confirmation bias**, in which you seek out information that confirms beliefs you already have and avoid information that might provide evidence to the contrary. This can range from reading news stories from outlets that you align with politically to only investing in companies you already believe to be promising or only favoring scientific data that supports your beliefs.

The **just-world fallacy**, yet another bias, is where you believe that people deserve what happens to them. In other words, people reap what they sow. This bias is associated with judging sick people as responsible for their illnesses and thinking that kids who are bullied deserve it.

The **halo effect** is a bias in which people rate others who make a positive impression on them (through their beauty, grooming, etc.) more positively than would be expected by their performance or other traits. For example, people rate essays that are paired with a picture of an attractive author as being better-written than those written by plain or unattractive authors.

Framing effects can also influence decision-making. Framing effects are a type of cognitive bias in which people make decisions based on how information is presented, such as a chance of success versus a chance of failure. For example, many people will register early for service when a penalty fee for late registration is emphasized, but fewer people will register early if the fee is presented as a discount for early registration.

3.2 Intellectual Functioning

Intelligence

Psychology defines intelligence in various ways. Almost every major researcher in the field of intelligence thought about intelligence differently, although each definition is relatively close to any other. In general, intelligence can be thought about as the ability of a person to solve new problems, learn from experience, and use existing knowledge to adapt to different environments. Charles Spearman defined **general intelligence** as the ability to score well on mental aptitude tests. Louis Thurstone separated mental abilities into categories and defined intelligence accordingly. Howard Gardner thought there were nine different types of intelligence. Robert Sternberg narrowed Gardner's different categories down to three.

For a little over a hundred years, standardized tests designed to quantify a person's intelligence have been developed by psychologists and put into widespread use. These tests are called **IQ tests**, or intelligence quotient tests. The founder of the modern IQ test, **Alfred Binet**, in conjunction with Theodore Simon, came up with these tests to predict which children may have difficulty learning material in school. The term intelligence quotient comes from how the test was originally scaled, which compared a child's "mental age" to his or her actual age and was calculated by dividing the mental age by the actual age. Binet himself stressed that the test could not possibly capture all facets of intelligence and warned against trying to completely quantify human intellectual ability.

$$\text{IQ} = \frac{\text{Mental Age}}{\text{Physical Age}} \times 100$$

The Binet IQ formula compares a person's mental age (intellectual functioning) with their chronological age.

Shortly after their invention in France, IQ tests made their way over to the United States and were reformatted and administered to broad swaths of the US population. The primary adapter of Binet's mental age test was **Lewis Terman.** He removed the original mental age quotient and replaced it with scores distributed on a bell curve, which is how IQ scores are formatted today. The updated version created by Terman was named the **Stanford-Binet intelligence test** and was the most popular IQ test used in the United States for decades.

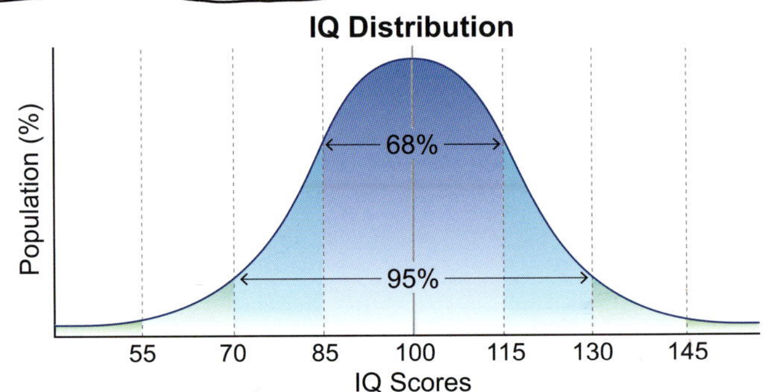

Starting with the earliest IQ tests and continuing to today, it has been found that different factors on intelligence tests tend to correlate with each other for any given test-taker. This means that if someone scores highly on the logic subsection of an IQ test, it is likely that other subsection scores will also be higher than average. This doesn't mean that people don't have strong and weak abilities, but that when two people are compared, if you look at the difference between one pair of their subscores, there will likely be a similar difference found between each of the other subscores as well. This has led researchers to believe that there may be a single factor underlying intelligence called the **g factor**. Originally described by Charles Spearman in the early 1900s, the g factor is a central part of most modern theories of intelligence and has been repeatedly found to correlate with measures of life success, such as level of education, income, job attainment, and job performance.

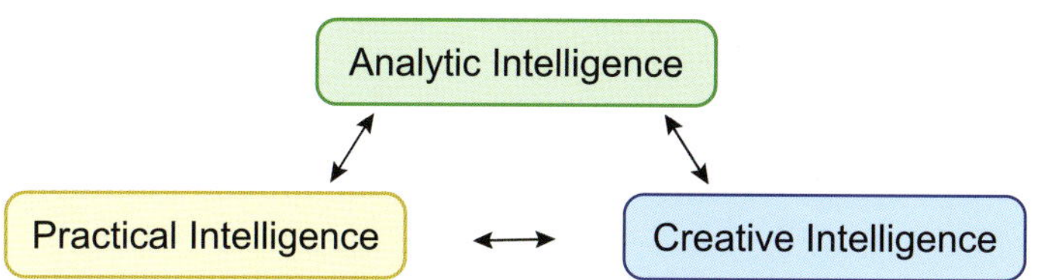

Triarchic Theory Of Intelligence

Other modern theories of intelligence include not one but multiple factors that make up separate types of intelligence. Most prominent is the **triarchic theory of intelligence**, which was created by Robert Sternberg. This theory splits intelligence into three types: **analytic intelligence**, **practical intelligence**, and **creative intelligence**. Analytic intelligence is what is tested on IQ tests, practical intelligence is the ability to solve real-world problems and use common sense, and creative intelligence is the ability to solve novel problems, adapt to new situations, and generate new ideas.

Another multifactor theory of intelligence is L.L. Thurstone's **theory of primary mental abilities**. Instead of one g factor explaining variations in human intelligence, the theory of primary mental abilities splits intelligence into seven factors. These factors are all closely related to what might be called analytical intelligence and have all been found to vary together statistically, which suggests that there is a single factor underlying differences between these seven factors. Thurstone also helped standardize IQ tests and invented new techniques for factor analysis, which helped verify the results of later cognitive tests.

Gardner's Theory Of Multiple Intelligences

Similarly, Howard Gardner's **theory of multiple intelligences** split intelligence into first seven, then nine independent factors. Some factors appear to be similar to what is tested on IQ tests, such as logical-mathematical intelligence and verbal-linguistic intelligence. Other factors are completely unrelated to what might be called analytical intelligence, such as musical, naturalist, and existential intelligence. Like Thurnstone's theory of primary mental abilities, many of Gardner's factors of intelligence have been found to correlate with the g factor, and it is thought that the factors that do not correlate with g are probably not empirically testable.

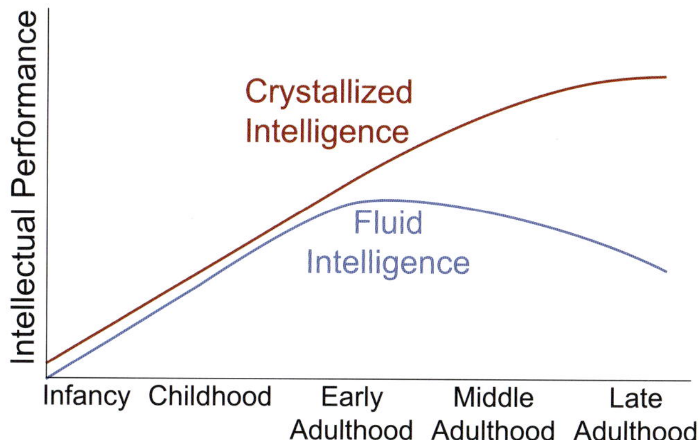

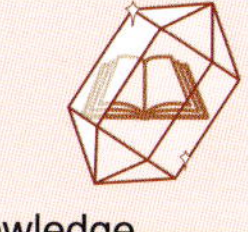

Crystallized Intelligence

- Use of learned knowledge
- Vocabulary and acquired skills
- Affected by experience (nurture)

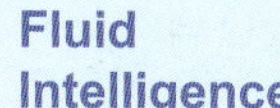

Fluid Intelligence

- Use of logic and abstract reasoning
- Novel problem solving
- Affected by genetics (nature)

Although almost every modern IQ test assumes that there is a single g factor, the g factor itself can be split into multiple subdomains representing different facets of cognitive processing. The two main divisions popularized by Raymond Cattell are **crystallized intelligence** and **fluid**

intelligence. Crystallized intelligence (Gc) is the ability to make decisions based on previously learned material and tends to increase or stay the same with age. In contrast, fluid intelligence (Gf) refers to the ability to make decisions when confronted with entirely new material and tends to decline with age. Both crystallized intelligence and fluid intelligence correlate with the g factor and are thought to be subfactors, instead of independent factors, of intelligence.

There are different standards for scoring that each IQ test follows, but most modern IQ tests, including the Stanford-Binet, Wechsler Intelligence Scale for Children (WISC), and Wechsler Adult Intelligence Scale (WAIS), have a median score of 100 and a standard deviation of approximately15. Raw test scores are normalized to fit into a normal distribution, and percentiles are assigned to each normalized score.

Like nearly all human traits, intelligence comes both from a person's genes and from his environment. IQ has been estimated to be from about 50% to almost 90% heritable, meaning that between 50% and 90% of the variation between people's IQ scores is likely due to heritable factors. Although genetics have a large impact on intelligence, no single gene has been linked to higher intelligence in individuals. Instead, it is thought that intelligence is based on hundreds or thousands of genes, each making a small contribution to intelligence.

The contribution to intelligence that does not come from genes comes from a person's environment. Many factors that have been linked to lowering a person's IQ, such as malnutrition, poor education, and poverty. Other factors, such as being breastfed as an infant, the length of time spent in school, and high socioeconomic status, have been linked to higher IQs. However, the factors that can cause negative effects tend to be much stronger than the factors that can cause positive effects. For example, iodine deficiency in children can cause IQ to drop almost 15 points, which in most tests is a full standard deviation. In contrast, being breastfed as an infant can cause an increase of between two or three IQ points.

Remember, correlation does not equal causation.

Although IQ correlates positively with a number of important life factors, such as wealth, educational achievement, age at death, and happiness, it is not the only variable that affects these factors. A person's outlook toward intelligence is also important. People who have a **growth mindset** regarding intelligence, meaning that they view intelligence as something changeable with effort and perseverance, tend to enjoy more career success than people who have a **fixed mindset** regarding intelligence. People with a fixed mindset view intelligence as something that is unchanging and something that a person either has or does not have.

3.3 States of Consciousness

Consciousness is the awareness of yourself and of at least some of the internal and external stimuli affecting you. The psychologist and philosopher William James spoke about "a stream of consciousness," wherein consciousness meanders from one direction to the next without ever stopping. There is no known structure in the brain that is responsible for consciousness; rather, it is thought to be somehow created by neural pathways working together.

There are four states of consciousness: alertness, daydreaming, drowsiness, and sleep.

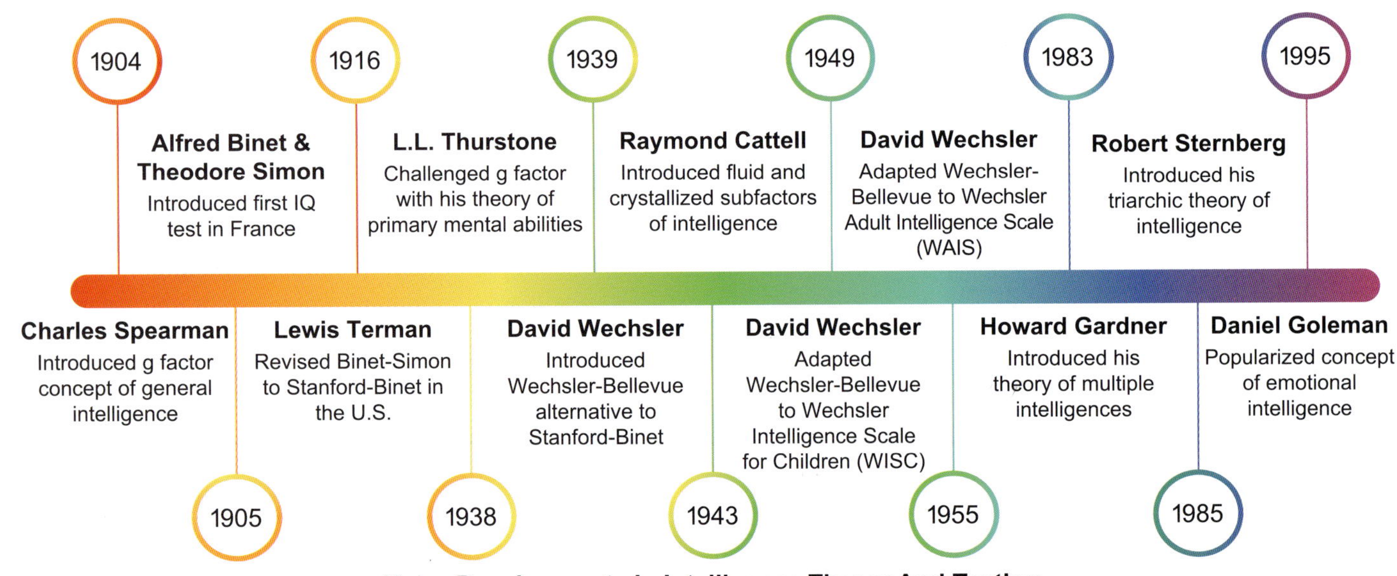

Major Developments In Intelligence Theory And Testing

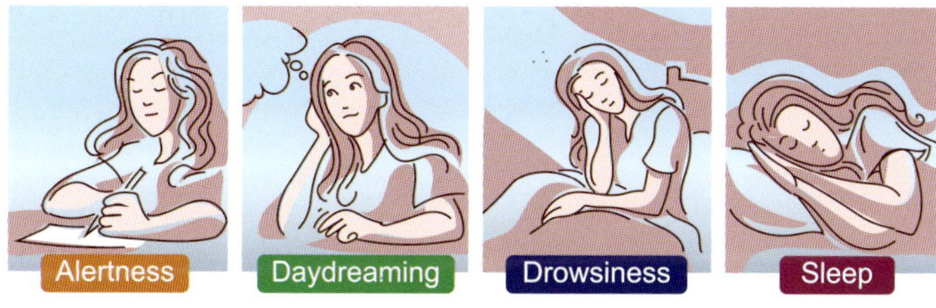

Four States of Consciousness

Alertness comes with an awareness of who you are and what is going on around you. It is also the state you are in when you are focusing on something or trying to remember something.

Daydreaming occurs when the mind wanders, and you generally feel more relaxed and less focused than when you are alert. People spend about 50% of their time awake daydreaming—this can either be unintentional or self-induced with meditation.

Drowsiness occurs just before falling asleep and just after waking up and can also be induced by deep meditation.

Sleep is the state of consciousness in which the awareness of the self or the world around you is significantly decreased.

Notice that sleep falls under the definition of being conscious.

An **electroencephalogram (EEG)** is a test that measures electrical activity in the brain. The test represents this activity as wavy lines called brain waves. Brain waves vary in amplitude and frequency. Four different types of brain waves are distinguished by their frequency. From highest frequency to lowest they are:

1. **Beta:** associated with focused alertness.
2. **Alpha:** associated with daydreaming and relaxation.
3. **Theta:** associated with drowsiness and light sleep.
4. **Delta:** associated with deep sleep and coma.

There is no precise point that distinguishes sleep from wakefulness. There are four main stages of sleep: N1, N2, N3, and REM. "N" stands for non-REM sleep.

N1 (Stage 1) sleep is characterized by the presence of both alpha and theta waves. People also experience **hypnagogic hallucinations**, which depending on the person's situation can range from seeing dots of light to extremely vivid images. If a person has been engaged in a repetitive task before bed, especially one that is new to him, that experience may recur in hypnagogic hallucinations. For example, if a person plays Tetris for several hours before going to bed, he may see the blocks falling again before falling asleep—this is called the **Tetris effect**. People may also feel like they're falling, leading to involuntary muscle twitches called **hypnic jerks**.

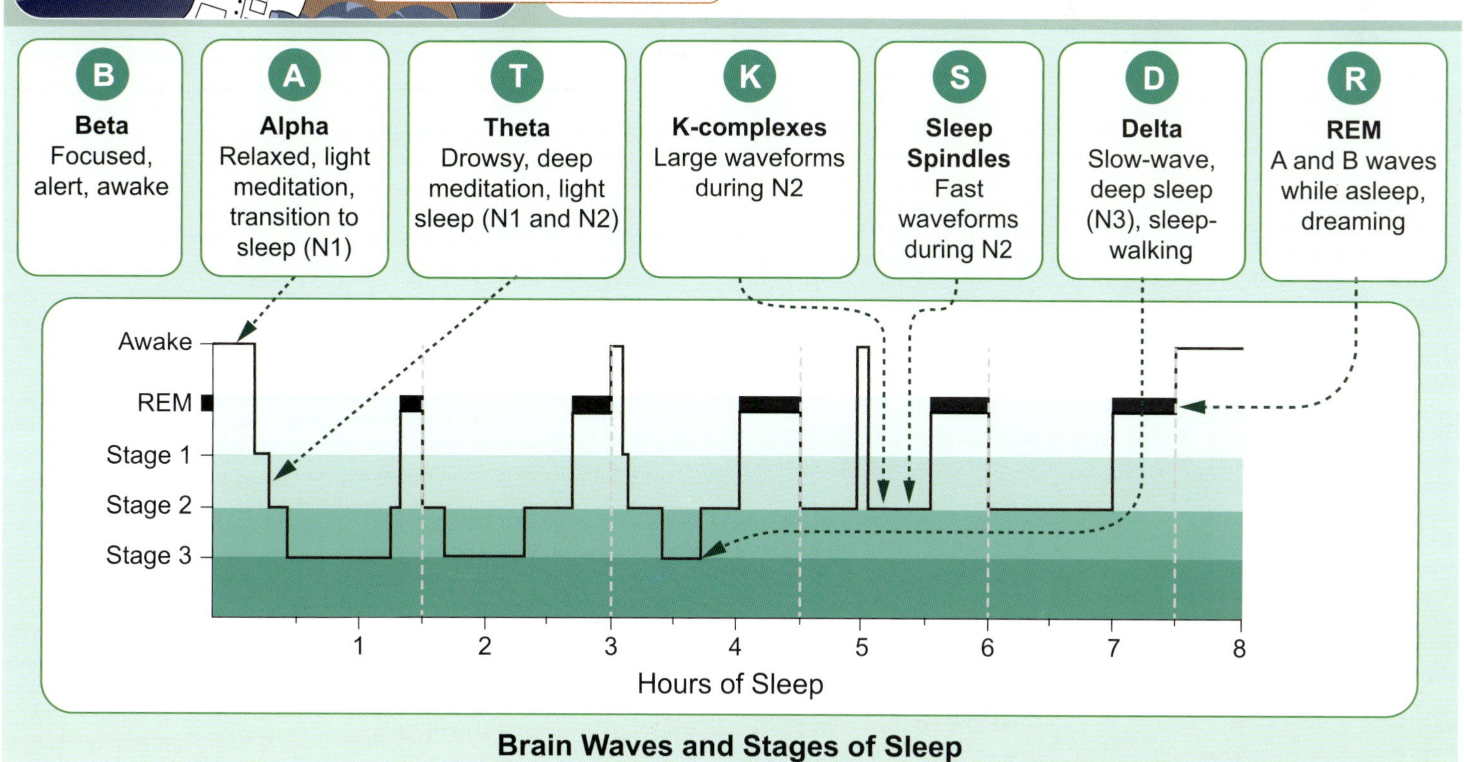

Brain Waves and Stages of Sleep

N2 (Stage 2) sleep is a deeper stage of sleep, with more theta waves and almost no alpha waves. Patterns called **K-complexes** and **sleep spindles** also appear.

K-complexes are thought to help keep people asleep and help memory consolidation during sleep. K-complexes can be natural or induced by other stimuli, such as gently touching a person's skin with a feather while he's sleeping.

Sleep spindles are probably important in both sensory processing and long-term memory consolidation. Sleep spindles appear as rapid bursts of activity and often follow shortly after K-complexes.

N3 (Stage 3) sleep is deep sleep, also known as **slow-wave sleep (SWS),** and is characterized by delta waves. People in N3 sleep are very difficult to wake up, and they can exhibit behaviors such as sleepwalking and sleep-talking.

REM (rapid eye movement) sleep is a deep sleep where most dreaming occurs. It is characterized by a mix of alpha and beta waves, appearing fairly similar to EEG patterns taken while awake. If you look at a person's eyes during REM sleep, you may be able to see the eyes moving around as if they are looking at something, which is where this stage gets its name. Most other muscles are paralyzed during REM sleep, which prevents people from acting out their dreams while asleep.

REM sleep is particularly important for memory consolidation, especially that of procedural memory, emotional memory, and spatial memory.

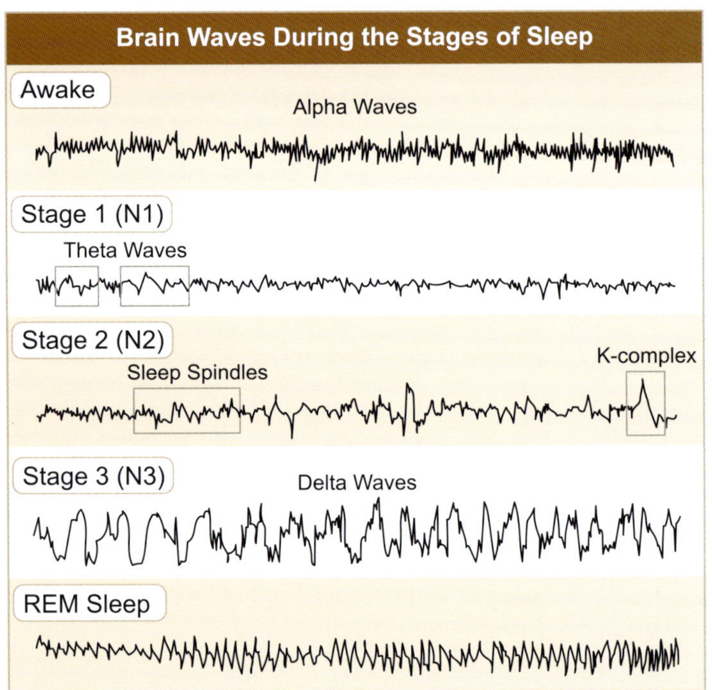

The entire sleep cycle is typically repeated four or five times each night, with a full cycle lasting about 90 minutes each. The order of the cycle typically goes as follows: N1 to N2 to N3, then back to N2, then to REM. Afterward, the cycle repeats, starting from either N1 or N2.

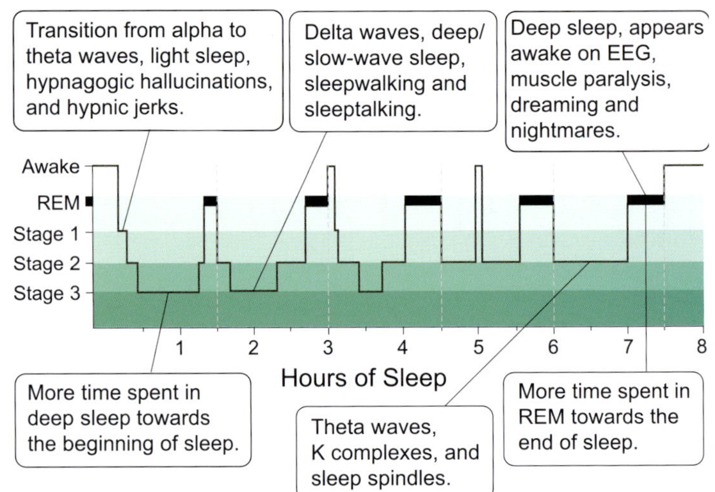

The length of REM sleep periods increases through the night, while other stages shorten. Overall, about 20-25% of sleep is REM sleep for young adults. The amount of time in each stage varies with age. Infants spend more time in REM sleep. The amount of REM sleep remains fairly constant into late adulthood, but older adults spend more time in N1, which may account for waking up more often during the night. Total sleep time declines with age.

Nature displays predictable rhythms that are tied to the orbit of the earth. The tides, the seasons, the phases of the moon, and the days are in sync. Life evolved under these circumstances, so it is no wonder that they play an important role in human biology. Human biology is underpinned by rhythmical behavior called **circadian rhythms.** Circadian rhythms are loosely tied to a 24-hour cycle. These cycles affect physical and cognitive performance, including short-term memory and sleep. Going to bed and waking up at irregular times can put your circadian rhythms out of sync, resulting in physical and mental health issues.

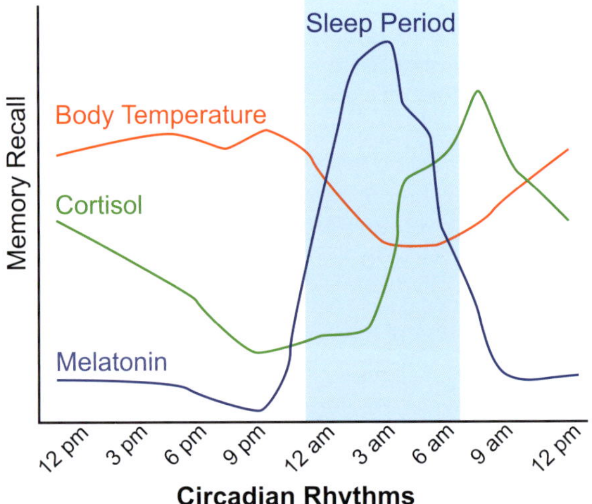

Although almost entirely absent from the body during daytime, the hormone melatonin, which is created by the pineal gland from the precursor substance serotonin, begins to be released after exposure to dim light. Other indicators used to measure the timing of a person's circadian rhythm are body temperature and the level of cortisol, a steroid hormone, in the blood.

Dreaming

Dreaming is likely a universal human phenomenon. Although REM sleep is closely associated with dreaming, dreams can also occur during non-REM sleep, but dreams during non-REM sleep tend to be less vivid and less easily recalled than dreams experienced during REM sleep. When a person is dreaming, most of the electrical activity measured in his brain is similar to that seen when he is awake. However, the activity in the prefrontal cortex—the region most associated with logical thinking—tends to be lower during dreams. This may help explain why we do not notice how strange dreams can be while we are experiencing them.

There are many theories as to why dreams occur. For example, **Sigmund Freud's theory of dreams** hypothesizes that dreams result from our unconscious thoughts and desires, most of which stem directly from early childhood memories and experiences. He also believed that experienced clinicians could interpret dreams.

To Freud, a dream has both manifest and latent content. **Manifest content** is what is literally happening in the dream, such as the dreamer falling off a building. **Latent content** is the hidden, true significance of the dream. In the above example, the latent content could be a fear of failure.

Freud's Dreaming Theory

Carl Jung also believed that the content of the dream was related to the dreamer's unconscious thoughts and desires. However, instead of focusing on early childhood memories and professional interpretation, Jung believed that dreams act as messages and can be used to help resolve emotional or religious problems.

There are also several neurobiological theories of dreaming. The **activation-synthesis theory** of dreaming holds that dreams result from brain activation during REM sleep. The brainstem releases neural impulses, while the cortex synthesizes them. So, dreams are the result of the brain trying to find meaning from meaningless brain activity.

Another theory is the **threat simulation theory**, which looks at dreams from the perspective of evolutionary biology. According to this theory, there is an evolutionary advantage to dreaming since the brain can simulate stressful or dangerous interactions, such as escaping predators or interacting with mates. Evolutionary biologists have also proposed that dreams confer an evolutionary advantage by helping problem solving, or that they have no purpose at all.

3.4 Sleep-Wake Disorders

Dozens of disorders involving sleep-wake cycles have been identified. **Sleep deprivation** can cause deficits in attention and working memory, driving ability, and other cognitively demanding tasks. Sleep deprivation is also linked to weight gain, lower levels of human growth hormone, and type II diabetes. When a person is sleep-deprived, he can usually return to normal function after a full night's sleep, which is often called paying off "**sleep debt**."

The amount of sleep a person needs is highly dependent on both his age and other individual factors. For example, newborns need between 14 and 17 hours of sleep per day, teenagers need between 8 and 10, and adults need between 7 and 9. In general, the older a person gets, the less sleep he needs to function normally.

The stimulatory nature of the fight-or-flight stress response is one cause of sleep deprivation. If stress is chronic, it's hard to pay off the resulting sleep debt. Exercise and otherstress management strategies will help me get better sleep and reduce the likelihood of this issue worsening to the point of diagnosable insomnia.

The chronic inability to fall asleep, difficulty remaining asleep, and/or perpetually waking up too early are symptoms of **insomnia**. Insomnia is commonly treated with prescription medications, but these drugs tend to lead to tolerance and dependence in the long run. For most people, lifestyle changes such as exercising regularly, limiting the use of alcohol, nicotine, and other drugs, and removing cell phones and other electronic devices from bedrooms are effective for preventing insomnia.

Narcolepsy, on the other hand, is characterized by excessive sleepiness throughout the day and by involuntarily falling asleep for brief periods of time. The sleeping fits are usually brief, lasting 8 minutes or fewer. Although there is no cure for narcolepsy, some medications can help reduce the severity of sleeping fits. The same sleep hygiene techniques used to prevent insomnia can also help people with narcolepsy.

Another common sleep disorder is **sleep apnea**. Sleep apnea is a disorder in which a person does not take in enough oxygen while asleep, causing him to wake up. He stays awake just long enough to breathe, then falls back asleep, often without realizing that he has woken up. Sleep apnea can lead to chronic sleep deprivation, vision problems, diabetes, and liver damage.

There are two types of sleep apnea: **obstructive sleep apnea (OSA)** and **central sleep apnea (CSA)**. Obstructive sleep apnea is caused by the soft tissues surrounding the airway constricting the airway during sleep, while central sleep apnea is caused by instability in the body's feedback mechanisms that control breathing.

The treatments for OSA are mostly preventative and include losing weight, avoiding nicotine and alcohol, and sleeping on one's side. Both OSA and CSA are also treated using a **CPAP (continuous positive airway pressure) machine**, which supplies pressurized air that holds a person's upper airway open.

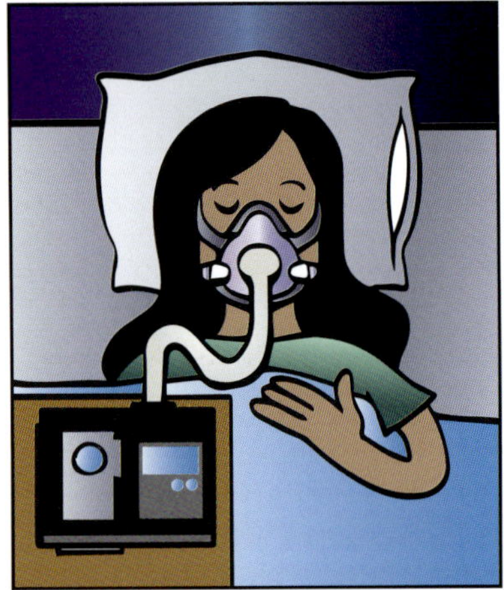

CPAP Machine for Sleep Apnea

Hypoventilation syndrome, another sleep disorder, is also treated with a CPAP machine. It occurs when a person loses the ability to get rid of the CO2 in the bloodstream, and can increase the risk of hospitalization and death due to cardiovascular problems.

Although it may seem strange, **sleepwalking** and **sleep-talking** are classified as sleep disorders. Sleepwalking and sleep-talking happen during N3 sleep and are thought to have a strong genetic component for risk. Although most actions that a person performs while sleepwalking or sleep-talking are harmless, such as sitting up, consuming food, and cleaning, it is also possible for people to cook, drive a motor vehicle, and commit homicide while sleepwalking.

Induced States of Consciousness

Most states of consciousness that people experience in their daily lives do not have to be induced—rather, they happen naturally and without effort. For example, you do not have to expend conscious effort to fall asleep or daydream. However, some states of consciousness must be induced either by psychoactive drugs or by making a conscious effort to do so.

Hypnosis is an induced state of consciousness that involves focused attention to the exclusion of other stimuli, as well as an enhanced response to suggestion. When someone is being hypnotized, they are generally told to focus on a rhythmic stimulus, such as their own breath or the movement of a pendulum. When they have become relaxed enough, they are more susceptible to **suggestion**, or having their thoughts, feelings, or behavior guided by another person.

Contrary to the popular perception of hypnosis, it does not work if a person does not want to be hypnotized. However, if the person is willing, hypnotism can both increase focus and concentration during hypnosis and effect long-term changes in a person's behavior. Hypnosis is useful for pain management, depression, anxiety, and a laundry list of other psychological problems.

High Hypnotic Suggestibility **Low Hypnotic Suggestibility**

There are two prevailing theories for why hypnosis works: the **social influence theory** and the **dissociation theory**. According to the social influence theory, hypnotism does not induce an altered state of consciousness, but instead describes people conforming to behavior that is expected of them. The dissociation theory holds that hypnosis is an altered state of consciousness that should be separated from "normal" conscious experience.

EEG scans of people experiencing hypnosis show more alpha waves than normal, suggesting that hypnosis is a state of relaxation.

Another induced state of consciousness is **meditation**, which involves the training of the mind in attention and awareness, with the added effect of creating a clear and stable mental state. Many meditation techniques focus on a particular object, such as the meditator's breathing or an image of an object, but some meditation techniques do not take anything as the object of focus.

Like hypnosis, meditation can produce more alpha waves on an EEG compared to a non-meditative state. In deep meditation, more theta waves can be seen—however, deep meditation is seen most often in people who have been meditating regularly over many years.

Because the definition of meditation is disputed, not to mention the ties that many meditation techniques have to specific organizations, much of the research on meditation is of poor quality. However, some studies performed on expert meditators show increased activity in parts of the brain involved in attentional control.

3.5 Types of Consciousness-Altering Drugs

Psychoactive Drugs

An especially potent and reliable way to effect induced states of consciousness is by using **psychoactive drugs**, which are drugs that alter our conscious experience and perception. They are classified into four main categories: depressants, stimulants, hallucinogens, and opioids.

Category	Main Effects and Examples
Depressants	↓ CNS Activity (↓ Blood pressure, Heart rate, Cognitive functioning) ↑ GABA (Alcohol, Benzodiazepines, Barbiturates)
Stimulants	↑ CNS Activity (↑ Blood pressure, Heart rate, Alertness) ↓ Adenosine (Caffeine), ↑ Acetylcholine (Nicotine), ↑ Monoamines (Cocaine)
Hallucinogens	↑ Sensation, Perceptual changes, Shifted consciousness ↑ Serotonin & Dopamine (LSD), ↑ Serotonin (Psilocybin)
Opioids	↓ CNS Activity (↓ Blood pressure, Heart rate), Analgesia, Antidiarrheal ↑ Endogenous Opioid Receptor Activation (Morphine, Heroin, Fentanyl)

Psychoactive Drugs

Depressants are drugs that depress, or lower the activity of, the central nervous system. Typically, they lower blood pressure, heart rate, and the general speed of cognitive function. There are three main types of depressants: alcohol, benzodiazepines, and barbiturates.

Alcohol is one of the most commonly used drugs in the world, and the global average consumption per person over the age of 15 is over 6 liters of pure alcohol every year. Alcohol is a neurotoxin that causes general impairment of brain function over the short-term, causing deficits in cognition, reaction time, inhibition, and many other areas. At high doses, alcohol can cause anterograde amnesia, also known as blackouts. High doses of alcohol can also lead to vomiting, unconsciousness, coma, and death. It is estimated that as much as 5% of the global population has an alcohol use disorder—in other words, they suffer from alcoholism.

Benzodiazepines, also known as "benzos," were as recently as 40 years ago the most prescribed drugs in the world. Benzodiazepines are often prescribed to treat anxiety, seizures, and insomnia, though they are also used to treat alcohol withdrawal. There are three types of benzodiazepines: short, intermediate, and long-acting. Short and intermediate-acting benzodiazepines are often prescribed for insomnia, though they can be used to treat seizures and as anesthetics. Long-acting benzodiazepines are more often used to treat anxiety and alcohol withdrawal.

Both alcohol and benzodiazepines bind to **GABAA receptors** in the central nervous system. When they bind, the receptors open, allowing chloride anions (Cl-) ions to pass down their electrochemical gradient. This, in turn, causes the affected neurons to become harder to activate, so the effects of alcohol and benzodiazepines are said to be inhibitory for most neurons.

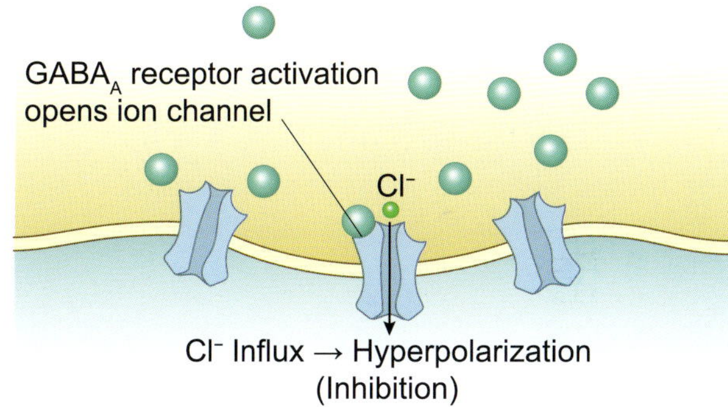

Barbiturates, like benzodiazepines, are used to treat insomnia or reduce anxiety. They can also be used to treat seizures and as anesthetics. Like alcohol and benzodiazepines, barbiturates activate GABAA receptors in the central nervous system.

In contrast to depressants, **stimulants** activate the central nervous system, increase blood pressure and heart rate, and make people feel more awake and alert. Although the subjective effects of stimulants and depressants are opposite, the mechanisms by which they work on a molecular level are different, so when both stimulants and depressants are taken simultaneously their effects do not cancel out, but instead overlap one another. Some examples of stimulants are caffeine, nicotine, cocaine, and methamphetamine.

> While they're opposite in many ways, depressants and stimulants do NOT cancel each other out!

Caffeine is the most popular psychoactive drug in the world. People use caffeine for many reasons, including alleviating or preventing drowsiness and improving cognition. Caffeine blocks adenosine receptors in the nervous system. In people who are awake and alert, almost no adenosine is found in their central nervous systems. However, as time passes, adenosine begins to accumulate and bind to adenosine receptors, leading to a cellular response that is ultimately perceived as drowsiness.

As you study, adenosine builds up in the brain and makes you feel drowsy. Caffeine blocks adenosine from binding, resulting in a stimulating effect.

Caffeine (Stimulant)
Chocolate Tea Energy Shot
Soda Coffee

Nicotine is another popular stimulant, often being consumed in the form of cigarettes, but also in cigars, electronic cigarettes, pipes, gums, and patches. Like caffeine, nicotine is consumed to prevent drowsiness and enhance cognitive function. Nicotine is also sometimes used for weight loss since it reduces appetite. However, nicotine is significantly more addictive than caffeine, with faster delivery methods carrying a higher likelihood of addiction.

Nicotine works by binding to nicotinic acetylcholine receptors in the central nervous system. When nicotine binds, the levels of several neurotransmitters in the brain increase. At lower doses, nicotine has a stimulating effect, but at higher doses, it has a sedative effect instead.

Cocaine is a particularly strong stimulant. Cocaine is most often snorted but can also be smoked or taken intravenously. Most people who use cocaine use it recreationally, and cocaine use can cause intense feelings of happiness, a loss of the feeling of reality, and excitement. Because of its potency, physical symptoms associated with cocaine are more severe than those of other stimulants, including very high blood pressure, very high heart rate, sweating, and dilated pupils.

Cocaine works by blocking the reuptake of dopamine, serotonin, and norepinephrine. When these neurotransmitters cannot be taken back up after they are released by neurons, they begin to build up in synapses. This causes postsynaptic neurons to fire, making the drug rewarding and promoting compulsive use of the drug.

Methamphetamine, also called "meth," is another powerful stimulant most often used recreationally, but it is also used to treat obesity and attention-deficit/hyperactivity disorder (ADHD). The effects of methamphetamine last for several hours and lead to severe crashes, in which users experience insomnia, irritability, and depression.

Although methamphetamine is occasionally prescribed for severe ADHD, amphetamines like Adderall are much more commonly prescribed for this condition.

Meth is extremely addictive, and long-term meth users may lose the ability to produce normal levels of dopamine. This is because meth causes the release of high levels of dopamine, and over time the body gets used to it and continually tries to ramp up baseline dopamine production—past a certain point, the body cannot make even a baseline level of dopamine on its own.

Hallucinogens are drugs that cause hallucinations, changes in perception, and other significant changes in consciousness that are not typically experienced due to other drugs in a person's daily life. Hallucinogens have been used in various medicinal and religious traditions for thousands of years—hallucinogens used in this context are known as **entheogens**.

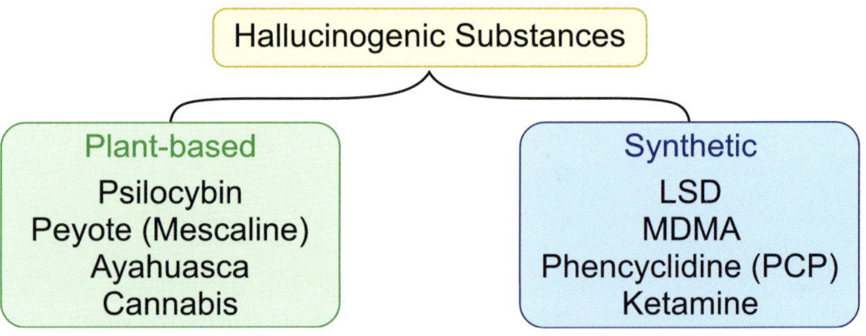

Substances with Hallucinogenic Properties

Perhaps the best-known hallucinogen is **lysergic acid diethylamide**, or **LSD**. The effects of LSD last between 6 and 14 hours, and at low doses can include mild visual hallucinations, feelings of euphoria, and sensory enhancement. At higher doses, there are significant changes in consciousness. Profound spiritual experiences, the loss of the feeling of "self," and changes in perspective can also occur.

Similarly, at low doses users may experience anxiety, nausea, delusions, and paranoia. Negative symptoms tend to get worse at higher doses, and can lead to overwhelming fear, unpleasant flashbacks, and panic.

LSD is thought to function by activating serotonin and dopamine receptors in the central nervous system. LSD is not physically addictive, but heavy users can develop a tolerance and psychological dependence on the drug. However, the risk for developing dependence is lower for hallucinogens than any of the other major categories of drugs.

MDMA, also called "molly," "ecstasy," or "E," is a drug with effects like those of hallucinogens and stimulants. MDMA works by increasing serotonin, dopamine, and norepinephrine, which leads to feelings of euphoria. MDMA use also causes high blood pressure and heart rate and can lead to dangerous dehydration and overheating.

MDMA is often used recreationally and is well known for producing feelings of closeness and empathy with other people, as well as reducing inhibitions and increasing self-confidence. Although MDMA is not used as often as other recreational drugs, usually once a week at maximum, long-term MDMA use at these levels may be neurotoxic.

Cannabis, also known as "weed," "marijuana," and many other names, is a drug that has characteristics of hallucinogens, stimulants, and depressants. For example, it can reduce inhibition, provoke anxiety, and cause mild hallucinations. It is consumed both recreationally and for medical purposes.

> Like MDMA, cannabis does not fall neatly into a single category. Both can have hallucinogenic and stimulant effects, but cannabis can also cause depressants effects.

Cannabis has special receptors in the brain that it binds to, called cannabinoid receptors. Cannabinoid receptors are G protein-coupled receptors that when activated decrease the activity of adenyl cyclase, calcium channels, and potassium channels.

Cannabis is less likely than other commonly consumed drugs, such as tobacco and alcohol, to cause addiction, but addiction is still possible. Additionally, heavy cannabis use, especially in young adolescents, has been linked to the development of schizophrenia, memory problems, and broad cognitive deficits in adulthood.

Opioids are a class of drugs that work on opioid receptors in the brain. They are commonly prescribed to treat pain, especially acute pain, but can also be used to treat diarrhea and opioid addiction. Some examples of opioids include morphine, heroin, and fentanyl.

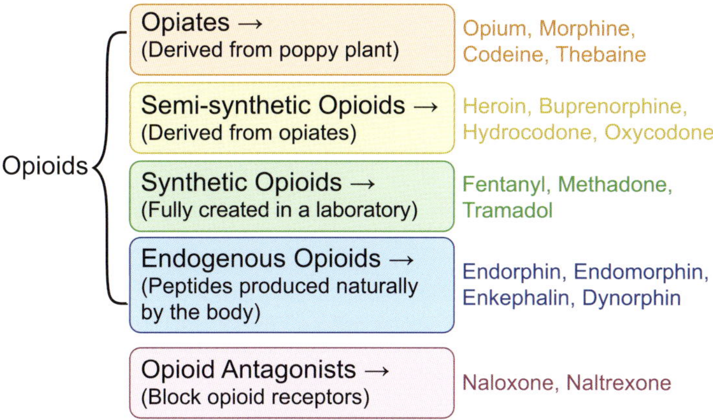

Opioid Classification

Opioid receptors respond to compounds the body makes on its own that cause pain relief, including endorphins, endomorphins, and dynorphins, as well as to synthetic opioids.

Opioid use, especially without medical supervision, often leads to addiction and can have many harmful side effects. Opioid overdose can be fatal, and if a person survives, he may experience permanent brain damage. In the case of an overdose, naloxone is used to block the effects of opioids—it takes between 2 and 5 minutes to be effective.

3.6 Drug Addiction and the Reward Pathway

Many widely used drugs, including drugs prescribed by doctors, can cause **drug addiction**. Drug addiction is a biopsychosocial disorder that involves compulsive drug-taking and drug-seeking behaviors, despite serious adverse effects.

> In psychology, the diagnosis for a drug addiction is called substance use disorder.

The method a person uses to take drugs, called the route of drug entry, has a significant effect on how addictive a drug can be. The faster the route of drug entry, the more addictive the drug tends to be.

> Remember that the faster the drug reaches the brain, the more addictive it tends to be!

Drugs taken through the skin are called **transdermal** drugs. Because the skin is an effective barrier to most compounds, transdermal drugs take several hours to be absorbed into the bloodstream. Many kinds of drugs are administered via transdermal patches, including nicotine, contraceptives, and narcotics.

> Transdermal drugs are designed for systemic treatment and are absorbed through the skin into the bloodstream. Topical drugs are designed for local treatment on the surface of the skin or mucous membranes.

Oral ingestion of drugs is one of the slower routes of drug entry since the drug must go through the gastrointestinal tract to be absorbed. This process takes anywhere from thirty minutes to several hours.

Inhalation quickly gets drugs into the lungs, and can include smoking, breathing in, and snorting. After inhalation, the drug enters the bloodstream and goes to the brain, making inhalation a much faster route of drug entry than transdermal or oral ingestion. Inhaled drugs take between 10 and 15 seconds to reach the brain.

Injection is the fastest method of drug entry. Most injected drugs are taken **intravenously**, meaning that they are shot directly into a vein. Injected drugs take only a few seconds to start working. Injecting drugs carries severe risks, such as bacterial infections. If users share needles, they can also transmit bloodborne diseases to one another, including HIV and hepatitis.

Term	Definition	Opioid-specific Example
Route of Administration	The location in which the substance enters the body	
Transdermal	Applied to skin and absorbed through skin into bloodstream	Fentanyl patch
Oral	Swallowed and primarily absorbed through GI tract into bloodstream	Methadone pills
Inhalation	Breathed in through mouth or nose and absorbed through lungs into bloodstream	Smoked heroin
Injection (IV)	Injected with a needle directly into the bloodstream (intravenous)	IV-administered morphine
Mechanism of Action	How a substance produces its effects	Bind at endogenous opioid receptors & increase dopamine
Intoxication	Acute physiological and behavioral signs of substance use	Analgesia, decreased blood pressure and heart rate, euphoria, sleepiness, constricted pupils, constipation
Tolerance	Adaptation to a substance results in diminished effectiveness	Cells rapidly become less responsive to opioid stimulation
Cross-tolerance	Tolerance to a different substance with similar pharmacological properties	Tolerance to one opioid causes tolerance to other opioids
Withdrawal	Symptoms caused by stopping or reducing dose of substance (sign of dependence)	Pain, elevated blood pressure and heart rate, dysphoria, insomnia, dilated pupils, diarrhea (notice these are often opposite of the intoxication effects!)
Substance-induced Disorder	Conditions caused by the use/disuse of the substance	Opioid-induced sexual dysfunction (erectile dysfunction, lack of sexual desire or arousal, lowered sexual satisfaction, trouble reaching orgasm)
Substance Use Disorder	Problematic pattern of substance use that is difficult to control despite negative consequences (addiction)	Opioid use disorder (problematic pattern of opioid use, including: taken in larger amounts or for longer than intended, unsuccessful effort to cut down or control use, strong craving, recurrent use despite significant consequences [work, school, relationships], tolerance, and withdrawal or continued use to avoid withdrawal)
Treatment	Approaches that seek to reverse an overdose or support someone in overcoming addiction (medications, therapy)	**Medications** Naloxone: fast-acting opioid antagonist that can reverse an overdose; naltrexone: long-acting opioid antagonist that reduces craving and blocks euphoria if an opioid is used; buprenorphine: opioid partial agonist that is a milder substitute for the problematic opioid; methadone: opioid full agonist that produces less euphoria and eliminates withdrawal and craving for the problematic opioid **Therapy** Individual Therapy: cognitive behavioral therapy (CBT) Group Therapy: Heroin Anonymous (HA) or Narcotics Anonymous (NA)

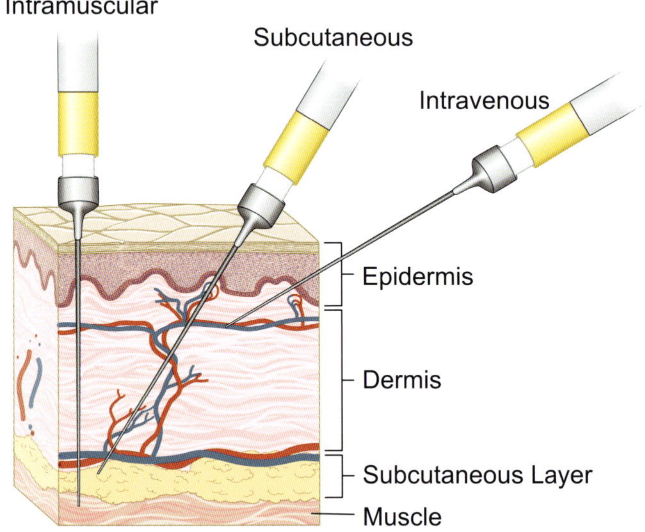

Another injection type is subcutaneous, which is administered into the subcutaneous tissue between the dermis and muscle.

Route of Administration	Speed	Examples
Transdermal (Skin)	Slow	Fentanyl patch, nicotine patch, progesterone cream
Oral (Swallow)	Slow	Birth control pills, cough syrup, dextromethorphan
Inhalation (Breathe)	Fast	Albuterol inhaler, cigarette smoke, nebulized antibiotics
Injection (Intravenous)	Fastest	IV heroin, IV chemotherapeutics, IV fluids
Injection (Intramuscular)	Depends	Long-acting injectable antipsychotics, hepatitis vaccine

Routes of Administration

Intramuscular injection is where the drug is injected directly into muscles. Although muscles have good access to blood vessels, a much smaller volume of drug can be injected intramuscularly than intravenously. Intramuscular injection can be either a fast or slow delivery. For example, haloperidol, an antipsychotic used to treat schizophrenia, works relatively quickly. In contrast, most vaccines that are administered intramuscularly work much more slowly.

Drug addiction occurs due to a combination of psychological and biological factors. When people engage in pleasurable activities, such as eating food, having sex, or being complimented, the brain releases **dopamine**. Dopamine is a neurotransmitter produced in the **ventral tegmental area** in the midbrain and is associated with motivational salience—in other words, it acts as a signal to indicate how enticing or repulsive an action is.

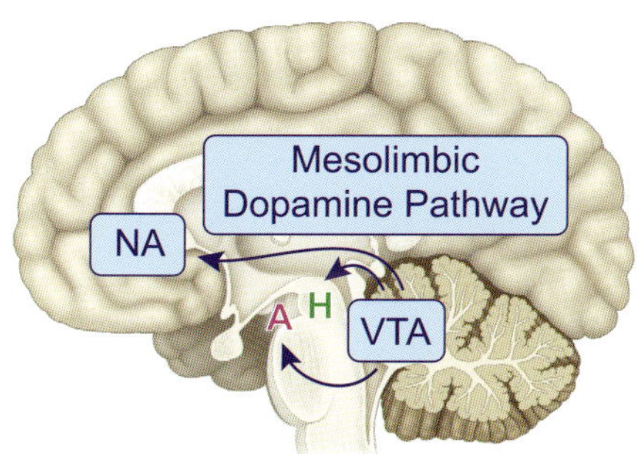

Reward Pathway

From the ventral tegmental area, dopamine is sent to various regions in the brain, including the nucleus accumbens, the amygdala, and the hippocampus. Combined, these regions make up the **mesolimbic pathway**, also known as the reward pathway.

When the reward pathway is stimulated and dopamine is released, the expression of certain genes involved in the mesolimbic pathway also change. Additionally, as more dopamine is released, less serotonin is released. **Serotonin** is a neurotransmitter that is partially responsible for feelings of contentment and satiation. When dopamine is released in this context, feelings of pleasure or euphoria are also common.

Aside from the reward pathway, which is a large biological factor in drug addiction, there are also psychological and environmental factors that influence addiction. Traumatic events experienced during childhood, extreme poverty, and adolescence are known to increase the likelihood of drug addiction. Additionally, being around people who are addicted to drugs, having a parent who is addicted to drugs, and a person's attitude toward drug use are also factors that influence whether a person will become addicted to a drug or not.

Drugs are formally called **substances**. When a person uses enough of a substance to affect him psychologically or biologically, he is **intoxicated**. What qualifies as intoxication depends on the drug in question: being intoxicated due to alcohol, or "drunk," is different from a "trip," which is intoxication due to a hallucinogen.

Substance use can cause a person to develop **substance-induced disorders**, which refer to conditions caused by the substance itself. For example, abusing benzodiazepines can directly cause depression or mania.

Delirium that occurs as a result of alcohol withdrawal is an example of a substance-induced disorder, whereas abusing alcohol despite it causing significant problems is characteristic of a substance use disorder.

Substance use disorders occur when a person continues to use a substance despite serious negative consequences. For example, a person's substance use can cause him to struggle in school or at work, damage his relationships, or interfere with his life goals.

Not everyone who uses substances develops a substance use disorder. Instead, psychologists and psychiatrists examine multiple aspects of a person's substance use to make a diagnosis. In general, medical professionals look for substantial life impairment, high tolerance, and withdrawal symptoms to be present before diagnosing a person with a substance use disorder.

Tolerance is the need to use more of the same drug to get a similar effect the next time a person takes it. Tolerance occurs because the brain adapts to some drugs, either by shutting down receptors or speeding up drug degradation. Thus, the next time a person takes the drug, the effect is weaker.

Some drugs cause **cross-tolerance**, or tolerance to related kinds of drugs as well as the drug itself, to occur. Usually, drugs that cause cross-tolerance are chemically similar, either acting on the same receptors or affecting the activity of the same neurotransmitters.

When a person stops taking a substance for an extended period of time, he can experience **withdrawal**. In order for a drug to cause withdrawal symptoms, it must also cause **dependence**, or changes in the body that cause it to rely on the drug. Withdrawal happens when a drug the body has become dependent on is stopped or taken at a lower dose.

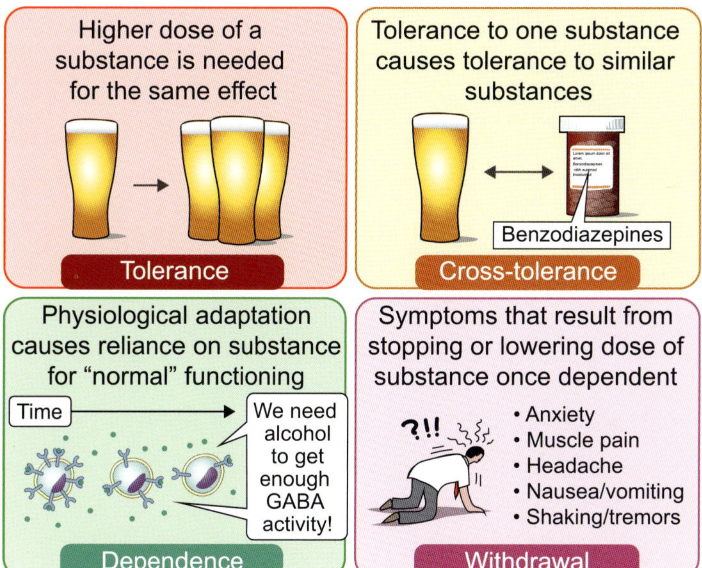

Withdrawal is often an unpleasant process, and in severe cases it can be fatal. The two stages of withdrawal are acute and post-acute.

Acute withdrawal lasts between several days and up to several weeks after quitting a substance. The symptoms in this period tend to be more physical, though the exact symptoms depend on the substance in question. For example, acute alcohol withdrawal can cause sweating, shaking, and tachycardia, while acute nicotine withdrawal can cause anger, irritability, anxiety, and depression.

Post-acute withdrawal can last many years, with symptoms tending to be psychological rather than physical. It is common for people to experience mood swings, irritability, and poor sleep quality, among dozens of other symptoms. Because these symptoms last so long and tend to come in waves, many people are discouraged from quitting substance use since it feels like they will never feel normal again. However, with time, symptoms tend to become less severe and less frequent, until they vanish entirely.

Because drug addiction is a biopsychosocial disorder, it has both physiological and psychological aspects. This makes treating drug addiction both challenging and important since addiction can result in physical and psychological harm to those affected.

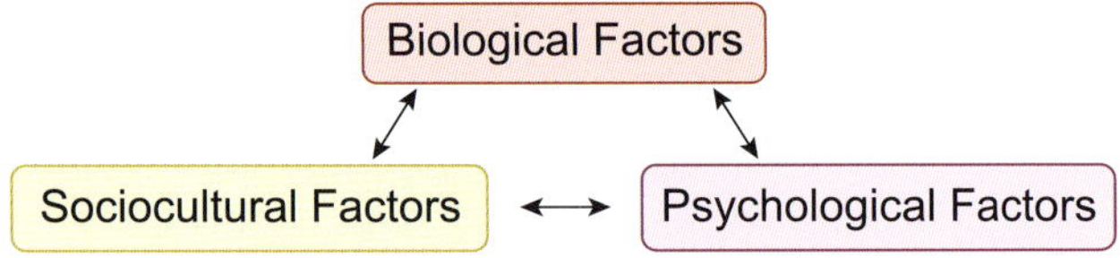

Biopsychosocial Model of Addiction

In most cases, drug addiction is treated with non-pharmaceutical interventions, though medication can also be used if needed. The primary goals of drug addiction treatment are to help a person quit drug use and prevent **relapse**, where the patient starts using the drug again.

Cognitive behavioral therapy, or **CBT**, is the cornerstone of most modern psychological therapy and is as effective as medication in treating many disorders, such as anxiety, PTSD, and substance use disorders. As the name suggests, CBT addresses both the cognitive and behavioral aspects of drug addiction and helps the patient recognize harmful thought patterns and behaviors associated with substance use.

Using CBT, people can learn to recognize their thought patterns associated with substance use. For example, a person trying to quit smoking might notice that he feels the need to smoke when he is stressed or hungry, and he uses tools other than cigarettes to feel better, such as exercise and chewing gum.

Similarly, a person can begin to recognize behaviors that make them more likely to use drugs. Many smokers want to smoke when they drink alcohol, so learning to avoid alcohol can be helpful for not triggering cravings.

An Example of CBT for a Substance Use Disorder

In the end, CBT is a way to give patients tools to help combat addiction on their own, and the psychologist's role in the therapy is to teach the patient how to cope and to provide him support.

Other types of therapy are also used to treat drug addiction, including group meetings and motivational interviewing.

Group meetings are often associated with groups like AA, or Alcoholics Anonymous. These groups act as support networks for people with addiction problems to talk about their experiences and guide people on a path to recovery, often following a 12-step path.

Motivational interviewing is a technique similar to CBT, but focuses more on the patient's internal motivation to change rather than other factors involving addiction. Motivational interviewing is often used to build trust between the patient and the psychologist, which can then lead to the patient pursuing other treatment options, such as medication or CBT.

Sometimes, patients must stay in the hospital to receive medical treatment, which is called **inpatient care**. When patients can stay at home most of the time and come into the hospital occasionally, this is called **outpatient care**. Particularly serious or sensitive cases of drug addiction usually start as inpatient care routines and transition into outpatient routines as the patient gets better.

Medications for treating drug addiction are also used, especially when the addiction is more severe. The type of medication used depends on the substance being abused and on the patient's circumstances, including means and tolerance of side effects.

Medications for addiction are often cross tolerant with the substance of abuse. For example, alcohol use disorder treatment may include benzodiazepines and heroin use disorder treatment may include other opioids, like methadone and buprenorphine.

Benzodiazepines are considered the gold standard for pharmaceutical treatment of alcohol addiction. Since benzos activate the same receptors in the CNS that alcohol does, the reward pathway gets activated without people drinking alcohol. The next step after quitting alcohol is to slowly taper off the dosage of benzodiazepines until the person no longer needs them.

There are many pharmaceutical methods used to help people stop smoking, but most of them focus on delivering nicotine to the patient in different forms that can gradually be reduced over time. For example, nicotine patches provide a slow but constant supply of nicotine to patients, decreasing their urge to smoke.

Medications used to treat opioid addiction work by binding to opioid receptors and staying bound to them for a long time. This results in a high, but one with less euphoria than commonly abused opioids. It also prevents patients from getting as high off of other opioids, since the receptors are blocked by the medication.

Some examples of this kind of medication include methadone and buprenorphine.

3.7 Language

As children grow and develop, they become able to interact with others around them and express themselves through language. How they do so has been hotly debated, and theories fall into three major camps: nativist, interactionist, and behaviorist.

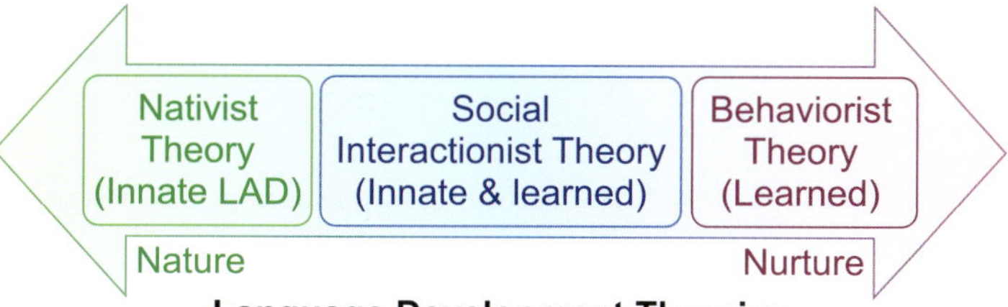

Language Development Theories

The **nativist theory** of language development proposes that all humans are born with the ability to acquire language. They are able to do so because they possess an **LAD**, or **language acquisition device**, in their brains that helps decode **universal grammar**—elements of language that are innate to human speech, such as nouns and verbs.

According to this theory, the language acquisition device is only active for a **critical period** of about nine years after birth. After this period ends, acquiring language becomes much more difficult. The nativist theory is most associated with **Noam Chomsky** and **Steven Pinker**.

The **social interactionist theory** of language development, or **SIT**, holds that in order for children to learn language, it is crucial that they interact with adults around them. Because children want to be able to communicate, they learn language through repeated social interaction. The SIT was created by Soviet psychologist **Lev Vygotsky**.

The **behaviorist theory** of language learning holds that children are not born with an innate ability to acquire language and instead learn through operant conditioning. For example, for a child to learn what the word "up" means, he would have to hear it and repeat it. For it to stick, he would have to be picked up after he says "up," so he can learn to associate the word with the action. The behaviorist theory was created by **B.F. Skinner**.

Language and the Brain

What parts of the brain are involved in speaking, reading, and writing? For most people, but not all, the **left hemisphere** of the brain is more active when processing and producing speech. Regardless of which hemisphere is more active, there are several brain regions that have drawn the attention of language researchers.

Wernicke's area (pronounced Ver-ni-kuhz) is a region of the brain located in the temporal lobe that is involved in the comprehension of both written and spoken language. When Wernicke's area is damaged, it can cause a condition called **Wernicke's aphasia**. **Aphasia** is a general term for a disorder involving language and is usually caused by stroke or head trauma, though it can also be the result of brain tumors or dementia.

People with Wernicke's aphasia are usually able to speak fluently and can form grammatically correct sentences. However, they are less able to understand both spoken and written speech than people without the disorder. Additionally, patients may make up new words, called neologisms, and are not able to notice when they are saying things that don't make sense or when they are making mistakes in word usage.

In contrast, people with **Broca's aphasia** can understand spoken and written language just fine but have difficulty producing speech at all. In severe cases, people with Broca's aphasia can only produce one-word utterances when asked questions. Unlike people with Wernicke's aphasia, people with Broca's aphasia tend to be aware of their speech problems and are more prone to depression than patients with other aphasias due to their difficulty communicating with other people.

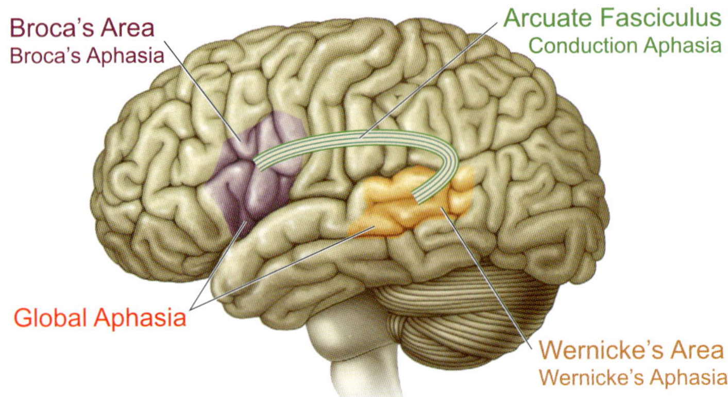

It is possible for both Broca's and Wernicke's areas to be damaged in a patient—this is called **global aphasia** and is almost always caused by a stroke or brain lesions. People with global aphasia show difficulty both in understanding and producing speech. Only 20 percent of people with global aphasia achieve functional use of language again, and this tends to be limited to daily conversations with familiar topics.

Conduction aphasia can occur when a person sustains damage to the **arcuate fasciculus**, a bundle of axons that connects Wernicke's area to Broca's area. People with conduction aphasia can fully understand speech but have difficulty repeating phrases given to them. Additionally, people with conduction aphasia can speak fluently, but tend to have **paraphasic** speech patterns, meaning that they mix up syllables and insert unwanted words and phrases when speaking.

Related to aphasia are anomia, agraphia, and anarthria.

Anomia is the inability to think of the right name for an object. Patients with anomia will often talk around the word that they are trying to say or require a cue to recall the word they were looking for. Patients with anomia will often know other properties of an object but will not be able to remember its name. For example, if given an apple, the patient will know that it can be peeled, sliced, or eaten, but will not be able to recall what it is called.

Agraphia is the inability to write, either through motor dysfunction associated with writing or through an inability to spell.

Anarthria is the total loss of speech due to motor dysfunction and is often caused by stroke, traumatic brain injury, or multiple sclerosis.

Anomia is a common deficit across the different aphasia conditions that is characterized by persistent difficulty with word finding and naming objects.

Here's a helpful mnemonic for the four aphasia conditions:

Wernicke's = Word salad

Broca's = Broken speech

Global = Got both (W + B)

Conduction = Can't repeat

Condition	Description
Wernicke's Aphasia	Impaired comprehension, intact speech fluency but nonsensical words (unaware)
Broca's Aphasia	Impaired speech fluency due to production problems (aware), intact comprehension
Global Aphasia	Impaired comprehension & speech production fluency (Wernicke's + Broca's)
Conduction Aphasia	Impaired repetition of phrases, paraphasic speech, intact comprehension
Anomia	Impaired word finding & naming, intact knowledge of object meaning/description
Agraphia	Impaired ability to communicate in writing (can be a linguistic or motor issue)
Anarthria	Total loss of speech abilities due to severe neuromuscular dysfunction

Aphasia Types and Related Conditions

Linguistic Theories

Thought and language are inseparable concepts for most people—after all, most people have a constant internal monologue, even if they are not always aware of it. For example, up until this point, most of the text should be fairly easy to read. It may feel automatic, but reading uncommon words like "zeugma" or "syzygy" tends to trip people up enough for them to notice that they were reading aloud in their head the whole time.

Which determines the other, thought or language? In other words, does how people think shape language, leading to basic principles that underlie all human language, or does language influence how people think?

Universalism holds that what people think dictates the language that they develop. That is, if a group of people can think about a concept, they will develop words or phrases to express that concept. For example, before the Japanese word "umami," often translated into English as "savory," became commonly used, a person taking a universalist approach to language might have said that English speakers did not have the concept of "umami."

Piaget's theory of cognitive development includes the development of language in children, which then extends to ability in adulthood. According to Piaget, when a child becomes able to understand certain concepts, such as object permanence or conservation, he begins to acquire the meaning of words that relate to that concept. For example, a child able to understand object permanence, or that objects still exist if they go out of sight, would be able to understand words like "lost," "gone," etc. As the child develops and becomes able to understand more and more complex concepts, he can understand and use words that relate to them.

Vygotsky's social interactionist theory (SIT) proposes that language and thought start out as separate entities and converge through social interaction. So, when a child is young he has the capacity for both thought and language; through **socialization**, or interaction with adults who already know a language, the two abilities combine into one.

Linguistic determinism, also known as the **linguistic relativity hypothesis**, is the theory that language influences how people think.

The belief that language has some influence on thought, but does not entirely determine how people think, is called **weak linguistic determinism**. For example, it has been found that native English speakers tend to think about time as a horizontal line, with the past being "left" and the future being "right" of the present. In comparison, native speakers of Mandarin Chinese tend to think about time as a vertical line, with the past being "up" and the future being "down." However, both Mandarin Chinese and English speakers share the concept of linear time—the differences in thought brought about by their languages are small.

The more extreme version of linguistic determinism is called **strong linguistic determinism**, or the **Sapir-Whorf Hypothesis**. According to this theory, the language a person speaks completely determines his thoughts. Hypothetically, if a person were to grow up speaking a language that had no words for numbers but instead expressed quantity in terms close to "few" and "many," he may be completely unable to learn arithmetic.

Universalism (Thought determines language)	**Piaget** (Thought influences language)	**Vygotsky** (Thought and language develop independently before converging)	**Weak Linguistic Determinism** (Language influences thought)	**Strong Linguistic Determinism (Sapir-Whorf)** (Language determines thought)

Linguistic Universality (Thought → Language)

Linguistic Relativity (Language → Thought)

Spectrum Of Linguistic Theories

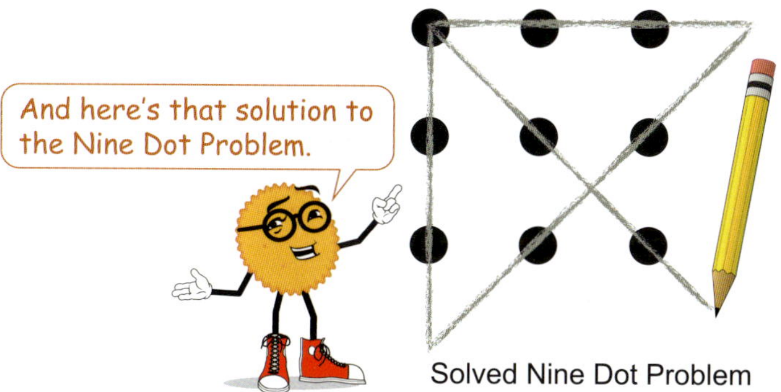

Solved Nine Dot Problem

PSY

Emotions, Stress, and Group Behaviors 4

4.1 Components of Emotion

Emotions are biological states that arise from neurophysiological changes. Emotions have three components.

1. Physiological (the way your body reacts)
2. Behavioral (the way you react)
3. Cognitive (what you think)

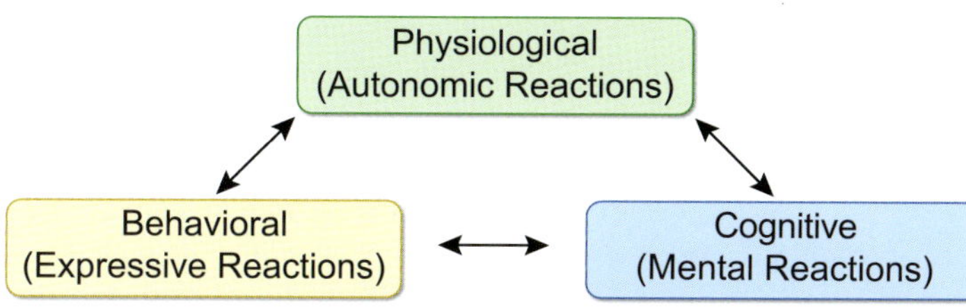

Emotion Triangle

All three components are typically intertwined in a single emotional experience.

I'll show you how I feel using three types of responses:

Physiological

Behavioral

Cognitive

	Contempt	Sadness	Anger
Physiological	This one has no agreed-upon responses. I'll skip it.	My chest gets tight, my limbs feel heavy, and my eyes water.	I'm hot and sweaty. My muscles are tense. My fists and jaw are clenched.
Behavioral	I sneer, roll my eyes, puff up my chest, and say "Heh," or "Hah."	Posture hunched, lip corners down, inner eyebrows up and together, eyes down, upper eyelids drooped.	I lean forward and jut my chin. I stare hard with my eyes wide open.
Cognitive	I'm morally superior to you.	It's so upsetting to think of never seeing them again.	I will not stand for this injustice!

	Disgust	Fear	Surprise	Happiness
Physiological	I feel nauseous and/or I start to gag.	I feel cold, I'm short of breath, and I tremble.	I feel attentive and aroused.	I feel calm, contented, and/or relaxed.
Behavioral	I turn my head away, hunch over, lower my eyebrows, and wrinkle my nose.	I freeze or I want to run or fight. My eyebrows are raised and close together and my eyelids are tense.	I step back and drop my jaw with my eyebrows raised and I raise my upper eyelids.	I narrow and wrinkle my eyes, raise my cheeks, pull my lips back and show my teeth.
Cognitive	Ew. Yuck! I cannot tolerate how gross that is!	This is a terrifying experience!	I could never have seen that coming!	This is such exciting news!

Physiological components of emotion are changes in the body's physiological state during an emotion. They do not include behaviors or conscious thoughts and are mostly autonomic. When a person is angry, for example, his rib cage tenses and his heart rate increases. He may sweat more than usual, and his blood pressure may rise.

Behavioral components of emotion are how the emotion is outwardly expressed. They include body language and nonverbal and verbal noises, such as swearing. They are overt expressions of emotion that are recognizable by other people. For example, a person who is sad might frown, hold his head in his hands, or cry. Behavioral components of emotion are dependent on cultural norms and vary from one individual to another.

Cognitive (a.k.a. subjective) components of emotion are conscious interpretations of feelings. They are the thoughts that accompany an emotional state, including preconceptions about a situation, an appraisal of the situation, and thoughts about the event that triggered the emotion.

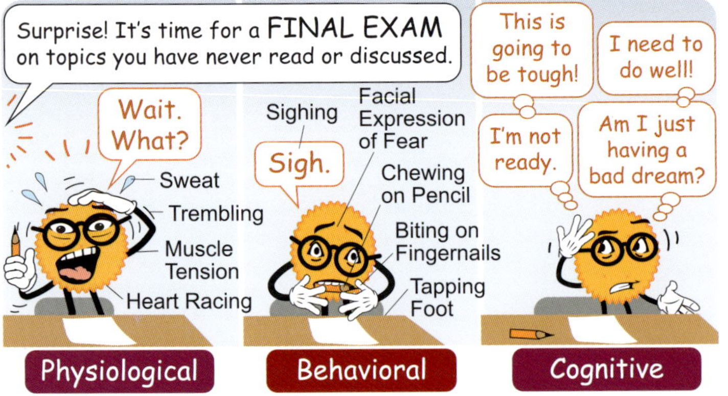

4.2 Universal Emotions

The psychologist **Paul Ekman** originally hypothesized that there are six **universal emotions** found across all human cultures: **sadness**, **anger**, **disgust**, **fear**, **surprise**, and **happiness**. The AAMC also lists joy as a universal emotion, but many consider it interchangeable with happiness. The American Psychological Association lists a seventh, **contempt**, which Ekman's research has provided strong evidence to support. A universal emotion is an emotion capable of being felt and facially expressed by all human beings. The concept of universal emotions is based on facial expressions and has been tested across disparate cultures.

The seven universal emotions mnemonic is Cold SAD FiSH: Contempt, Sadness, Anger, Disgust, Fear, Surprise, and Happiness.

Because some emotions appear to be universally recognizable, biologists have proposed that emotion is an **adaptive** trait that is evolutionarily favored. Emotions have a behavioral component. Behavior affects fitness. Predictable emotional responses lead to modification of behavior within social groups, altering the fitness of groups and individuals.

Crouton knows that if he runs into the street, I will get really angry. My emotion helps my offspring survive, making me more fit in a Darwinian sense.

4.3 Theories of Emotion

One of the oldest theories of emotion is the **James-Lange Theory of Emotion**, which holds that the experience of emotion arises directly from physiological and behavioral responses that follow a stimulus. In other words, a stimulus creates physiological and behavioral responses, which in turn create the conscious experience of a particular emotion, the cognitive response. For instance, trembling and running, a physiological and behavioral response to seeing a bear, is followed by the cognitive response of interpreting the emotion as fear.

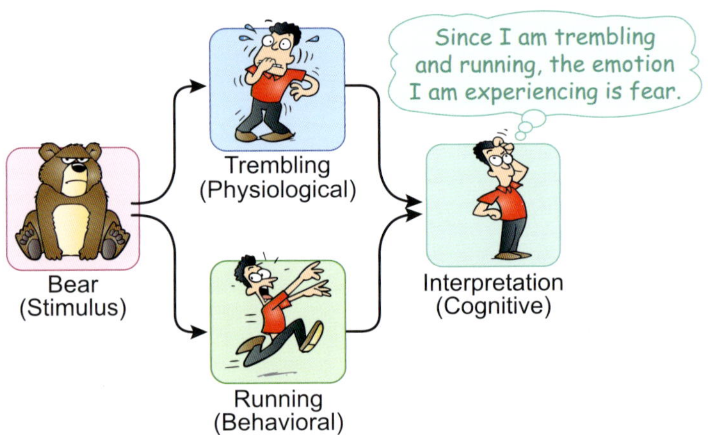

James-Lange Theory of Emotion

Created in direct response to the then-popular James-Lange theory, the **Cannon-Bard Theory of Emotion** argues that instead of the physiological response preceding the emotion, both the physiological response and the cognitive response of the emotion occur at the same time. So, instead of feeling fear after trembling, the feeling of fear occurs simultaneously with trembling.

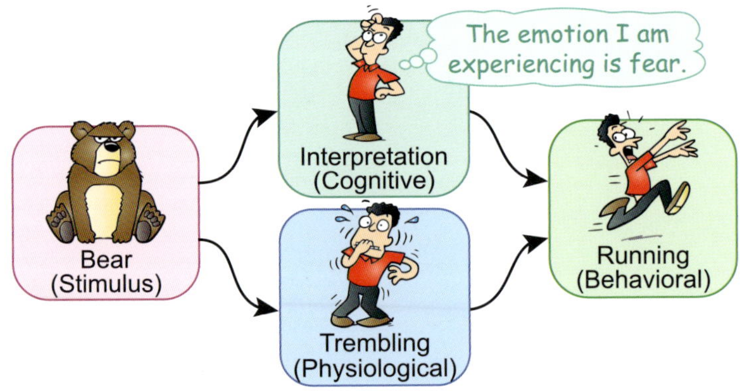

Cannon-Bard Theory of Emotion

One problem with the Cannon-Bard theory is that it doesn't explain how a behavioral response can intensify an emotion, such as how smiling may increase happiness.

The **Schachter-Singer Theory of Emotion**, also called the *two-factor theory of emotion*, holds that physiological changes due to an event are followed by a second factor, cognitive appraisal, interpreting the context of the event before assigning an emotion. Like in the James-Lange theory, emotion arises from a physiological change. However, unlike in the James-Lange theory, the mind must determine which emotion is experienced based on context and experience. Only then is the emotion consciously felt.

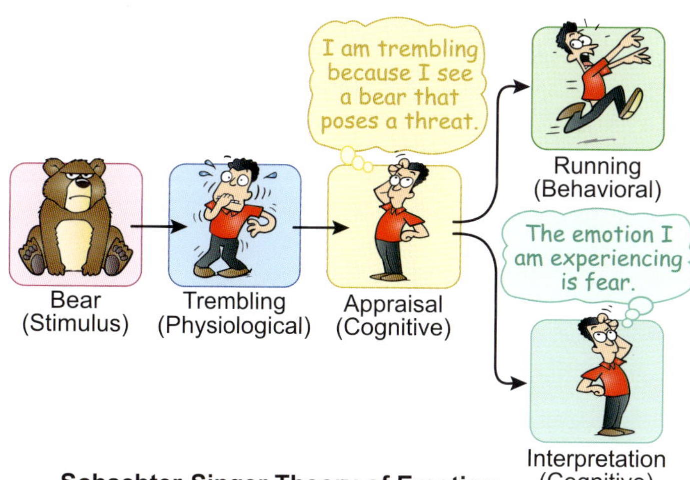

Schachter-Singer Theory of Emotion

How can you remember the three theories of emotion and their names?

"Lange" rhymes with "strange," and the James-Lange theory is a bit strange because it proposes that I tremble and run BEFORE I feel fear.

Imagine the "cannon" of Cannon-Bard firing back at the "strange Lange" theory, arguing, "Wait a minute! I run BECAUSE I feel fear. AND I don't need to tremble to realize that I am afraid".

"Schachter" rhymes with "factor" as in the need for a second factor, cognitive appraisal of the physiological response, when deciding if I am afraid. Thus, the trembling is followed by the recognition that there is a bear that is causing the trembling, and therefore fear is the appropriate emotion.

Theory	Stimulus	Response	Mnemonic
James-Lange	**Acceptance to Medical School** CONGRATULATIONS! You have been accepted to Salty Medical School.	Heart Racing (Physiological) + Smiling (Behavioral) → "Since my heart is racing and I am smiling, I am feeling excited!" (Cognitive) + = Excited	James-Lange is strange to think that you feel excited because your heart is racing and you are smiling.
Cannon-Bard	**Acceptance to Medical School** CONGRATULATIONS! You have been accepted to Salty Medical School.	Heart Racing (Physiological) + "I am feeling excited!" (Cognitive) → Smiling (Behavioral) + Excited =	Like a cannon firing back at the strange Lange theory, Cannon-Bard states that you smile because your heart is racing and you feel excited.
Schachter-Singer	**Acceptance to Medical School** CONGRATULATIONS! You have been accepted to Salty Medical School.	Heart Racing (Physiological) ↓ "My heart is racing because I was accepted into medical school." (Cognitive Appraisal) → I am feeling excited!" (Cognitive Interpretation) ↗ Smiling (Behavioral) = Accepted = Excited =	Schachter rhymes with factor, which should help you remember that it's a two-factor theory (there are also two names that start with the same letter)! Schachter-Singer says you feel excited and smile because your heart is racing and in this context, you determine that means that you are excited (not scared).

4.4 Biology of Emotion

Although all parts of the brain are active to some extent during emotional experiences, some areas seem to be more involved than others. The **insular cortex**, which lies beneath the junction of the frontal, temporal, and parietal lobes, is activated when we consciously experience emotion.

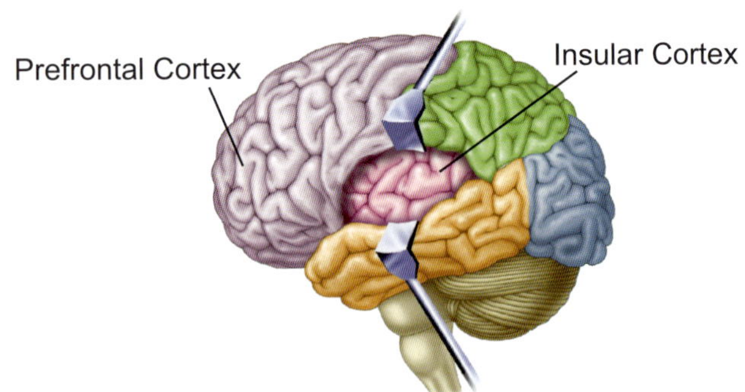

The **prefrontal cortex** is crucial for higher-level brain function, such as problem solving, decision making, cognitive inhibition, and working memory.

The **limbic system** is the part of the brain between the brainstem and both halves of the cerebral cortex. It is involved in emotional regulation, motivation, and memory. The limbic system is made up of the hippocampus, the thalamus, the amygdala, the hypothalamus, the cingulate cortex, and the olfactory bulb. Neurotransmitters such as dopamine, norepinephrine, and serotonin also play a key role in the response of the limbic system.

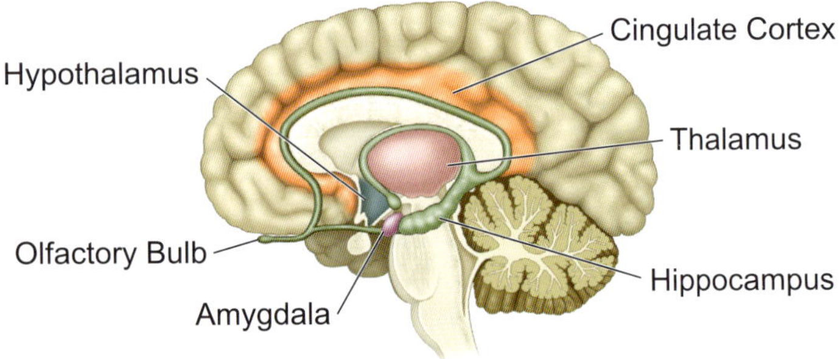

The Limbic System

The **hippocampus** is probably the best understood part of the limbic system and is essential in forming new **episodic** or **autobiographical** memories. However, it does not seem to be important for forming procedural memories, such as learning how to play a new musical instrument.

The hippocampus also encodes emotional content, which it receives from the amygdala and other brain regions. While episodic memories are being formed, both the actual event being encoded into memory and the context surrounding the event combine. This is why returning to the place where an emotional event happened can trigger that emotion again.

Another helpful way to remember the role of the hippocampus is to imagine a hippopotamus camping by a campfire with a birthday cake in his lap. The hippo is happy because it is his birthday. His birthday (an episodic event) and his happiness (an emotion) will help you recall that the hippocampus is involved in episodic memory and emotion.

Because the brain has two halves (with a hippocampus in each half), damage to one hippocampus does not normally cause a significant loss of function. However, if both hippocampi are damaged, it normally causes **anterograde amnesia**, or difficulty forming new memories. This kind of damage can also cause **retrograde amnesia**, where memories formed before the damage occurred become more difficult or impossible to recall.

The **thalamus** acts as a relay system for sensory information that gets passed on to the cerebral cortex for processing. All types of sensory input pass through the thalamus EXCEPT for input associated with the sense of smell, which goes from the olfactory bulb to the amygdala, hippocampus, and other regions. Because sensation comes hand in hand with emotional experience, the thalamus is an important mediator in the genesis of emotions.

Ancient Athens was a thalassocracy, and they had dominion over the seas. This is not where the word thalamus comes from, but it helps me remember that, just as the sea allows for the transport of goods, the thalamus allows for the transport of sensory information.

The **amygdala** plays a large part in the formation and storage of emotional memories. Patients whose amygdalae have been damaged have a harder time remembering the details of frightening events, such as the contents of a horror film. The amygdala is involved in both negative and positive conditioning, and it projects to the hypothalamus and other regions. The amygdala receives input from every sensory system, including the olfactory system.

Whenever I need a good scare, I just go to the closet, pull out my amygdala, and open it up. That's where I keep my emotional memories.

When parts of the medial temporal lobe, which contains the amygdalae and several other structures, are damaged, a condition called *Klüver-Bucy syndrome* can result. Klüver-Bucy syndrome is characterized by compulsive eating, inappropriate sexual behaviors, and hyperorality, or the insertion of inedible objects into the mouth.

The **hypothalamus**, so named because it sits below the thalamus, is a tiny region of the brain in humans – about the size of a pearl. The hypothalamus is highly interconnected with other regions of the brain and is tasked with releasing hormones, coordinating circadian rhythms, and controlling food intake patterns. It is also responsible for regulating many automatic behaviors, such as body temperature, hunger, thirst, and the fear response.

The **cingulate cortex**, a region of the brain located in the middle of the cerebral cortex, is another important part of the limbic system. The exact role of the cingulate cortex is still being debated.

The cingulate cortex is divided into two main sections: the *anterior cingulate cortex* and the *posterior cingulate cortex*. The anterior cingulate cortex seems to be involved in attention control, emotional stability, and empathy, among other processes. The posterior cingulate cortex appears to handle some aspects of spatial memory and mediating interactions between emotion and memory.

The **olfactory bulb** receives information about smell from the olfactory system and passes it on to other regions of the brain, such as the amygdala or the hippocampus. The primary role that the olfactory bulb plays in emotion is through its connections with other brain regions, as the experience of smell can be integrated into the emotional content of a memory.

It has also been found that removing the olfactory bulb can cause symptoms of depression in rats, indicating a link between emotion and the olfactory bulb, but the full purpose of the olfactory bulb in emotion is unknown.

When a person is experiencing emotion, unconscious physiological changes tend to occur simultaneously with the conscious aspects of an **emotional experience**. The response outside of the person's control is managed by the **autonomic nervous system** (ANS).

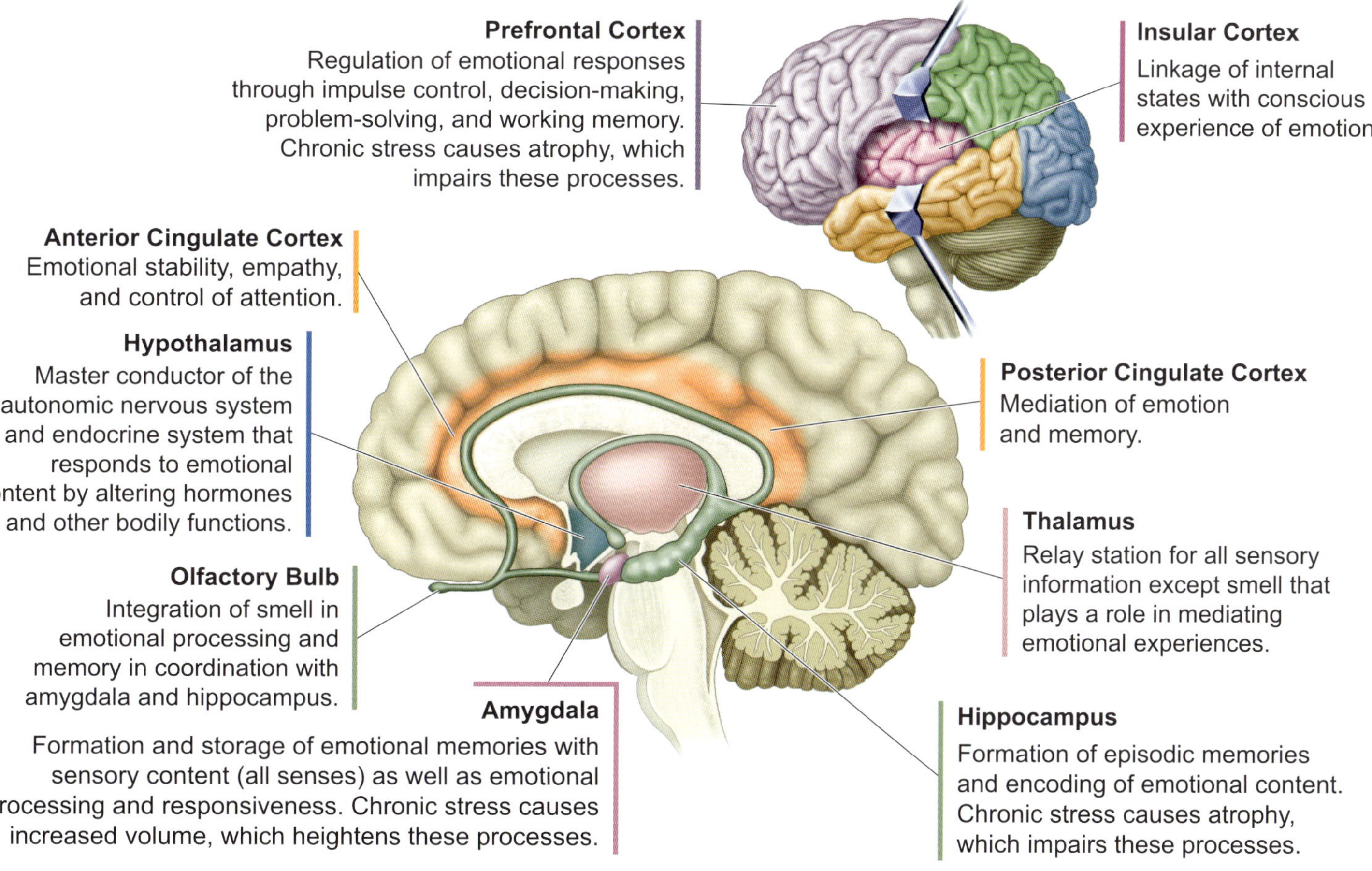

Emotion Areas of the Brain

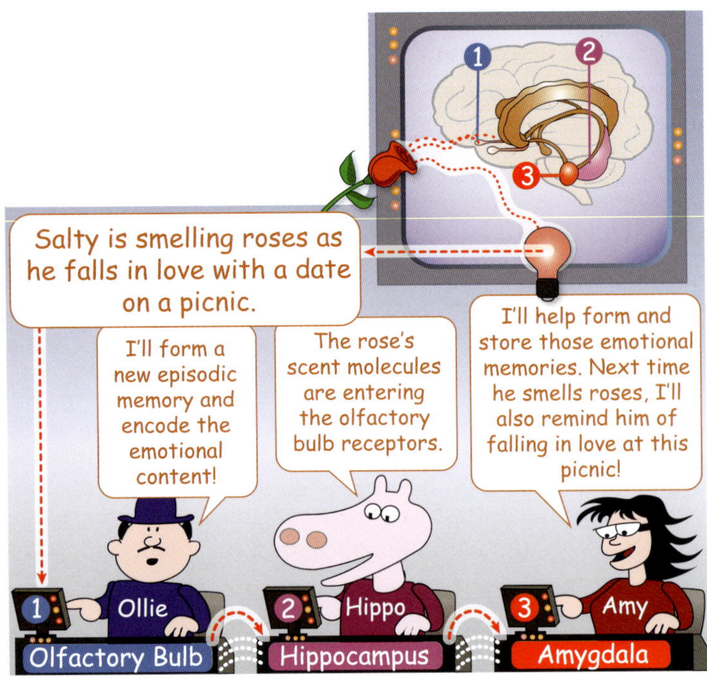

Salty's Olfactory Assembly Line

Physiological markers of emotion are the physiological manifestations of emotion, such as changes in heart rate, sweating, and even brainwave patterns.

Although many physiological markers of emotion are vague and subjective, such as the feeling of "butterflies in the stomach," some telltale aspects of emotion can be directly measured and quantified. For example, EEG and skin conductance data can be combined to form an electrical pattern associated with the startle response, or how people react to being surprised. Changes in skin conductance, heart rate variability, and various biochemical stress markers (think hormones, like cortisol) are all used to measure physiological signs of emotion.

4.5 Stress and Stressors

Stress is a response to demand upon an individual. The demand may be **physiological** (caused by the environment), **psychological** (caused by how the environment is perceived), or both.

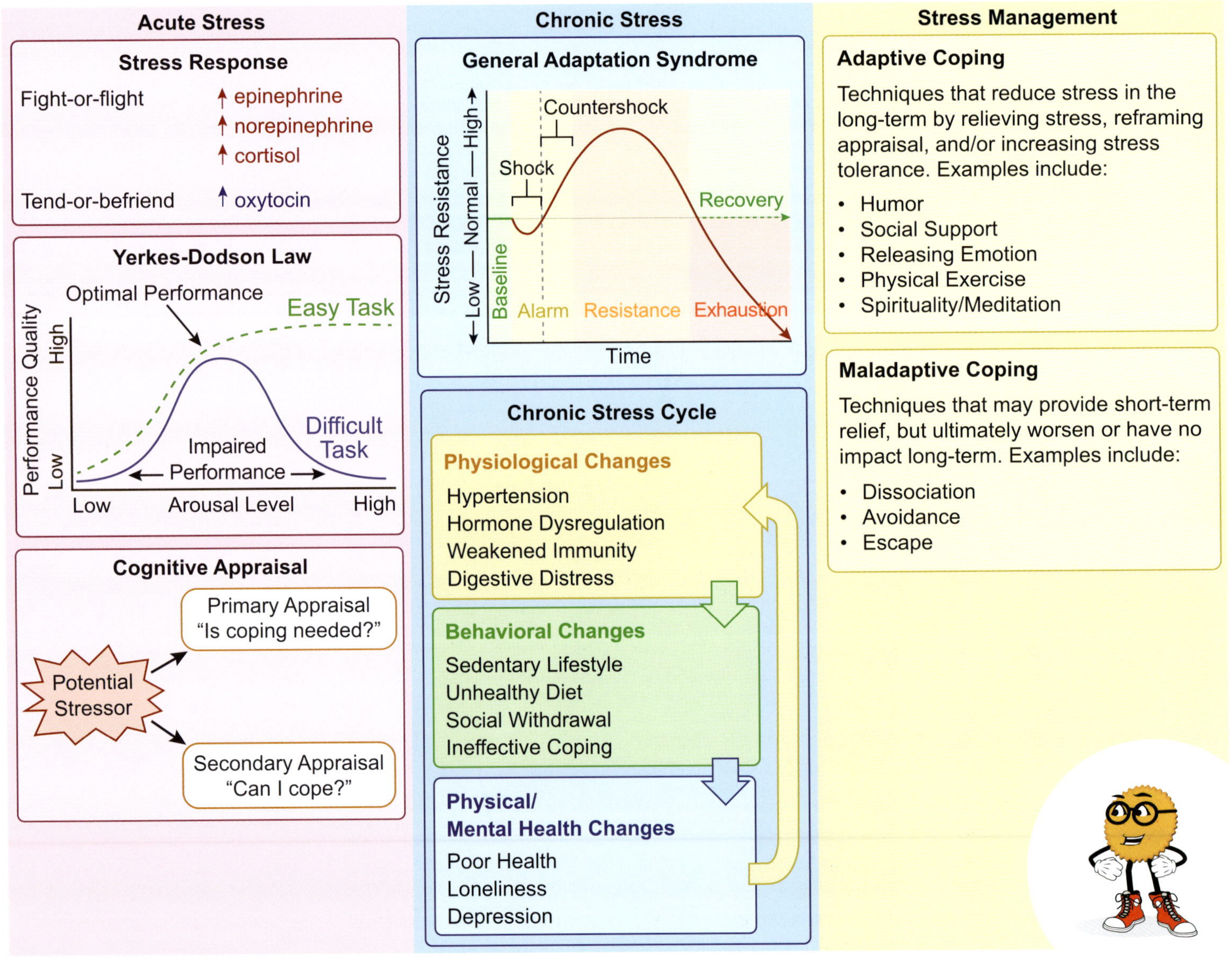

Acute Stress

Stress Response

Fight-or-flight	↑ epinephrine ↑ norepinephrine ↑ cortisol
Tend-or-befriend	↑ oxytocin

Yerkes-Dodson Law

Optimal Performance
Easy Task
Difficult Task
Impaired Performance
Performance Quality (Low – High)
Arousal Level (Low – High)

Cognitive Appraisal

Potential Stressor → Primary Appraisal "Is coping needed?"
Potential Stressor → Secondary Appraisal "Can I cope?"

Chronic Stress

General Adaptation Syndrome

Countershock
Shock
Recovery
Baseline
Alarm
Resistance
Exhaustion
Stress Resistance (Low — Normal — High)
Time

Chronic Stress Cycle

Physiological Changes
Hypertension
Hormone Dysregulation
Weakened Immunity
Digestive Distress

Behavioral Changes
Sedentary Lifestyle
Unhealthy Diet
Social Withdrawal
Ineffective Coping

Physical/ Mental Health Changes
Poor Health
Loneliness
Depression

Stress Management

Adaptive Coping

Techniques that reduce stress in the long-term by relieving stress, reframing appraisal, and/or increasing stress tolerance. Examples include:

- Humor
- Social Support
- Releasing Emotion
- Physical Exercise
- Spirituality/Meditation

Maladaptive Coping

Techniques that may provide short-term relief, but ultimately worsen or have no impact long-term. Examples include:

- Dissociation
- Avoidance
- Escape

A **stressor** is the event that causes the stress. There are two types of stressors.

1. **Cataclysmic events**
2. **Personal events**
    a. Major life events
    b. Daily stressors
    c. Ambient stressors

Cataclysmic events (catastrophes) are large-scale, unpredictable, and non-specific stressors, meaning that they cause nearly everyone who experiences them to feel stress. They include events like natural disasters, wars, and pandemics. Cataclysmic events are less common than other stressors but tend to be more severe.

Types of Stressors

Major life events are significant shifts in how a person lives from day to day. Regardless of whether they are "positive" or "negative" events, the uncertainty that comes with new situations tends to be stressful. Some examples of major life events are marriage, death of a spouse, personal injury, and getting fired. Because of their rarity, major life events are less likely to be significant causes of overall stress than other types of stressors.

Daily stressors, also called *micro-stressors*, are probably the biggest contributor to stress in a person's life. Daily stressors are stressful events that happen as a part of everyday life, such as making decisions, meeting deadlines, having disagreements with people, being late for work or school, etc. What qualifies as a daily stressor is highly individualized, since people vary more in what they find stressful in everyday life than during a natural disaster. For example, one person might find walking his dog enjoyable, while another might find it irritating.

Dependent stressors, like interpersonal conflict, partially **depend** on what I do, think, and feel, while independent stressors, like being struck by lightning, are **independent** from my behavior and personal characteristics.

Ambient stressors are stressors that are an unavoidable part of the environment in which a person lives. They can include ambient noise, pollution, traffic, and crowding. Ambient stressors tend to be chronic, low-level, yet perceptible stressors. They can negatively impact a person's level of stress without him being aware of it.

Stressors may also be divided into two categories: independent and dependent stressors. **Independent stressors** occur regardless of a person's actions or disposition, while **dependent stressors** are clearly linked to a person's behavior. For example, being involved in a train accident would be an independent stressor, while panicking after procrastinating on an assignment would be a dependent stressor.

4.6 Effects of Stress on Physiological Functions

Stress manifests itself physiologically. The physiological reaction to stress starts with the activation of the "**fight-or-flight**" system, which involves the activation of the sympathetic nervous system and the release of several hormones.

When the sympathetic nervous system is activated, both heart rate and breathing rate increase. At the same time, blood vessels in the periphery of the body constrict, forcing blood into major organs such as the heart, brain, and lungs. The net effect is to increase the delivery of oxygen to important organs and tissues used for fight or flight.

Activation of the endocrine system during the fight-or-flight response leads to the release of catecholamines, such as **epinephrine** and **norepinephrine**. These hormones can bind to almost every type of cell in the body, and have different effects depending on which cell and which receptor type they bind.

Cortisol, a steroid hormone produced in the adrenal cortex, is also released during the fight-or-flight response. Cortisol is a type of glucocorticoid that stimulates gluconeogenesis, dampens the immune response, and can cause the breakdown of proteins and lipids over long periods of time.

Hormones are also released when the body is experiencing types of stress that fall outside "fight or flight" situations, such as **psychological stress**. In these times, people often fall back on support systems such as family and friends. This response is called the "**tend-and-befriend response**" and is characterized by an increase in nurturing behaviors and engagement in social networks during times of stress. This response is thought to be modulated by **oxytocin**, a hormone released during the tend-and-befriend response which helps dampen the stress response and promote social and romantic bonding. The effects of oxytocin are enhanced by estrogen, while androgens inhibit the release of oxytocin.

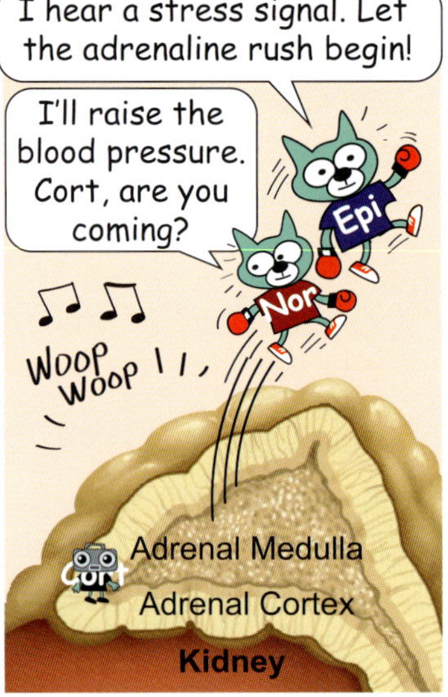

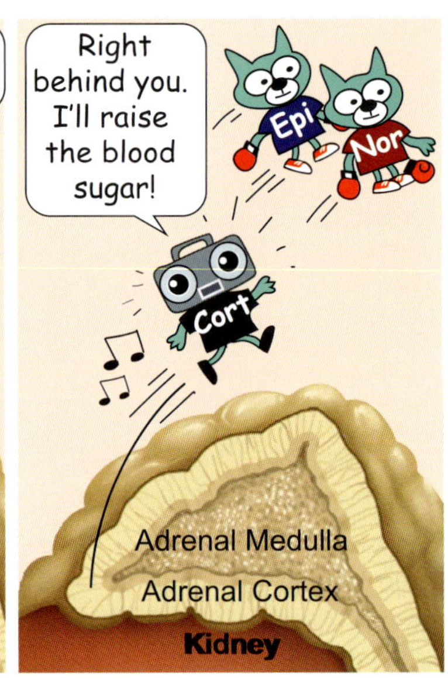

There are three distinct stages of the stress response as outlined by Hungarian-Canadian endocrinologist **Hans Selye** in the **general adaptation syndrome**.

1. Alarm
2. Resistance
3. Exhaustion (or recovery)

During the **alarm phase**, the body reacts to a threat by starting the stress reaction. At first, the body is in a state of "*shock*," and several systemic values can drop, such as blood volume, blood sugar, and the amount of solute in the blood. This can lead to circulatory shock.

After the alarm phase comes the **resistance phase**, characterized by system-wide changes to deal with a stressor. The type of response depends on the stressor and the individual: for example, if a person is starving, his body might lower its resting metabolic rate, reduce the desire for exercise, and maximize nutrient absorption from food.

The body's goal in the resistance phase is to restore homeostasis in the short term. If the stressor can be overcome, the body returns to normal and can adapt or change to be better prepared for the stressor in the future. This process is called **recovery** and is the third stage in the general adaptation syndrome.

If, however, the body cannot return to baseline functioning after the resistance phase, a different third stage occurs: **exhaustion**. Exhaustion can happen after a long period of unresolved stress. The body's resources deplete, and immune function declines. Blood vessels may become constricted to the point that tissues can no longer get enough blood, leading to necrosis. In severe cases, organs can fail, or *decompensate*, causing death.

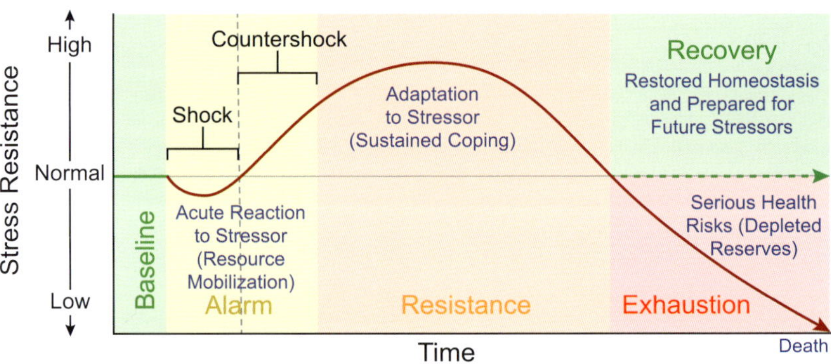

General Adaptation Syndrome

According to the **general adaptation syndrome** theory, the human stress response is nonspecific—the physiological response for all individuals to any given stressor is the same, though the degree of the response may vary and the behavioral response may vary.

When the body never receives a clear signal that a stressor is gone, it can experience a constant stress response, known as **chronic stress**.

Chronic stress negatively affects nearly every major body system.

The **cardiovascular system** responds to the constant activation of the sympathetic nervous system and the endocrine system by increasing blood pressure, blood volume, and heart rate. In the long term, this forces the heart to work harder to move blood around the body. Sustained high blood pressure, also called **hypertension,** can lead to **myocardial infarction** (heart attack), stroke, and abnormal heart rhythms.

The **reproductive system** is also impacted by chronic stress. Men and women experience different reproductive problems when stressed.

Chronic stress in men can decrease the production of **testosterone**, the primary male sex hormone. In adults, low levels of testosterone can lead to decreased muscle and bone mass, increased body fat, decreased libido, and the inability to maintain an erection. Chronic stress in men can also negatively impact sperm production and quality, making it more challenging to conceive children. The impact of stress on the immune system can make infections of the reproductive system more likely.

Chronic stress in women affects the levels of several reproductive hormones, especially **FSH**, **LH**, and **estrogen,** the primary female sex hormone. Stress in women can lead to irregular or absent menstrual cycles, painful periods, and changes in cycle duration. Stress can also worsen *premenstrual syndrome*, or *PMS*, and this in turn may become an added source of stress.

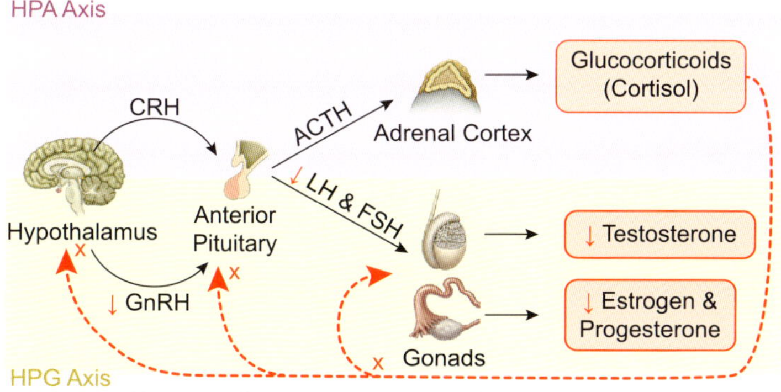

Chronic Stress Impact on Sex Hormones

Women experiencing chronic stress are more likely to have difficulties conceiving, and fetal and childhood development can be hindered by chronic stress. The symptoms of menopause are made worse by stress, and menopause itself can be a significant stressor. Stress can also worsen existing reproductive diseases such as herpes or polycystic ovarian syndrome (PCOS).

The **immune system** is especially prone to damage by chronic stress. Short-term exposure to stressful events – on the scale of several minutes—causes a burst of "first responder" activity and several signs of weakening function. When the stress is extended over several days, weeks, or months, which is common in daily life, all aspects of the immune system suffer.

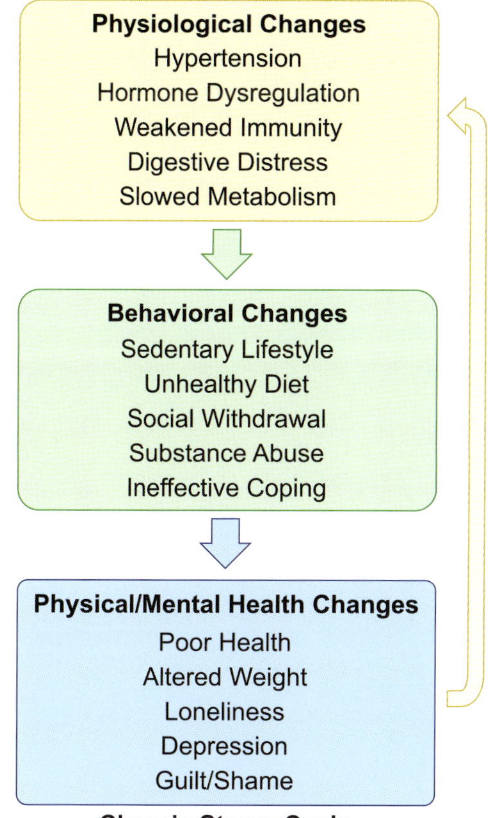

Chronic Stress Cycle

People who are older or sick tend to be more susceptible to stress-related immune problems. In older people, sub-clinical depression can suppress the immune system over several months. Young people are no less susceptible to chronic stress but tend to have higher baseline immune function.

The duration of stress matters more than the severity when it comes to the immune system. Long-term stress also tends to be associated with other chronic issues, such as loneliness and depression, which build on each other and worsen over time.

The **digestive system** can be affected by chronic stress. The digestive system is in constant communication with the brain, and both signals sent by the brain and by the bacteria in the gut can influence digestive symptoms. Stress can make people more attentive to gut pain, bloating, and general discomfort. Changes in gut bacteria can influence mood, which in turn modulates a person's response to stress.

When a person is stressed, he may use tobacco or drink alcohol more than usual, which can lead to acid reflux or heartburn. Stress may cause a change in appetite, which can lead to changes in mood. Stress can also affect digestion itself by weakening the intestinal barrier that keeps gut bacteria out of the rest of the body, causing chronic low-level inflammation.

Metabolism is also affected by chronic stress. During the stress response, the body secretes cortisol and epinephrine. Over the long term, these hormones reduce insulin sensitivity, which can lead to diabetes. Additionally, high levels of cortisol may favor the development of central obesity (fat accumulating in the torso).

4.7 Behavioral and Emotional Responses to Stressors

The effects of stress are not limited to physiological changes but can also affect **behavior** and **emotion**. Stress-related behavioral changes are thought to be in part caused by chronically high levels of glucocorticoids, such as cortisol, which are released in response to stress.

Although glucocorticoid receptors are found in nearly every cell in the body, they are not distributed equally across all cells. In the brain, the prefrontal cortex, the hippocampus, and the amygdala all have high concentrations of glucocorticoid receptors and are involved in the behavioral changes caused by stress. After experiencing chronic stress, these areas can shrink or undergo other permanent changes.

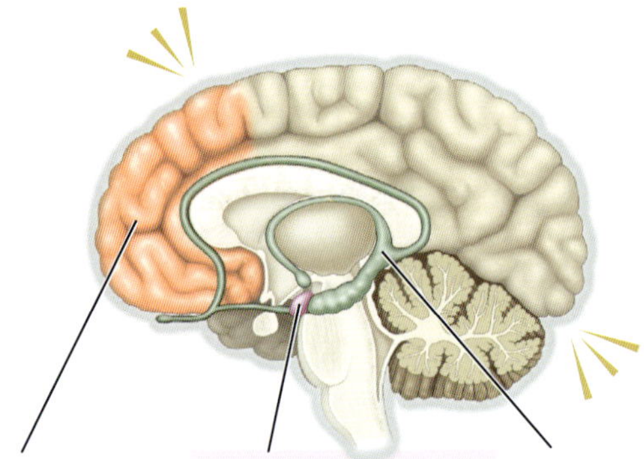

Prefrontal Cortex	Amygdala	Hippocampus
Designed to downregulate stress response via higher-order functions, such as cognitive appraisal. Chronic stress leads to atrophy, which impairs impulse control, decision making, and working memory.	Designed to upregulate stress response via detection of emotional stimuli and distress signaling to the HPA axis. Chronic stress leads to volume enlargement, which heightens stress perception and reactivity further.	Designed to downregulate the stress response via glucocorticoid receptors that inhibit HPA axis (negative feedback). Chronic stress leads to atrophy, which impairs HPA feedback and contextual episodic memory formation.

The Brain Under Stress

Chronic stress is strongly linked to the development of depression. In patients with depression, the amygdala and the subgenual cingulate tend to be overactive, while the prefrontal cortex is underactive. Additionally, the hippocampus shrinks, though this can be partially reversed with antidepressants.

Depression seriously affects a person's daily life, leading to a chronic low mood (sometimes called dysthymia), low self-esteem, lack of pleasure (called anhedonia), and/or low energy. Emotional states such as sadness or anger may also become more common. **Learned helplessness**, or losing the ability to cope when consistently subjected to stressors outside of one's control, is also thought to contribute to depression.

Learned helplessness can be prevented in rats through regular exercise. This may be why **exercise** helps alleviate symptoms of depression as well as prevent depression in the first place.

More generally, stress can affect both mood and daily activities. Feelings of anxiety and depression (though not necessarily to the point of disorder), irritability, and lack of motivation are common. Social withdrawal, over or undereating, and substance abuse can also be brought on by stress.

Stress does not always have a negative effect on behavior. **Eustress** is a type of stress that a person interprets as being positive. Instead of being a source of mental or physical discomfort, the response to eustress is more often a feeling of meaning or hope.

The highest state of eustress is **flow**, or a feeling of total immersion in an activity with little to no awareness of one's surroundings. Often called being "**in the zone**," flow states are commonly experienced by musicians, athletes, and gamers. Flow states are inherently pleasurable and motivating, and they are correlated with high levels of performance in artistic and scientific fields, athletics, and general learning.

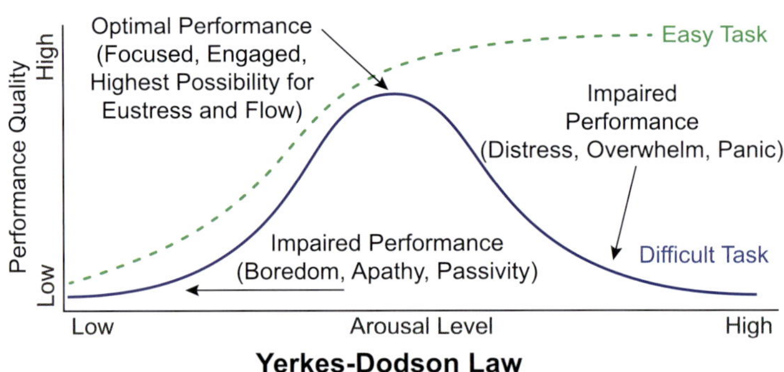

Yerkes-Dodson Law

A person's performance on mental tasks, such as focused attention, decision-making, and multitasking is affected by his level of arousal or by the amount and type of stress he is under. The relationship between arousal and performance is known as the **Yerkes-Dodson law** and shows two trends: for simple tasks, such as fear conditioning, performance goes up with the level of stress. For difficult tasks, the level of performance follows a bell curve, with low-stress and high-stress environments leading to low performance and moderate levels of arousal leading to optimal performance.

4.8 Stress Appraisal

How a person thinks about an event can influence the extent to which he finds it stressful. This is called the **appraisal theory of stress** and was popularized by the psychologist **Richard Lazarus** in tandem with Susan Folkman. The process by which a person labels an event as stressful is called **appraisal** and has two stages: primary and secondary appraisal.

Primary appraisal involves assessing stress in the present moment. There are three categories into which primary appraisals may fall.

1. Irrelevant
2. Benign/positive
3. Stressful

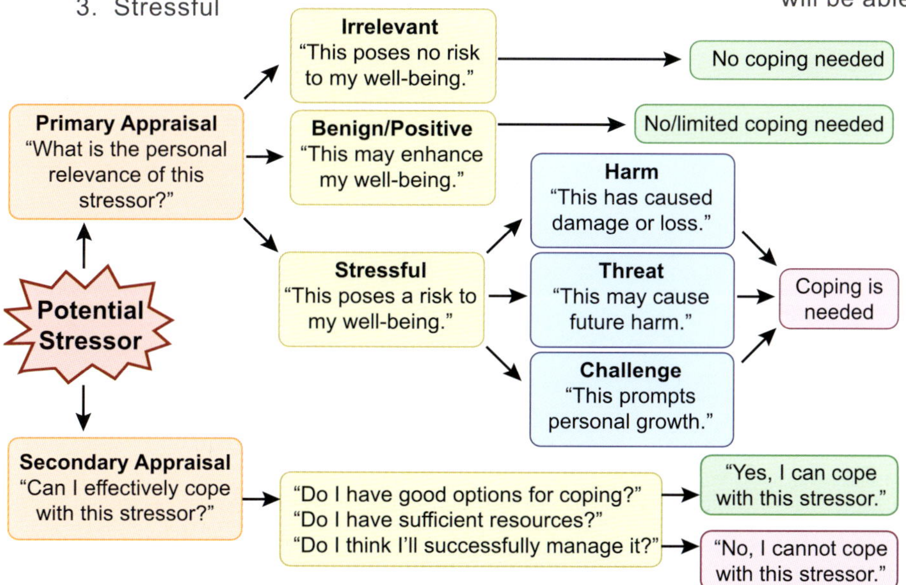

Cognitive Stress Appraisal

Irrelevant events carry no importance to the person experiencing them. No matter their outcome, none of the person's values, needs, or commitments are infringed upon, and nothing would be gained or lost no matter how things play out.

Benign/positive events are events that a person views as benign or positive. These events almost always come with some negative feeling, such as fear that the benefit from the event will go away or that some later harm will come as punishment for feeling good.

Stressful events are events that actively harm a person, provoke fear that he will be harmed, or that encourage him to mobilize resources for growth. Often, these thoughts occur together – for example, a student who finds out that he failed a test can simultaneously feel shame about his performance, feel anxiety about the consequences of failure, and desire to do better next time. These facets of stressful events are called *harm*, *threat*, and *challenge* respectively.

Secondary appraisal is an evaluation of a person's ability to deal with the event being appraised. Secondary appraisal involves taking into account what options are available to deal with an event, the likelihood that a given strategy will work, and the likelihood that the person appraising the event will be able to implement it.

Because the words "primary" and "secondary" are used to describe these processes, it is understandable to assume that primary appraisal is more important than secondary appraisal or that primary appraisal comes before secondary appraisal. However, neither are true: both types of appraisal are equally important in evaluating events, and the processes happen simultaneously, not one after the other.

4.9 Managing Stress

Stress is something that comes with being alive. It is unwise to try to avoid stress completely, for doing so is impossible—simply attempting to avoid all stress can be stressful in itself. Stress can also be a useful indicator of parts of one's life that might need to change. Thus, strategies for **managing stress** are important to leading a balanced and fulfilling life. Coping strategies have the effect of solving problems that lead to stress, minimizing existing stress, and helping a person tolerate stress when it occurs.

At its core, methods for managing stress are, in the words of psychologist Albert Ellis, "what works best for you." There are almost as many strategies for coping with stress as there are psychologists to recommend them.

Humor is a common and effective coping mechanism, with about 40% of people using it to deal with stress. How humor works to cope with stress is not fully known, but it may function by affecting how people appraise stressful events. Another possibility is that humor can increase the experience of positive emotions, and yet another is that a good sense of humor leads to positive social interactions, which promote **social support**.

Releasing emotion is another good method for coping with stress. People who inhibit emotional expression tend to have higher blood pressure than those who do not, and the act of inhibiting emotion is linked to increased stress and autonomic arousal. There is also some evidence that simply expressing emotion, whether through writing a diary or talking to someone, can lead to better immune function and general health.

Regular **physical exercise** is one of the most important habits a person can build for both stress management and general health and well-being. Not only does physical exercise directly improve mood and make dealing with stress easier, but the dozens of other positive effects on your body can reduce the number and severity of stressful situations due to poor health.

Religious and spiritual practice correlates with and probably causes positive health outcomes in their practitioners. Other factors not directly related to the practice itself, such as social support, less frequent consumption of alcohol, and improvement in mood, may also improve health, which has a large effect on stress. The effects of religious and spiritual practice on health become greater the more religious a practitioner is. In other words, people who consider their religious or spiritual practice an important part of their lives are more likely to enjoy positive health outcomes than those who rate their practice as less important.

Meditation and related practices, such as mindfulness and Christian contemplation, can reduce stress and improve physiological markers associated with stress, such as blood pressure, heart rate, and levels of stress hormones. Slowed breathing, blood pressure, and heart rate along with lower stress hormones indicate **relaxation**, which in and of itself, is helpful for managing stress.

All the coping techniques listed above are called **adaptive coping techniques** because they reduce stress levels in the long term, either by helping a person become stronger against stress or by changing a person's thinking patterns.

In comparison, **maladaptive coping techniques** are coping techniques that work in the short term but worsen or have no effect on long-term stress levels. There are almost as many maladaptive coping techniques as there are adaptive coping techniques, and unfortunately maladaptive techniques tend to be more effective in alleviating short-term symptoms of stress than adaptive coping techniques are.

Some examples of maladaptive coping techniques include dissociation—where a person tries to separate himself from reality, anxious avoidance—where a person seeks to avoid any and all stressful situations, and escape—where a person attempts to use media or substances to forget reality.

4.10 Social Psychology and Human Behavior

People act differently in the presence of others compared to when they are alone. The field of **social psychology** aims to describe and explain these differences in behavior.

Group Behavior

Social facilitation refers to the tendency of people to perform differently on tasks when other people are watching them. When a task is simple/well-practiced, people generally perform better around others than alone. When the task is complex/unfamiliar, however, people tend to perform worse when other people are watching.

Social facilitation has been linked to levels of arousal. Presumably, the presence of others while doing a task increases arousal, enhancing people's performance on easy tasks and making hard tasks even harder. This relationship resembles the **Yerkes-Dodson law** discussed earlier.

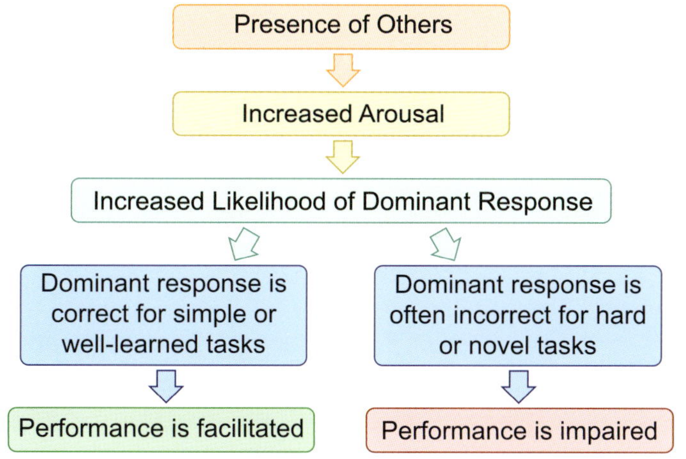

Social Facilitation vs. Social Inhibition

Related to social facilitation is the **Hawthorne effect (a.k.a. the observer effect)**, which states that people change their behavior when they know that they are being observed. The Hawthorne effect is broader than social facilitation, since it has been observed in situations where people are not trying to perform specific tasks.

Hawthorne Effect (Observer Effect)

Expectation Bias (Observer Bias)

> Be sure to not confuse the Hawthorne effect with observer bias. The Hawthorne effect is where people behave differently when they're being watched, while observer bias is where a researcher unconsciously influences the results of an experiment when he knows which group (e.g. control or experimental) a subject belongs to.

Deindividuation is the loss of self-awareness when in a crowd or in otherwise anonymous situations. This effect can lead to people behaving in ways they would not if they were alone, since they are unlikely to be personally identified by others. Deindividuation can manifest in both positive and negative ways—for example, people are more likely to donate large sums of money to charity while in a group, but they are also more prone to cyberbullying others when they believe they are anonymous.

The **bystander effect** is the observation that a person is less likely to help someone when he is part of a group. The larger the group, the less likely a given bystander is to volunteer to help.

Bystanders respond differently to different situations. They are more likely to step in and help when the situation is dangerous, when the perpetrators are still present (if there are any), and when the cost to the bystander is physical—that is, they risk their bodily safety instead of money or their time.

Social loafing is where people put in less effort when working in a group than when working alone. Many potential explanations for where it comes from have been put forth, including deindividuation, feeling that their contribution will not make much of a difference, and attempting to not be "suckered" into doing more of the work than other people.

A phenomenon called the **diffusion of responsibility** contributes to deindividuation, the bystander effect, and social loafing. Diffusion of responsibility is where people take less responsibility for their actions (or lack thereof) when others are present—people assume that other people have already acted or will take responsibility for their own actions.

Diffusion of Responsibility

The Psychology of Control

Like many of the terms used in sociology, the definition of **social control** is both vague and controversial. In a broad sense, social control refers to all social processes that cause conformity—these can range from teaching children how to behave in school to social media posts from national agencies urging people to get their flu shots.

Conformity is the act of matching actions or beliefs to those of other people. Conformity is encouraged by **social influence**, which is *how* people change their beliefs in response to social pressures—in other words, it is the mechanism by which conformity occurs. There are two main types of social influence: normative social influence and informational social influence.

Normative social influence involves a person looking to a group of people to decide how to act, even when he already has an idea as to what he should do. The primary motivation behind normative social influence is fitting in with the group, as people tend to fear rejection if they do not conform to the behavior of the group.

Informational social influence occurs when someone copies the behavior of a group when he himself does not know how to act. Instead of representing an attempt to fit in, informational social influence reflects the assumption that groups of other people have a better understanding of ambiguous situations than an individual does—as such, a person tends to copy the actions of those around him when he is not sure how to behave.

Normative Social Influence

Informational Social Influence

When you conform after knowing what to do, that's normative social influence. When you conform because you don't know what to do, that's informational social influence.

Even when people conform **publicly**, meaning they match their behaviors with those of the group when they are being observed, they do not necessarily conform **privately**. That is, people are less likely to conform when nobody else can see them.

Another method of grouping the types of conformity splits it into three categories: compliance, identification, and internalization.

Compliance is where a person pretends to agree with social norms but privately holds views that contradict them.

Identification is conforming to the beliefs of someone trusted or respected. It is a deeper type of conformity than compliance.

Internalization involves a person conforming both publicly and privately to a social norm. It is the deepest type of conformity, and is difficult to change once it occurs.

If social influence is *how* conformity occurs, **peer pressure** is the root cause of conformity. Peer pressure is the influence on a person's behavior that comes from his peers—people that he believes to be similar to himself in some way.

Everyone can be affected by peer pressure, but most of the research on the phenomenon has been concentrated on children and adolescents. Children as young as preschoolers respond to peer pressure, but tend to only conform publicly. In adolescents, peer pressure seems to be a particularly strong predictor of whether teens will engage in risky behavior. Adults are less likely to conform due to peer pressure than children and adolescents, but they can also be swayed by peer pressure.

Adult Peer Pressure

Obedience is another type of social influence. Obedience involves a person following instructions from an authority figure. It has been shown that people generally obey authority figures, though religious and moral beliefs can override commands from those in power.

Studying Conformity and Obedience

Some of the most famous experiments in all of psychology have centered on studying conformity and obedience.

Solomon Asch carried out a series of experiments in the 1950s that were designed to test conformity. Fittingly, these have come to be known as the **Asch conformity experiments**. All of these experiments had the same basic structure: take one unsuspecting study participant, put him in a room with seven **confederates** (actors working with the researcher), and ask them to say which line on the right image (A, B, or C) is the same length as the line on the left image.

Piece of cake, right? The wrinkle in these experiments, however, is that at some point the seven confederates would all give the same *incorrect* answer to this question. In the original line study, after hearing seven other people give the wrong answer, most (about 60%) study participants gave the correct answer anyway, contradicting the confederates. However, the remaining nearly 40% conformed to the incorrect answer given by the confederates.

This process was repeated in the same study with different images, though all of them were versions of the same simple comparison setup. Only 5% of people always conformed, meaning that 95% of the participants disagreed with the confederates at some point. However, only 25% of study participants never agreed with the confederates, meaning that 75% of people conformed at least once.

The results of the Asch line experiments have been put forth to support both normative and informational social influence. Some researchers claim that people conformed to the confederates in order to fit in and avoid rejection, while others believe that study participants were genuinely unsure of which answers were correct, and conformed because they assumed the confederates knew something they did not.

The **Milgram obedience experiments**, which began in the 1960s and were created by **Stanley Milgram**, aimed to test people's tendency to obey authority figures.

Study participants were recruited to help with a psychological experiment in which they would be shocking a "learner" with electricity. This learner was a confederate, and only pretended to be receiving shocks. They were overseen by a scientist who directed them on when to shock the learner, as well as the voltage they should use to do so. Study participants started off with low voltage "shocks", then were asked by the scientist overseeing them to ramp them up as time went on. These "shocks" eventually reached voltage levels that, if the shocks were real, would have killed the learner.

The learner matched his reactions to the amount of voltage he was supposed to be receiving. For instance, he might yelp in pain at low voltage, scream and ask to stop at higher voltages, and stop responding at the highest voltage, implying that he had lost consciousness or died. Study participants were clearly made uncomfortable by these reactions, but were told by the scientist that they had to continue the experiment. About 60% of study participants continued through to the end of the trial, a figure that has been replicated in other studies, and every single participant in the original study delivered a shock over 300 volts.

The primary takeaway from the Milgram experiments is that obedience to authority is normal, even when the people obeying feel deeply disturbed by their doing so. It has been proposed that obedience to authority is a type of conformity, and might function through normative influence, informational influence, or a combination of both types. Alternatively, people might internalize the idea that their purpose in interactions with an authority figure is to be useful, and try to help the authority figure as much as possible, even if they have reservations about specific actions they are asked to do.

The **Stanford prison experiment**, led by **Philip Zimbardo** in the early 1970s, was set up to study how people's behavior would change in a simulated prison. Study participants were randomly assigned to be either prisoners or guards and were effectively left alone from that point on—guards were not allowed to physically harm prisoners, but almost everything else was allowed. Almost immediately, guards began to abuse their prisoners, and in response the prisoners began resisting the guards. The actions of both groups escalated in severity over a period of days, and Zimbardo ended the experiment after just six days.

Zimbardo's conclusion from the experiment was that **situational attribution**, or assuming that people's actions are best explained by their situations and not by any fundamental part of their personality, is a better explanation for how people behave than **fundamental attribution**, in which people believe that the behavior of others is caused by some core aspect of who they are as a person.

Participants may also have **internalized** their roles as either prisoners or guards and changed their behavior to match how they thought a guard or prisoner should act. Participants may also have undergone **deindividualization**, where the differences between people are intentionally erased in order to weaken their sense of identity. It has also been proposed that the guards experienced **cognitive dissonance** when they mistreated "prisoners" that they knew were their fellow students.

The Zimbardo prison experiment would not pass an ethics board today. Additionally, there are two serious problems with trying to extrapolate its results to a larger population: demand characteristics and selection bias.

Major Limitations of the Stanford Prison Experiment

Demand characteristics occur when participants in an experiment figure out the point of the experiment and subconsciously change their behavior to assist the researchers. Every study participant was briefed on what the experiment was studying beforehand, and it is likely that some of them changed their behavior to better fit their ideas of what Zimbardo and his team were looking for.

Selection bias is where the sample of study participants does not represent a random sample of the broader population. In the newspaper ad Zimbardo put out to advertise the study, he mentioned that the experiment was a study of "prison life." What kind of people voluntarily sign up to be in a simulated prison?

As it turns out, it is likely that the people who signed up for the experiment scored higher in personality measures of narcissism, social dominance, and aggression, among other related traits, than the general population.

Factors that Affect Conformity

In general, people that live in cultures that are more individualistic (focused on the individual instead of the group) are less likely to conform to a group than people from collectivist (focused on the group more than the individual) cultures.

As people age, they tend to be less likely to conform than younger people. Men appear to be less likely to conform than women, especially in scenarios where people know they are being observed. Additionally, the larger a group gets, the more likely people are to conform to it.

A number of situational factors have also been found to influence people's likelihood to conform. Being surrounded by attractive group members, wanting to please the group, and a feeling of group cohesion (members feel strongly linked to one another) all increase conformity.

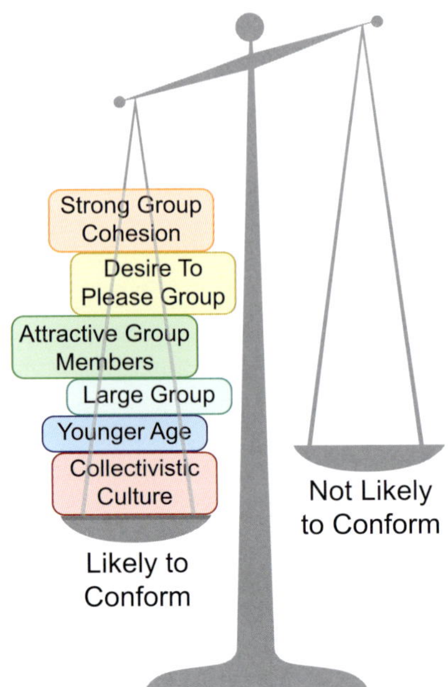

Conformity Factors Scale

How Groups Make Decisions

Groups behave differently than individuals. When groups make decisions, two main effects come into play: group polarization and groupthink.

Group polarization is the tendency of groups to come to more extreme conclusions after a discussion than the individuals who make up the group had originally intended. For it to occur, members of the group must have a shared understanding of the topic at hand when starting out. Additionally, there must be views that are initially more dominant than others. Over time, the opinions of the group trend towards more radical positions.

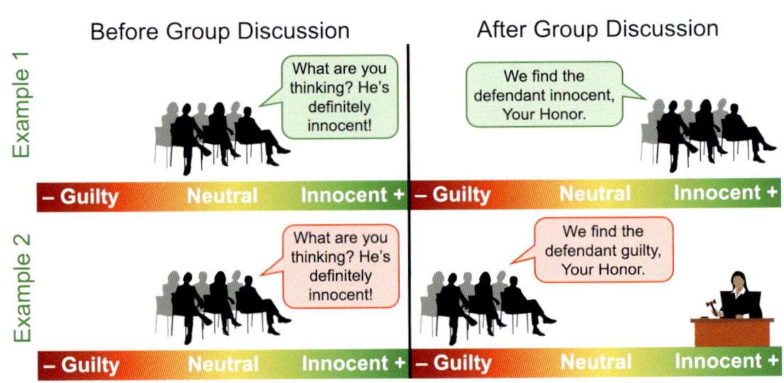

Group Polarization

Group polarization is driven by a couple of factors. The first is **group identity**, or the feeling that being part of a particular group is an important part of who a person is.

Feelings of group identity tend to increase after talking with people who share similar views to a group a person identifies with.

The second factor that drives group polarization is **in-group/out-group affiliation**. When a person is exposed to views that contradict those of the group with which he identifies, he tends to label the person promoting it as part of the out-group—a group with which he does not identify. When the same person encounters views that support the group he identifies with, he labels the person promoting those views as part of the in-group—a group with which he identifies. A person is more likely to be influenced by members of an in-group than those of an out-group.

Groupthink is a mode of thinking that occurs when people are making decisions in a group that prioritizes harmony over realistic solutions to a given problem. It is most common in small, tightly-knit groups (i.e., in-groups that have a strong sense of group identity) and almost invariably leads to bad decisions.

Imagine a meeting of members of Heroin Anonymous (HA), a twelve-step recovery program designed for people to beat heroin addiction. HA meetings tend to be small and personal, with members getting to know each other extremely well over a long period of time.

Suppose that in one of these groups most members express the view that heroin addiction cannot be overcome—thus, there is no point in trying to get clean. If one person argues against this view, the other members may gang up on him, trying to convince him to give up. If he falls prey to groupthink, he will change his mind to match the other members and continue using heroin, despite the entire point of HA meetings being to escape heroin addiction.

Groupthink can be avoided by inviting experts into the group to comment on its direction, asking group members to honestly voice their opinions, and asking a random group member to play "devil's advocate" at every meeting.

Social Norms and How to Break Them

Social norms are customs, values, laws and standards that regulate how people behave. They are shared among members of a group, dictate which actions are acceptable and unacceptable, and form the basis of social life.

Norms are enforced via **sanctions**, which are rewards and punishments given out by the group when people either uphold or break social norms. **Positive sanctions** are given for following social norms, while **negative sanctions** are given for breaking social norms.

Both norms and sanctions can be formal or informal. **Formal norms/sanctions** are generally written down, recognized, and enforced by institutions. **Laws** are an example of a formal norm, and **fines/prison sentences** are some formal sanctions.

Informal norms/sanctions are not recognized by institutions, and tend to be more vague than their formal counterparts. Refraining from screaming in public is an example of an informal norm, while gossip is an example of an informal sanction.

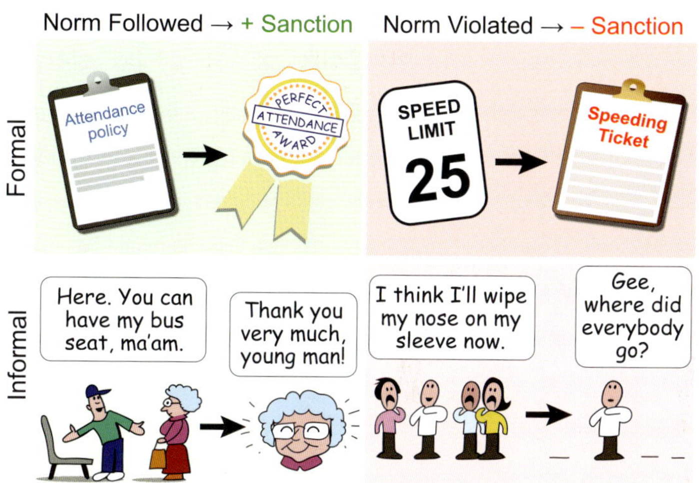

Social Norms and Sanctions

There are two main groups of norms.

1. Folkways
2. Mores

Folkways (also called customs) are the largest group of norms. They are actions a person is expected to do in a given situation, but there are usually only minor consequences for breaking any one of them. Some folkways in the United States include eating three meals a day, covering one's mouth and nose when one sneezes, and calling one of man's best friends a "dog" instead of a "woofer."

Mores are norms based on moral principles, and have much greater consequences for breaking them. They tend to be more abstract than folkways, and include such concepts as being loyal or showing compassion. Mores are generally expressed in a positive way—that is, mores are things you should do, not things you should not.

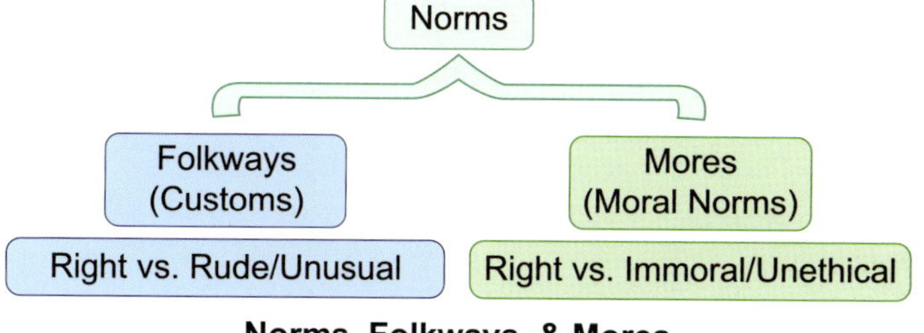

Norms, Folkways, & Mores

Taboos are mores expressed in a negative way. In other words, taboos are moral principles based on things you should not do, not things you should do. Some common taboos are incest, infidelity, and cannibalism.

Anomie is the breakdown of social norms between an individual and his society. It is thought to come from conflict between deeply-entrenched belief systems, and it can cause a person to experience social dysfunction, and even to act in an antisocial manner. This is because when a person no longer accepts the norms of the groups he is a part of, he has no reason to conform to them—his actions can be viewed as civil disobedience or treason, depending on who is judging him.

Deviance

When a person experiences anomie, he is prone to break social norms. Defying social norms is called **deviance**, and multiple theories have been created to classify and explain it. Four of these are:

1. Labeling theory
2. Strain theory
3. Neutralization theory
4. Differential association theory

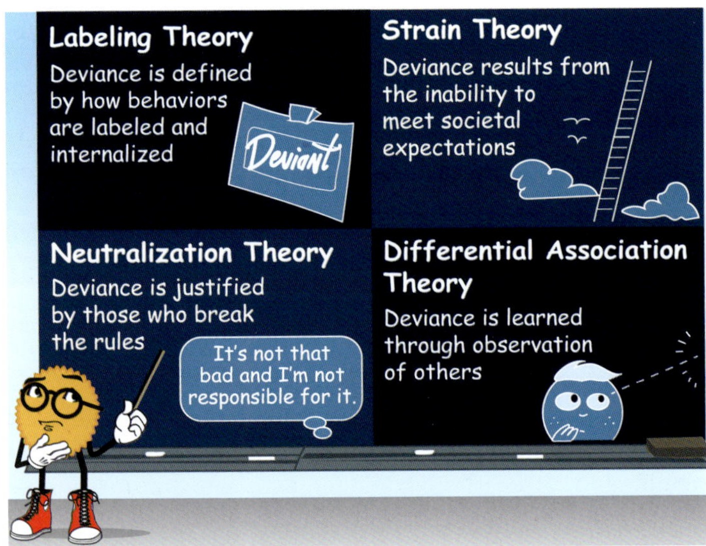

Labeling theory states that how behaviors are labeled changes people's tendency to perform them. Instead of deviance being something inherent in an act, groups tend to label minority behaviors as deviant or "bad" while labeling majority behaviors as "good."

This theory notes that labels and specific behaviors do not always go together, and that labels can create stigma that is not necessarily warranted. The label of "blond," for example, has come to be associated with stupidity for many people. Thus, a person with blond hair might be treated as if he is dumb, even if his behavior does not match the stereotype.

Labeling theory has divided deviance into two types: primary and secondary deviance.

Primary deviance occurs when people break social norms but only receive minor punishments for doing so. This first deviant act is noticed by others, but does not generally lead to stigma or the labeling of the person breaking norms as a "deviant."

Secondary deviance is when people do something bad enough to be labeled as a "deviant." This can happen after people break the same norms over and over, or if they violate mores or commit taboos without showing remorse. Once the label of "deviant" is applied to an individual, he is more likely to be ostracized or stigmatized by those around him.

Strain theory argues that people turn to deviance when they cannot live up to societal expectations. Both an individual and the people around him expect him to act in a certain way, but some standards are simply too high for him to achieve.

Strain Theory

American culture tends to give a high status to people who are "successful," which generally means that they are wealthy or have a high income. Success seems to be respected even if wealthy individuals break social norms to gain their wealth, and most Americans are held to this high standard. Poor people, for whom this standard is less easily attainable, usually conform to social norms and try to "make it" via culturally approved means. Some people, however, accept the cultural standards of success but violate norms in order to achieve it, such as through scamming other people or selling illegal drugs.

Neutralization theory posits that people justify deviant actions to themselves so that they avoid feeling guilt or shame for performing them. This theory holds that people have a good idea of what the norms of their groups are, as well as what will happen when they break them. People bend the rules for themselves temporarily to get what they want, and come up with a reason that they use to defend themselves afterward.

Imagine that you are doing homework and get a text message from a friend asking for a photo of your work so far. If your professor has banned sharing notes or working together on homework assignments, you might feel conflicted about granting your friend's request. If you do end up sending him or her the photo, neutralization theory predicts that you would create a reason for breaking the norm of integrity, such as, "my friend needed my help—what else was I supposed to do?"

Neutralization Theory

Differential association theory claims that people learn deviant behaviors from watching others who perform them. The more deviant actions a person sees performed, the more likely he is to carry them out himself. Conversely, if a person is surrounded by people who uphold social norms, he is more likely to avoid deviant actions.

If a kid grows up in a neighborhood where he sees crime on an everyday basis, differential association theory predicts that he is at higher risk of becoming a criminal than a kid raised in an environment with less crime.

Collective Behavior

Collective behavior sounds suspiciously like group behavior, but the two concepts are different. Collectives are short-lived, have low barriers to entry (generally limited by physical proximity to the collective), and have more relaxed social norms than groups usually do. Collective behavior tends to break social norms, and range from such harmless occurrences as fads to mass panic.

Fads are collective behaviors that spread quickly and widely, only to burn out and be forgotten as rapidly as they had spread.

Most fads are unlikely to cause lasting damage to people who participate in them. Some fads, however, are more dangerous—some recent ones include the benadryl challenge, where people film themselves taking huge doses of diphenhydramine (an allergy medication) and the milk crate challenge, in which people climb up and down structurally unsound "stairs" made of milk crates.

Riots occur when a violent collective forms in response to disagreements or complaints. Property damage due to riots is common, though violence against other people is by no means uncommon. Some of the most well-known riots of the past few years developed out of protests following the murder of George Floyd—although most of these protests did not involve property damage or interpersonal violence, demonstrations that turned violent caused a total of at least one billion dollars in damage.

Mobs are similar in origin to riots, but tend to target individuals instead of property. Mobbing can be violent, as in the case of lynch mobs, or non-violent, such as social media mobs.

Mass hysteria is the rapid outbreak of atypical actions, thoughts, or feelings in a collective that is manifested in unusual behaviors or experiences. One example is **mass psychogenic illness (MPI)**, which is where illness spreads through a collective with no identifiable infective agent—instead, MPIs are passed on to others socially.

Recently, people have been developing "Tourette-like" behaviors after consuming online content made by people who claim to have Tourette syndrome—patients can often name specific "influencers" they follow. However, the symptoms they have do not align with those of Tourette syndrome, and are both extremely numerous and complicated, changing with the release of every weekly set of videos.

Socialization

Socialization is the process through which people learn social norms. People learn these norms from various sources, including their parents, friends, romantic partners, mass media, etc. These sources are called **agents of socialization**.

Agents of Socialization

Parents, and to a lesser extent other members of the family, contribute most to an individual's socialization. This is due in large part to the sheer amount of time an individual spends with his parents before starting school, as well as to the close bonds between parents and their children.

When a child starts school, he is exposed to a larger, less tightly-knit group of people from which to learn how to behave. These can be his **peers**, who are fellow classmates around his age, and adult authority figures who are not his parents, such as teachers. The importance of peers in socialization grows until a child leaves school.

Socialization in the **workplace** can be thought of as a continuation of the socialization process in schools. Adolescents and adults interact with their coworkers, both their superiors and subordinates, and learn appropriate behavior through doing so.

Mass media is playing an increasingly important role in socialization. In 2015, teenagers spent an average of nearly nine hours a day consuming media, and most families have experienced an increase in this consumption during the COVID-19 pandemic. Many young people spend more time consuming media than any other kind of activity on a daily basis, and in the process pick up social norms from watching how others act on screen.

Agents of Socialization

Social Facilitation vs. Inhibition

Hawthorne (Observer Effect)

Since I'm anonymous, I'll conform to the group.
I'm not responsible—I'm just part of the group.
Not my problem to solve.
He's probably just napping.
I'm sure security's been called.
I'm not doing one second more work than anyone else.
The teacher doesn't know our individual contributions anyway.

Deindividuation | Bystander Effect | Social Loafing

Diffusion of Responsibility

Group Behavior

How it occurs: Normative social influence
Informational social influence

Why it occurs: Peer pressure

A B C

Asch Experiment | Milgram Experiment | Zimbardo (Stanford Prison) Experiment

Major Studies

Conformity & Obedience

Does everyone agree?
Yeah, of course...
We find the defendant innocent, Your Honor.
– Guilty | Neutral | Innocent +
We find the defendant guilty, Your Honor.
– Guilty | Neutral | Innocent +

Groupthink | Group Polarization

Group Decision-making

Norm Followed → + Sanction | Norm Violated → – Sanction

Formal: Attendance Policy → Perfect Attendance Award; Speed Limit 25 → Speeding Ticket

Informal: Here. You can have my bus seat, ma'am. → Thank you very much, young man!; I think I'll wipe my nose on my sleeve now. → Gee, where did everybody go?

Social Norms and Sanctions

Folkways & Mores

Social Norms & Violations

Labeling Theory
Deviance is defined by how behaviors are labeled and internalized
Deviant

Strain Theory
Deviance results from the inability to meet societal expectations

Neutralization Theory
Deviance is justified by those who break the rules
It's not that bad and I'm not responsible for it.

Differential Association Theory
Deviance is learned through observation of others

Deviance Theories

Be sure to say 'please' and 'thank you'.
Salty, you have so many pencils, you should really share them!
Love your suit, Salty!
HA HA

Parents | Peers | Workplace | Mass Media

Agents of Socialization

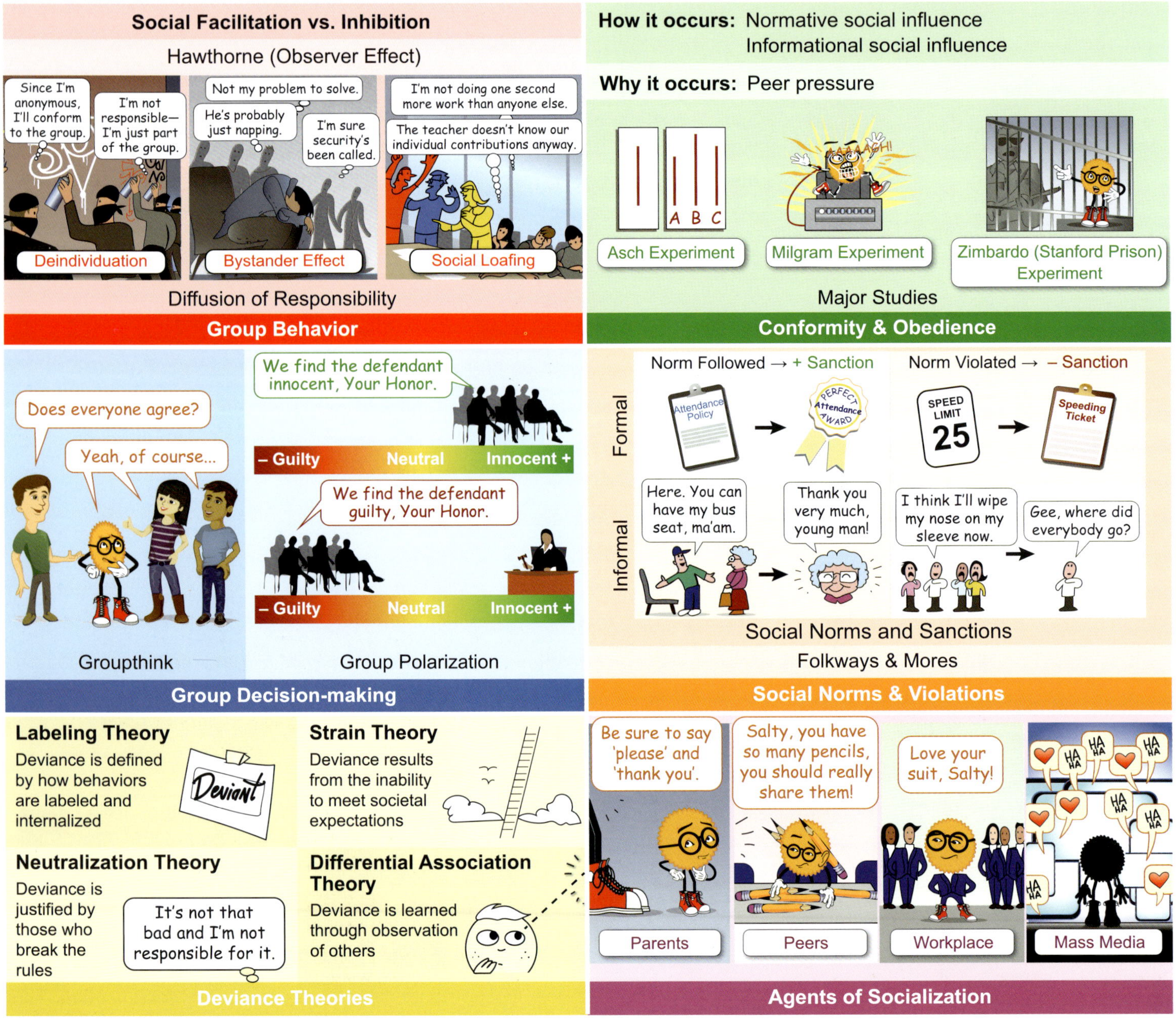

PSY

Nervous System, Traits, and Development

5

5.1 The Nervous System

The **nervous system** is split into two parts: the **central nervous system** and the **peripheral nervous system**.

The Central Nervous System

The central nervous system is made up of the **brain** and **spinal cord**.

The brain is composed of three parts, called the cerebrum, the cerebellum, and the brainstem.

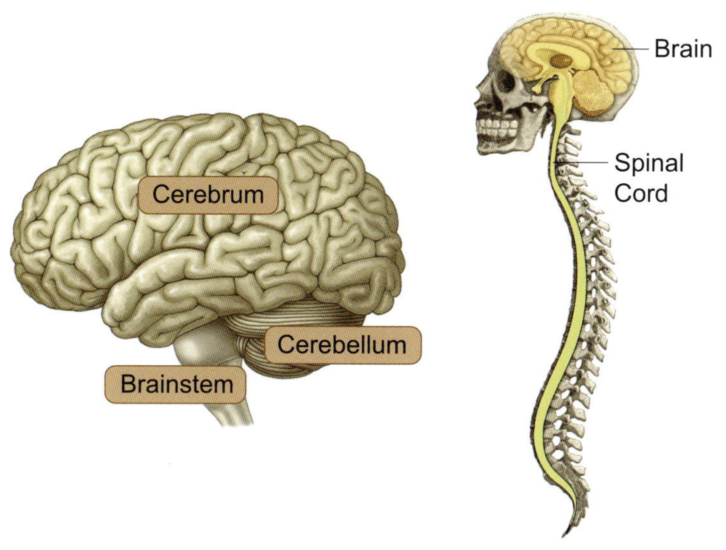

The **cerebrum** (forebrain) occupies over 80% of the brain's volume. It is split into a left and right hemisphere.

The largest part of the cerebrum is the outermost layer called the **cerebral cortex**. The cerebral cortex is composed of **gray matter**, which contains the bodies of neurons (somas), dendrites, and synapses. The surface of the cerebral cortex is not smooth, but covered in folds with ridges and valleys called gyri and sulci, respectively. Folds increase the surface area of the cortex without adding to its overall volume.

The cerebral cortex contains four different **lobes**.

1. Frontal lobe
2. Parietal lobe
3. Temporal lobe
4. Occipital lobe

Pet The Old Frog:
Parietal, Temporal, Occipital, Frontal

The **frontal lobe** is responsible for higher mental functions, such as cognition (thinking) and motor control (movement). Some areas of the frontal lobe include the prefrontal cortex, the motor cortex, and Broca's area.

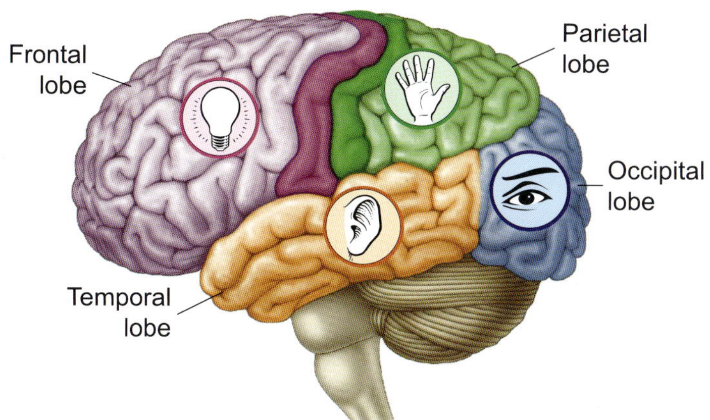

The **prefrontal cortex** is associated with many of the mental processes associated with executive functioning, which refers to the ways our brain works to control behavior. Some examples of executive functions are planning, fluid intelligence, working memory, and attentional control.

The **motor cortex** is the region of the brain that controls voluntary movements, while **Broca's area** is linked to the production of spoken language.

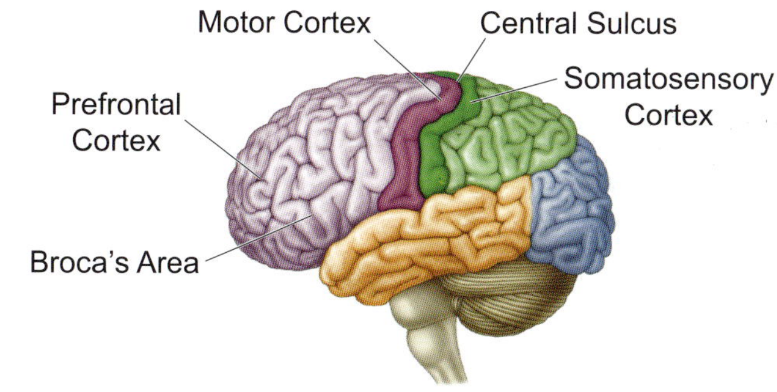

The **parietal lobe** is responsible for processing tactile sensory information (touch), as well as a limited processing of taste and visual information. The region of the parietal lobe that handles most of this processing is called the **somatosensory cortex**.

The **occipital lobe** is concerned with processing visual information and is the brain's primary visual processing center.

The **temporal lobe** has many functions, chief among which are auditory and olfactory processing, but which also include learning and memory.

While there are four main lobes, recently there has been increased acknowledgement about two other potential lobes. The **insular lobe**, also called the insular cortex or the insula, is located beneath the junction of the frontal, parietal, and temporal lobes. It has roles in conscious awareness, emotion, and gustatory processing. The **limbic lobe** refers to areas of the cortex that are involved in the limbic system, including the cingulate cortex and the entorhinal cortex.

The parts of the cerebrum that are located "under," or are surrounded by, the cerebral cortex are called the **subcortical cerebrum**. This includes portions of the telencephalon and all of the diencephalon. Some of these structures are listed below.

The **limbic system** is a group of interconnected structures that are involved in regulating emotion and memory. Two main structures are the amygdala and hippocampus, which are part of the telencephalon and are located deep within the medial part of the temporal lobe.

The **basal ganglia** (or **basal nuclei**) are groups of neurons involved in controlling motor functions. The largest component is the corpus striatum, which contains the caudate and putamen. The corpus striatum is part of the telencephalon, but like the limbic system, other structures are distributed throughout the brain.

Many subcortical structures are made up of **white matter**, which is composed of **tracts**—bundles of neuronal axons. These tracts connect individual regions of the brain to other regions and to the spinal cord. White matter gets its distinctive white color from the presence of **myelin**, which coats the axons that come together to form white matter.

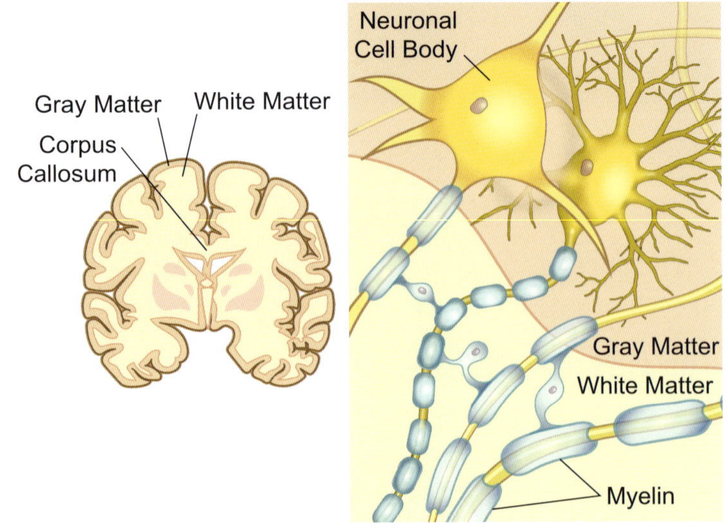

The two hemispheres of the cerebrum are connected by a structure called the **corpus callosum**, a thick bundle of nerve fibers that allows for communication between the two hemispheres.

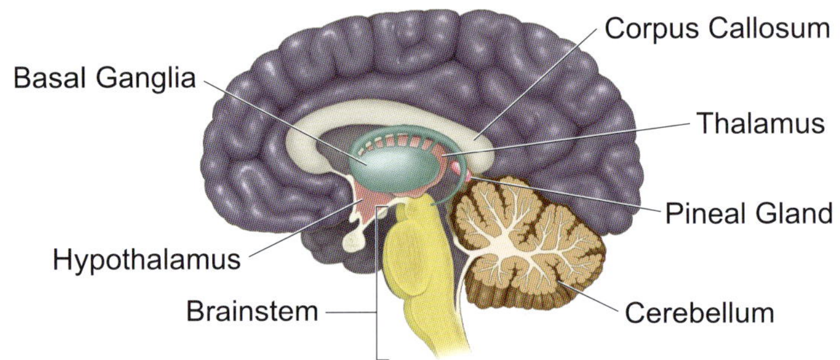

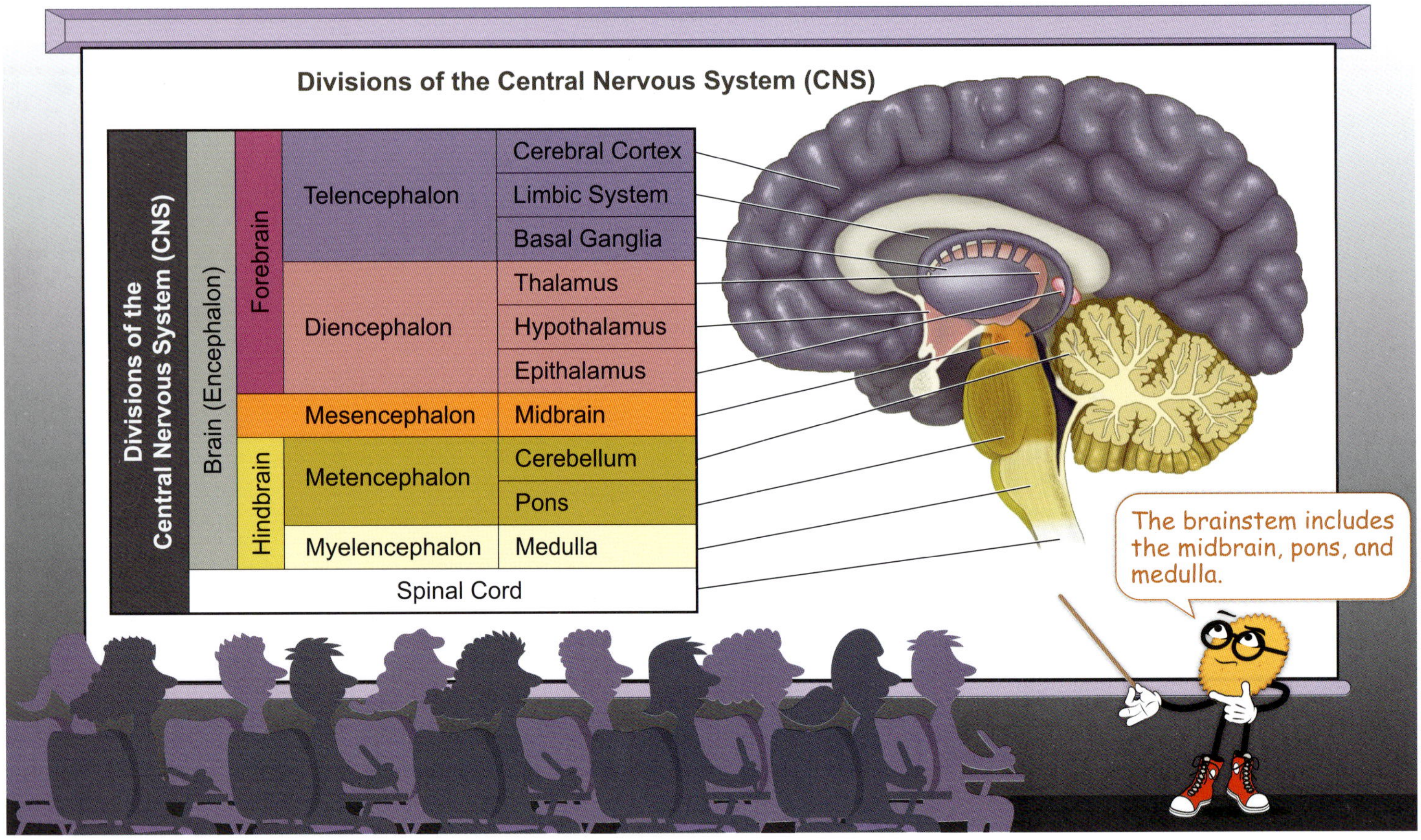

Divisions of the Central Nervous System (CNS)

Divisions of the Central Nervous System (CNS)				
Brain (Encephalon)	Forebrain	Telencephalon	Cerebral Cortex	
			Limbic System	
			Basal Ganglia	
		Diencephalon	Thalamus	
			Hypothalamus	
			Epithalamus	
	Mesencephalon		Midbrain	
	Hindbrain	Metencephalon	Cerebellum	
			Pons	
		Myelencephalon	Medulla	
Spinal Cord				

The brainstem includes the midbrain, pons, and medulla.

The **diencephalon** is a part of the brain located beneath the corpus callosum and contains several structures, including the **thalamus**, the **hypothalamus**, and the **epithalamus**.

The **thalamus** acts as a routing station for all sensory information (except for smell) that is carried to the brain. In addition to passing information to other parts of the brain, it seems to be important for integrating this sensory information.

The **hypothalamus**, so named because of its location below the thalamus, helps regulate the function of the autonomic nervous system, as well as to serve as a link between the nervous and endocrine systems. It also mediates several key biological urges, often called "the four F's." These are fighting, fleeing, feeding, and fornicating.

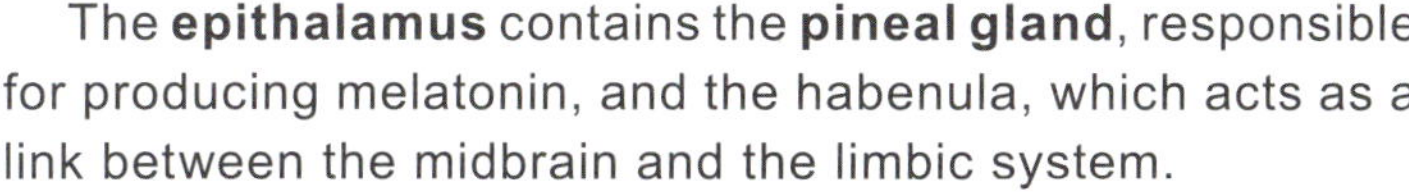

Because it conducts the autonomic nervous system, Salty blames the hypothalamus when he's feeling "hangry!"

The **epithalamus** contains the **pineal gland**, responsible for producing melatonin, and the habenula, which acts as a link between the midbrain and the limbic system.

The **basal ganglia** (or **basal nuclei**) are a group of neurons located laterally, or to the sides of, the thalamus and are involved in controlling motor functions.

Moving on from the subcortical cerebrum, we come to the cerebellum. The **cerebellum** is a brain structure located under the occipital lobe in humans, and it is most clearly responsible for motor control and coordination. Different parts of the cerebellum handle movement for different regions of the body, with some sections regulating the trunk, others controlling the limbs, and still others that are involved in speech and eye movements.

The **brainstem** is both the smallest major region of the brain and the most essential for life—damage to it through physical trauma or stroke are much more likely to result in death than similar injuries in other regions. It contains many different substructures, some of which are the midbrain, the pons, and the medulla.

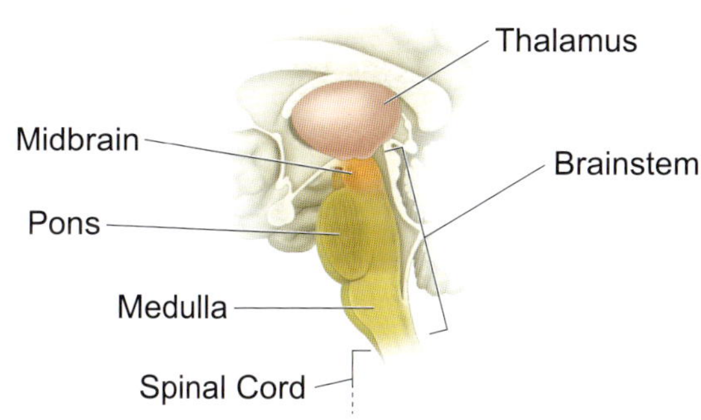

The **midbrain** is associated with controlling our awareness of pain, processing auditory input, and regulating fine motor control, among many other functions.

The **hindbrain** contains the pons, medulla, and cerebellum (the cerebellum is not, however, part of the brainstem).

The **pons** contains cranial nerve nuclei, which are collections of neurons that associate with cranial nerves. Neurons that carry information to and from the cranial nerves synapse with these nuclei, which then pass the signal to other regions of the brain. Because of this, the pons is involved in sleep, respiration, bladder control, and all the functions that require input from the cranial nerves that synapse with nuclei in the pons.

The **medulla** (or **medulla oblongata**, its full name) is similar to the pons in that it also contains cranial nerve nuclei. These nuclei are involved in regulating a wide variety of basic physiological functions, including blood pressure, heartbeat rate and force, breathing.

Cranial nerves are nerves that originate from either the cerebrum or the brainstem. There are twelve pairs of cranial nerves, two of which (the olfactory and optic nerves) are attached to the cerebrum, with the other ten pairs connected to the brainstem.

The Motor Cortex and Upper Motor Neurons

The area of the brain that coordinates motor function is called the **primary motor cortex**. It is located in the back part of the frontal lobe.

Much like the somatosensory cortex discussed previously, different parts of the primary motor cortex oversee different parts of the body. Instead of receiving sensory input, however, the primary motor cortex coordinates voluntary movements.

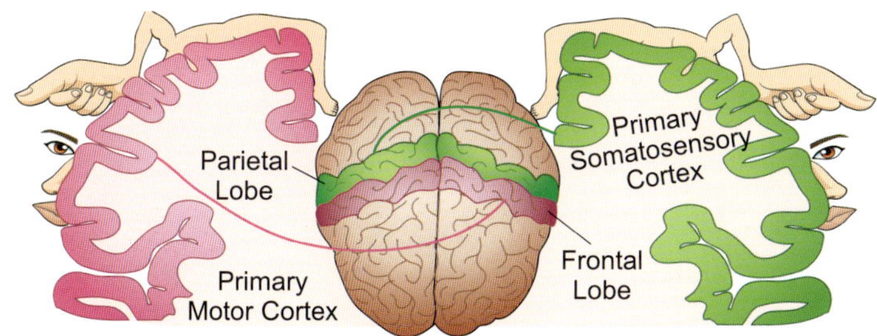

Primary Motor Cortex and Somatosensory Cortex

The neurons that connect to the primary motor cortex and carry information out of the brain are called **upper motor neurons (UMNs)**. These upper motor neurons either lead to the brainstem or the spinal cord.

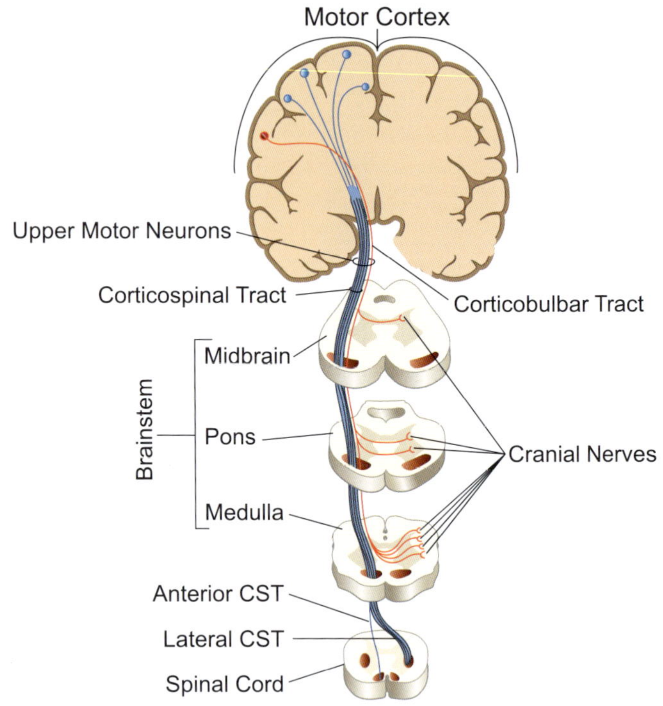

The UMNs that lead to the brainstem make up the **corticobulbar tracts**. The corticobulbar neurons synapse with cranial nerve nuclei.

Most UMNs leave the brain and travel through the spinal cord. About 80% of these neurons cross over to the other side of the body and form the **lateral corticospinal tract.** The remaining 20% of these neurons do not cross over until they reach the level in the spine where they terminate, and make up the **anterior (ventral) corticospinal tract**.

The main role of UMNs is to control lower motor neurons, which will be discussed later in this chapter. They can also connect to **interneurons**, which are neurons that enable communication between different brain regions or neurons from different parts of the nervous system.

Neural Development

When the nervous systems of human embryos and fetuses are developing, they progress through a series of stages before birth. About four weeks after conception, the neural tissue that will eventually become the brain has split into three different regions. From back (caudal) to front (rostral), they are:

1. The rhombencephalon, or the future hindbrain.
2. The mesencephalon, or the future midbrain.
3. The prosencephalon, or the future forebrain.

By the time a baby is born, all of these regions have changed significantly. The **hindbrain** becomes the cerebellum, the medulla, and the pons. The **midbrain** does not divide further, but instead matures. The **forebrain** develops into the cerebrum.

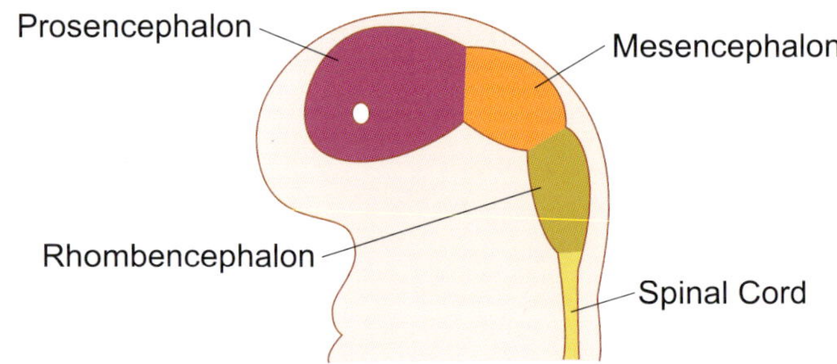

Lateralization of Cortical Functions

At a glance, the halves of the brain look pretty symmetrical. On closer inspection, however, some differences start to appear—for example, left-handed people may have relatively larger right hemispheres compared to right-handed people. While not consistently replicated, many studies suggest that left-handed people also have less lateralized brain functions compared to right-handed people. Beyond differences related to handedness, though, there are functional differences between the two hemispheres.

With the exception of olfactory (smell) information, and to a lesser extent auditory (sound) information, sensory information is processed **contralaterally**, meaning that it is processed in the hemisphere on the opposite side of the body. For example, visual information from the left side of the visual field is processed in the right cerebral cortex. In general, motor functions are also controlled by the hemisphere on the opposite side of the body—so, moving your left hand is orchestrated by your right hemisphere. This phenomenon is called **contralateral control**.

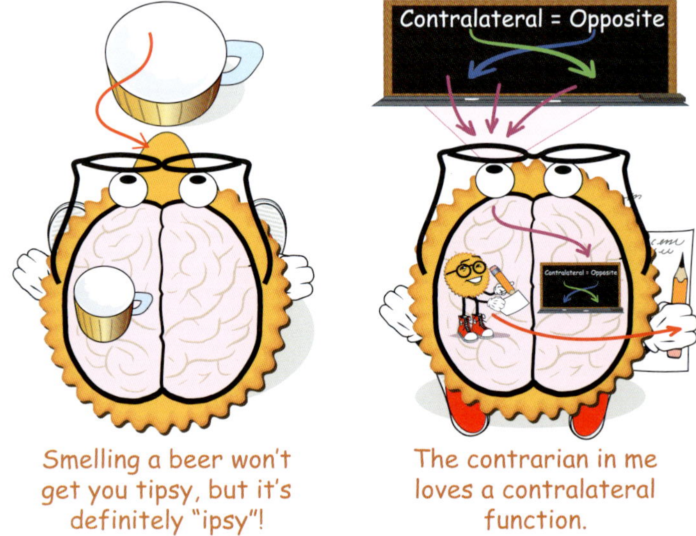

Smelling a beer won't get you tipsy, but it's definitely "ipsy"!

The contrarian in me loves a contralateral function.

Olfactory and some auditory information, however, is processed **ipsilaterally**, meaning on the same side of the body. This means that olfactory information from the left side of the nose is processed in the left hemisphere.

Methods Used in Studying the Brain

In the long ago, before the advent of MRI, CT scans, or PET imaging, physicians and scientists looking to study the brain had very little material to work with. Simple x-ray machines were used in medicine only a year after their invention in the late 1800s, prompting a frenzy of research and studies of clinical applications on their utility and effectiveness.

However, the soft tissues that make up the brain do not show up well on x-ray images, limiting their usefulness in studying brain function in living patients. For this reason, the early methods of investigating brain function relied heavily on **autopsies**. Because there was no practical way to look inside a living patient's brain, researchers would examine the brains of people after they died and correlate neurological problems they experienced in life with changes in the brain seen after death. These changes could be due to traumatic accidents, tumors, or events like strokes.

Another method for studying the brain is a **lesion study**. Lesion studies can refer to two types of experiments. In the first type, researchers create lesions in the brains of test animals, such as mice or non-human primates, using a variety of different techniques. They then observe which functions are disrupted by the lesions and use this data to make inferences about what the affected brain areas might do in humans. This disruption in function can be permanent, such as when researchers burn holes into the animals' brains, or reversible, like when they cool down neurons in the brain so much that they stop firing for a while.

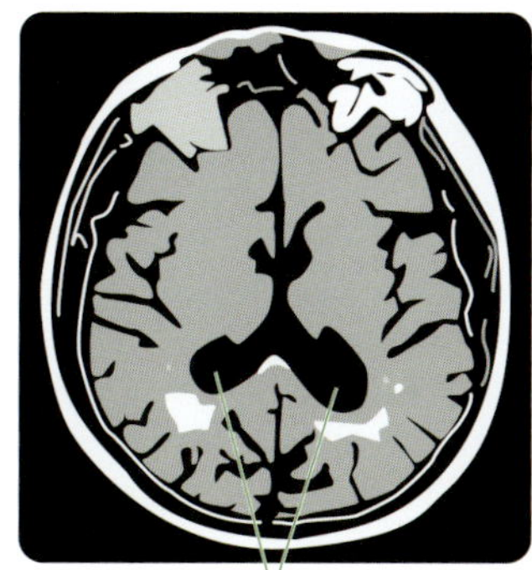

Alzheimer's Disease White Matter Lesions

The second type of lesion study uses modern imaging techniques to study people affected by brain lesions over a long period of time. After a lesion is identified, participants are carefully monitored for changes in mental function. This type of study is observational, not experimental—researchers do not create the lesions in these patients, as they do in the first type of lesion studies.

Modern imaging techniques have made brain imaging something that can be done safely in real-time. The two workhorses of modern medical imaging, the **CT scan** and the **MRI**, were invented within a few years of one another in the early 1970s. CT scanning, or computerized tomography scanning, combines a rotating x-ray machine with computer software that converts the data generated by the machine into tomographic, or cross-sectional, images.

MRI, or magnetic resonance imaging, uses strong magnetic fields and radio waves to generate images of structures inside the body. It is used more often than CT scanning for imaging the brain because it allows for better visualization of the brainstem and cerebellum, as well as improved contrast between gray and white matter.

Both CT and MRI are extremely useful for showing changes in brain structures, but they cannot give us any information about how the brain is functioning—at least, not on their own.

Other techniques are used to get an idea of what is going on in the brain on a functional level. The oldest of these is **electroencephalography**, or **EEG**. The data recorded during EEG is compiled into a document called an electrogram.

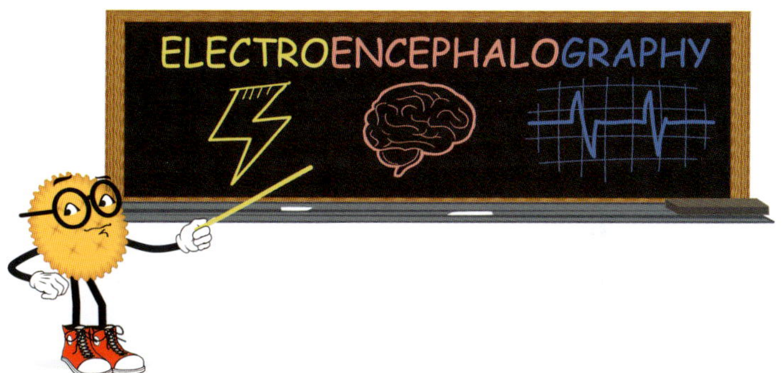

The word electroencephalography can be broken down: electro, meaning electricity, encephalo, meaning brain, and graphy, meaning a writing or a measurement. So, an EEG is a measure of electrical activity in the brain.

EEG works by measuring the changes in electrical activity on the skin caused by brain activity of the outer layers of the cerebral cortexes. This technique does not produce images, instead yielding patterns of electrical signals that can be read to see if someone has epilepsy, a sleep disorder, or various other conditions. EEGs are usually performed by putting gel-covered electrodes on a person's scalp and hooking those electrodes up to a machine that converts the data into a form understandable by a computer.

There are more complicated ways of measuring electrical activity in the brain. One of these is called **magnetoencephalography**, or **MEG**. Instead of measuring changes in voltage using electrodes on the scalp, MEG measures changes in the magnetic fields in the brain. It does this by using devices called **SQUIDs**, or **superconducting quantum interference devices**. These devices are extremely sensitive to changes in the strength of magnetic fields that pass through them and can measure these changes very quickly.

MEG can be used to classify the electrical patterns associated with a number of disorders, such as multiple sclerosis and Alzheimer's disease. However, it is not yet used to diagnose these conditions.

The word magnetoencephalography can also be broken down into parts: magneto, meaning magnetic, encephalo, meaning brain, and graphy, meaning a writing or measurement. In other words, magnetoencephalography is a measure of magnetic fields in the brain.

The flow of electric current produces magnetic fields. When neurons fire, they create these electric currents. So, both EEG and MEG measure the same thing: the electrical activity produced by neuronal action potentials. They just measure different aspects of the same phenomena.

The two methods of studying brain function discussed so far work by measuring the electrical activity produced by the outer edge of the brain's cerebral cortexes. These methods are useful, but work best when combined with other approaches to studying the brain.

The most widely-used of these methods is called **fMRI**, or **functional magnetic resonance imaging**. In addition to the high-resolution images of the brain that can be taken with normal MRI scans, fMRI allows researchers to see which parts of the brain are active at any given time.

fMRI works by measuring slight differences between oxygenated and deoxygenated hemoglobin in the blood—when certain areas of the brain are activated, the tissues in those areas use more oxygen. By matching up the spikes in oxygenated blood flow with tasks that test subjects perform during an fMRI scan, we can see which brain regions are active during those tasks.

PET (positron emission tomography) scans are another method physicians and scientists use to study brain function. A PET scan can show where blood is flowing in the brain or highlight areas that are using a lot of glucose over a period of time.

PET on its own produces a fairly low-resolution image that can be difficult to interpret. This is why PET is often combined with another imaging technique, such as CT or MRI, to produce images that are much easier to read. A combined scan looks like this:

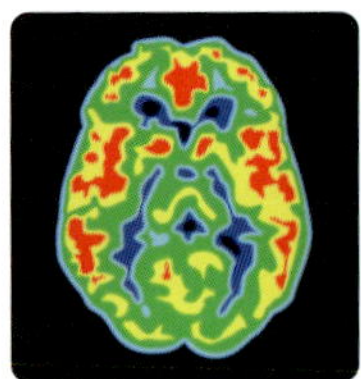
Axial Plane

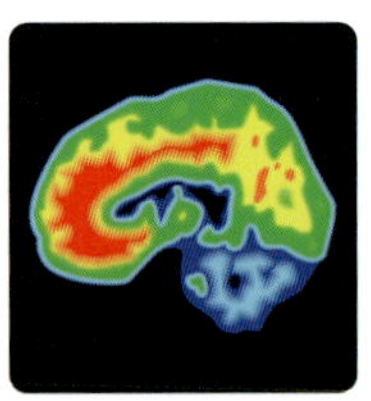
Sagittal Plane

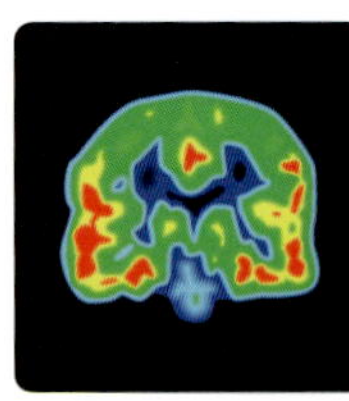
Coronal Plane

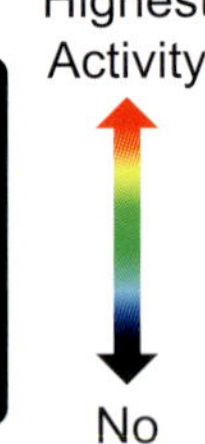

In order for a PET scan to work, the patient being imaged has to swallow a liquid that contains molecules that have a radioactive label attached to them. The most commonly used radiolabeled molecule for imaging the brain is called fluorodeoxyglucose (18F). It is made of a glucose molecule attached to a radioactive isotope of fluorine named fluorine-18.

The Spinal Cord

The **spinal cord** is a long tube of neural tissue that runs from the brainstem to a little bit below waist level. It is encircled by the **spinal canal**, a series of holes in the vertebrae that make up the spine, which helps protect the spinal cord and serve as a barrier between it and the rest of the body.

The spinal cord can be thought of as an extension of the brain, and its main job is to connect the central nervous system to the peripheral nervous system. This involves passing motor information from the brain to the nerves in the rest of the body and relaying somatosensory information to the brain that comes from the peripheral nervous system, among other functions.

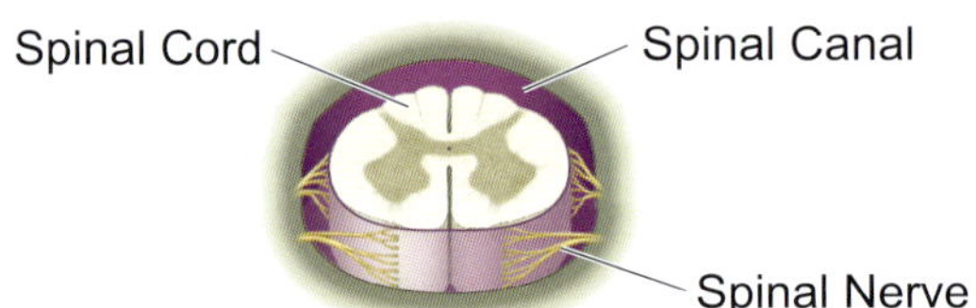

Functions of the Central Nervous System

The central nervous system is responsible for coordinating all of our senses, movement, and reflexes. With the exception of voluntary movements, most of these functions are automatic and do not require conscious effort. These functions are known by many names, such as lower functions, basic functions, etc.

Functions that require conscious input, such as thinking, feeling emotion, and planned movement are often called higher functions. These functions lie at the heart of our experience as humans, and how these functions combine to produce consciousness is currently a mystery.

Higher functions do not necessarily require conscious input—for example, the unconscious processing of information in the brain is generally considered to be a higher function.

The Peripheral Nervous System

All nerves and ganglia outside the brain and spinal cord are part of the peripheral nervous system. The peripheral nervous system, much like the central nervous system, has two main divisions: the somatic nervous system and the autonomic nervous system.

The **somatic nervous system (SoNS)** is the branch of the peripheral nervous system that allows you to sense the world around you and to move your body. The nerves in the somatic nervous system are connected to sensory receptors and to skeletal muscles.

As discussed in the sensation material, information from somatosensory receptors is transmitted to the PSC (primary somatosensory cortex) in the brain via somatosensory pathways.

The nerves directly connected to skeletal muscles are called **lower motor neurons (LMNs)**. These lower motor neurons are controlled by upper motor neurons, or UMNs, which are ultimately controlled by the brain.

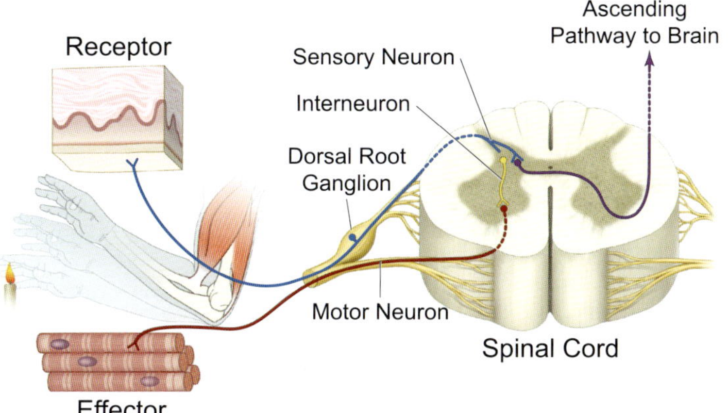

Somatic Sensory Motor Pathways

The **autonomic nervous system (ANS)** is responsible for maintaining homeostasis at a broad level in the body. It innervates almost every body system, and it regulates many of the body's most important functions, from heart rate to smooth muscle to endocrine gland function. Like its name suggests, the autonomic nervous system works without conscious control.

It's no coincidence that *autonomic* sounds like *automatic*!

There are two divisions of the ANS: the sympathetic and parasympathetic nervous systems.

The **sympathetic nervous system (SNS)** is often called the "fight or flight" branch of the ANS. In other words, the SNS helps get the body ready to respond to stressful or dangerous situations. In doing so, it inhibits digestion, increases heart rate, moves blood from the periphery of the body into the trunk, among other things.

The **parasympathetic nervous system (PSNS)** is also known as the "rest and digest" branch. Instead of ramping the body up, it is involved in winding the body down, helping to conserve energy and other resources. The PSNS promotes digestion by increasing stomach acid secretion, slows heart rate, and lowers blood pressure.

Some presentations of the ANS include a third branch called the enteric nervous system. Capable of functioning independently from the brain, the enteric nervous system is a network of nervous tissue that runs through nearly the entire gastrointestinal tract, spanning from the esophagus to the anus. Because it contains all of the elements of a nervous system, it is often called the "second brain." Although it can function independently, many of its functions are carried out with input from the CNS. It is involved in regulating digestive processes, such as digestive tract motility (how quickly digestion and peristalsis occurs) and blood flow to the digestive system.

Even just the thought of a bear triggered the sympathetic nervous system into action!

Neurotransmitters

Neurotransmitters are chemicals released from the **axon terminal** of a neuron into a **synapse** where they are taken up by other **receptors** on nearby cells.

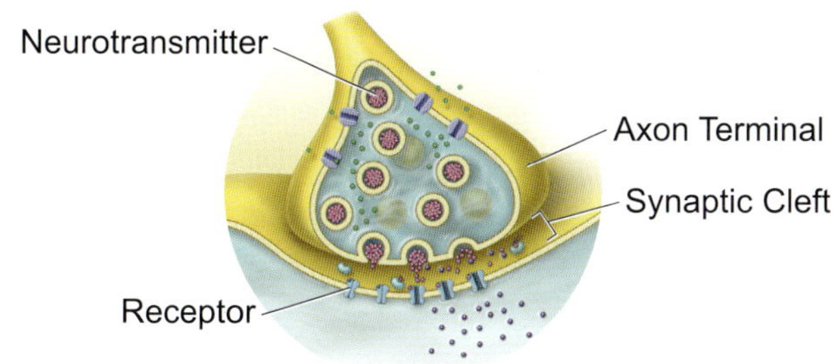

There are many different types of neurotransmitter, and they are usually sorted into several different groups. Three of these are:

1. Monoamines
2. Amino acids
3. Peptides

The **monoamine** neurotransmitters include dopamine, serotonin, epinephrine, and norepinephrine, among others.

Dopamine in the brain acts as a neurotransmitter, and it is involved in four main pathways called dopaminergic pathways. Two of these pathways originate from an area of the brain called the **ventral tegmental area (VTA)**, a region of neurons in the midbrain that has been implicated in motivation, cognition, and the brain's reward system.

The VTA contains **dopaminergic neurons**, which are neurons that make dopamine. These neurons are connected to many other brain areas, especially regions in the frontal lobe such as the prefrontal cortex.

Some of these neurons project to an area of the brain called the **nucleus accumbens**. The VTA and nucleus accumbens are the primary regions targeted by addictive drugs, like nicotine, cocaine, and ethanol. The addiction and reward pathways are discussed in more detail in other sections of the book.

Dopamine is also used in some pathways in the brain that regulate motor function, such as those in a region called the **substantia nigra**. Damage to the dopaminergic pathway associated with this region, called the nigrostriatal pathway, can cause symptoms of Parkinson's disease. This is why drugs that are broken down in the body to become dopamine are often used to treat the disease.

Serotonin is another major neurotransmitter in the brain. Serotonergic neurons, or neurons that produce serotonin, are localized in small areas of the brainstem called **raphae** (singular raphe, pronounced ray-fee). Despite this, projections from these raphae are extensive, making them difficult to study. On top of this, only a few of the neurons in these raphae even produce serotonin, and drugs that specifically target serotonin receptors are not yet commonly used.

> While Sir Raphael produced paintings, the raphe nuclei produce serotonin.

For these reasons, the specific functions of serotonin are poorly understood. Serotonin has been linked to both physiologic functions, sleep, temperature control, and pain, and psychological disorders like psychosis and GAD (generalized anxiety disorder).

Perhaps because of serotonin's wide range of function and its ubiquity in the brain, many different classes of therapeutic drugs target serotonin receptors. Some of these

Neurotransmitter	Molecular structure	Major functions	Associated disorders
Serotonin		Mood Sleep	Depression ↓
Acetylcholine		Learning/ memory Movement	Alzheimer's disease ↓
Norepinephrine		Arousal Concentration	ADHD ↓ PTSD ↑
Dopamine		Reward motivation Movement	Parkinson's disease ↓ Psychosis ↑
Histamine		Arousal Appetite	Allergies ↑
Endorphins (β)		Pain relief	Chronic pain ↓

Major Neurotransmitters of the CNS

include antidepressants, antipsychotics, and anxiolytics (anti-anxiety medications).

Epinephrine is a minor neurotransmitter produced in the brain by the medulla and seems to be involved in regulating some basic bodily functions, such as breathing. There is weak evidence that it might also be used in the retina, muscle and blood vessel function, and neural pathways linked to depression.

Norepinephrine is produced mainly by neurons in the medulla and the pons. One region of the pons called the **locus coeruleus** contains about half of the noradrenergic neurons (neurons that produce norepinephrine) in the brain. Although the overall number of these neurons is fairly low, neurons from this area are responsible for providing almost all the norepinephrine used by the cerebral cortex, as well as parts of the spinal cord.

Dopamine | Norepinephrine | Epinephrine

Fun fact: the "fight-or-flight" response is largely due to the high levels of epinephrine and norepinephrine coursing through the body!

The activity of norepinephrine has been linked with the sleep-wake cycle, behaviors related to survival (e.g. eating and drinking), and regulation of physiological arousal. It has been suggested that norepinephrine might be involved in the development of both PTSD (post-traumatic stress disorder) and ADHD (attention-deficit/hyperactivity disorder).

There are many different amino acids that also act as neurotransmitters in the brain. The most important excitatory amino acid neurotransmitter is glutamate, while the most common inhibitory neurotransmitters are GABA and glycine.

Receptors for glutamate, the anionic form of the amino acid glutamic acid, are found in practically every nervous system cell. Glutamate is always excitatory, meaning that it makes the neurons that take it up more likely to fire.

Partially due to its wide distribution in the nervous system, glutamate's precise functions have been difficult to study. Glutamate seems to be important in learning and memory, and problems with either glutamate release or with the receptors that take it up have been linked to many different disorders, such as schizophrenia, diabetes, and autism.

Glutamate

GABA & Glycine

Glutamate is the major excitatory (on-switch) neurotransmitter compared to GABA and glycine, which are the major inhibitory (off-switch) neurotransmitters. Together, they facilitate tight regulation of neurotransmission in the central nervous system.

GABA (**γ-aminobutyric acid**) is the primary inhibitory neurotransmitter in the brain. It is thought to play a role in brain development, as well as to regulate anxiety. GABA activity is also linked with a number of different conditions, like alcoholism and epilepsy.

Glycine is another inhibitory neurotransmitter, and its function is mainly localized in the brainstem and spinal cord, though it plays an important role in auditory and visual processing. It may be possible to use medications that modify glycine release or uptake to treat some disorders, such as epilepsy or schizophrenia.

Over a hundred types of **peptide neurotransmitters**, also called **neuropeptides**, have been identified. Thankfully, only a few of these are relevant to the MCAT.

One group of peptides that might come up on the test are the **endorphins**. Endorphins bind to the same receptors in the brain that morphine and other opioids bind to, and unsurprisingly endorphins have similar effects to morphine and other drugs like it. Some effects of endorphins include inhibiting the pain response, alleviating symptoms of depression and anxiety, and facilitating social bonding.

Acetylcholine is a neurotransmitter that does not fit very well into the three categories outlined so far. Nevertheless, it is integral to the functioning of both the central and peripheral nervous systems.

From learning and memory to conscious motor activity to resting and digesting, acetylcholine has a lot of balls in the air to juggle.

In the central nervous system, acetylcholine binds to two types of receptors: muscarinic and nicotinic receptors.

Some muscarinic receptors in the CNS are linked to learning and memory. Others are involved in controlling motor functions, and still others help control the production and release of acetylcholine.

Nicotinic receptors, as their name suggests, are good at binding to nicotine. Although this might suggest that nicotinic receptors are related to addiction, it seems that under normal circumstances nicotinic receptors are important for regulating arousal and attention.

Acetylcholine is used by both branches of the peripheral nervous system. In the ANS, it seems to function by lowering heart rate, increasing gastric motility (how quickly digestion occurs), and constricting the airways. Acetylcholine is also the neurotransmitter released by the lower motor neurons of the SoNS (somatic nervous system) at the **neuromuscular junction**. This means that all conscious motor function relies on acetylcholine activity.

Histamine is another molecule that does not fit well into most categories. Aside from its role as a neurotransmitter, it has over twenty different functions in the body, including regulating blood pressure, controlling the release of gastric acid, and promoting libido.

Histamine is made all over the body. In the brain, histamine is produced in one region of the hypothalamus and sent throughout the brain and spinal cord. Histamine functions as a neurotransmitter to help regulate the sleep-wake cycle, learning, and memory.

The Endocrine System and Behavior

The anatomy of the structures involved in the endocrine system is discussed in the Biology book.

Some of the behavioral effects of the endocrine system are pretty clear: for example, during the fight or flight response, adrenaline contributes to raising your heart rate and making you sweat. These physiological changes are associated with emotions you might feel under stress, like fear or anger. You tend to make different decisions when you're afraid or angry—thus, adrenaline activity can cause changes in behavior.

Watch out! When stressed, the adrenaline rush can lead to road rage!

However, other hormones also affect behavior, though they tend to have subtler effects or a less clear mechanism of action. The following list of hormones is not meant to be comprehensive, but to instead give some examples of how hormones can influence how we act.

Oxytocin can cause milk letdown, or the release of breast milk from the nipple. This effect is most obvious (and important) to breastfeeding mothers. It usually takes a few minutes for milk to come out of the breast while breastfeeding, even when the baby is already suckling. When the baby latches on to your breast, both oxytocin and **prolactin**, a hormone that increases milk production, are released in the brain. These hormones, not the mechanical action of suckling, are what drive breastmilk production and release.

Some women experience episodes of either depression or mania after giving birth—these conditions are called postpartum depression and postpartum mania respectively. Although why this occurs is not clear, it is thought that **estrogen**, **prolactin**, and **cortisol** may play a role in their development. It is possible that treatment with either agonists or antagonists of receptors for these hormones could be used to treat these conditions.

Ghrelin is a hormone known to increase feeding behaviors. This is due in part to its ability to increase hunger, as well as its role in modulating the sensation of taste and reward behaviors. Ghrelin works by activating some areas of the hypothalamus and the VTA (ventral tegmental area), and is thought to play some part in people becoming addicted to palatable (high sugar / high fat) food.

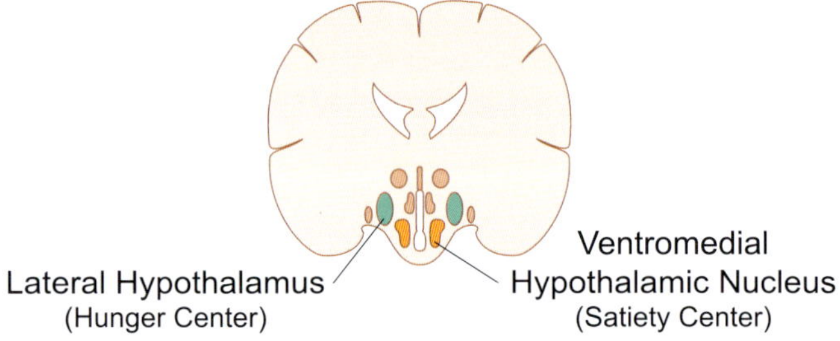

Another hormone involved in the regulation of food intake is **leptin**. The best-studied function of leptin is to regulate how much fat is stored in the body, though it probably has many other functions. The levels of leptin in the blood correlate with a person's body weight, and leptin levels tend to decrease with weight loss.

Some endocrine compounds that affect behavior are not hormones, but other types of molecules. One of these is **proopiomelanocortin (POMC)**. POMC is what is known as a precursor polypeptide, meaning that it is broken down into other peptides in the body. In this case, these peptides are hormones.

Neurons that produce POMC express the serotonin $5HT_{2C}$ receptor on their surfaces. This receptor modulates the release of melanocortin, another peptide hormone involved in regulating feeding behaviors. Drugs that activate the serotonin $5HT_{2C}$ cause weight loss, while drugs that block the receptor cause weight gain. It is possible that melanocortin agonists would be helpful in treating obesity, but no large clinical trials with these agonists have been performed yet.

5.2 Behavioral Genetics and Measuring Heritability

The question of why people are different from one another has probably been asked as long as humans have existed. One of the oldest known answers to this question comes from the history of Ancient China. Chen Sheng, a military captain who led a rebellion in China over two thousand years ago, is said to have proclaimed, "Kings and nobles, generals and ministers—such men are made, not born!"

Was he correct? The answer to this question has proven to be unclear and polarizing. In the 19th century, it was widely believed that a person's genetics were the primary determinant of a person's character, with this view reversing throughout much of the 20th century.

Behavioral genetics attempts to use the study of genetics to explain why people behave differently from one another.

Modern behavioral geneticists generally believe that both nature (biology) and nurture (environment) play an important role in human behavior.

Genes, Temperament, and Heredity

Heredity is the passing on of traits from parents to their children. From a biological perspective, heredity involves the transfer of genetic and epigenetic information. Some scientists consider cultural inheritance, such as customs passed down through multiple generations of a family, to be an example of heredity as well.

Traits refer to a characteristic that can be used to differentiate people. These traits can be **inherited traits**, which come from our parents, or **acquired traits**, which come from our interactions with the world around us.

Inherited Traits

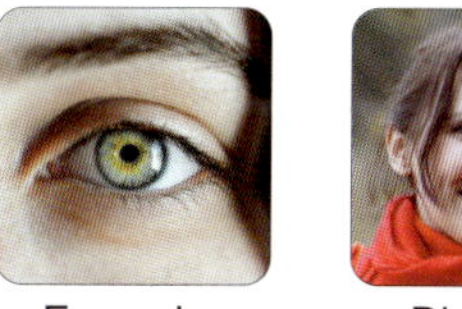
Eye color

Dimples

Acquired Traits

Ear piercing

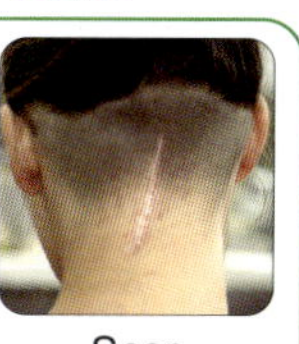
Scar

The genetic mechanisms that underlie the expression of some traits are understood. These are often called **simple traits**, and they are often linked to the expression of a single gene or of a small group of genes. Some examples of simple traits are oculocutaneous albinism (where the eyes, skin, and hair lack pigmentation) and cystic fibrosis, a disorder that causes damage to many of the body's organ systems.

The vast majority of traits are **complex traits**, which tend to involve large groups of genes that interact with the environment in complicated ways. There are too many of these to list here, but some examples are height, intelligence, and the likelihood of developing certain diseases, such as coronary heart disease and rheumatoid arthritis.

One of the groups of traits that psychologists are most interested in is **personality**. Personality refers to a person's combination of judgements (decisions that affect behavior), thoughts, and affects (observable markers of an emotion). Some traits that make up personality tend to be stable throughout a person's adult life, while others undergo almost constant changes.

It is not yet known why some traits are relatively fixed while others are malleable. Despite this, a person's personality has been shown to be correlated with many major life outcomes, including social status, relationship satisfaction, job performance, and a person's political affiliation.

Temperament is a concept often confused for personality. In contrast with personality, which includes both the biological and environmental components that influence a person's behaviors, thoughts, and emotions, temperament only refers to the differences in traits that are biologically based. In other words, a person is born with his temperament, while a person's personality changes over time as he interacts with his environment.

The degree to which a trait varies from person to person due to genetics is called **heritability**. Heritability is a statistical measure and is widely used in the field of behavioral genetics.

In more formal terms, heritability is a quantitative measure of the variation of a phenotypic (observable from the outside) trait within a population.

Heritability is only useful for finding out how much genetics contribute to differences in a trait in populations, or groups of two or more people. It can't be used to show how important genes are in contributing to a trait in an individual.

How can studies be designed to measure heritability? There are many different study designs that can be used, but the most common are:

1. Family studies
2. Twin studies
3. Adoption studies
4. Genome-wide association studies

Family studies compare trait differences between people from one family to people who are not closely related to each other. Although these studies are relatively simple to perform, they are limited by the large number of confounding variables associated with this technique. People in the same family can be raised in dramatically different environments, and one individual shares at most about half of their DNA with their family members (excluding identical twins).

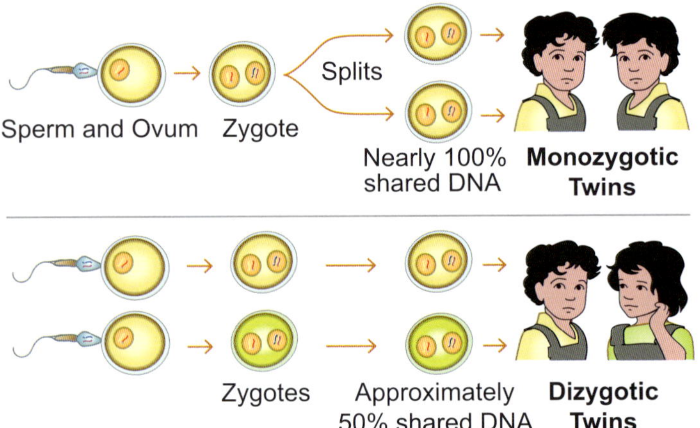

In family studies, the control group is made up of unrelated individuals, while the experimental group is members of the same family.

Twin studies involve comparing traits in pairs of twins. These studies can examine both **identical twins**, who share almost the same DNA, and **fraternal twins**, who share about half of their genes with each other.

Because identical twins share nearly identical DNA and have very similar environments, both before birth and as they grow up, differences in traits between them are less common than between fraternal twins or siblings born at different times. In contrast, fraternal twins share similar environments but only about half of their DNA with each other.

Twin studies are most useful when they observe large groups of both identical and fraternal twins. For example, a researcher might want to predict the contribution of genetics to the development of gallstone disease. After collecting the rates of gallstone disease in all study participants, she would then compare the concordance rate (likelihood that if one twin develops the disease that the other twin will too) between the identical and fraternal twins.

If the concordance rate is higher in identical twins than fraternal twins, she might conclude that gallstone disease is genetically linked. If both identical and fraternal twins share similar environments when growing up, differences in the concordance rate is likely genetic. Alternatively, if there is no difference in concordance rate between identical and fraternal twins, it is likely that the trait being studied is not influenced by genetics.

In twin studies, the control group is identical twins, while the experimental group is fraternal twins.

If a trait has a large genetic component, identical twins will be more similar than fraternal twins in that trait. If the trait is mainly controlled by the environment, identical twins and fraternal twins will show similar differences in that trait.

Adoption studies are often used as a supplement to twin studies. They are carried out by studying people, usually monozygotic twins, who were separated from their biological parents and raised in adoptive households. These studies assume that because the twins are raised in different environments, similarities in traits or other life outcomes between the twins are attributable in large part to genetics.

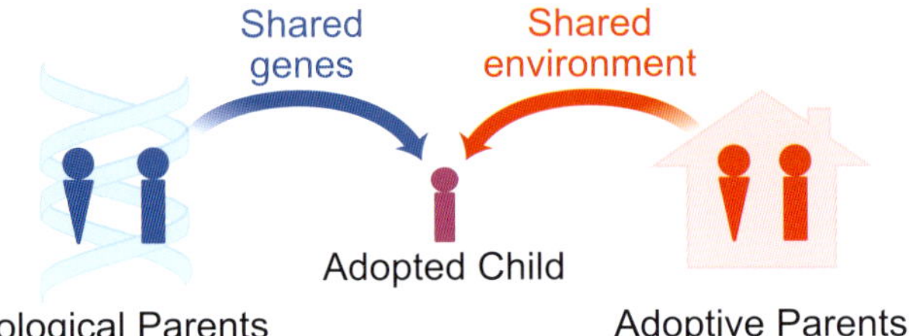

Adoption studies have been used to estimate the genetic components of disorders like schizophrenia and bipolar disorder, as well as behavioral trends, such as criminality.

Some adoption studies look for similarities between an adopted child and both their adoptive and biological parents. Others compare non-biological siblings who are raised by the same families.

If groups of identical twins raised together and groups of identical twins raised in different households share a similar expression of a trait, that trait probably has a large genetic component. If the same groups show different expressions of a trait, its expression is probably regulated by the environment.

Similarly, if a person who has been adopted resembles their biological parents more than their adoptive parents in a trait, that trait is likely to have a strong genetic component. If that same person resembles their adoptive parents in a trait, that trait is probably environmentally mediated.

Genome-wide association studies (GWAS) look across the entire genomes of different individuals to try to determine if genetic differences are associated with different traits. Most GWAS examine single nucleotide polymorphisms (SNPs), which are substitutions of a single A,C,T, or G for another nucleotide. GWAS can examine hundreds of thousands of these SNPs, which are then compared to trait differences in the subjects' genomes. The SNPs that are shared by people who exhibit the trait in question are usually further investigated to determine how they affect the trait's expression.

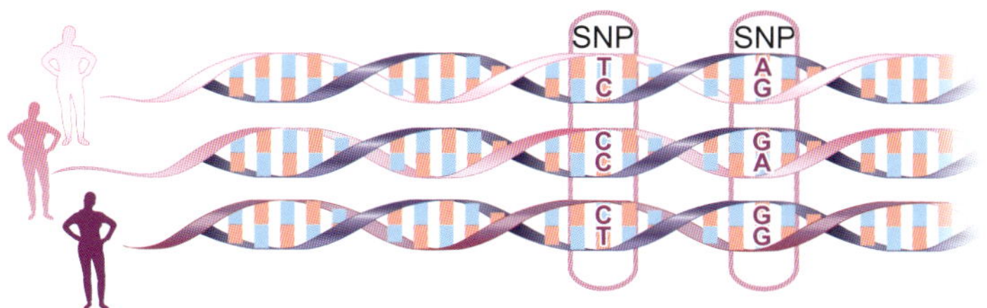

GWAS have been used to find genes associated with the development and severity of common conditions, such as type-2 diabetes and schizophrenia. They have also contributed to the expansion of personalized medicine, where patients' genetic data is used to customize their treatment plans. This data can be used in the treatment of certain types of cancers and respiratory disorders like asthma and COPD (chronic obstructive pulmonary disease).

In GWAS, the control group is a large group of people who do not have the condition being studied, while the experimental group is made up of people who do have the condition.

5.3 Behavioral Traits and Development

Adaptive Value of Traits and Behaviors

Adaptive value is a term that comes from evolutionary biology, and it refers to how useful a trait is for allowing an organism to survive and reproduce in its environment.

Evaluating survival and reproduction directly is less common in psychology than in biology, and is generally the domain of evolutionary psychology, a subdivision of psychology. Despite this, many behavioral traits in humans have been proposed to have adaptive value.

The study of behavioral traits in animals is called **ethology**. Unsurprisingly, the study of human behavior is called **human ethology.**

Ethologists (scientists who specialize in ethology) have sorted behavioral traits into three main categories.

1. Innate behaviors
2. Learned behaviors
3. Complex behaviors

Innate behaviors are actions that people perform that do not have to be learned. These behaviors are thought to be genetically inherited, and are exhibited even by people raised in near-total isolation from other humans. They do not change significantly after birth.

Reflexes are one example of innate behaviors. Unlike the reflexes covered in the Biology book, these reflexes involve input from the brain, not just the spinal cord. Some of these reflexes stay with us throughout our lives, while others (the primitive reflexes) usually go away as we develop.

The photic sneeze reflex gets me every time!

The photic sneeze reflex, which causes some people to sneeze when they look at bright light, is an example of a reflex that persists through adulthood. The Moro reflex, one of the primitive reflexes, is where infants quickly abduct (spread out) and then adduct (pull back in) their arms when dropped.

Fixed-action patterns (FAPs) are a lot like reflexes, but they tend to be more complex actions. Although FAPs have been best-studied in other vertebrate species, some behaviors, such as yawning, have been identified as FAPs in humans.

The last main type of innate behavior is **orientation movements** (or **taxes**, singular **taxis**). Orientation movements require coordinated actions to be performed, such as a goose's rolling of an egg back into a nest from which the egg has been removed.

If human infants are placed on their mother's belly right after they are born, they know how to move their legs to push themselves up to her breast. When they reach the breast or are placed on it, they are able to search for the nipple, latch on to it, and begin sucking without breathing in the milk. The motor actions that accompany these behaviors are orientation movements.

Learned behaviors are actions that must be learned, and are thus not present at birth or inherited genetically. They can be changed, modified, and improved with practice.

Many social skills are considered to be learned behaviors, since people who grow up in isolation from other people tend not to display them. Children who grow up without meaningful social contact are sometimes called feral children—many of these children have neither acquired a first language nor developed senses of personal property or situational awareness.

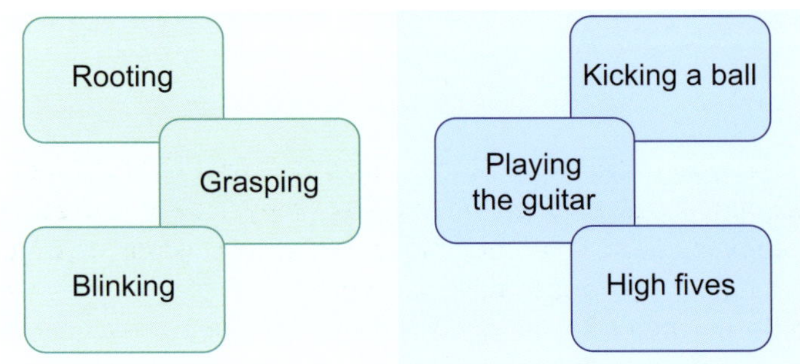

Innate Human Behaviors **Learned** Human Behaviors

Complex behaviors are behaviors that are combinations of both innate and learned behaviors. It is likely that most human behaviors fall into this category. An example of a complex behavior is walking—although babies have a reflex that enables them to perform walking motions, they only develop the ability to walk on their own with time and practice.

Behaviors that can be observed by other people in any way are called **overt behaviors**, while behaviors that are only observable by the person performing them are called **covert behaviors**.

Overtly, I'm all smiles, but covertly, I'm nervous about getting it done.

Like all phenotypic characteristics, behavior is acted on by natural selection. Behaviors that enhance an organism's fitness are more likely to be passed down than behaviors that decrease it. While many human behaviors have clear benefits to fitness, such as language and our social abilities, other behaviors are harder to analyze.

The Moro reflex discussed earlier in this section is thought to be inherited from our non-human primate ancestors. Because these ancestors were primarily arboreal (lived in trees), a reflex that causes infant apes to grab back on to their parents if they were to fall would be extremely useful. However, modern humans do not usually live in trees, nor do infant humans cling to their mother's belly fur. As such, there may be no benefit in humans retaining the Moro reflex.

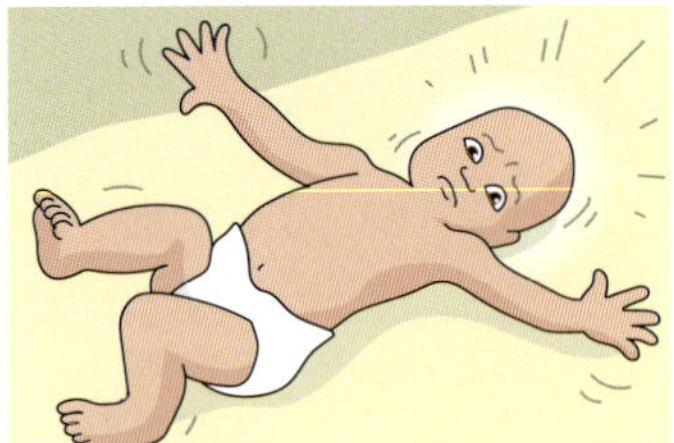

The Moro (Startle) Reflex

Heredity and the Environment

As mentioned earlier, views on how genes and the environment affect behavior have changed over time. The current consensus is that both genetics and environmental factors influence how we act. Additionally, our environment can change how our genes are expressed, and our genes can cause us to seek out specific environments.

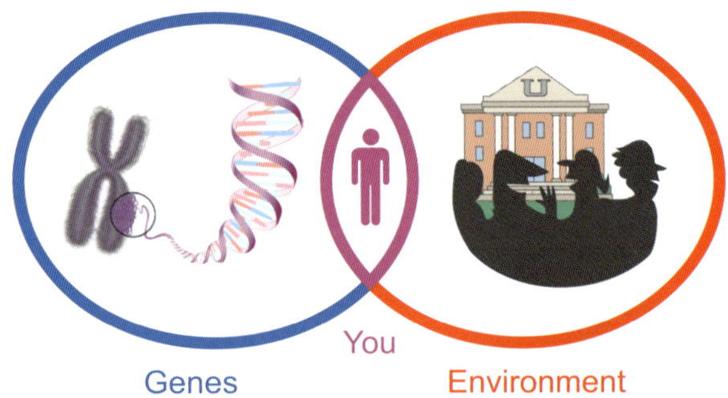

In the late 1940s, it was standard practice to give supplemental oxygen to infants who were born prematurely, as it had been shown to reduce infant mortality. Unbeknownst to them, the levels of oxygen being delivered were high enough to damage blood vessels in the babies' retinas, which were not yet fully developed. This damage causes a disease called retinopathy of prematurity, or ROP, which in severe cases causes blindness. When the medical community realized what was happening, they scrambled to find a solution to the problem, and a combination of revised standards and technologies like the ventilator brought ROP levels back under control.

Hyperoxia, or the presence of too much oxygen in the body, changes the expression of some genes that are critical for blood vessels to develop properly. Hypoxia, or too little oxygen, is also a risk factor for ROP and changes how the same genes are expressed in the retina. Although ROP is now much less common, it serves as a reminder of the powerful effect the environment can have on genetic expression.

Personality has been shown to be partially genetic, with different personality scales estimating its heritability between 17 and 65%. In other words, between 17 and 65 percent of the difference between two people with the same genome comes from their genes, while the remaining 35 - 83 percent is due to the environment.

People's personality traits are associated with their behavior. For example, people who score high on measures of introversion are more likely to attempt suicide than other people, while those who score high on extraversion are more likely to exercise regularly than low scorers.

Most studies investigating the link between personality and behavior report that the contribution of a given personality trait to a behavior is low. Because personality is only partially genetic, it is likely that individual genes play an extremely minor role in modulating specific behaviors. Despite this, it is clear that a person's genetic makeup influences how he acts.

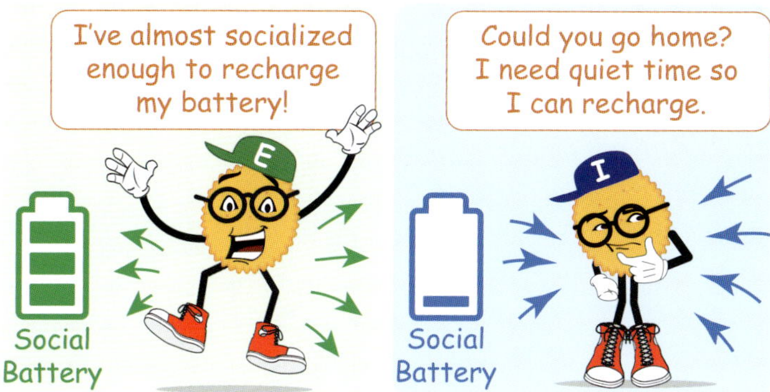

Another complicating factor to determining the relationship between genes and personality is the fact that people can fall in the middle of the spectrum of a personality trait. The middle of extraversion and introversion, for example, is called ambiversion. Ambiverts display extraverted and introverted tendencies.

Regulatory Genes and Behavior

The proteins that are responsible for regulating gene expression are covered in the Biology book. These proteins are themselves coded for by genes called **regulator genes**. Through their role in the production of regulatory proteins, regulator genes can affect how an organism behaves.

Infection of mice with a variant of influenza, the virus that causes the flu, has been shown to affect the activity of certain regulator genes, as well as to cause the mice to behave anxiously. While this design cannot separate the effects of the virus from the effects of upregulating regulator genes, it seems likely that these regulatory genes are crucial for maintaining normal behavior. A different infection, one with a coronavirus, causes changes in murine (mouse) regulator genes that lead to neuronal degeneration and paralysis.

Epigenetic modifications to the genome can also change an organism's behavior. Problems with adding acetyl groups to the amino acid tails attached to histones can cause problems with learning and memory, while issues with DNA methylation have been linked with disruption in the balance between excitatory and inhibitory activity in the brain.

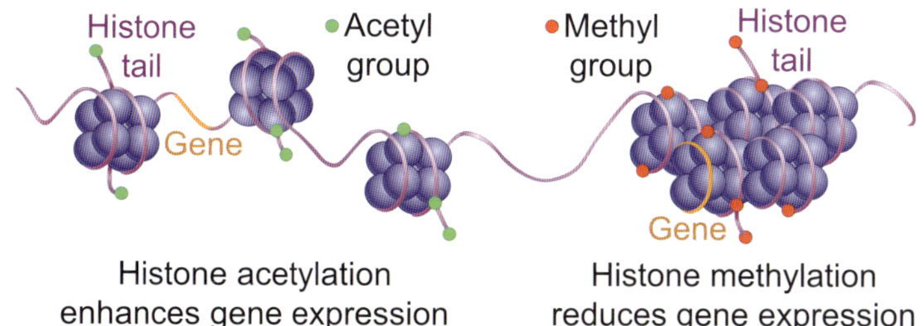

Motor Development

As mentioned earlier, babies are born with an impressive array of reflexes.

Newborns have practically no ability to control their motor functions. As they grow, however, they slowly but surely begin to learn voluntary movements. The order in which they pick up these skills is remarkably similar between different children, as is the timing at which they develop these abilities.

It is not necessary to memorize these milestones or exactly when they occur. Instead, it is better to have a general idea of what behaviors come before others and approximately when they develop.

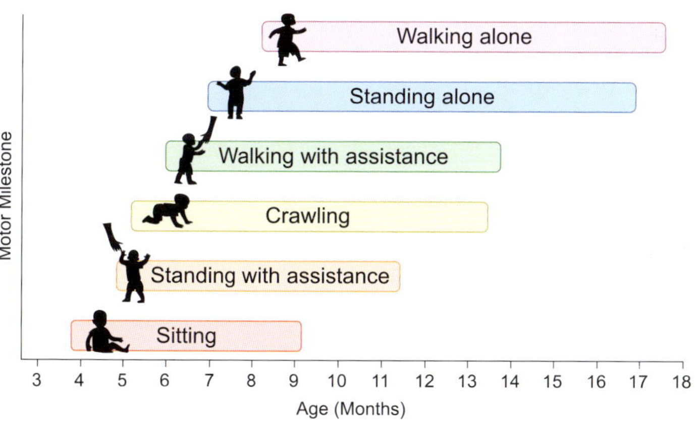

The mechanisms that drive motor development in children are not well understood. It is clear that most movements children make (excluding reflexes) are coordinated and probably purposeful, and they represent attempts to accomplish goals. The movement patterns that a child performs lay the foundation for more complex motions he learns as he grows, and a number of factors from a child's experiences to his parental environment to his genetics likely play a role in his motor development.

Developmental Changes in Adolescence

Adolescence and puberty are two different but related ideas. In Western countries, **adolescence** is generally defined as the period that spans from 10 years of age to about 18 or 19. This period involves a number of social, psychological, and physical changes. The most important of these physical changes is **puberty**, the process through which a child's body matures into that of an adult.

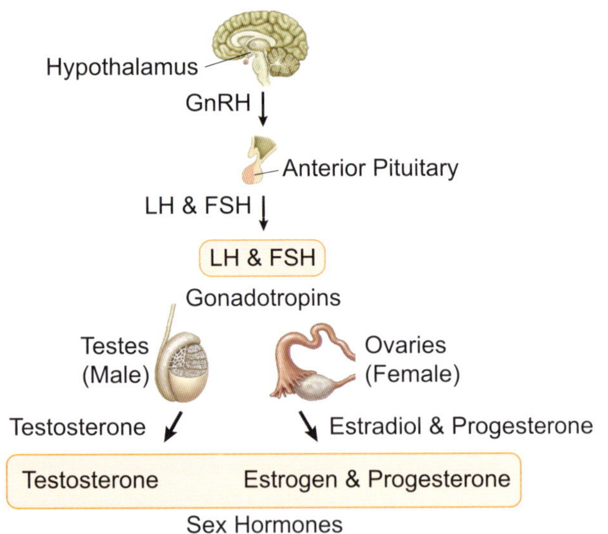

Most of the physical changes in adolescence are driven by puberty. The average age to start puberty is different for boys and girls, and different changes tend to occur at different times. For example, girls tend to start developing breasts and experiencing a growth spurt at around the age of 10, whereas boys generally are 12 years old or so before undergoing growth spurts and testicular maturation. On average, all of the physical changes associated with puberty occur about two years earlier in girls than in boys.

Puberty brings with it an increase in the height and body weight of adolescents, as well as the development of sexual organs in both sexes. There are also psychological, social, and cognitive changes associated with adolescence.

Most adolescents are more concerned with their body image, or how their body looks, than younger kids or adults are. In general, adolescent girls worry more about their appearance than boys their age do, and are more likely to be dissatisfied with how they look—this leads to girls spending more time comparing themselves to their peers. Boys, on the other hand, do not seem to be as concerned about what their peers think of their appearance, but are more worried about conforming to an ideal body image, i.e. one that is muscular and symmetrical.

The social changes that come with adolescence are many and profound. They can include the solidifying of personal identities, changes in self-esteem, development of sexual and romantic relationships, and the entrance into the workforce. Drug use, mental illness, and delinquency are also common.

Although the brain develops most quickly during infancy, a second surge of growth occurs during adolescence. Brain areas like the prefrontal cortex get larger, while the structures of the limbic system are activated in different ways than in children or adults. The prefrontal cortex, which is implicated in long-term planning, impulse control, and other executive functions does not finish developing until people are about 25. This may help explain why adolescents tend to show deficits in these abilities. The activity of the limbic system characteristic of adolescents might help explain why teens and young adults tend to experience mood swings and rely on emotions to guide their thinking.

Adolescence also marks the second main period of **synaptic pruning**, which involves the elimination of synapses from various places in the nervous system. It is thought that this happens in the process of learning—as some neural pathways are used over and over again when a memory is being formed, synaptic pruning might strengthen these connections by getting rid of unneeded synapses. This pruning was once thought to stop at adulthood, but has been shown to continue well into a person's 20s.

6 Personality, Attitudes, and Disorders

6.1 Personality

Each individual has thoughts, feelings and behaviors that remain fairly consistent throughout his life and distinguish him from others. This consistency and distinctiveness lead to a unique set of behavioral traits that form his **personality**.

While personality is considered to be relatively stable, it is also **situationally specific**. This means that outside factors, such as hunger, fatigue, other people, and the situation itself, influence the expression of personality at a given time. For example, someone who is typically easy-going may be high-strung the morning of the MCAT or someone who is generally patient may snap at the grocery store clerk when they're already late for work.

Psychoanalytic Perspective

In the early 1900s, Sigmund Freud published works on his psychoanalytic theory of personality. **Psychoanalytic (psychodynamic) theory** explains personality (and psychological disorders) through conflicts in the unconscious mind that arise during childhood experiences. These conflicts are typically over how the individual deals with primitive urges. Freud identified three entities within the human mind that he proposed acted outside conscious awareness to influence personality and behavior: the id, the ego, and the superego.

The **id** is present from birth and seeks instant gratification, avoiding pain without consideration of social norms. The raw biological urges (eating, sleeping, sex, etc.) reside in the id. The id exists entirely within the unconscious. The **ego** desires gratification as well, but is also concerned with reward and punishment. The ego delays the gratification of the *id* until a socially acceptable way of fulfilling urges is found. The ego makes decisions using reason, considering social norms and seeking to avoid negative consequences. The **superego** arises from the ego at about 3 to 5 years old. The superego understands and is driven by higher principles. It internalizes social norms into a moral code. While the ego simply seeks to obey social norms in order to avoid punishment, the superego understands and even desires to abide by moral principles.

According to Freud, behavior is a battle between the id, the ego, and the superego. For instance, right now your id may be telling you to take a nap, while your ego is weighing the real consequences of such an action. At the same time, your superego is concerned about the 'rightness' of being self-disciplined.

Freud believed that there were two main factors that drove people's behavior: libido and the death drive.

Libido, in Freud's view, is the energy that people devote towards love and other positive drives. It also includes sexual desire and the urge to feel other kinds of physical pleasure. The **death drive** is its opposite, representing the instincts for aggression, self-harm, and compulsive repetition of behaviors.

Freud divided awareness into three layers.

1. **Conscious**: Thoughts of which you are immediately aware (thoughts like "I am studying for the MCAT." or "I love this online course.")
2. **Preconscious**: Thoughts that you can easily summon into your conscious awareness (thoughts of your anticipated date this evening, or what you had for supper last night)
3. **Unconscious**: Thoughts of which you are unaware, yet influence your behavior (thoughts generated by childhood trauma or suppressed sexual desires)

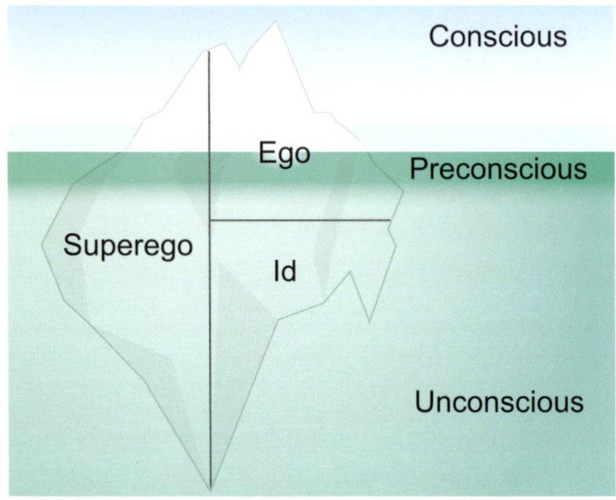

Freud believed that there were far more unconscious thoughts than conscious thoughts. Think of Freud's theory as an iceberg with 90 percent of thoughts below the surface. Additionally, the activities of the ego and superego are most available to observation, while the id is almost entirely inscrutable.

Conflict between the id, ego, and superego creates anxiety. **Defense mechanisms** are an effort to relieve anxiety. Defense mechanisms have been divided into four different categories.

1. Psychotic defense mechanisms
2. Immature defense mechanisms
3. Neurotic (intermediate) defense mechanisms
4. Mature defense mechanisms

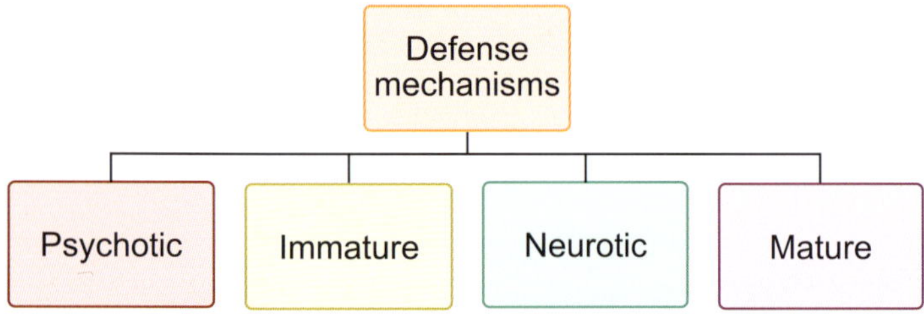

Although adults can use mechanisms from any of the four categories, they tend to use mechanisms from some categories more than others. The overuse of certain mechanisms can become pathological, meaning they are associated with mental illnesses.

Psychotic defense mechanisms, like their name implies, are commonly seen in people experiencing psychosis, which is a severe loss of contact with reality. Some of these mechanisms are.

1. **Denial**: A refusal to accept the world around you because it is too frightening (I'm the best poker player in the world and I'll never need to sleep again!)
2. **Distortion**: Extreme warping of reality to fit personal needs (I'm in the hospital because the Communist Gangster Computer Gods are afraid of my psychic powers.)

Immature defense mechanisms are common in adults, but are not effective in building a person's ability to cope with stress and anxiety.

1. **Projection**: Projecting your own bad thoughts onto someone else (I don't like you. I don't enjoy feeling like I don't like you, so I think that I actually do like you and it's just you who doesn't like me.)
2. **Hypochondriasis**: A preoccupation with the idea of having a serious illness, despite evidence to the contrary (I don't care that the doctor said my stomach ache isn't cancer. I'm sure it is!)

Neurotic (intermediate) defense mechanisms are also common in adults, but have some short-term utility in coping with life.

1. **Repression**: Holding feelings inside (a case of amnesia after a bad experience)
2. **Displacement**: Displacing your feelings onto a more convenient target (I am angry with my husband, so I will yell at the kids.)
3. **Reaction formation**: Doing the opposite of what you feel (I feel guilty for cheating, so I buy flowers for my girlfriend.)
4. **Regression**: Immature behavior, even when appropriate responses are known (throwing a temper tantrum instead of having a level-headed conversation.)
5. **Rationalization**: Making excuses for destructive behavior (I might as well play because studying won't really change my MCAT score.)

Mature defense mechanisms are consciously selected coping behaviors, and are most common in emotionally healthy adults.

1. **Sublimation**: Doing a good thing because if you don't you are going to do something socially unacceptable (going for a jog instead of beating your noisy neighbor to death)
2. **Suppression**: Delaying thinking about a stressful situation in order to process it at a later time (I'm having a bad day…I don't want to think about my GPA right now.)
3. **Humor**: Avoiding talking earnestly about a subject in an enjoyable way, distancing yourself from the stressful nature of the topic (joking that you're unsuccessful with men instead of seriously thinking about why that is)

Freud also identified certain principles to explain why people behave differently from one another. Some examples of these are the pleasure and reality principles.

The **pleasure principle** describes how the id operates, and says that the id seeks the immediate satisfaction of its urges. In contrast, the **reality principle** explains the function of the ego—the ego serves to delay gratification of the id's urges until a reasonable solution can be found.

Carl Jung was a contemporary of Freud and was strongly influenced by him, though he felt that Freud's theories had been too centered on sex. Carl Jung spoke of a personal unconscious and a collective unconscious. The personal unconscious was like Freud's unconscious. The collective unconscious, however, was a collection of latent memories inherited from an individual's ancestors; supposedly people retained not only the memory of their parents and grandparents, but archetypes, which are akin to memories of the entire human race. Archetypes were images with Hermetic meaning to all humans. They appeared in dreams and became cultural symbols.

Alfred Adler, another contemporary of Freud, believed that the human drive for superiority, and not sex as Freud had argued, was the driving force behind personality. The feeling of inferiority as a child leads people to compensate by acquiring new skills and behaviors. This led Adler to propose the inferiority complex in individuals whose feelings of inferiority had become excessive.

The theories of Freud, his followers, and most of his contemporaries fall into the psychodynamic perspective. The most important contributions from the psychodynamic perspective can be summarized in four statements.

1. Behavior is influenced by the unconscious mind.
2. Behavior is influenced by internal conflict.
3. Behavior is influenced by early childhood experiences.
4. Defense mechanisms are a normal way of dealing with anxiety.

The psychoanalytic theory is a psychodynamic theory.

Behaviorist Perspective

Critics of the psychodynamic perspective found it unscientific, having too little evidence, too few samples, and being untestable. Adopting the **behaviorist perspective** to study personality, **John B. Watson** abandoned the study of the mind in itself and considered only observable behavior. In contrast to the psychodynamic perspective, in the behaviorist perspective external environmental factors, rather than internal psychological factors, become important in understanding personality. From a "pure" behaviorist perspective, internal mental processes are assumed to be unknowable. A person is like a black box whose inside is unknowable. The behaviorist studies only what goes in and what comes out of the black box.

Behaviorists explain personality through learning experiences that lead to predictable behaviors. To understand personality, they took personality theory into the laboratory and studied animals.

B.F. Skinner's principles of operant conditioning were not originally intended to explain personality, but they have been applied to personality theory. Skinner argued that behavior is *determined* by the environment. Any consistency in an individual's personality is due to response tendencies that are learned through experience. According to Skinner, personality development continued throughout life in no particular stages. For Skinner, environmental consequences determine behavior in three ways:

1. **Reinforcement**: Desirable consequences encourage certain behavior. (If people laugh at your jokes, you will tell more jokes.)
2. **Punishment**: Undesirable consequences discourage behavior. (If people ridicule your blue shirt, you will wear a red shirt.)
3. **Extinction**: A response ceases due to lack of consequence. (If people stop laughing at your jokes, you will stop telling jokes. If they stop ridiculing your blue shirt, you start wearing it again.)

Skinner's proposed mechanism for learning is called **operant conditioning**.

Skinner and Watson were some of the first researchers to build on the behaviorist approach of **Ivan Pavlov** in the West. Pavlov's work in **classical conditioning** laid the foundation for behaviorism.

Social Cognitive Theory

Albert Bandura argued that cognitive processes distinguished humans from other animals. Conditioning was not a passive process in humans, but was, instead, an active process shaped by an individual's mind. Still a behaviorist theory, **social cognitive theory** added cognitive influence (influence of the mind) to personality development. A person doesn't learn only from the consequences of his own experiences but can also learn by observing the experiences of others. This is called **observational learning.** One child who witnesses another being punished for lying may learn to be truthful without actually experiencing the punishment himself; in this way, his cognitive process is seen as important in the development of his personality. Both social cognitivists and pure behaviorists agree that personality is shaped by learning.

Don't confuse observable behavior with observational learning. The first refers to actions by individuals or groups that can be seen and measured by researchers. The second is how individuals learn through observing other people's actions. Observational learning distinguishes cognitive theory from pure behaviorist theory.

Humanistic Perspective

Humanistic theory challenged the dehumanizing and deterministic aspects of pure behaviorist theory. Humanists believe that humans do more than simply respond to external stimuli—humans have free will. Humanistic theory also rejected the pessimism of psychodynamic theory. Humans are not slaves to conflicts within their unconscious minds. Instead, humans have a desire for personal growth.

Humanistic theory is an optimistic approach. In terms of personality, subjective viewpoints become even more important than reality—if you think of yourself as brave, then you will behave bravely, even if you really are frightened. Finally, humanists tend to focus on the conscious aspects of personality since we have less control over our subconscious mind.

Carl Rogers was a humanist who viewed personality development through what he called the "self". This "self" was a person's mental picture of himself. Today we call it **self-concept**. Rogers' self was subjective; it did not have to agree with reality. For example, it is possible for a person to view himself as handsome even while others find him ugly. When a person's self-image does not align with reality, **incongruence** occurs. Too much incongruence leads to anxiety, while **congruence**, the opposite of incongruence, allows for personal growth.

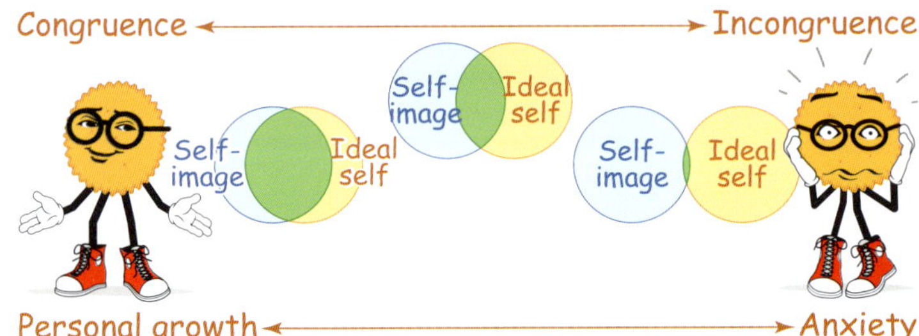

Because these ideas were developed over time and because there is no absolute consensus, different books may define different "selves" (e.g. actual self, true self, ideal self, self-image, self-worth, self-esteem, etc...). Sometimes there are three "self" circles aligning, sometimes there are two. For the MCAT, just remember that when the "selves" align, there is congruence (happiness); when they don't, there is incongruence (anxiety).

Rogers believed that **authenticity**, or living in an open and self-accepting way, was key to developing congruence. He also argued that **acceptance** from other people was necessary for this development to occur.

Abraham Maslow presented a humanistic theory that is often referred to as the 'hierarchy of needs' where more basic needs (physiological needs at the bottom) must be met before higher order needs are pursued. The highest need on this scale is **self-actualization**, the desire to achieve one's full potential. Self-actualization is the natural goal of every person, though obstacles can impede his path towards achieving it.

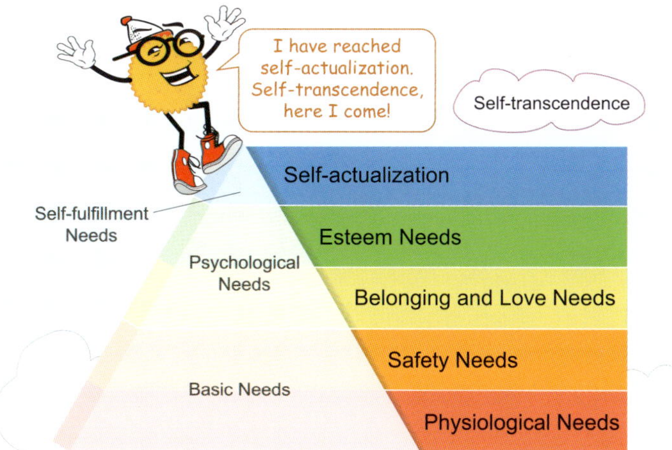

Just before his death, Maslow wanted to add self-transcendence, finding meaning and identity beyond oneself, to the top of the hierarchy.

Both Rogers and Maslow agreed that congruence is necessary for personal growth, but disagreed about how congruence could be achieved. Rogers thought that acceptance and authenticity on their own were enough, while Maslow posited that self-actualization was also required.

Biological Theory

The **biological theory** of personality asserts that a person is born with much of his personality hardwired—his personality is written in his genes. It is hypothesized that evolution has acted upon personality by naturally selecting for and against certain traits.

The first major biological theory of personality was created in the early 1950s by **Hans Eysenck**. He came up with it after observing that identical twins tended to have more similar personalities than fraternal twins, and he suggested that some aspects of personality were inherited from people's parents. He also proposed that different levels of cortical arousal were associated with different personality features.

Jeffrey A. Gray challenged Eysenck's theory in the 1970s, proposing his own **biopsychosocial theory of personality**. While he accepted the idea that some aspects of personality were inherited, he argued that a different biological mechanism controlled people's personalities. He called them the **behavioral inhibition system (BIS)** and the **behavioral activation system (BAS)** respectively. The BIS is activated in response to unpleasant events and signals a person to avoid them, while the BAS responds to positive events and prompts people to seek them out.

In the 1980s, **C. Robert Cloninger** developed yet another biological theory of personality. He believed that different dimensions of personality were associated with different neurotransmitters—for instance, novelty seeking (the tendency to try new things) was linked with reduced activation of dopaminergic neurons. He proposed that the personality dimensions were managed by different brain systems, an idea which has been supported by fMRI studies.

Twin studies provide evidence for this theory. Such studies compare monozygotic (identical) twins to dizygotic (fraternal) twins. Higher levels of similarity between monozygotic twins indicate greater genetic influence in personality development. Studies of cases where twins have been separated at birth have led to even greater insight, since similarities can no longer be attributed to a shared environment in such cases. Such studies support the biological theory. Studies of infants with apparent genetic predispositions toward certain behaviors also supports the biological theory. But the theory isn't all nature over nurture. As the individual grows, environmental factors presumably modify these traits to create a fully developed personality.

Trait Theory

Trait theory describes what many people think of when they define personality. Trait theory states that personality consists of **personality traits** that distinguish individuals and that are stable over a lifetime. The extent to which individuals express such traits exists on a continuum and are affected by situational factors. For instance, a person may be extroverted, introverted, or he may fall somewhere in the middle, and as explained earlier in this section, the specific expression of their personality trait is influenced by many external factors, including their mood, environment, and current circumstances. Therefore, it's important to consider situational explanations of people's behaviors.

One of the first trait theories of personality was created by **Gordon Allport**. After going through a dictionary to find every word that might be used to describe a person's personality, Allport came up with a classification that separates these traits into three groups.

Cardinal traits are pervasive patterns of behavior that show through in almost everything an individual does—a person may have one or two of these truly defining features.

Central traits are slightly less definitive than cardinal traits, and encompass features that we all share to some degree, such as aesthetic interest or leadership.

Secondary traits tend to be less obvious and consistently expressed than either cardinal or central traits.

The most widely-used model of trait theory today is the **five-factor ("Big 5") model**, which describes personality based upon five traits that can be remembered using the OCEAN mnemonic.

1. **Openness to Experience**—How curious, imaginative, and flexible are you?
2. **Conscientiousness**—How diligent, well-organized, and disciplined are you?
3. **Extraversion**—How much stimulation do you need? (Are you assertive and adventurous?)
4. **Agreeableness**—How sympathetic, cooperative, and modest are you?
5. **Neuroticism**—How anxious, insecure, and hostile are you?

Raymond Cattell came up with the predecessor to the Big 5 model, called the 16 Personality Factor (PF) questionnaire. It was through analyzing his work that the five personality dimensions that make up the Big 5 were originally discovered.

Hans Eysenck's theory of personality also has some components of trait theory. He argued that people have three main dimensions that can be used to describe their personalities: extraversion, neuroticism, and **psychoticism**. The first two of these are used similarly in the Big 5 model, while psychoticism describes how much a person tends to experience reality in a way that the majority of people do not.

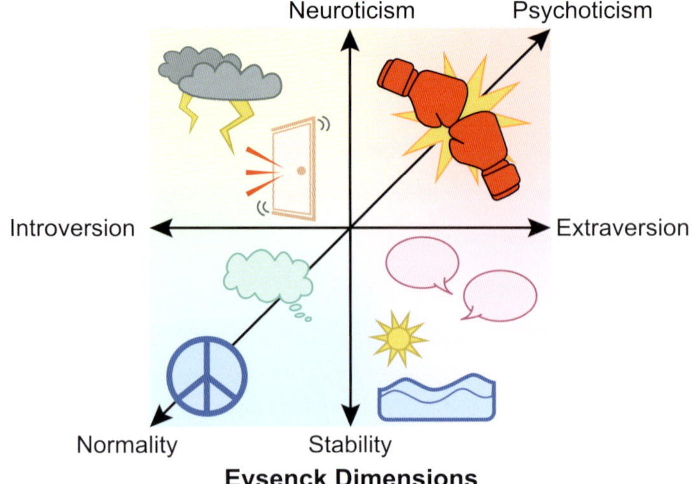

Eysenck Dimensions

Most modern trait theories of personality have been created using **factor analysis**. At its core, factor analysis is a statistical technique that seeks to explain why some variables in a data set covary, or move up and down with other variables. It does so by supposing that there are other hidden variables that influence the variables that vary together—these hidden variables are called **factors**.

Imagine that you had access to an infinitely large library of statements about someone's personality. These might include phrases like, "Being around other people makes me feel energized" or, "I like being the center of attention." You could then give a random set of 100 of these statements to 100 different people and ask them to rate how much they agree or disagree with these statements on a scale of 1 to 10, with complete agreement being a 10 and complete disagreement being a 1. If the group of people you're testing tends to rate some statements similarly, it can be said that these statements covary.

If people's responses to these statements reliably covary, factor analysis assumes that they covary due to one underlying factor. In other words, the reason that people respond to these statements similarly is because they reflect an idea that unites them all.

The Big 5 model was generated by performing the example experiment on a large scale. After making a large library of questions related to personality and using them to test thousands of people, researchers used factor analysis to see how people's answers to these questions were related. They found five main groups, but didn't yet know what they might represent. After examining which questions tended to be answered similarly across the study population, they assigned the labels of openness, conscientiousness, extraversion, agreeableness, and neuroticism to the five factors they found. These factors were found by two independent teams of researchers at almost the same time, and serve as the basis for the most widely used tests of personality in modern psychology.

Perspective	Major Theorist	Major Associated Terms and Contributions
Psychoanalytic	Sigmund Freud	Id, ego, superego, levels of consciousness, defense mechanisms
Behavioral	Ivan Pavlov	Classic conditioning (unconditioned/conditioned stimulus/response)
Behavioral	B.F. Skinner	Operant Conditioning (reinforcement, punishment, extinction)
Social Cognitive	Albert Bandura	Observational learning (learning through observation)
Humanistic	Carl Rogers	Self-concept, congruence, authenticity, acceptance
Humanistic	Abraham Maslow	Hierarchy of needs, self-actualization, self-transcendence
Biological	Jeffrey Gray	Behavioral inhibition system, behavioral activation system
Biological	C. Robert Cloninger	Neurotransmitters (low dopamine ⟶ novelty seeking)
Biological/Trait	Hans Eysenck	Cortical arousal, extraversion, neuroticism, psychoticism
Trait	Gordon Allport	Cardinal traits, central traits, secondary traits
Trait	Raymond Cattell	Factor analysis, 16 Personality Factor (PF) questionnaire
Trait	"Big 5" (many theorists)	OCEAN (openness to experience, conscientiousness,extraversion, agreeableness, neuroticism)

Personality Perspectives and Theorists

6.2 Motivation

Motivation is what drives people to behave in a certain way. There are different factors that have been proposed to influence motivation, including instincts, arousal, drives, and needs.

Factors that Influence Motivation

In the earliest theories of motivation, **instincts** were used to explain the source of nearly all human behaviors. These theories are most closely associated with **William James** and **William McDougall**, both of whom were psychologists working in the early 20th century.

Both thinkers viewed instincts as influenced by heredity and learning—for example, there might be some genetic basis for "shyness" that a baby is born with, and as he grows and develops he learns appropriate times for being shy. However, instincts are generally considered to be innate (and thus independent of learning) by modern psychologists. As such, the instinct theories of motivation are no longer widely used to explain human behavior.

Other theories sought to explain motivation through the concept of **arousal**. According to these theories, both emotion and motivation arise from the activation of the central nervous system. Different actions are associated with different levels of activation—for example, people tend to be less aroused while in a coma than when they're awake. The most prominent promoter of these theories was **Donald Hebb**.

The original arousal theories of motivation have been strengthened over time by the work of **Hans Eysenck** and **John Lacey**. However, there are several unresolved problems with the arousal theories, and they too have largely fallen out of favor.

Drives have also been used to clarify where motivation comes from. Although the first **drive reduction theory** was published at about the same time as the first arousal theory, they did not become popular until the mid-20th century.

Drive reduction theories argue that humans have **needs**, or behaviors that must be performed in order to maintain homeostasis. These needs are generally physiological, simple, and essential for survival—they include such things as water, food, and sleep. When a drive is fulfilled, the need temporarily goes away.

For example, if a person needs water, the drive of thirst naturally occurs. The goal of thirst is to reduce the need for water. Thirst motivates him to drink until the need for water disappears. Thirst is an example of a **negative feedback loop**. The more a person drinks, the less thirsty he becomes, and when the body recognizes that the need for water has been eliminated, the drive of thirst stops.

There are two types of drives: primary drives and secondary drives. **Primary drives** are innate and do not have to be learned—they include hunger and thirst. **Secondary drives** are not innate and must be learned—they include a desire for money or affirmation from other people.

Additional Theories

Several theories of motivation build on the ideas of needs and drives. One of these, **Maslow's hierarchy of needs**, argued lower level needs, like basic survival and security-related needs as well as psychological needs like love, belonging, and esteem, generally need to be satisfied before moving on to higher levels of needs, like self-actualization and transcendence.

Incentive theory represents a natural outgrowth of the behaviorist perspective on human behavior. It states that people are motivated by incentives (rewards). If a person is rewarded after performing a certain action, he is motivated to keep performing that action. If he is instead punished for performing a behavior, he becomes less likely to perform that behavior in the future.

Cognitive theories of motivation emphasize the rational and logical thought processes that drive human behavior. These approaches tend to focus on goal-setting, interpersonal relationships, and tend not to view motivation as instinctual or only mediated by physiological drives.

The dominant understanding of motivation in psychology today draws from all of the theories listed above, and the study of motivation has mainly fallen under the umbrella of I-O (industrial-organizational) psychology. This branch of psychology studies how people behave in the workplace, and motivation is a key driver of productivity in companies and other organizations.

Motivators that Regulate Behavior

Even the most deeply rooted human drives are influenced by both biological and sociocultural factors. These factors contribute to our experiences of hunger, sex drive, and substance addiction, among others.

Several different brain areas have been implicated in regulating hunger, including the arcuate nucleus and the paraventricular nucleus, which are regions of the hypothalamus. Many endocrine hormones, especially ghrelin, leptin, and insulin are also known to mediate hunger. Eating, and by extension hunger, is also deeply social, and people take cues from one another about how and what to eat. For example, people tend to eat more food if they are eating with others, and the foods consumed across human cultures show tremendous variability—try finding chitlins in India or balut in Azerbaijan.

Our libidos (sex drives) are also partially controlled by our hormones. Over half a dozen endocrine compounds, including testosterone, the estrogens, serotonin, norepinephrine, and others, have been identified as important in regulating libido. Psychological factors like mental illness also affect libido. Some social factors also influence libido, but comparatively less scientific research has been devoted to studying these factors.

Many of the drugs that have the tendency to cause serious problems in the lives of their users are addictive. The biological mechanisms that underlie drug addiction are covered in more detail elsewhere. Social factors can also factor into drug addiction—some of these include friends and family using drugs, experiencing abuse and neglect, peer pressure, and bullying.

6.3 Attitudes

Attitudes are ways of thinking and feeling about objects that shape behavior. These objects can be concrete, like people and things, or abstract, such as goals and ideas.

There are three components of attitude that combine to form the **ABC model of attitude**.

1. Affective
2. Behavioral
3. Cognitive

Affective

"I feel excited"

Behavioral

"I'm jumping up and down"

Cognitive

"I think I nailed the MCAT"

ABC Model Attitude Blocks

Affective components are the feelings or emotions we have that are relevant to a given object. For example, you might feel anger towards the concept of traffic, which in turn influences how you think about it.

Behavioral components are the behaviors we direct at an object. We might avoid traffic, or curse when we are stuck in it—these behaviors also shape how we think about traffic.

Cognitive components are the perceptions we have of an object. One might hold the belief that traffic is boring—this thought combines with affect and behavior to form an attitude about traffic.

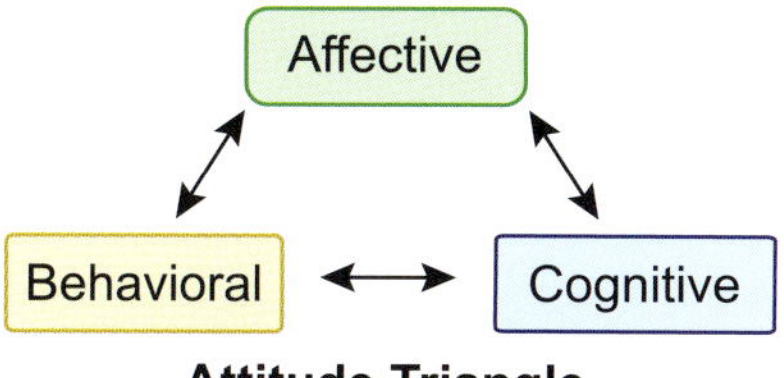

Attitude Triangle

Attitudes and behavior affect each other in a reciprocal manner—in other words, our attitudes affect how we behave, and our behavior affects our attitudes as well.

Attitudes can be explicit or implicit. A person is aware of his **explicit attitudes** and unaware of his **implicit attitudes.**

Attitudes and Behavior

If you are familiar with the phrase, "give him an inch and he'll take a mile," you have already been introduced to one of the ways that our behavior can change how we think. A more formal statement of this idiom is known as the **foot-in-the-door technique**. In general, people are more likely to agree to a large or important request after agreeing beforehand to a smaller one. For example, asking people to put a small, inconspicuous "please drive safely" sticker on their window makes them more likely to agree to putting a big, ugly sign in their yard later on.

Related to the foot-in-the-door technique is the **door-in-the-face technique**. Instead of asking people for a small favor, then a larger one later, the door-in-the-face technique reverses the order. Someone employing this technique first asks for a large, inconvenient favor with the expectation that they will be rejected. They then later ask for something much more moderate or reasonable. People are more likely to agree to the second request if they rejected a much larger one beforehand.

Door-in-the-face techniques are used commonly in sales and retail. For example, a waitress at a restaurant might ask you if you would like to order dessert before she gives you your check. If you refuse, she might ask if you want a smaller item, like a tea or coffee. The act of asking you about dessert makes you more likely to buy the tea or coffee.

Role-taking can also influence people's attitudes. When people take on new roles, they tend to feel out of their depth or as if they do not belong. As people continue to function in this role, be it as a student, parent, or employee, they generally lose the anxiety they once felt and become more comfortable. Over time, acting in a certain role can change a person's attitude concerning that role. This has been shown in several experiments involving positions of authority—randomly assigning people to roles of strength and weakness causes them to change their beliefs about both themselves and other people.

Our attitudes can also change how we behave—there are four major theories that try to explain how this works.

1. The elaboration likelihood model
2. The attitude to behavior process model
3. The theory of planned behavior
4. The prototype willingness model

The **elaboration likelihood model (ELM)** states that there are two pathways by which people are persuaded to do something: the central route and the peripheral route.

When someone is convinced via the **central route**, he is paying attention to the factual information and rational argument presented by the person persuading them—the degree to which his attitude changes depends on how strong he thought the argument was.

In contrast, when someone is convinced via the **peripheral route**, he focuses on the other information associated with the person persuading them. This can include anything from the flashiness of the presentation to the credentials of the presenter.

Persuasive Message
Central Route
Peripheral Route
Deep Processing (Arguments)
Superficial Processing (Surface Cues)
Lasting Attitude Change
Temporary Attitude Change

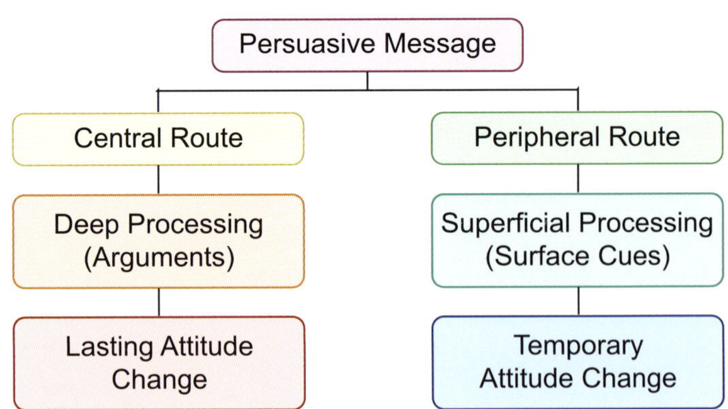

According to the ELM, people persuaded via the central route are more likely to experience a lasting change in attitude, while people convinced via the peripheral route tend to undergo a short-lived shift in attitude.

The **attitude to behavior process model** argues that events, attitudes, and past experience combine to influence our behavior. In short, something happening to you triggers an attitude related to that event. You then remember past experiences of similar events and use both your attitude and memories to decide how to respond to what is currently happening to you.

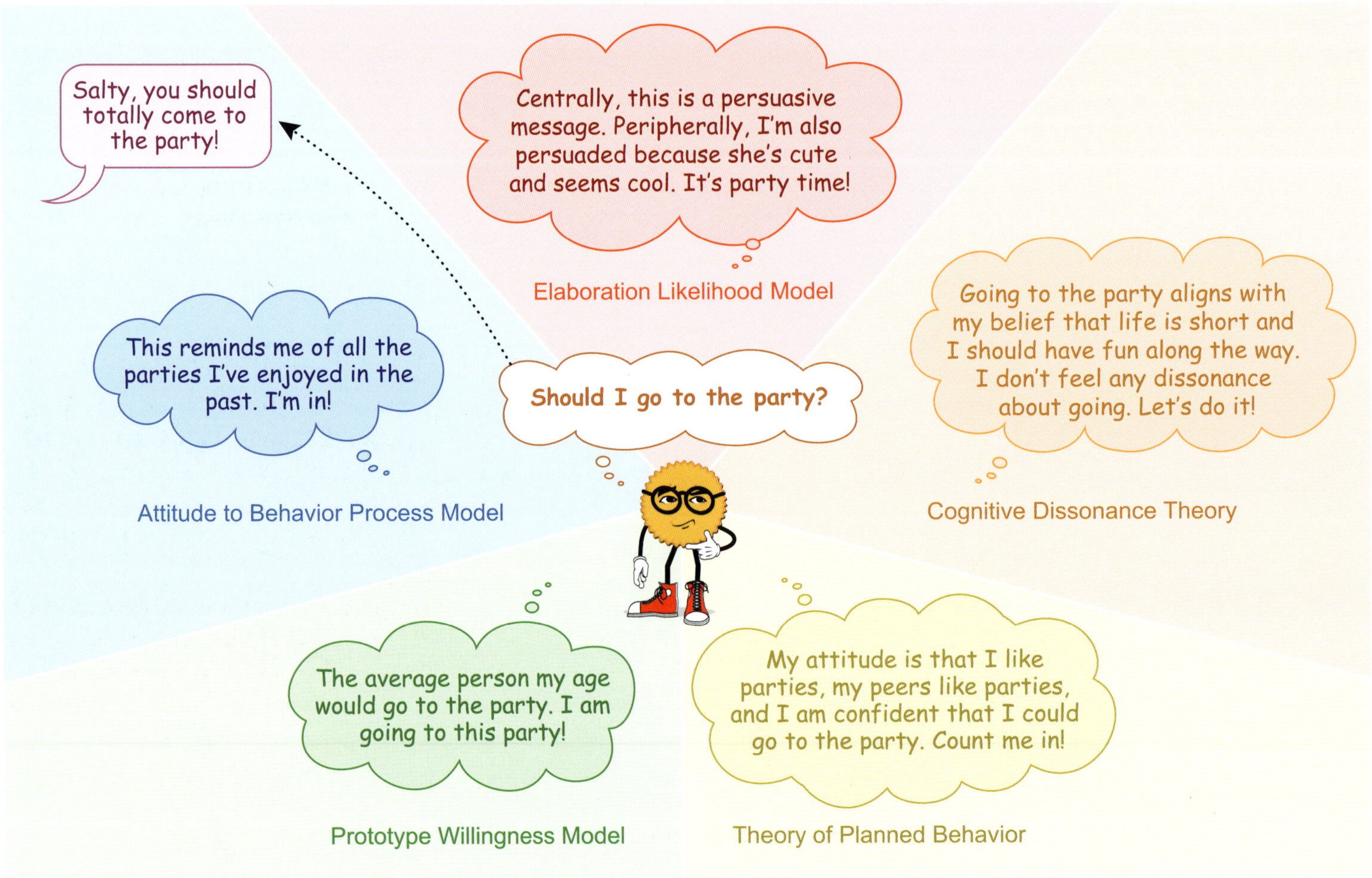

Salty, you should totally come to the party!
Centrally, this is a persuasive message. Peripherally, I'm also persuaded because she's cute and seems cool. It's party time!
Elaboration Likelihood Model
This reminds me of all the parties I've enjoyed in the past. I'm in!
Attitude to Behavior Process Model
Should I go to the party?
Going to the party aligns with my belief that life is short and I should have fun along the way. I don't feel any dissonance about going. Let's do it!
Cognitive Dissonance Theory
The average person my age would go to the party. I am going to this party!
Prototype Willingness Model
My attitude is that I like parties, my peers like parties, and I am confident that I could go to the party. Count me in!
Theory of Planned Behavior

Imagine being woken up in the middle of the night by a loud noise (the event). You might feel fear or apprehension (attitude), and you might also have investigated similar noises before and found nothing (past experiences). Your fear and memories of nothing being wrong interact and potentially change your response to this event—perhaps you would ignore the noise and go back to sleep.

The **theory of planned behavior** says that our intentions drive our behavior. Our intentions are influenced by three different factors: our attitudes towards a behavior, subjective norms, and perceived behavioral control (how much control we think we have over a behavior).

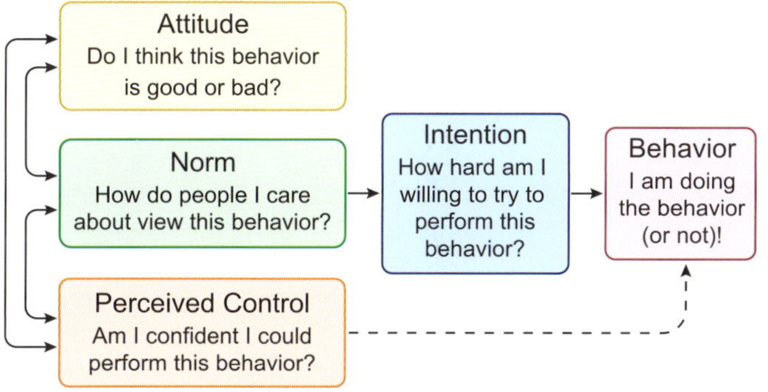

Theory of Planned Behavior

Consider deciding whether or not to cook dinner. You might feel positively about cooking but have friends that think cooking is boring. Additionally, you might feel that cooking is inherently challenging because you have a small kitchen. All of these elements work together to influence your decision to cook dinner.

The **prototype willingness model** posits that a total of five factors influence people's behavior. They are attitudes, subjective norms, behavioral intention, behavioral willingness, and **prototypes**.

Prototypes are cognitive representations of people or ideas that we extrapolate to aid in decision making. For example, when adolescents are deciding whether or not to engage in risky behaviors, they tend to compare themselves to their images of a *typical* risk-taker their age and not to a particular person they know.

Prototype

Attitudes and behavior don't align perfectly. For instance, a person can disapprove of swearing and still swear. Attitudes can change behavior, and behaviors can change attitude. Other than persuasion, some of the factors involved are:

1. **Experience**—Does the person have experience in a topic with which the attitude is concerned?
2. **Expertise**—Does the person have expertise in a topic with which the attitude is concerned?
3. **Repetition**—Does the person repeatedly express the attitude?
4. **Cognitive consistency**—Does the person think in a manner consistent with the attitude?
5. **Behavioral consistency**—Does the person behave in a manner consistent with the attitude?
6. **Consequence**—Is the person rewarded by having the attitude?
7. **Societal norms**—Is the attitude the norm in society?

If you can honestly answer "yes" to most of the questions above about a given attitude, the attitude is probably strongly held and likely to influence a person's behavior. It would be difficult to persuade such an individual to change that attitude.

Don't memorize these factors—just think about them.

Cognitive Dissonance Theory

Cognitive dissonance is the uncomfortable feeling that arises when holding conflicting beliefs and/or acting in ways that conflict with beliefs.. This process is normally stressful, and it prompts people to reevaluate their current thought patterns and/or behaviors to relieve their feelings of stress.

There are three main strategies that people use to resolve cognitive dissonance—they can change their beliefs, modify how they think about their beliefs, or change their behaviors.

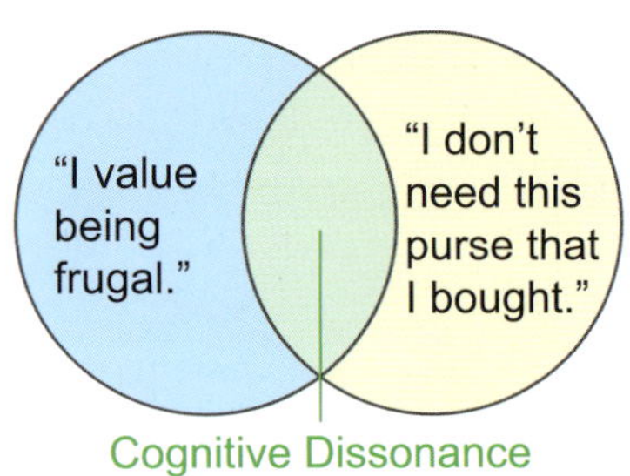

Take for example a person who has been told by his physician that he needs to reduce his sugar intake—this means giving up ice cream for the foreseeable future. This person is struck by cognitive dissonance as he considers having a pint of ice cream after dinner. On one hand, he wants the ice cream—on the other, he has been told that continuing his high sugar intake will harm him.

He has several options open to him. He can tell himself that he doesn't want the ice cream—this is a kind of denial at first, but will hopefully become what he truly believes with time. He can also lower the importance of the physician's warning in his mind and convince himself that his high sugar intake isn't all that bad. He can also bring in more beliefs to justify eating the ice cream—for instance, he might tell himself that all of his family members eat ice cream, so there's no reason why he shouldn't. He might also flatly deny that his physician is reliable and say that high sugar intake won't hurt him. Finally, he might choose to eat less ice cream.

To make cognitive dissonance go away, you can change your behavior. Alternatively, you can trivialize, supplement, or deny any of the beliefs that are stressing you out.

6.4 Psychological Disorders

Psychological disorders are more commonly called **mental disorders**. Mental disorders are patterns of behavior or thought that cause the person experiencing them distress or harm.

Historically, the main method of understanding mental disorders has been the **biomedical model**. This model focuses on the biological causes of these disorders and generally seeks to treat them with drugs. The **biopsychosocial model**, on the other hand, looks at both the physiology and the cultural and social factors that play a role in the disorder, and often combines medicine with therapies and other non-pharmaceutical interventions.

There are two main systems used to classify mental disorders. The first is the **ICD (International Classification of Diseases)**. The ICD is created by the World Health Organization and is currently on its eleventh revision, called the ICD-11.

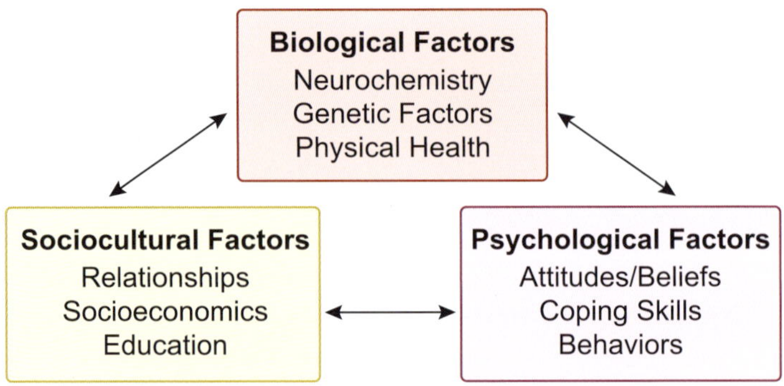

Biopsychosocial Model of Mental Health

The ICD is an international classification, while the second widely-used system is American. It is called the **DSM (Diagnostic and Statistical Manual of Mental Disorders)** and was last updated in 2022 to its revised fifth edition, the DSM-5-TR.

Both of these systems are maintained by large teams of experts in psychiatry, psychology, and other fields related to mental health, and are generally treated as the authoritative texts for the diagnosis of mental disorders. However, there is significant disagreement concerning what should be considered a disorder, what defines each disorder, and whether mental health issues can even be fit into distinct categories. Nevertheless, clinicians will generally refer to one or both of these manuals when considering which diagnosis, if any, is appropriate to give one of their patients.

Because of the complexity and controversy involved in diagnosing and classifying mental disorders, estimating how common a psychological disorder is has proven to be difficult. It is estimated that about 20% of all adults in the US have had a mental disorder in the past year, with young people, women, and people who report belonging to two or more racial groups having higher rates of disorder than other groups.

Types of Mental Disorders

The DSM-5 is nearly a thousand pages long, and it breaks mental disorders into 22 major categories. The most important disorders to know for the MCAT will be introduced here.

Neurodevelopmental disorders are disorders caused by abnormalities during the development of the nervous system. They include intellectual developmental disorder, language and speech disorders, autism spectrum disorder, and ADHD (attention-deficit/hyperactivity disorder), among others.

Schizophrenia is a disorder associated with **psychosis**, which is a loss of touch with reality. The symptoms of schizophrenia are generally sorted into three different categories: positive, negative, and cognitive.

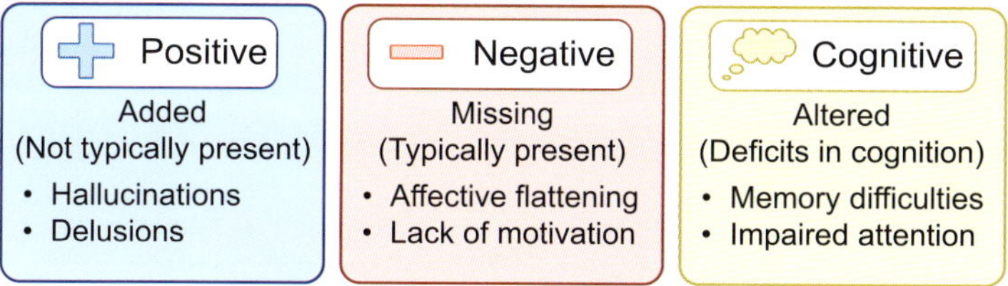

Symptoms of Schizophrenia

Positive symptoms do not get their name from their effect on a person's well-being, but instead from the fact that they represent "additions" to a person's experience. Hallucinations, delusions, and movement disorders are all examples of positive symptoms—things that start happening when a person has schizophrenia.

Negative symptoms are things that stop happening in many people with schizophrenia. In other words, they represent the loss of some abilities present in average people. Affective flattening (the loss of the ability to express emotions), avolition (the loss of the desire to accomplish goals or solve self-motivated problems), and alogia (loss of the ability to express oneself clearly verbally) are some of the negative symptoms of schizophrenia.

Cognitive symptoms are changes in a person's core thought processes and thinking abilities. These symptoms tend to be extremely resistant to current treatments, and include memory deficits, problems with paying attention, and impaired executive functioning.

Schizophrenia affects less than 1% of the population, and men tend to be diagnosed earlier than women are. People are normally diagnosed between the ages of 16 and 30, though both children and the elderly can develop the disorder. Before a person with schizophrenia has a psychotic episode, there tends to be a long period where mild delusions, hallucinations, etc. get worse and worse—this period is called the **prodrome**.

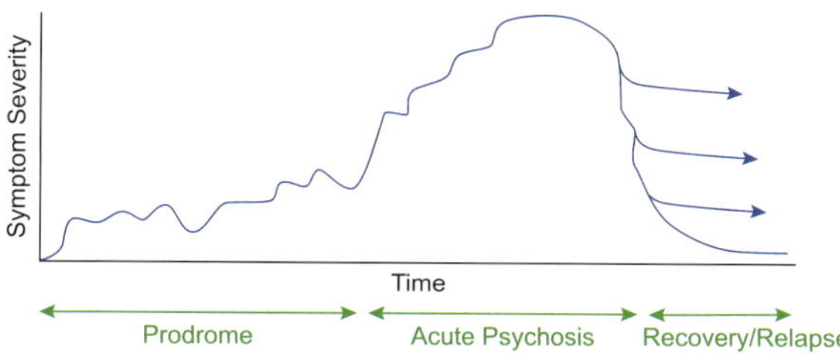

Psychosis Stages

Schizophrenia is associated with a greatly reduced life expectancy—about 20 years less than healthy individuals. This reduction in lifespan is almost entirely due to increased rates of suicide among people with schizophrenia—being male, having a high IQ, abusing drugs, and having other mental disorders all increase the risk of suicide.

Mood disorders, also known as affective disorders, is a category in which the primary symptoms are related to pervasive and marked disruptions in emotion. The two main subcategories are bipolar disorders and depressive disorders. The lifetime prevalence of any mood disorder among adults is approximately 20%.

Bipolar and related disorders are characterized by periods of depression and mania or hypomania. Mania is where a person has such high arousal (general energy levels) that it causes major problems in their life. People experiencing a manic episode tend to sleep less, develop grandiose thoughts (thinking they're capable of doing things they absolutely cannot do), and become easily distracted. Mania can also involve psychotic breaks, where a person loses touch with reality. Hypomania is less severe than mania in terms of intensity and thus involves less social and occupational disruption than mania. Bipolar I disorder requires at least one full manic episode, while bipolar II disorder requires at least one hypomanic episode, but never a full manic episode. The lifetime prevalence of bipolar I and bipolar II disorders are similar at approximately 0.5-1% each.

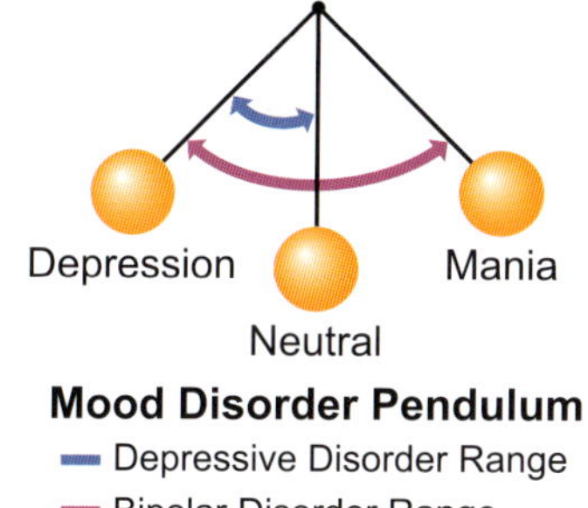

Mood Disorder Pendulum
- Depressive Disorder Range
- Bipolar Disorder Range

Depressive disorders are marked by problems caused by excessive feelings of sadness, emptiness, or irritability/anger. These feelings must last for two or more weeks to be considered disordered, but most depressive episodes last much longer than that. There are several different types of depressive disorders, and they are set apart from each other by their duration and severity. Major depressive disorder (MDD) is the most common and well-known. It has a lifetime prevalence of approximately 12%.

Anxiety disorders are diagnosed when people regularly experience excessive fear and worry. These symptoms can happen in response to specific triggers, such as using public transportation or seeing blood—this is called a (specific) **phobia**. Excessive anxiety can occur for no easily-observable reason, which is known as **generalized anxiety disorder**.

Generalized anxiety disorder is characterized by excessive and uncontrollable worries.

The symptoms of anxiety can be overwhelming, sudden, and inappropriate, presenting as a **panic disorder**. In addition to terror, people with panic disorders can experience symptoms that resemble a heart attack, including heart palpitations (feeling that your heartbeat is abnormal), chest pain, and a sense that they are about to die.

The lifetime prevalence of anxiety disorders in the U.S. adult population is the highest of any mental disorder at approximately 28.8%. The most common anxiety disorder is specific phobia (12.5% lifetime prevalence), followed by social anxiety disorder (12.1% lifetime prevalence), which is essentially a phobia related to social embarrassment. Generalized anxiety disorder (5.7% lifetime prevalence) and panic disorder (4.7% lifetime prevalence) are less prevalent, but still affect a large number of adults compared to most other mental disorders.

Obsessive-compulsive disorders are marked by, unsurprisingly, both obsessions and compulsions. Obsessions are strong thoughts or urges that are both persistent and hard to control, and compulsions are activities associated with these obsessions. For example, a person may have a recurring thought that he is physically unattractive, and this obsession causes him to excessively check his appearance in the mirror—an example of **body dysmorphic disorder**.

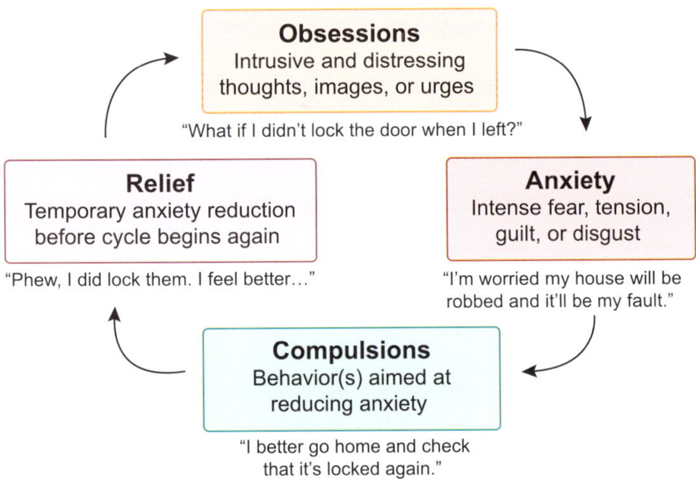

The OCD Cycle

Trauma-and stressor-related disorders are disorders that form after traumatic events. The most common of these disorders is **PTSD (posttraumatic stress disorder)**. Symptoms of PTSD can vary from vivid, unwanted memories of the traumatic event, to avoidance of triggers that prompt those memories, to negative changes in emotional regulation and sleep.

Dissociative disorders are typified by unpleasant or distressing changes in a person's identity or memory. These include forgetting important information about oneself in response to trauma, constantly feeling that one is an outside observer of one's own life, or exhibiting two or more distinct personalities.

Somatic symptom and related disorders are conditions associated with physical symptoms that are believed to be psychological in origin. In other words, the symptoms of these disorders resemble non-psychiatric illnesses, but the medical cause of their symptoms cannot be identified. An example of this is **conversion disorder (functional neurological symptom disorder)**, where patients experience neurological symptoms like paralysis or blindness that have no known medical cause and are linked to a psychological event.

It is also possible for people to falsify, exaggerate, or even create injuries or illnesses in themselves or others.. This somatic symptom disorder is technically called factitious disorder, but is often referred to as **Munchausen syndrome**. People with this condition are not consciously deceiving themselves or health care providers about their symptoms. It is very difficult to tell apart from **malingering**, where people knowingly invent symptoms in order to benefit themselves. The major difference is that the primary, albeit unconscious, goal of factitious disorder is receiving attention and sympathy as part of the "sick role," whereas the conscious goal of malingering is to receive secondary gains, such as insurance compensation following a car accident.

This flowchart below demonstrates the core differences between conversion disorder, factitious disorder, and malingering using an unexplained neurological symptom as an example (only conversion disorder requires neurological symptoms):

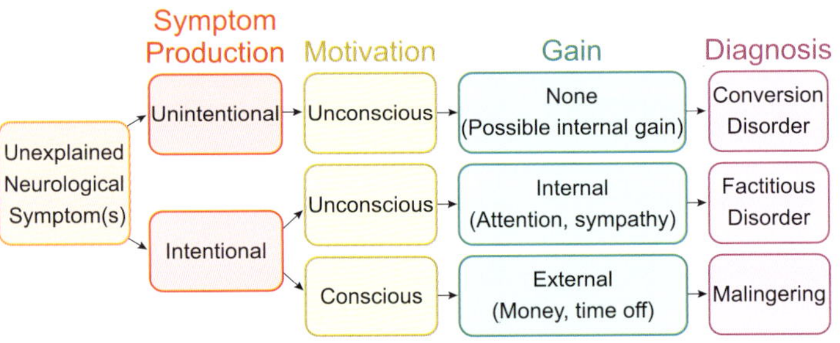

Feeding and eating disorders occur when people experience significant behavioral abnormalities related to the consumption of food. Some examples are anorexia nervosa, where people have an extreme fear of gaining weight, bulimia, where people eat large quantities of food at once and subsequently try to get it out of their bodies, and pica, in which people eat objects that are not food.

Distorted body image is a common feature of eating disorders, especially anorexia.

Sleep-wake disorders happen when a person's sleep is regularly disturbed to the point that it causes him issues and is not caused by external factors like environmental noise. Insomnia, narcolepsy, and obstructive sleep apnea are examples of sleep-wake disorders.

Neurocognitive disorders are disorders that affect learning, memory, and other aspects of cognition. Alzheimer's disease is the most common neurocognitive disorder.

Personality disorders are diagnosed when patients exhibit personalities socially unacceptable enough to cause stress or disability. They are characterized by enduring patterns of behavior and inner experiences that deviate significantly from an individual's cultural norms. The lifetime prevalence of any personality disorder is approximately 10%. These disorders are grouped into three categories, called cluster A, B, and C respectively.

People with **cluster A** personality disorders are generally viewed by others as strange or eccentric. The disorders in cluster A are:

1. **Paranoid personality disorder**, in which people are distrusting of others to an extreme degree.
2. **Schizoid personality disorder**, where people have nearly no interest in relationships with other people and do not display strong emotion.
3. **Schizotypal personality disorder**, characterized by strange beliefs, magical thinking, and "odd thinking and speech."

Cluster B personality disorders are linked by a tendency for people diagnosed with them to be seen as impulsive, dramatic, or self-destructive. The cluster B disorders are:

1. **Antisocial personality disorder**, where people show a near-total disregard for how their actions affect other people. It is associated with aggression, deceitfulness, and a lack of remorse.
2. **Borderline personality disorder**, typified by frantic efforts to avoid abandonment, self-destructive impulsivity, anger, and recurrent suicidal behavior.

Borderline personality disorder involves unstable mood and relationships.

3. **Histrionic personality disorder**, characterized by theatricalism, discomfort if not at the center of attention, and shallow / inconsistent emotions.
4. **Narcissistic personality disorder**, in which people have an inflated sense of self-importance, display entitlement, lack empathy, and are preoccupied with high status and success. It is perhaps the defining personality disorder of our time.

Cluster C personality disorders manifest to other people as excessively fearful or worried. They are:

1. **Avoidant personality disorder**, in which people consistently avoid situations because they are concerned about getting criticized.
2. **Dependent personality disorder**, where people are extremely reliant on other people, seek constant reassurance, avoid judgment, and are afraid of being alone.
3. **Obsessive-compulsive personality disorder**, which is *different* from OCD (obsessive-compulsive disorder). It is characterized by perfectionism, a preoccupation with rules, lists, etc., excessive devotion to work or productivity, miserliness, and a tendency towards hoarding.

Biological Bases of Nervous System Disorders

Almost every nervous system disorder is caused by a combination of factors. These ultimately boil down to genetics and the environment, both of which can cause changes in a person's physiology—different changes are associated with different disorders.

The Biology of Schizophrenia

The brains of people with schizophrenia have been shown to be structurally different from people without the disorder. Some brain regions, such as the hippocampus, amygdala, thalamus, and nucleus accumbens are smaller than in healthy individuals, while other regions are larger. Additionally, the cerebral cortexes of people with schizophrenia tend to be thinner than those of healthy people, and the brain tends to have less volume in people with schizophrenia than in average people.

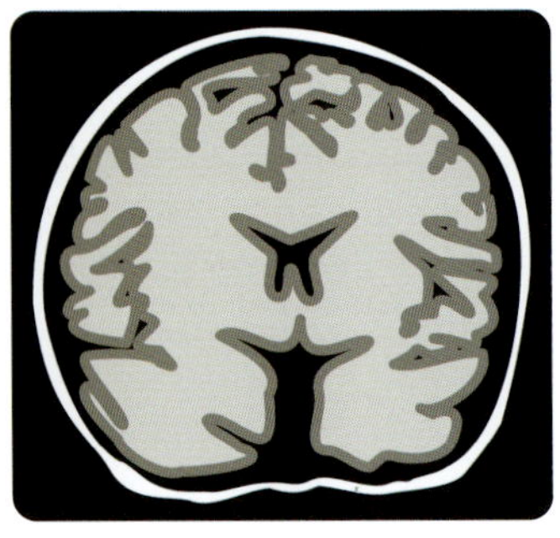

Control (healthy)

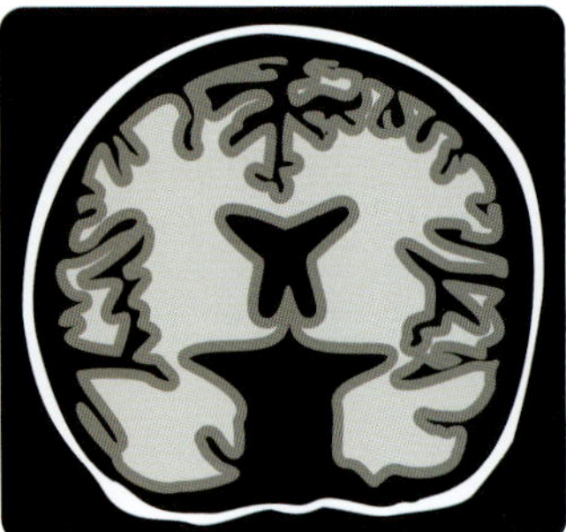

Schizophrenia

There are also changes in brain activity observed in schizophrenia, as well as differences in the amount of neurotransmitters in the brain. Patients with schizophrenia tend to have lower levels of activity in their prefrontal cortexes, thalamae, and other areas. They also tend to have more dopamine receptors and fewer glutamate receptors, leading to two different theories to explain the cognitive changes associated with schizophrenia. These are called the dopamine hypothesis of schizophrenia and the glutamate hypothesis of schizophrenia respectively.

The **dopamine hypothesis of schizophrenia** links excessive dopaminergic signaling to the positive and negative symptoms of schizophrenia. That is, the neurons that are supposed to fire when they take up dopamine are firing more often in people with schizophrenia than in healthy people. The positive symptoms are tied to abnormal activity in the **mesolimbic (reward) pathway.** while the negative symptoms are connected to dysfunction in the **mesocortical pathway**—one of the four dopamine pathways mentioned earlier in this chapter.

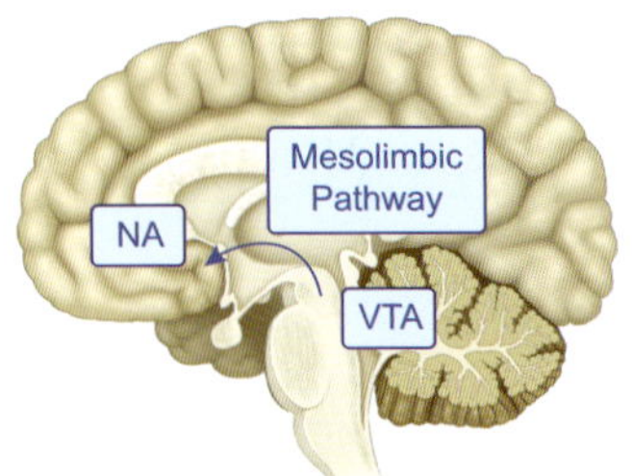

Mesolimbic Pathway (Positive Symptoms)

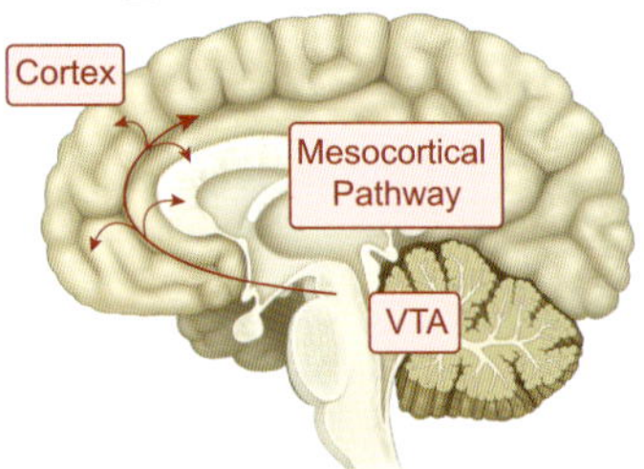

Mesocortical Pathway (Negative and Cognitive Symptoms)

Schizophrenia Dopamine Symptoms

The **glutamate hypothesis of schizophrenia** proposes that both dopamine and glutamate work together to cause the symptoms of schizophrenia. It came about after researchers found that people with schizophrenia tend to have reduced glutamatergic signaling in their brains, and has been supported by fMRI and genetic evidence.

The causes of schizophrenia are currently unknown. It is thought that both genetic and environmental factors contribute to its development, and a number of specific risk factors have been identified. However, most people with a genetic predisposition for schizophrenia do not go on to develop the disorder—the same is true for people raised in environments that increase the risk of schizophrenia.

The Biology of Depression

Over the years, many different theories have been made to explain where depression comes from. Along the way, differences between the brains of depressed people and healthy people have been found. At a structural level, depression is associated with decreases in gray matter in the prefrontal cortex and some subcortical areas, such as the structures of the limbic system. It is also linked to degradation of white matter in certain areas, especially the corpus callosum. Many of the areas that tend to be different between depressed people and healthy people are connected with emotional regulation and responding to stress.

The neural pathways involved in depression are extremely complicated. Historically, their activity in depression has been explained by the **monoamine hypothesis of depression**, which argues that depression is caused by deficits in monoamine neurotransmitters, such as dopamine, serotonin, and norepinephrine. This theory has been challenged by two other theories: the neuroplasticity hypothesis and the neurogenesis hypothesis.

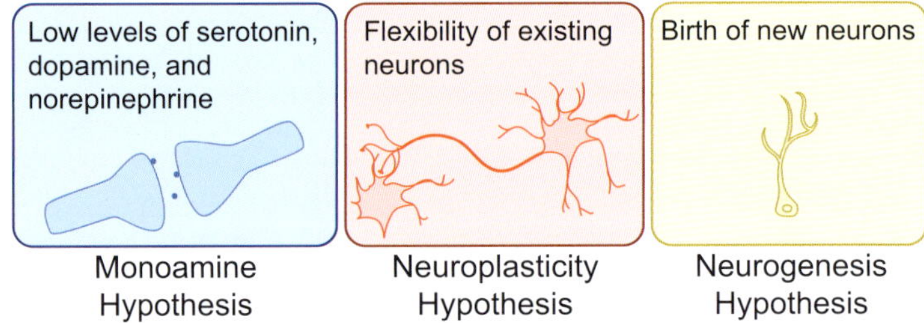

Biological Depression Theories

The **neuroplasticity hypothesis** posits that the chronic stress caused by depression causes neurons in the brain to atrophy (weaken and die) and that antidepressants work by reversing this process. The **neurogenesis hypothesis** states that depression prevents new neurons from being made (neurogenesis) in the brain and that antidepressants indirectly promote the creation of new neurons.

Like with schizophrenia, the causes of depression are unclear at present. Depression seems to be partially hereditary, and the risk is passed down both genetically and epigenetically. Environmental factors, like childhood abuse, neglect, and family dysfunction all increase the risk of depression. Serious adverse life events and some medications can also make someone more likely to become depressed.

The Biology of Alzheimer's Disease

Alzheimer's disease (AD) is thought to be caused by the buildup of **amyloid plaques** and **neurofibrillary tangles** in the brain. Amyloid plaques are mostly made up of **beta (Aβ) proteins** that accumulate in the brain's gray matter, while neurofibrillary tangles are composed of hyperphosphorylated **tau proteins** located on the inside of brain cells. These plaques and tangles interfere with neuronal function and communication, and the more of them that form, the worse the disease tends to get.

Why these plaques and tangles form in the first place is unknown. Some lifestyle factors, such as regular exercise, cognitive activity (playing chess, etc.), and having a large social network are associated with a reduced risk of dementia. There is no cure for AD, but some medications have been developed to help treat symptoms of the disease.

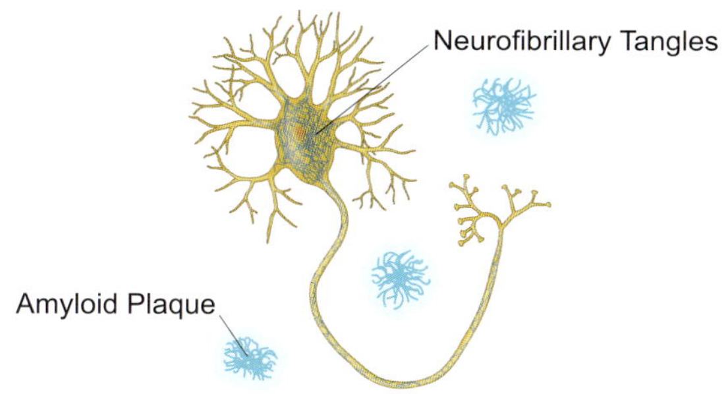

The Biology of Parkinson's Disease

Parkinson's disease is a progressive (gets worse over time) nervous system disease. It usually affects motor functions first, causing slow movements and a distinctive "pill-rolling tremor," before eventually leading to postural instability, increasing the risk of falls. Cognitive and behavioral changes are common, especially in later stages of the disease. Most people with Parkinson's will go on to develop dementia—many patients will also suffer from deficits in executive functioning and from psychosis. Parkinson's is inevitably fatal, and patients live about ten years on average after being diagnosed with the disease.

Parkinson's disease is probably caused by the death of dopaminergic (dopamine-secreting) neurons that project from the substantia nigra to the **basal ganglia**, which results in insufficient dopamine available for motor functions. When these neurons are examined, clumps of a protein called **α-synuclein** are visible inside—these clumps are called **Lewy bodies**.

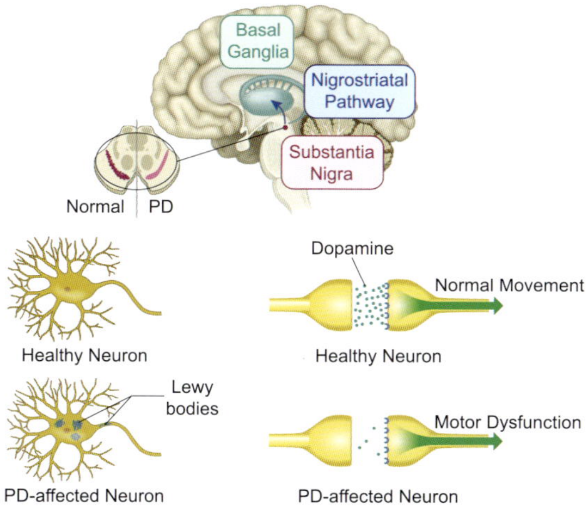

Parkinson's disease cannot be cured, but it can be treated. The most common medication used for this purpose is L-dopa, which is a precursor of dopamine that gets broken down into dopamine in the brain. Both genes and some environmental factors, such as drinking well water or pesticide exposure, have been linked to the development of Parkinson's.

Because Parkinson's disease is thought to be caused solely by the death of dopaminergic neurons in the brain, scientists are trying to find a way to replace the lost neurons. The most promising method of doing so is by using **stem cells**. These cells are able to differentiate into different types of cells, including dopaminergic neurons. However, generating stem cells that do not become cancerous has proven challenging, and while stem cell grafts have been successfully performed on animals, these treatments have not yet been carried out on humans.

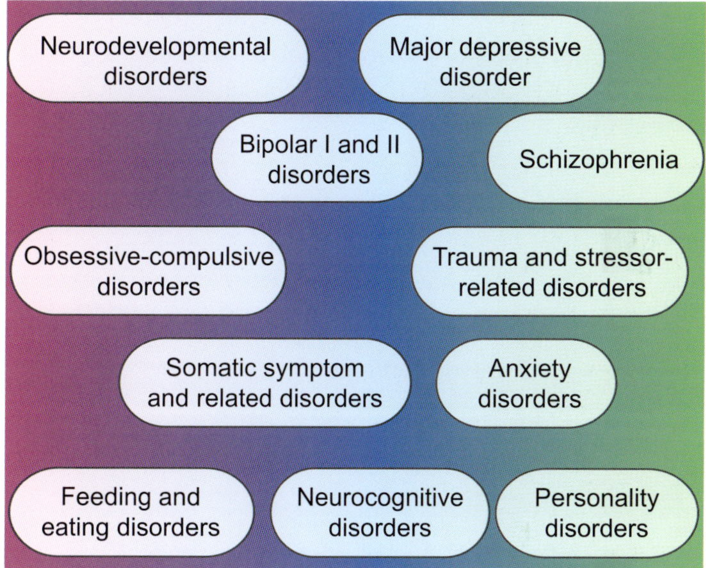

PSY

Learning and Identity Formation

7

7.1 Learning Theories

Nonassociative and Associative Learning

"Learning" is an imprecise term whose meaning changes depending upon what theory is being addressed. A behaviorist definition for "learning" is an adaptive physical change in the nervous system resulting in changes in behavior. The changes are evoked by a stimulus. Once learning has occurred, exposure to the same stimulus results in a different response. A **stimulus** can be anything that can be sensed by an individual.

> Don't forget that theories in psychology evolve and change. This means that definitions must be flexible as well. Don't expect each theory to agree perfectly with the last.

> Learning starts with a stimulus. It causes a physical change in your nervous system. This physical change causes you to behave differently in the future when you are exposed to that same stimulus again.

Nonassociative learning is an increase or decrease in response due usually to repeated applications of a single stimulus that is not linked to any other stimulus. Habituation, dishabituation, and sensitization are types of nonassociative learning.

Nonassociative Learning

Sensitization

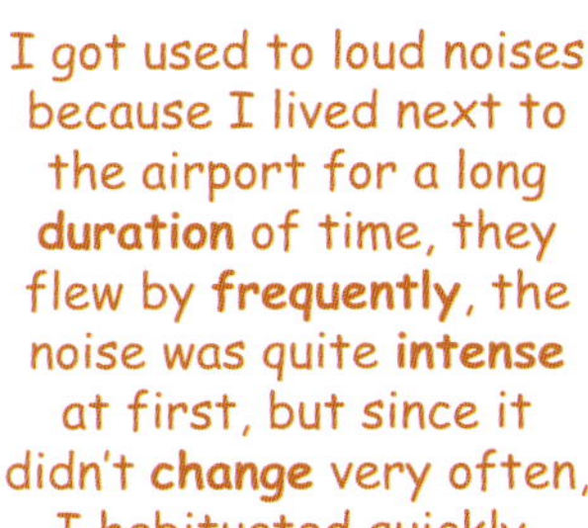

Habituation

Associative Learning

Classical Conditioning

Operant Conditioning
(Reinforcement s & Punishments)

Operant Conditioning
(Schedules of Reinforcement)

Nonassociative learning usually takes place gradually. A notable exception is sometimes seen in the case of sensitization, but we'll talk about that later.

Associative learning occurs when new information is acquired due to a connection between two things. The two things might be two stimuli, as in classical conditioning, or a consequence and a stimulus, as in operant conditioning.

The "nonassociative" part of nonassociative learning is tricky. Classical conditioning has an association between two stimuli. Nonassociative learning involves only one stimulus, so there can be no association.

Habituation, Dishabituation, and Sensitization

Upon repeated and prolonged applications of an irrelevant stimulus, an individual's response gradually decreases. This is known as **habituation** and is an example of nonassociative learning.

Imagine loud construction taking place outside a person's window while he is trying to study. At first it interferes with his concentration, but once he has been studying for a while he habituates to the noise—he is no longer aware that he hears it.

Habituation occurs in the presence of an unchanging repeated stimulus without punishment or reward. It is one of the simplest and most common forms of learning. It allows an individual to ignore unimportant, repetitive stimuli in favor of more important, sporadic stimuli. Habituation does not require intent or even awareness. It always involves a decrease in response, and never an increase. It can last hours, days, or even weeks, but recovery is spontaneous—in other words, if the stimulus is stopped, the response automatically returns to normal over time.

Four factors affect habituation.

1. **Duration**—If the stimulus is not applied for a long enough duration, reintroduction will produce *spontaneous recovery* of the response.
2. **Frequency**—The more frequent the stimulus, the faster the habituation.
3. **Intensity**—The more intense the stimulus, the slower the habituation.
4. **Change**—Changing the intensity or duration can erase the effect of habituation.

The more often it happens, the more I get used to it. But if it's really harsh, or it keeps changing, I just can't habituate to it.

During the process of habituation, a new stimulus can temporarily remove the effects of habituation. For instance, a person working near a construction site may become habituated to the sound of constant hammering. However, if some other obtrusive construction noise arises and then vanishes, the person may suddenly notice the hammering again. This temporary phenomenon of renewed response to the habituated stimulus is called **dishabituation**. Dishabituation is another example of nonassociative learning.

Think of dishabituation as the sudden temporary removal of habituation due to another stimulus.

Don't confuse dishabituation with extinction. Dishabituation is not just the return of a response due to the removal of the habituated stimulus. Dishabituation requires a NEW stimulus that draws attention to the habituated stimulus.

Sensitization occurs when the repeated application of a stimulus leads to a progressively stronger response. An example of sensitization happens in neurons involved in learning and memory. When groups of neurons fire at the same time, those same groups of neurons become more likely to fire together again later—this process forms a positive feedback loop. Sensitization is also a type of nonassociative learning.

7.2 Classical Conditioning

Classical conditioning is a form of associative learning that changes involuntary behavior. It was first described by Ivan Pavlov. In classical conditioning, an unconditioned stimulus transfers its conditioned response to a neutral stimulus. An **unconditioned stimulus (UCS)** is a stimulus that naturally (without learning) produces a response. When a dog sees a piece of meat, he salivates. The meat is an unconditioned stimulus. Salivation is an **unconditioned response (UCR)**—no conditioning is required for the meat to produce salivation.

On its own, ringing a bell does not automatically make a dog salivate. The bell ringing starts out as a **neutral stimulus (NS)**—it does not evoke the desired response. But when bell ringing is paired with the sight of meat, the dog salivates. When the bell ringing is paired with the meat over and over again, the dog learns to associate the bell ringing with the sight of meat, and the dog will salivate when he hears the bell ringing, even though he doesn't see the meat. The salivation has now become the **conditioned response (CR)**—the dog has learned (been conditioned) to respond by salivating when the bell rings. The bell ringing is now a **conditioned stimulus (CS)**—a stimulus that evokes a learned behavior. Each exposure to the stimulus is called a **trial**. **Acquisition** is the point when the NS becomes the CS.

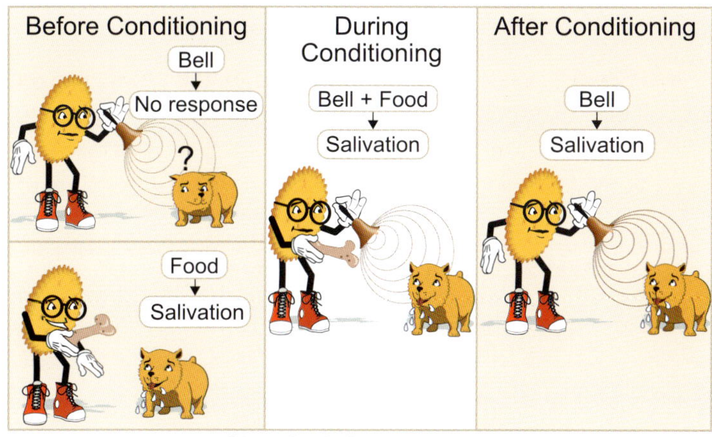

Classical Conditioning

"Conditioned" is another word for "learned". "Unconditioned" means that it happens naturally without learning. Notice that the bell ringing has gone from a neutral stimulus to a conditioned stimulus. Salivation is an unconditioned response when evoked by the meat, but is a conditioned response when evoked by the bell ringing.

As the bell rings over and over without the dog seeing the meat, the salivation gradually decreases and eventually disappears altogether. This extinguishing of the CR is called **extinction**. However, if the dog is allowed to rest following extinction, the CR may return spontaneously. This is called **spontaneous recovery**. Repeating extinction and spontaneous recovery leads to a decrease in the intensity of the CR.

I used to salivate whenever I heard a bell, but now it's totally extinct.

Ah, but have you tried to elicit the renewal effect by returning to the lab?

Interestingly, if the CR is extinguished in a different environment than it was acquired, it may come back upon returning to the original environment. This phenomenon is called the **renewal effect**. For instance, if the dog is removed from the laboratory, he will eventually stop salivating when he hears a bell ringing. But, if the dog is returned to the laboratory, the salivation might return spontaneously due to the renewal effect.

Stimulus generalization is when a different (yet similar) stimulus evokes the CR. For instance, if the bell ringing were replaced by a buzzer that sounded somewhat similar to the bell, the dog might still salivate. If so, that would be an example of stimulus generalization. The buzzer becomes a CS, even though it was never paired with the meat.

Stimulus generalization should not be confused with **higher-order conditioning**. In higher-order conditioning, a

CS can be used to condition an NS. The bell ringing evokes salivation, so, just like the meat was used to condition the dog to salivate when he heard the bell ringing, the bell ringing can be used to condition the dog to salivate whenever he sees a red light. The red light (the NS) is acquired as a new CS without reliance upon the meat (the UCS).

Don't confuse stimulus generalization with higher-order conditioning. In the dog experiment, stimulus generalization happened because the buzzer and the bell ringing were similar and the dog basically confused the two. Higher-order conditioning happened because the dog was classically conditioned a second time to associate the bell ringing with the red light.

Stimulus discrimination is the opposite of stimulus generalization. **Stimulus discrimination** is the ability to learn to discriminate between similar CSs. In another experiment with dogs, the dogs were conditioned to salivate at the sight of a circle. In an example of stimulus generalization, they salivated at an ellipse as well. When the ellipse was not paired with the meat, the dogs learned to discriminate between the circle and the ellipse and only salivated at the sight of the circle.

Classical Conditioning and Therapy

Classical conditioning is used in various therapies. **Aversive conditioning** attempts to change a behavior by associating an undesired behavior NS with an unpleasant experience UCR. For instance, to stop someone from biting their nails (NS) the nails might be painted with a bad tasting polish (UCS) that causes disgust (UCR). If the nail biting becomes associated with the bad taste, the nail biting becomes the CS and the disgust becomes the CR. The behavior is discouraged.

Graduated exposure therapy or **systematic desensitization** gradually substitutes the anxiety response with a relaxation response. It is a treatment for phobia. There are three phases.

1. Reciprocal inhibition: a relaxation response replaces the anxiety response;
2. Fear hierarchy list: exposures are listed in graduated order from least anxiety producing to most anxiety producing;
3. Actual exposure: the patient works his way up the list while practicing replacement of the anxiety response with the relaxation response.

While systematic desensitization (graduated exposure) goes through all of these stages, implosive therapy begins at 3a and flooding begins at 3b.

When aversive therapy is done suddenly, it is called flooding or implosion therapy. The two techniques are not the same. In **flooding**, the patient is usually exposed to the actual object of his fear or an image of the object. In **implosive therapy**, the patient is typically asked to imagine the object of his fear. Additionally, implosion therapy relies upon psychodynamic approaches to deal with the accompanying anxiety.

Counterconditioning is where an unwanted response to a stimulus is replaced by a desired response. This is done by observing the original stimulus/response pair and adding a second stimulus designed to counteract the original stimulus.

For example, imagine a child learning what different animals look like. When he's in the learning process, if pictures of the animals are paired with pictures of scared human faces, he will come to associate the animals with being scary. After this association is formed, it can be reversed through counterconditioning—instead of pairing the animal pictures with a scared face, they can be paired with a smiling face. Over time, the child will associate the animals with smiling instead of being scary.

7.3 Operant Conditioning

Operant conditioning is a type of associative learning that focuses on voluntary behavior. It was first described by B. F. Skinner as, "active behavior that operates upon the environment to generate consequences." In operant conditioning, a response is followed by a consequence. The response is active voluntary behavior, and the consequence shapes the response.

For example, the response might be a rat in a Skinner box (a box that can both detect a desired behavior and reward the animal inside for doing so) pushing a lever. The consequence is that the rat is rewarded with a food pellet. The rat learns to associate the response with the consequence—the consequence shapes the response.

In operant conditioning, the consequence is really just an anticipated stimulus that comes after the response. The sooner after the consequence that the response occurs, the better operant conditioning works.

There are two types of consequences: reinforcement and punishment. Reinforcement is intended to encourage behavior or make a response more likely. Punishment is intended to discourage behavior or make a response less likely. Each type of consequence can be positive or negative. **Positive** means that a stimulus is added, **negative** means that a stimulus is removed.

Reinforcement makes a response more likely by rewarding it. The reward can be positive, the addition of something positive like food, or negative, the removal of something causing pain. In order to teach a rat in a Skinner box to push a lever, each time he pushes the lever either a food pellet can be given (positive reinforcement) or an electric shock can be discontinued (negative reinforcement).

Punishment makes a response less likely by punishing the response. The punishment may be positive, addition of something unpleasant like a beating, or it may be negative, such as the removal of privileges.

Reinforcement and punishment both work to shape behavior, but studies indicate that positive reinforcement is a much more effective tool than punishment for establishing desirable behavior patterns. If you want to teach Fido to sit, you should reward him with a treat immediately after he sits, rather than chiding him for standing up.

Reinforcement encourages, punishment discourages. Positive adds, negative subtracts. Reinforcement: I add something good or subtract something bad. Punishment: I add something bad, or subtract something good.

Reinforcers and punishments can be primary or secondary. A **primary reinforcer** is natural or innately rewarding, such as food, sleep, and sex. A **secondary reinforcer** requires conditioning to be rewarding. Secondary reinforcers are things like money, attention, and praise. A **primary punisher** is naturally or innately unpleasant, like pain, extreme heat, and bodily harm. A **secondary punisher** requires conditioning to be unpleasant. Secondary punishers are things like criticism, demerits, and mean looks.

Secondary reinforcers are sometimes called conditioned reinforcers because they are only rewarding because the individual has been conditioned to think so.

Acquisition in operant conditioning takes place through a process called **shaping**. In shaping, reinforcers are given for approximations of the desired response. The desired response is called the **target response**. Over time, the approximations must become more accurate representations of the desired response in order to earn a reinforcer. Eventually, the desired response is acquired.

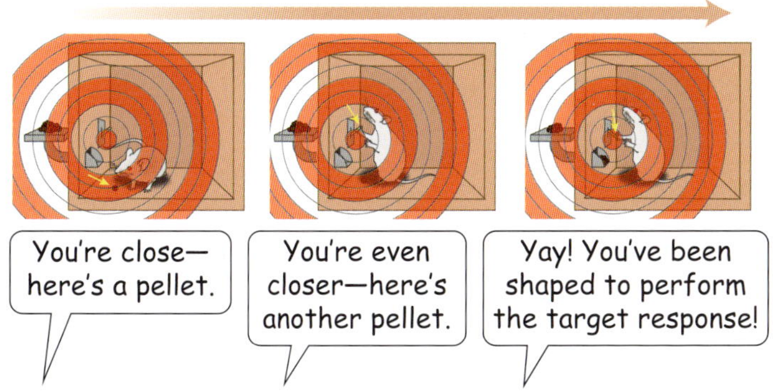

An example of shaping might be as follows: the target response is for a rat to push a lever. When the rat is first placed in the Skinner box, he is given a reinforcer for approaching the lever. As he learns to approach the lever, he is gradually only given a reinforcer for touching the lever. As he learns to touch the lever, he is gradually only given a reinforcer for pushing the lever. His behavior has been shaped to achieve the target response of pushing the lever.

Extinction also occurs with operant conditioning. When the reinforcer is removed, there may be a brief increase in the response before it gradually extinguishes (referred to as an **extinction burst**). Extinction bursts are evident in human behavior.

For instance, imagine someone trying to quit smoking. His doctor prescribes him the medication varenicline, which binds to the same receptors in the brain that nicotine does. This prevents the association of smoking with a pleasant feeling, and generally leads to the individual lowering his tobacco consumption.

After several days of tapering off cigarettes, however, an individual may end up smoking more tobacco than he did before starting treatment for a short period of time. Effectively, he is binging on cigarettes, even though the medication he's taking stops him from enjoying smoking—this is the extinction burst. After it ends, he is likely to quit smoking for good.

When an individual acquires a response that decreases or ends an unpleasant stimulus, he has exhibited **escape learning.** A person who learns to walk away from conversations whenever they turn unpleasant is exhibiting escape learning.

Avoidance learning is similar to escape learning, but the response occurs before the aversive stimulus is applied. In **avoidance learning**, the individual responds in order to avoid an aversive stimulus. A man who wants to avoid arguments with his wife may recognize cues from his wife that indicate that a discussion is about to become an argument. If he responds by walking away, he is exhibiting avoidance learning. Both avoidance learning and escape learning result from negative reinforcement, because they are rewarded by the removal of something bad.

Avoidance behaviors can be addictive because they are intrinsic reinforcers (the behavior is the reinforcer). Individuals who practice avoidance behavior are rewarded for never responding in the alternative. Whether or not the unpleasant consequence would have occurred is unknown and remains untested as long as the avoidance behavior is practiced. Perhaps the cues given by the wife no longer accurately foreshadow an argument. The man is unlikely to ever find out because he is rewarded for never finding out. Avoidance behavior demonstrates why phobias can be difficult to cure. Someone who has a phobia of dentists, for instance, is rewarded for avoiding the dentist (at least until he gets a bad cavity!)

> Phobias are not caused by avoidance behavior. They are simply made more difficult to cure by the avoidance behavior. Phobias are caused by classical conditioning.

Reinforcement and Punishment Schedules

Reinforcement and punishment schedules are the rules specifying when a reinforcer or punishment is provided as a consequence. An example of a reinforcement schedule would be the number of times that the rat must push the lever in order to receive a pellet.

Reinforcement and punishment can be continuous or intermittent. In either case, reinforcers are only provided upon performance of the target response. **Continuous** means that the reinforcer is provided each time the target response is performed. A continuous schedule is useful when training a new behavior because it creates a strong association between the behavior and the target response. A drawback to continuous reinforcement is that saturation may occur where the reinforcer loses its appeal. Extinction also tends to happen more rapidly after a continuous schedule.

Intermittent (also called partial) means that sometimes when the target response is performed, the reinforcer is not provided. Intermittent schedules are more common in everyday life. For instance, most people get paid at regular intervals rather than every time they show up for work.

Intermittent schedules can be divided into ratio schedules and interval schedules. Ratio schedules are based on the number of target responses, while interval schedules are based on time. Both of these are divided again into fixed and variable schedules. Each type of reinforcement schedule has an identifiable pattern of responses.

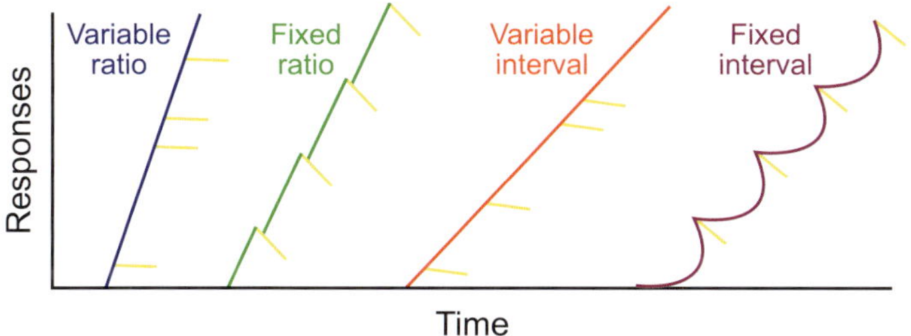

In a **fixed-ratio schedule** the target response earns a reinforcer every nth time it is performed. There is a fixed ratio of unreinforced to reinforced target responses. For instance, a three-to-one ratio means that three target responses are required before a fourth target response produces a reinforcer. A fixed-ratio schedule results in a brief drop-off of responses after each reinforcer, followed by an increase until the next reinforcer. Some sales bonuses are on fixed-ratio schedules where the salesman is paid for every third or fourth sale.

Ratio = # of Responses

In a **variable-ratio schedule** the target response earns a reinforcer, on average, every nth time it is performed. For instance, a three-to-one variable-ratio schedule earns three reinforcers for 12 target responses, but the three target responses to be rewarded are chosen at random. They could be the 1st, 5th, and 9th responses, or the 2nd, 9th and 12th responses. The only certainty is that there will be, on average, one reinforcer per every four target responses. A variable-ratio schedule results in a rapid, steady response rate and is the most resistant to extinction of the reinforcement schedules. Gambling is an example of a variable-ratio schedule—this is one reason why gambling can be addictive.

Variable = Varies (changes)

Fixed-ratio

Variable-ratio

Fixed-interval

Variable-interval

In a **fixed-interval schedule**, only the first target response performed after a fixed interval of time earns a reinforcer. For instance, if the interval is two minutes, each time a reinforcer is given, no additional reinforcer may be given for any response for the next two minutes. After two minutes have elapsed, the next target response receives a reinforcer. A fixed-interval schedule results in a strong drop off after each reinforcer, followed by an increase until the next reinforcer. Pay periods are typically fixed-ratio schedules.

Fixed = consistent Format

In a **variable-interval schedule**, only the first target response performed after a variable interval of time earns a reinforcer. The time intervals will have a predetermined average. For instance, if the average interval is two minutes, then after any reinforcer is given, no reinforcer may be given for any response for a random interval of time. The average of the random time intervals must be two minutes. After the random interval of time, the next target response receives a reinforcer. A variable-interval schedule results in a steady response rate with a good resistance to extinction. Checking your email is typically done on a variable-interval schedule—receiving an email is the reinforcer.

InTerval = Time

Ratio schedules tend to produce more target responses in less time than interval schedules. Variable schedules tend to produce responses that are difficult to extinguish.

Variables can't be Vanquished, and Ratios are Rapid. So Variable Ratio schedules are Very Rapid.

Latent Learning

Latent learning occurs without stimulus or reward. Behavior change in latent learning is delayed, and the change is not expressed until it is required. Environmental cues are acquired from the environment passively. Individuals who live in an area for a period of time become familiar with the area without intentional memorization.

Edward Tolman investigated latent learning with his rat-maze experiment. Rats were divided into three groups. For ten days, the first group was given a reward for navigating a maze, while the other two groups were not. Of course, the first group quickly learned the maze. During the second ten days, the second group was also given a reward for navigating the maze. The second group learned the maze much faster than the first group had learned the maze. The performance of the third group, which had not been given a reward, remained negligible.

This result demonstrated that the second group had learned something about the maze during the first ten days despite receiving no reinforcers. Tolman argued that during the first ten days, they had created a **cognitive map** of the maze allowing them to navigate more quickly once a reinforcer made it desirable to do so. The formation of a cognitive map is an example of latent learning.

The Role of Cognition in Conditioning

As thinking in psychology evolves, theories change. Classical conditioning used to be thought of as an association between the stimulus and the response— the meat and the salivation. Toward the end of the 20th century, that thinking shifted to viewing classical conditioning as an association between the stimulus and the expected stimulus; the bell ringing and the meat. When the dog hears the bell, he expects to see the meat, and, as a result, he involuntarily starts to salivate. This process involves a cognitive process.

The same is true for operant conditioning. Originally thought of as an association between the response and the consequence absent any cognitive expectation, the association is now considered to be between the response and the expected outcome. The rat pushes the lever because he expects a pellet. This association also involves a cognitive process.

There is still disagreement as to whether or not all learning in humans requires cognitive processes, but there is probably no question that classical conditioning and operant conditioning, at least very often, involve cognitive processes.

When you think about how to identify the cognitive process in conditioning, the key word is EXPECTATION. Rather than simple reflex, there is thinking about the future; there is expectation.

7.4 Biological Processes Affecting Associative Learning

Innate learning or behavior refers to behavior controlled mostly by genes and receives little influence from the environment. Innate behavior is instinctual. Innate behaviors are "hard-wired," so, although they are likely to be performed correctly the first time, they are inflexible. Learned behavior, on the other hand, is less reliable, but is adaptable to the environment.

Most behavior is a combination of innate and learned elements. Since so many behaviors have strong innate elements, certain behaviors are more easily conditioned in certain animals.

Although it might seem that given enough time and pellets a rat can be conditioned to do anything, it turns out that **biological predisposition** (also called **biological preparedness**) both limits and facilitates learning within a given species. Associations that are part of an animal's natural world are easier to learn than those that are not. Animals have evolved to be genetically predisposed to certain behaviors. Such behaviors are more susceptible to conditioning.

Biological predisposition refers to the fact that there are some tricks that you just can't teach a rat.

Biology predisposition can interfere with conditioning through **instinctive drift**. Under certain conditions and over time, instinctual behavior tends to replace learned behavior. A dog trained not to bark may bark anyway when exposed to stressful conditions. The behavior of wild animals kept as pets is unpredictable due to instinctive drift.

Biological Predisposition in Taste Aversion

When an individual becomes ill after eating a food and afterward avoids that food, that is a classically conditioned **taste aversion**. One thing that makes this an unusual example of classical conditioning is that it requires just one trial. Another thing is that eating the food and the illness may occur several hours apart. The conditioning can occur even when the individual is certain that the food did not cause the illness. The condition can last from days to years.

Taste aversion is a type of classical conditioning to which most animals are biologically pre disposed.

The type of neutral stimulus plays an important role in taste aversion. In the wild, eating poisonous food is not a mistake an animal can afford to make too often. It is likely that taste aversion evolved as a protection mechanism against eating poisonous foods. Animals have become biologically predisposed to be conditioned in this manner.

If a taste has been previously tried and found NOT to cause illness, the taste is resistant to becoming a conditioned stimulus in taste aversion. Taste aversion is inhibited when the taste involved is not novel. This phenomenon is called **latent inhibition**. A latent memory for a taste inhibits the individual from associating that taste with the illness. The more familiar the taste, the greater the inhibition. This makes sense when considering taste aversion as a protection mechanism. Known tastes that have not caused illness in the past should not be poisonous now. Latent inhibition occurs in all types of classical conditioning, not just taste aversion.

7.5 Observational Learning

Learning is not limited to classical and operant conditioning mechanisms. In **observational learning**, an individual can change his behavior based on his observation of the behavior of another individual. In other words, a change in behavior (learning) can take place without direct experience with the classical conditioning stimulus or the operant conditioning consequence. Individual A learns by observing the learning process of individual B. In this case, individual B is called the **model**.

Observational learning proposed an important difference between itself and traditional theories of conditioning—observational learning emphasizes the importance of cognition in learning. Mediation between the stimulus and the response is an important cognitive process in observational learning. The observer does not automatically imitate observed behavior—there is thinking involved. As discussed above, nowadays, modern psychologists agree that cognition plays a role in classical and operant conditioning as well.

Albert Bandura proposed a **social cognitive theory** which identifies four mental processes that must take place after exposure to the stimulus and before learning takes place.

1. **Attention**: The observer must be paying attention. This may be influenced by the extent to which the observer identifies with the model.
2. **Retention**: The observer must remember the behavior.
3. **Production**: The observer must be able to produce the response. Physical or mental limitations may prevent the observer from attempting the behavior.
4. **Motivation**: The observer must be motivated to copy the behavior. Rewards and punishment will be considered here.

If Salty brings cookies to his boss, it demonstrates he was paying **attention** to the model; **retained** the memory that his boss loved when the model brought cookies; was able to **produce** the behavior by bringing in cookies, and **motivated** to do so because the model was rewarded.

PARM: **P**roduction, **A**ttention, **R**etention, **M**otivation. These four components represent the thinking process that distinguishes observational learning from conditioning, the cognitive model from the behaviorist model. Recall that in the behaviorist model, these processes are in the "black box" that can't be accessed, and so shouldn't be considered.

When an observer places himself in the position of the person (called the social target) who he is observing and believes he is feeling the same emotions as that person, those feelings are called **empathic emotions**. There are **mirror neurons** in humans (and all primates) that fire both when the person performs a behavior and when he sees another person perform the behavior. This phenomenon is called **mirroring**. There is a slightly different phenomenon called **mentalizing** that occurs when the observer feels the emotions that he thinks the social target *should* feel, but the social target may or may not actually feel. These feelings are called **vicarious emotions**. Empathic emotions are a subset of vicarious emotions.

For instance, the social target may be the joker at a party who unwittingly makes a fool of himself. While the observer is embarrassed for the social target, the social target is not embarrassed for himself. The observer may or may not understand the real feelings of the social target, but he still feels the embarrassment that he thinks the social target should feel. This is mentalizing, and the emotions are vicarious. If the social target is actually embarrassed, then this is mirroring, and the emotions are empathic.

HA HA HA! Okay, here's an even better joke! Did you hear the one about the...

Through mentalizing, my vicarious emotion right now is deep embarrassment. Talk about cringeworthy!

"Monkey see, monkey do." If you only remember one thing here, make it that vicarious emotions cause some of the same neurons to fire in the observer's brain as would fire if he were performing the behavior himself.

The discovery of mirror neurons lends support to social cognitive theory because if the same thing is happening in the brain of an animal being conditioned as in the brain of an animal observing that conditioning, both animals would be expected to be conditioned in the same way.

My behavior is based on reciprocal determinism—I did it because I personally think it's funny and the situation called for humor.

Ha ha!

Ha ha!

Hmm..

Ha ha!

Ha ha!

Observer

Model

I learned this by observing my sister. Using the PARM model, I Produced the behavior because I was paying Attention to the model, Remembered how to do the behavior, and was Motivated to reproduce it.

Ha ha!

Hmm..

Ha ha!

Model

Observer

Wow, I've started quite the diffusion chain!

Maybe I'm just mentalizing, but I'm vicariously proud.

I learned the behavior, but I don't feel like imitating them. This is the learning-performance distinction.

Ha ha!

Ha ha!

Model

Observational learning can spread via a **diffusion chain**, where one person observes a behavior and copies it. By copying that behavior, he becomes a model for others to do the same.

In a concept known as **reciprocal determinism**, Bandura pointed out that observational learning suggested that not only could the environment influence behavior and the individual, but behavior and individual factors, like thoughts and feelings, could influence the environment as well. This creates a three-way interaction between the environment, the person, and their behavior.

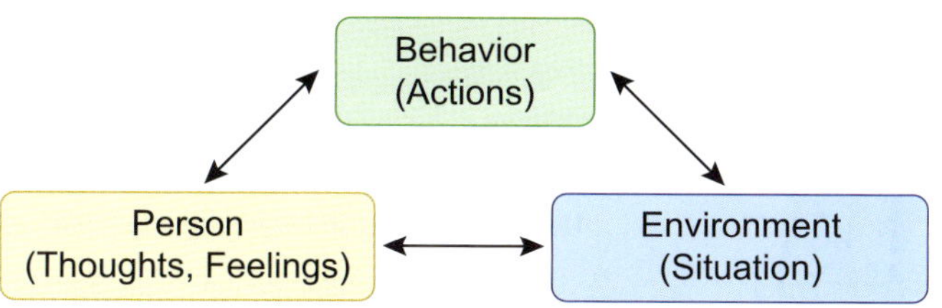

Reciprocal Determinism

In the nature vs. nurture argument, observational behavior emphasizes nurture. Your environment is more important than how you were born.

In the **Bobo doll experiment**, a filmed adult displayed aggressive behavior toward an inflated doll (called a Bobo doll). The film was shown to one group of children and not to another. The children were then placed into a room by themselves with a Bobo doll and other toys. Some of the children who had been exposed to the film reenacted the aggressive acts and even created novel aggressive acts not demonstrated in the video, including using toy guns. Children not shown the video showed less aggressive behavior toward the Bobo doll. This study is often cited as an indication of the effects of television violence on children.

No Bobo dolls were harmed during this experiment.

There were some children that did not imitate the behavior. After the experiment, Bandura bribed these children to imitate the behavior. The children were able to imitate the behavior. This demonstrated **learning-performance distinction**—just because you don't perform a behavior doesn't mean that you didn't learn it.

Understand these three things about social cognitive theory:

1. People learn by observing.
2. Mental states are important to learning—PARM.
3. Learning might not lead to behavior change.

Note that #3 means that the pure behaviorist definition of learning as a change in behavior no longer works here.

Insight Learning

Insight learning is the occurrence of an epiphany after deep contemplation. It does not arise through trial and error, and there is no stimulus-response relationship. The solution to a thought puzzle spontaneously arises after mental machinations. Previous experience plays a role, but it is accompanied by a sudden new appreciation of a logical sequence.

A well-known example of insight learning is of Sultan the chimpanzee. Sultan was given two sticks and a bunch of bananas were placed outside his cage, out of reach of even with one of the sticks. Sultan tried to reach the bananas with either stick, but eventually gave up. While playing with the sticks, he suddenly noticed that they could be fit together to make a longer stick that would reach the banana. Sultan reached the bananas, and from then on solved the problem immediately whenever presented.

There is no step-by-step process to insight learning. Insight learning is always accompanied by a preliminary deep-thinking stage, followed by a sudden realization. Insight learning brings about a long-lasting change.

7.6 Self-Concept, Self-Identity, and Social Identity

Be aware that almost none of the definitions used in this section are widely agreed upon among psychologists.

Self-concept is a person's mental image of himself. The modern usage of the term was popularized by Carl Rogers and Abraham Maslow.

Rogers believed that a person is born with the tendency to **self-actualize**, meaning that he is driven to become the best version of himself that he can, at least in his own eyes. This "best version" is his **ideal self**, and he requires an unshakeable sense of **self-esteem** to achieve it. The current version of himself is his "**real self**," also known as his **self-image**.

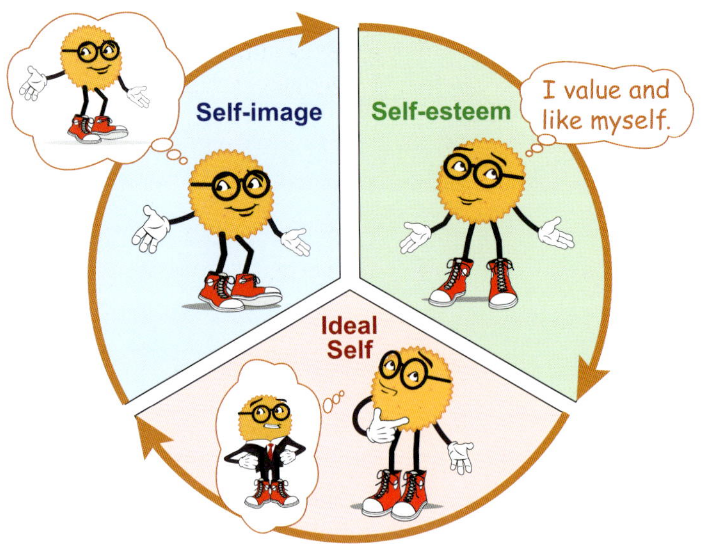

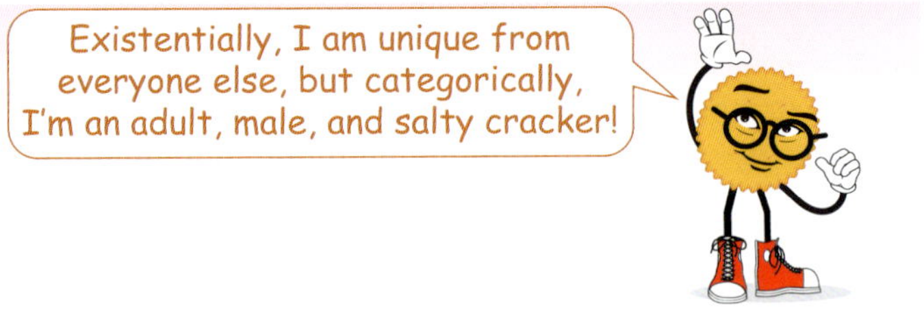

Psychologist Michael Lewis developed a different breakdown of the components that make up self-concept. He proposed that two elements, the existential self and the categorical self, combine to form a person's self-concept.

The **existential self** is the awareness that there is a self that is different from other people. Lewis estimated the development of the existential self to take place when a person is around three months old and wrote that the existential self does not change significantly throughout a person's life.

The **categorical self** is the ability of a person to use categories to define himself in comparison to the outside world. These categories change over time and are different across cultures, and seem to develop before a child reaches one year of age.

Social identity theory argues that self-esteem relies on two types of identity: personal identity and social identity.

Personal identity is the set of qualities that characterizes a person, and it does not include parts of his identity related to group identity. His **social identity** is made up of the groups to which he belongs and how he feels about being in them.

How does a person decide which groups he is a part of and what they mean to him? **Self-categorization theory** argues that groups are a fundamental part of human identity and that people use categories to make sense of the world around them.

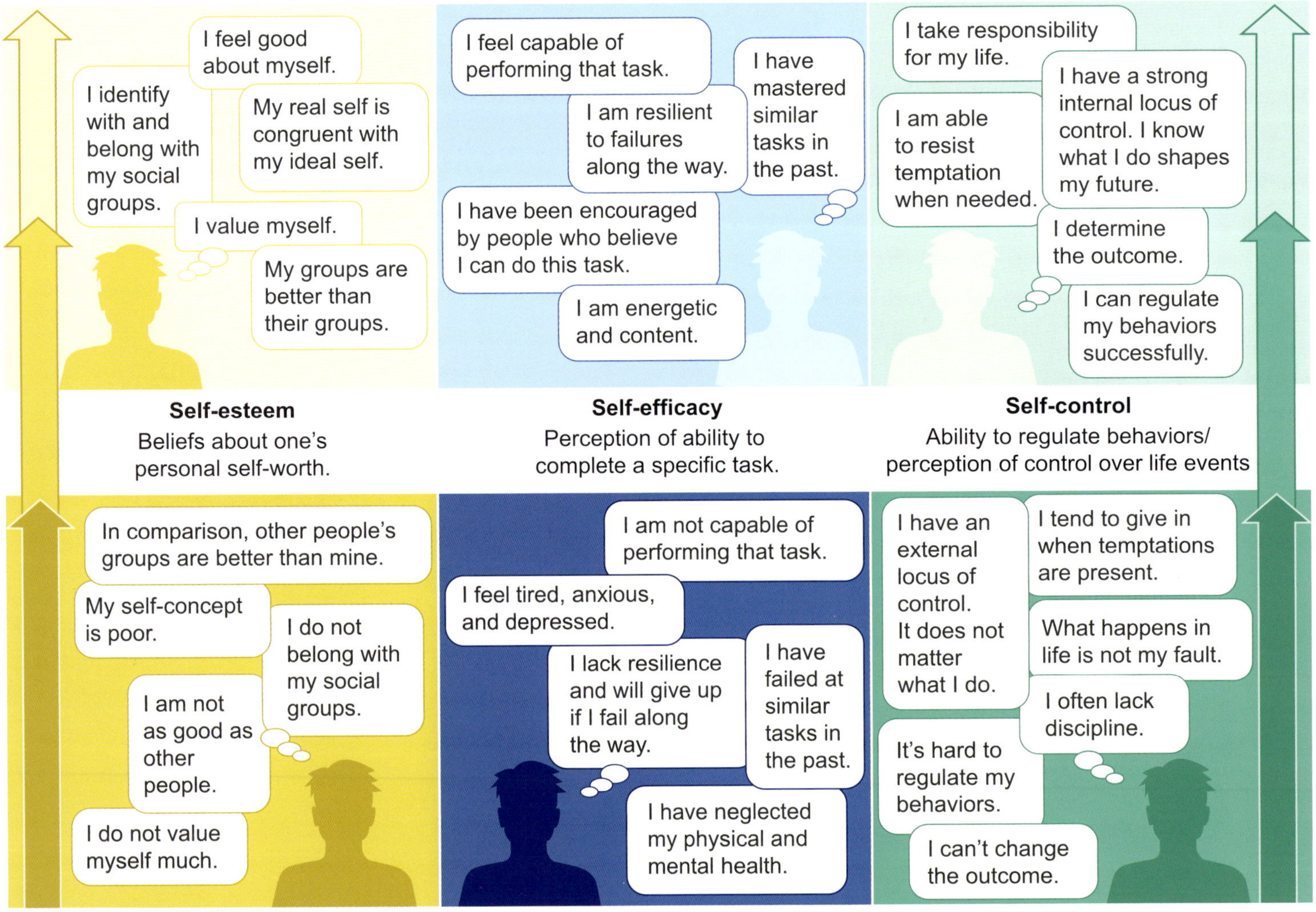

I feel good about myself.
I identify with and belong with my social groups.
My real self is congruent with my ideal self.
I value myself.
My groups are better than their groups.

I feel capable of performing that task.
I have mastered similar tasks in the past.
I am resilient to failures along the way.
I have been encouraged by people who believe I can do this task.
I am energetic and content.

I take responsibility for my life.
I have a strong internal locus of control. I know what I do shapes my future.
I am able to resist temptation when needed.
I determine the outcome.
I can regulate my behaviors successfully.

Self-esteem
Beliefs about one's personal self-worth.

Self-efficacy
Perception of ability to complete a specific task.

Self-control
Ability to regulate behaviors/ perception of control over life events

In comparison, other people's groups are better than mine.
My self-concept is poor.
I do not belong with my social groups.
I am not as good as other people.
I do not value myself much.

I am not capable of performing that task.
I feel tired, anxious, and depressed.
I lack resilience and will give up if I fail along the way.
I have failed at similar tasks in the past.
I have neglected my physical and mental health.

I have an external locus of control. It does not matter what I do.
I tend to give in when temptations are present.
What happens in life is not my fault.
I often lack discipline.
It's hard to regulate my behaviors.
I can't change the outcome.

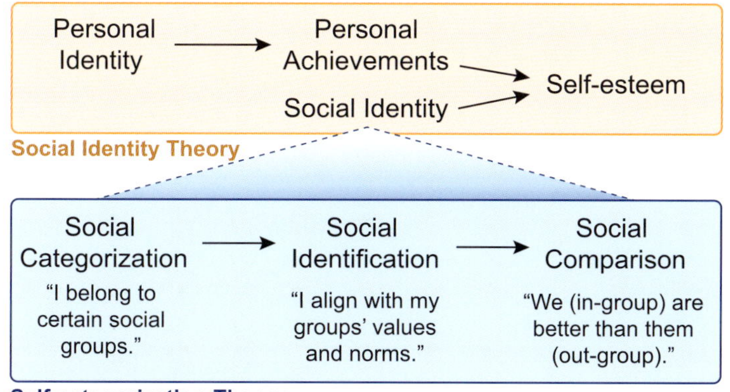

Social Identity Theory and Self-categorization Theory

First, people sort things (e.g. inanimate objects, people, ideas) into **categories**. The world is too complicated to treat every phenomenon as entirely unique, and treating things differently depending on which category they belong to is basically a heuristic—a mental shortcut used to save time when solving problems.

People also sort themselves into different groups, and these groups can be based on any element of someone's personal identity that they think is important. When people put themselves in groups, they tend to **identify** with the values and norms of these groups, as well as modify their behavior to match what they think a member of that group should do.

Another thing that people tend to do when sorting themselves into groups is **compare** the groups they are a part of to other groups. This is not usually an objective process, and people generally misrepresent groups they are not a part of. For example, a person might believe that another group is more homogenous (made up of similar people) than it really is or overestimate how different another group is from one that the person belongs to.

Social identity theory and self-categorization theory are closely related, but different, theories. However, most psychologists who accept one also accept the other, and researchers who use both theories are said to follow the **social identity approach**.

Self-Esteem and Self-Efficacy

Self-esteem is someone's perception of their own worth as a person. It is normally thought of as a relatively stable trait, though it can change over time.

Self-esteem is my perception of self-worth based on my self-evaluation. **Self-efficacy** is how confident I feel about successfully accomplishing a specific task or goal, like becoming a professional football player.

Self-efficacy is a more specific term than self-esteem and refers to a person's belief in their ability to accomplish a particular task. The concept of self-efficacy was created by Albert Bandura.

There are four main ways to increase self-efficacy for a given task or situation: mastery experiences, social modeling, social persuasion, and physical/psychological training.

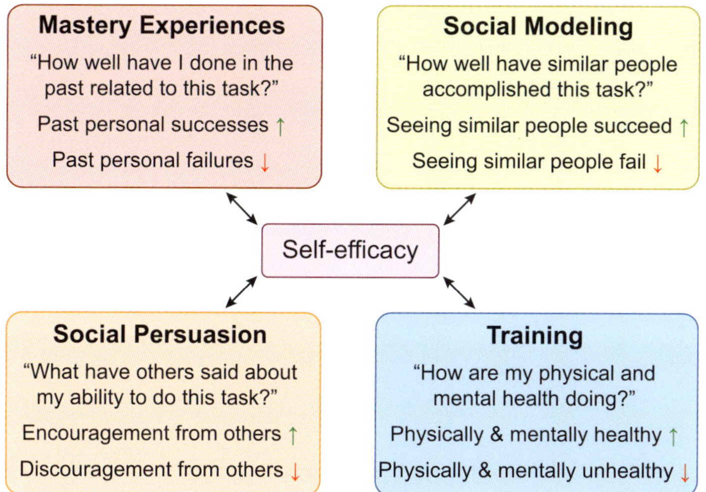

Mastery experiences happen when a person successfully completes a task and are the strongest drivers of self-efficacy. When people are trying to learn how to do something, succeeding after putting in consistent effort is crucial for building self-efficacy. In contrast, failure (especially early in the learning process) greatly reduces self-efficacy.

Social modeling is where observing others that a person identifies with changes their self-efficacy. In general, seeing someone similar to oneself succeed at a task increases self-efficacy, while seeing them fail decreases it.

Social persuasion is typically direct encouragement or discouragement that comes from other people. Encouragement tends to increase self-efficacy, while discouragement tends to decrease self-efficacy.

Physical/psychological training, which includes strength training, cardio, and psychotherapy, can help increase self-efficacy on a broad scale. This is because people rely on their physiological and mental states, among other factors, to judge what they can do and what they cannot. When people are fatigued, sluggish, or experiencing negative emotions, they tend to interpret their feeling as evidence that they cannot do a certain task—the opposite is true for people who are energetic and content.

People with high self-efficacy for a given task tend to set high goals and are firmly committed to accomplishing them. They usually attribute failure to a lack of effort, not a lack of skill, persevere in the face of adversity, and are generally more resilient than people with low self-efficacy.

Self-efficacy on the MCAT

People with low self-efficacy tend to set lower goals and are more likely to not follow through on them. If they fail at a task, they are likely to believe their failure came from a lack of skill and not a lack of effort, and are more discouraged by setbacks than people with high self-efficacy.

Self-Control

Self-control is a person's ability to override thoughts and emotions to regulate his own behavior. Put another way, it is the ability to ignore temptations in the pursuit of long-term goals.

Temptations are desires that conflict with a person's values or goals. A well-known test of children's ability to resist temptations is the **marshmallow experiment**, originally headed by Walter Mischel and some colleagues at Stanford.

In the experiment, 4-year-old children were given the choice between eating one marshmallow now or waiting fifteen minutes and receiving two marshmallows. Only about 30% of the children managed to wait the entire time without licking, nibbling, or eating the marshmallow.

Mischel Marshmallow Study

The kids tested in the original experiment were followed by the researchers for decades. Over time, they found that the children who were able to wait for the two marshmallows did better on the SAT, were more likely to get advanced academic degrees, and were less likely to be obese, among other positive life outcomes. However, it is likely that these effects are mainly the result of general cognitive ability (IQ) and the socioeconomic status of the families that kids grow up in, though self-control might play a role as well.

Closely linked to self-control is the idea of **ego depletion**. Presumably, self-control is a limited resource and depletes when people resist temptations. When people have low energy levels or have just completed a task that requires self-control, they are more likely to give up on a second activity that tests their self-control. However, large-scale studies on ego depletion have given mixed results, and despite over twenty years of research it is not yet clear whether ego depletion is a real phenomenon.

People think about their ability to control what happens in their life, including their own behavior, in different ways. People's beliefs about the level of control they have exist on a spectrum. One extreme, called an **internal locus of control**, is the belief that people have total control over, and thus complete responsibility for, everything that happens to them. The other extreme, called an **external locus of control**, is the view that people have no control over anything that happens to them.

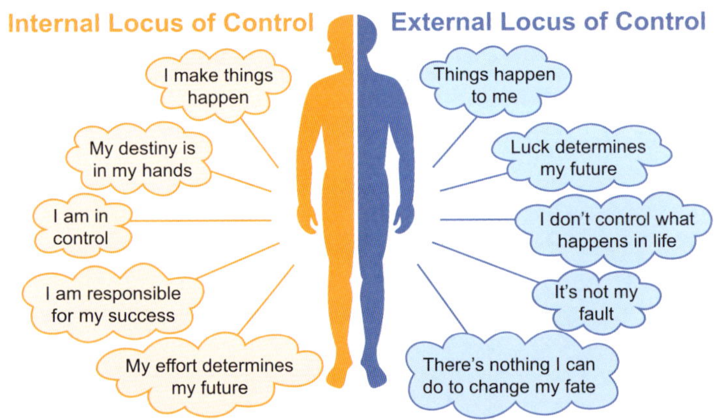

Most people sit between these two extremes. In general, having a more internal locus of control is correlated with better health and academic achievement, as well as a higher socioeconomic status and self-esteem than their external locus of control counterparts.

A strongly external locus of control can make people more likely to experience learned helplessness. **Learned helplessness** is where people stop trying to avoid unpleasant situations after repeated exposure to bad things that happen to them that are out of their control.

Learned helplessness affects people in many different ways. It has been implicated in the development of depression, anxiety about academic and work performance, and the tendency to believe misinformation, among other things.

While learned helplessness can be thought of as a response to having no choice in a situation, **choice overload** can occur when people have too much control over a decision they are trying to make. When people have too many options to choose from when trying to decide something, they both have a harder time making a decision and are more likely to regret the decision once they make it.

Types of Identity

There are a near-infinite number of ways that a person can divide his identity into smaller sub-identities. Some of these divisions have taken on special significance in society. The most widely-discussed of these are race, ethnicity, gender, age, sexual orientation, and socioeconomic status (class).

7.7 Formation of Identity

Theories of Identity Development

There are many different theories concerning how a person's identity develops, and they tend to focus on different aspects of identity, such as personality, cognition, and morality.

The first modern theory of identity development was the **psychosexual theory**, which was first dreamt up by Sigmund Freud. Freud was most interested in early childhood development, since he believed that a person's personality was more or less formed by the time he turned six. He proposed that children progress through a series of five stages that represent changes in where they direct their **libido**.

If a child gets stuck during one of these stages, he is said to be **fixated**. These fixations can show up as problems later in life, and generally manifest as an inappropriate focus on the psychosexual needs that dominate the stage(s) that the person got stuck on as a kid. There are five stages.

1. Oral
2. Anal
3. Phallic
4. Latent
5. Genital

One classic mnemonic for remembering these stages is: Old Age Parrots Love Grapes. Of course, the best mnemonic is one you remember easily—if you make your own, try to make them as bizarre and memorable as possible!

Stage	Age	Libido Focus/ Erogenous Zone	Developmental Task	Adult Fixations/ Traits
Oral (Old)	0–1	Mouth (sucking, biting, swallowing)	Feeding and weaning from breast or bottle	Oral fixation (smoking, overeating, nail-biting) Dependency or aggression
Anal (Age)	1–3	Anus (retaining or expelling feces)	Toilet training (develop control over bowels and bladder)	Anal-retentive (orderly) Anal-expulsive (messy) Obsessiveness
Phallic (Parrots)	3–6	Genitals (masturbation)	Resolve Oedipus (boy)/Electra (girl) complex by identifying with same-sex parent	Sexual dysfunctions Vanity/exhibitionism Competitiveness
Latent (Love)	6–12	None (dormant)	Develop social and intellectual skills	None
Genital (Grapes)	12+	Genitals (sexual intimacy with others)	Maturation of sexual identity and interests	Sexually mature Mentally healthy

Freud Psychosexual Stages

The **oral stage** lasts from birth until about one year of age. During this stage, a child's libido is centered around his mouth and drives behaviors like eating, drinking, and biting. If fixation occurs, a person might experience problems later in life like overeating, smoking, and nail-biting that is referred to as an oral fixation. Someone stuck in this stage may become overly dependent or highly aggressive.

The **anal stage** spans the ages of one to three years old. A child's libido during this stage is focused on his anus, which he is expected to learn to control during toilet training. Fixation during this stage can cause either an overly orderly or disorganized personality, called anal-retentive and anal-expulsive personalities respectively. People stuck in this stage become obsessive as adults.

The **phallic stage** occurs between the ages of three to six. Throughout this stage, a child's libido is concentrated on the genitals, driving masturbation. Freud believed that the **Oedipus complex**, a phenomenon in which a boy resents his father due to sexual desire for his mother, develops during the phallic stage. Later, the term Electra complex was added by Carl Jung, which is essentially the same concept, but for girls. Whereas boys experience castration anxiety, girls are said to experience penis envy. Both complexes are resolved by identifying with, and taking on characteristics of, the same-sex parent. Fixation during this stage can lead to sexual dysfunctions, confused sexual identity, vanity, exhibitionism, intense competitiveness, and many other apparent ailments.

Freud's Oedipus Complex

The **latent stage** lasts from age six until the beginning of puberty, usually around age 12. A child's libido is suppressed during this phase, and children direct their energies to learning how to interact with people outside of their families. Fixation does not occur during this stage.

The **genital stage** lasts from the beginning of puberty until death. In this stage, libido returns and is directed again towards the genitals. Instead of being directed to one's own genitals, however, the libido is focused on the genitals of others. If a person has no fixations remaining from the previous stages, he develops into a healthy, well-adjusted, and sexually mature adult. If fixations are left over, they tend to start causing major problems during the genital stage.

Often considered the first true theory of identity development, Erik Erikson's **psychosocial stages of development** is a series of eight stages that healthy people progress through during their lives. Each of these stages is marked by a **crisis**, which is a conflict between two competing psychological forces (e.g., identity vs identity confusion). If a person successfully overcomes the crisis for a stage, he gains a basic strength unique to that stage—if he fails to do so, he may develop an **antipathy**, or negative trait related to the central conflict for the failed stage.

Erikson's eight stages are:

1. Infancy: trust vs. mistrust
2. Early childhood: autonomy vs. shame/doubt
3. Play age: initiative vs. guilt
4. School age: industry vs. inferiority
5. Adolescence: identity vs. role confusion
6. Young adulthood: intimacy vs. isolation
7. Adulthood: generativity vs. stagnation
8. Old age: integrity vs. despair

Exact ages for each stage vary across sources. Use context clues to determine the best answer if unsure.

Stage	Age	Psychosocial Crisis	Developmental Task	Strength	Antipathy
1. Infancy	0–1	Trust vs. Mistrust (My)	Ensure basic needs are met	Hope (Hope's)	Withdrawal
2. Early childhood	1–3	Autonomy vs. Shame/Doubt (SoDa)	Explore environment and begin to establish independence	Will (Will)	Compulsion
3. Play age	3–6	Initiative vs. Guilt (Gas)	Try new things and plan ahead	Purpose (Provides)	Inhibition
4. School age	6–12	Industry vs. Inferiority (Internally)	Discover personal interests	Compe-tence (Coverage)	Inertia
5. Adoles-cence	12–20	Identity vs. Role Confusion (Really Caused)	Clarify identity and social roles	Fidelity (For)	Repudiation
6. Young adulthood	20–40	Intimacy vs. Isolation (Isolated)	Build intimate relationships and deeply connected friendships	Love (Lasting)	Exclusivity
7. Adulthood	40–65	Generativity vs. Stagnation (Stomach)	Contribute to their community	Care (Cash)	Rejectivity
8. Old age	65+	Integrity vs. Despair (Distress)	Reflect on legacy left behind	Wisdom (With-drawals)	Disdain

Erikson Psychosocial Stages

Since many of the psychosocial crises begin with the same letter, it's helpful to use the second word for the mnemonic. Again, the wilder, the better if you want to make your own!

Infancy, or stage 1, lasts from birth until about 18 months. Its crisis is that of **trust vs. mistrust.**

A child is completely dependent on his parents during this stage, and how he is treated during this stage plays a large role in how his sense of trust develops. If he is well-cared for—for example, if he is fed regularly, kept warm, safe, clean, and spends a good amount of quality time with other people, he is likely to develop **hope**.

In this context, "hope" basically means a sense that the future is somewhat predictable and something to look forward to, not something random and scary.

If his physical needs are not met or if he is neglected socially he may develop withdrawal, which is a tendency to not engage with the outside world due to fear or mistrust.

Early childhood, or stage 2, lasts from about the ages of 18 months to 3 years old. Its crisis is that of **autonomy vs. shame/doubt**.

This stage overlaps with the first small behaviors that parents expect children to take some responsibility for, such as eating, bathing, getting dressed, and going to the bathroom. If a child's parents are supportive during this process and he manages to shoulder these burdens, he develops **will**.

> "Will" is something like a sense of autonomy or a desire to be independent from other people. You can think of it as having willpower.

Erikson Stage 2

If a child's parents are never content with his efforts during this stage, he may develop compulsion, or the tendency to act on desires immediately and is likely to experience shame and doubt about himself.

The **play age**, or stage 3, occurs between the ages of about three to six years old. Its crisis is that of **initiative vs. guilt**.

In this stage, children exhibit behaviors that further assert their independence from their parents as they try new things and engage in goal-directed planning. This inevitably leads to some conflict between parents and their kids that needs to be resolved. If his parents are not too strict and handle this conflict in a non-destructive way, a child develops a sense of **purpose**. If a child's parents are overcontrolling, the child may feel guilty for acting out and might go on to have problems with his self-esteem that lead to inhibition rather than taking initiative.

The **school age**, or stage 4, spans from roughly six to 12 years of age. Its crisis is that of **industry vs inferiority**.

The school age stage is when people outside a child's immediate family, such as teachers and peers at school and clubs, take on an important role in his development. This environment is less nurturing than those of the previous stages, and pushes children to become productive and to value their accomplishments. If this process goes well, a child develops **competence**. If he underperforms academically, athletically, or socially, he might develop inertia, or an unwillingness to work towards goals.

Erikson Stages 3 and 4

Adolescence, or stage 5, lasts approximately from 12 to 20 years of age. Its crisis is that of **identity vs role confusion**.

This stage is where a child figures out what he wants to do with his life and how he fits into society. Adolescence takes center stage in Erikson's theory, and many other theories of identity development focus entirely on this process of coming-of-age. If a child completes this stage successfully, he becomes an adult with a clear personal identity and gains **fidelity**.

> "Fidelity" is the ability to trust yourself and others, as well as the ability to commit yourself to causes you believe in.

If a child fails to complete this stage, he may experience repudiation, which is the tendency to act rebelliously or to commit himself to deviant groups or causes.

Young adulthood, or stage 6, lasts approximately from the age of 20 to age 40. Its crisis is that of **intimacy vs isolation**.

During this stage, people tend to look for lasting, intimate relationships with other people. These are often romantic, though deeply connected friendships are also important in this stage. If a person manages to form close, long-lasting relationships with others over this time period, he gains the virtue of **love**. If he fails, exclusivity, or denying his love to other people or to himself, may occur, which can result in isolation and loneliness.

Adulthood, or stage 7, lasts from about 40 to 65 years of age. Its crisis is that of **generativity vs stagnation**.

This stage has the potential to be the most productive part of a person's life, both in a career and for building a family through raising children and preparing them for the hard road ahead of them. If a person successfully clears this stage, he develops **care**, which is a concern for and love of the generations of people to come and of the community he lives in. If he does not, he might experience rejectivity, meaning that he becomes so self-absorbed that he loses the ability to care for the people and to be a productive member of society.

Erikson Stage 8

Old age, or stage 8, lasts from approximately 65 years of age until death. Its crisis is that of **integrity vs despair**.

This is the stage during which most people retire, life slows down, and people start reflecting on their lives. If people can come to terms with how they lived before they pass away and avoid wallowing in bitterness and past mistakes, they gain **wisdom**. If they fail to do so, they may develop disdain for their fellow man and sink into despair.

Erikson's theory of identity development was deeply influential and inspired several other researchers to expand even further upon the older theory with a special focus on the stage of adolescence (identity vs. role confusion).

The best-studied of these theories is called the **identity status theory** and was created by James Marcia. Identity status theory argues that there are four main states that a person's identity can be in during adolescence. They are (in order of more mature to less):

1. Identity achievement
2. Identity moratorium
3. Identity foreclosure
4. Identity diffusion

Commitment (Devotion) \ Crisis (Exploration)	Yes	No
Yes	**Identity Achievement** "I know and like who I am."	**Identity Foreclosure** "I am who I was told to be."
No	**Identity Moratorium** "I'm struggling to figure out who I am."	**Identity Diffusion** "I don't know or care who I am."

Identity Status Theory

A person's identity status is determined by two factors: a crisis and a commitment. This crisis refers to the desire to actively question and explore one's own identity, while the commitment can be a devotion to values, life goals, or any other cause that requires some kind of effort or sacrifice.

Identity achievement occurs when an adolescent arrives at a sense of self and direction after considering many different options. This state is associated with having satisfying intimate relationships, high self-esteem, and higher levels of conscientiousness.

Identity moratorium is where an adolescent is still trying to figure out which commitments he wants to pursue and what kind of person he wants to be. In other words, he wants to form a strong sense of identity, but is not yet sure what he wants that identity to be.

Identity foreclosure happens when an adolescent is prematurely (that is, uncritically or unthinkingly) committed to an identity, typically one given to him by his parents or other authority figures. This state is linked to authoritarian and closed-minded attitudes.

Identity diffusion is the state in which an adolescent has neither an interest in developing his own identity nor any commitment to particular values, goals, etc. This state is marked by an increased likelihood of loneliness, hopelessness, and anxiety.

For most people, identity status is remarkably stable throughout early adulthood. However, when identity status does change, it tends to shift towards a more mature status, e.g., from identity foreclosure to identity moratorium.

The previous theories of identity development are based on psychoanalytic principles. The next few theories also concern identity development, but look at different facets of identity and at different forces that influence it.

Kohlberg's stages of development was created by Lawrence Kohlberg and focuses on how children develop a sense of morality. He split moral development into three main levels, each of which contains two smaller stages for a total of six stages.

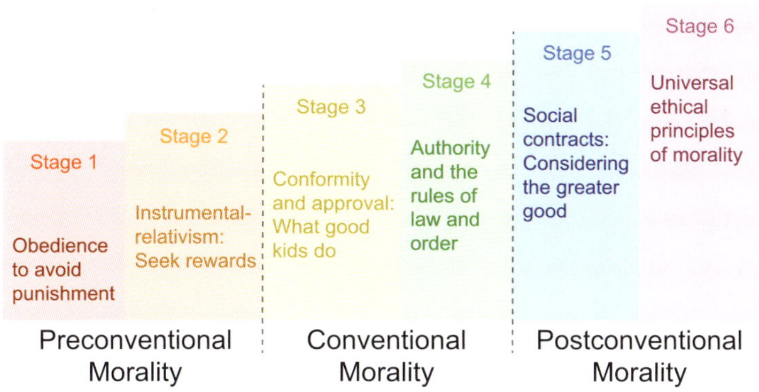

Stage 1
Obedience to avoid punishment
Stage 2
Instrumental-relativism: Seek rewards
Stage 3
Conformity and approval: What good kids do
Stage 4
Authority and the rules of law and order
Stage 5
Social contracts: Considering the greater good
Stage 6
Universal ethical principles of morality
Preconventional Morality
Conventional Morality
Postconventional Morality

Kohlberg's Stages of Moral Development

Kohlberg did not provide specific ages for each stage. Most sources suggest that preconventional morality lasts until around age nine to 12. From there, many people remain in conventional morality indefinitely, though very rarely adolescents and a bit more commonly adults can proceed to postconventional stages of morality.

The first level is called the **preconventional level** and is characterized by thinking about morality as something that is set entirely by an outside authority.

The first stage in this level is the **punishment-and-obedience stage**. In this stage, children perceive acts that get people punished as "bad" and acts that get people rewarded as "good." In this stage, children seek primarily to avoid punishment.

The second stage is the **instrumental-relativist stage**. This stage is where children develop the belief that actions that satisfy their needs and occasionally those of other people are "good," while actions that harm themselves or others are not. They are focused on maximizing rewards for themselves.

The second level is the **conventional level** and is marked by a person not only conforming to the moral norms of the groups he belongs to, but maintaining, identifying with, and enforcing them as well. Kohlberg did not include ages in his theory, but people will often proceed to the conventional level of morality between the ages of nine and 12 at the earliest. This level is typical of adolescents and some adults.

The first stage in this level (and the third stage overall) is the interpersonal concordance orientation, a.k.a. the **good boy—nice girl stage**. People in this stage tend to label behaviors that make others happy or that other people

Age	Freud Psychosexual	Erikson Psychosocial	Kohlberg Morality
0–1	Oral (Old)	Trust vs. Mistrust (My) (Hope) (Hope's)	
1–3	Anal (Age)	Autonomy vs. Shame/Doubt (SoDa) (Will) (Will)	Preconventional
3–6	Phallic (Parrots)	Initiative vs. Guilt (Gas) (Purpose) (Provides)	1. Avoid punishment (Avoid) 2. Seek rewards (Seeking)
6–12	Latent (Love)	Industry vs. Inferiority (Internally) (Competence) (Coverage)	Conventional
12–20	Genital (Grapes)	Identity vs. Role Confusion (Really Caused) (Fidelity) (For)	3. Conform for approval (Conformity) 4. Follow rules (Follow)
20–40		Intimacy vs. Isolation (Isolated) (Love) (Lasting)	Postconventional
40–65		Generativity vs. Stagnation (Stomach) (Care) (Cash)	5. Social contracts (Subjective)
65+		Integrity vs. Despair (Distress) (Wisdom) (Withdrawals)	6. Universal Ethical principles (Ethics)

Freud, Erikson, and Kohlberg Stages

approve of as "good." They also start to consider people's intentions when judging the morality of their actions. They typically conform to what they believe are other people's expectations of them in order to gain approval.

The second stage in this level (the fourth stage overall) is the **"law and order" stage**. During this stage, people show respect for authority because they believe that is the right thing to do, and try to maintain social norms and fulfill their duties just for the sake of doing so. They uphold rules because they believe they are supposed to do so and do not make exceptions or consider their internal ethical code. Rules are concrete and must be followed.

The third and final level is the **postconventional level**. This level is marked by attempts to define morality as something that exists outside of a person's group identity. In other words, people begin to think that morals are subjective, abstract, and are malleable depending on the circumstances involved. At this stage, people are guided by their moral compass rather than explicitly by laws and social conventions.

The first stage in this level (and the fifth stage overall) is the **social contract stage**. This stage is characterized by an understanding of morality as something that is negotiated between every member of a society. At this stage, people are more inclined to make decisions based on what promotes the greater good and is the best outcome based on the entirety of the situation.

In stage 6 of Kohlberg's stages of development, laws are important, but, ultimately, decisions should be based on abstract universal ethical principles.

The second stage in this level (and the sixth stage overall) is the **universal ethical principle stage**. In this stage, people believe that self-chosen ethical principles should determine what is right and what is wrong. The principles are abstract, not concrete, and are focused on ethical ideals, such as the sovereignty of the individual, the sanctity of human rights, and the inherent dignity of human beings.

Lev Vygotsky's **social interactionist theory** also takes a stance on identity development. As the name suggests, social interaction is central to this theory and is the driving force behind how children learn to think.

Vygotsky believed that all children are born with a set of abilities called **lower mental functions**—these are innate, biological capabilities, and include such things as sensation, attention, and memory. In contrast, **higher mental functions** like language, learning, and general cognition are not innate and must be learned. Children use a combination of lower mental functions and instruction from other people to develop the higher mental functions.

Children learn best when they are being taught by a **skilled other**, who can be an adult or peer that already knows how to do the task the child is trying to learn. A skilled mother can keep the child in the **zone of proximal development**, which is the range of difficulty for a given skill that the child can only handle with outside help.

Imagine trying to teach a kid how to catch a baseball. He might already be able to catch a ball that is dropped a few inches into his open palm, meaning that the task is too easy to be in the zone of proximal development. On the other hand, he might not even be able to see your best fastball pitch, let alone catch it—that'd be out of the zone of proximal development due to its difficulty. He might just be able to catch a ball thrown gently at his torso, and only with your help. That level of difficulty falls within his current zone of proximal development for the skill of catching a baseball.

Vygotsky believed that language development was the key to children's ability to think about themselves in a meaningful way. To him, children gaining **private speech**, or the ability to talk to themselves in their heads instead of out loud, is the cornerstone of their cognitive abilities maturing. They use this internal voice and interactions with the people around them to help shape their beliefs, behaviors, and ultimately who they are.

Influence of Social Factors on Identity Formation

As many of the theories concerning identity formation suggest, social factors play an important role in shaping our identities. Let's take a closer look at some of the individual and group factors that influence identity formation.

Imitation is the act of observing someone else's behavior and copying it. Babies appear to be born with the ability to imitate others—when tested, infants as young as a day old can imitate people's facial expressions. Imitation is crucially important in learning of all kinds, from the acquiring of motor skills to fitting in with social groups. Observing others, imitating them, and ultimately, identifying with them is one process by which culture and socialization influence identity development.

There is some evidence that our ability to imitate others is linked to **mirror neurons**, which are neurons in the brain that fire both when performing an action and when watching someone else perform the same action. However, most research on mirror neurons has been done on monkeys, not humans, and both the importance and existence of these neurons in humans is still not clear.

The **looking-glass self** is the image that an individual thinks that other people have of him. This idea of the self was created by **Charles Horton Cooley**, and he thought that three factors combined to produce it.

1. The imagination of one's own physical appearance to others.
2. How he imagines others judge his appearance.
3. Some kind of feeling related to the first two factors, such as pride or shame.

In other words, we do not respond to other people's actual opinions of us to form an identity, but instead change how we feel about ourselves based on what we imagine people think about us.

George Herbert Mead built on the idea of the looking-glass self with his own approach to identity that he called **social behaviorism**.

Mead believed that there were two main stages in the development of the self, called the play stage and the game stage. Prior to these stages, the child begins preparing themselves for the more complex social tasks that will follow. This is known as the preparatory stage.

In the **preparatory stage**, the child imitates adults without understanding the meaning behind their actions. This might involve pretending to vacuum or mimicking their parents by making comments that are beyond the child's understanding.

Mead's Play Stage

In the **play stage**, children engage in **role-taking** based on what they see adults acting out in society, such as "mother," "friend," "physician," etc. to see how those roles function. At this point, children form an understanding of how individual roles work, but lack a broader, integrated sense of self.

In the **game stage**, children gain an understanding of how roles function as parts of broader society. Instead of adopting one role at a time, children in the game stage adopt many roles simultaneously—additionally, these roles are all directly related to one another.

> Mead thought that kids were most heavily influenced by people close to them, like their siblings, parents, and friends.

Mead believed that these games are microcosms of society, and that people's ability to understand their role in smaller-scale games translates to developing a sense of self. This self has two interrelated components called the "me" (social self) and the "I" (response to the social self).

The "**me**" is the habitual part of the self that is formed through social interactions and reflects how the person believes the generalized other views them. The "I" is the active part of the self that responds to the "me." That is, the "me" reflects the internalization of societal expectations and attitudes, while the "I" is the spontaneous part that flexibly responds to those expectations and attitudes.

The "I" works within the framework laid out by the "me" and is the primary part of the self that makes a person's personality unique. According to Mead, a person with a "me" that is too strong simply adopts the beliefs of his family, friends, and neighbors, and is predictable and conforming to the point of being boring. A person with a well-developed "I," however, deviates from the views of the people around him in novel and interesting ways.

To Mead, the "I" and the "me" are in a dynamic balance and make up the **real self**.

Reference groups are the groups that an individual will compare himself to when evaluating his own behavior, status, or some other aspect of his identity. These comparisons can change how he acts or feels about a given topic. Reference groups are one way in which culture affects identity formation because it influences which reference groups we are exposed to and use as the standard for comparison.

For example, people who are told that they are making less money than their peers at work tend to feel dissatisfied with their wages, even if they are being paid significantly more than other workers outside their own company or in their industry in general. This is thought to be because these people are using their fellow employees as a reference group, and in doing so form the opinion that they are being underpaid for their work.

PSY

Behavior Attribution and Social Structure

8

8.1 Attributing Behavior to Persons or Situations

Attribution Theory

Attribution theory focuses on how people make judgements about their own and other people's behavior. When a person observes a specific behavior in himself or others, does he attribute that behavior to personality or to circumstance?

Dispositional (internal) attribution is when someone concludes that a person behaves a certain way due to his disposition, whereas **situational (external) attribution** occurs when someone attributes a person's behavior to his situation. In other words, dispositional attributions blame personality, while situational attributions blame circumstance.

Harold Kelley's **Covariation Model** relies on three factors to explain how people assess the behavior of others.

1. **Consensus:** If others engage in the same behavior, it is considered situational. ("Everyone was doing it, so there must have been something in the air. It certainly was NOT his personality.")
2. **Distinctiveness**: If the individual exhibits a behavior that is unusual for him, behavior is considered situational. ("He never behaves this way. It's just not his personality, so it was the environment.")
3. **Consistency:** If the individual engages in a behavior consistently, it is considered

Fundamental Attribution Error

I think an apple's bad decisions are a reflection of its character and personality.

Actor-observer Bias

I think my bad decisions are due to context and circumstance.

Group Attribution Error

I think one apple's attributes apply to all apples and the decision of one group of apples reflects the attitudes of all apples.

Self-serving Bias

I believe I succeed due to personal qualities and I fail as a result of circumstance. It protects my self-esteem.

Hostile Attribution Bias

I assume others' behaviors are hostile towards me even though they aren't. It can cause relational and reactive aggression.

False Consensus Bias

I think my beliefs are common. It's too stressful to imagine others might disagree with me.

Prejudice: Affect

Affect is how I feel.
I feel afraid of oranges.
I feel angry at oranges.
I feel pity for oranges.

Prejudice: Behavior

Behavior is what I do.
I harass oranges. I don't hire or promote oranges.
I refuse service to oranges.

Prejudice: Cognition

Cognition is what I think and believe. I believe oranges are shallow. I believe oranges are submissive. I believe oranges are irresponsible.

Ethnocentrism

In moments of ethnocentrism I analyze a different culture through the lens of my own culture, usually in a culturally superior or nationalistic way.

Cultural Relativism

In moments of cultural relativism I am more able to view members of another culture from the perspective of their culture.

dispositional. ("He always does that. It is just how he is. It is his personality.")

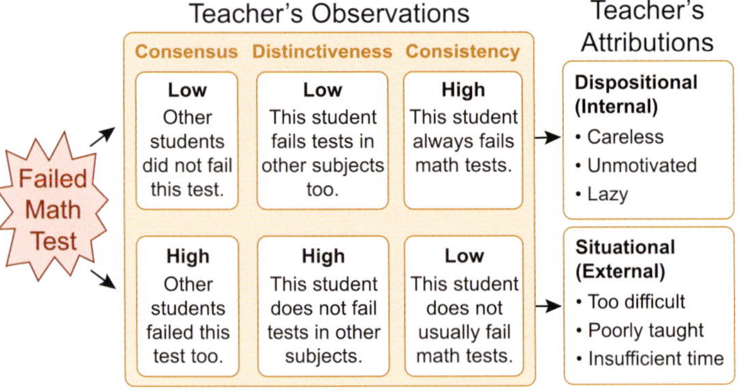

Kelley's Covariation Model

People are prone to error when judging both their own behavior and the behavior of others. These systemic errors are called **attribution biases**, and they affect all of us to some degree.

The **fundamental attribution error** is the tendency to think that other people's decisions reflect their personality or character. In other words, it's the belief that other people do things because, "that's just how they are," instead of attributing their actions to external factors.

Actor-observer bias is a complement to the fundamental attribution error, but it's applied to oneself rather than other people. In other words, people tend to think that their *own* behavior is mainly due to circumstance instead of anything essential to their character. Most sources refer to the actor-observer bias as the tendency to both make dispositional attributions about others and situational attributions about ourselves.

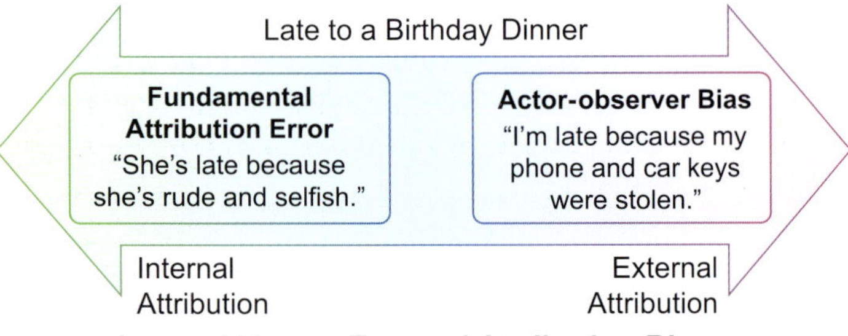

Internal Versus External Attribution Biases

Also related to the fundamental attribution error is **group attribution error**. This attribution bias can show up in two ways: either people assume that the attributes of an individual in a group apply to everyone in the group or people conclude that a group's decision reflects the attitudes of all the members of the group.

For example, a person might learn about an individual from a particular nation or culture. When he is later asked about what he thinks other people from that nation or culture are like, he is more likely to say that the other people are similar to the individual he learned about than if he hadn't been exposed to information about the individual in the first place.

Similarly, if a person is told that a group of people decided that sheep are the best animals on the planet he is more likely to believe that the individual group members all believe that sheep are indeed the best animals. He is more likely to believe this even in the face of evidence to the contrary, such as being told that the group's decision was not unanimous or that some people held more sway over the decision than others.

The **self-serving bias** is the belief that when we succeed it's because of our personal qualities, while our failures are mainly the result of our circumstances. It is thought to be a method to protect our self-esteem and is less common in older adults, people with depression, and people with an internal locus of control.

Hostile attribution bias is where people assume that other people's behaviors are hostile to them, even if their behaviors are completely harmless. This bias has been best-studied in children and is associated with both reactive and relational aggression. Reactive aggression is aggression in response to an event like a perceived insult or physical threat, while relational aggression includes acts like gossiping and excluding other people from social groups.

False consensus bias refers to people's tendency to believe that their beliefs are both common and appropriate in a given circumstance. In other words, people tend to think that other people both share their beliefs and think like they themselves do. This bias has been found in people's evaluations of everything from how they think others will vote in presidential elections to the interpretation of legal contracts. Like self-serving bias, it is thought to stem from a desire to maintain our self-esteem, since the perception that people disagree with us can be stressful.

Differences in how common and severe these biases are have been found between different cultures. For instance, people raised in East and South Asian cultures appear to be less susceptible to the fundamental attribution error, while some research has found that people from Europe and North America are more prone to self-serving bias.

Examples of Attribution Biases

Prejudice and Bias

Prejudice is an attitude held about a person or group of people that is not based on actual experience. **Bias** is an inclination for or against something that can be influenced by prejudicial attitudes. Put simply, bias is a preference or tendency. As an attitude, prejudice can be positive or negative and can be directed at anyone.

There are many factors that influence how prejudice develops and is expressed. Sociologists tend to focus on the related concepts of power, prestige, and class to explain where prejudices come from.

Power is the ability to change how other people act, **prestige** is respect given to people that have certain skills, knowledge, and "success" in general, and **class** is a level of social status associated with definite characteristics and values.

Prestige can be based on actual achievements (achieved status) or a person's position in a social hierarchy regardless of their performance or effort (ascribed status).

Some sociologists believe that people who enjoy a high level of power or prestige or are members of a high social class create prejudiced systems to maintain their social position. Other sociologists argue that prejudice is a group's response to a perceived threat from a different social group, and still others believe that prejudice is a reaction to people or groups that have different beliefs and values than a given individual or group.

Since prejudice is an attitude, it can be broken down into the same three components as other attitudes. According to the ABC model of attitude, they are the affective, behavioral, and cognitive components of prejudice.

Affective components of prejudice are the feelings and emotions that contribute to prejudice. Inducing anger in people is enough to make them more likely to form prejudices.

Behavioral components of prejudice are the actions related to prejudice. These actions are generally called **discrimination**.

Cognitive components of prejudice are thoughts and beliefs that inform prejudice. These can include categorization (sorting people into different groups), assimilation (accepting ideas about other people and oneself), and stereotypes, among other things.

Stereotypes are broadly-held beliefs that people who belong to a given group have particular characteristics.

Most stereotypes about groups that have been empirically studied by sociologists and psychologists seem to be accurate. That is, when a large number of people are asked questions with quantifiable answers about other groups of people, their answers are, on average, significantly closer to well-established values than can be explained by mere chance. This is especially true for stereotypes related to race, gender, and political views, while it seems to be less true for stereotypes about people from certain nations (national stereotypes).

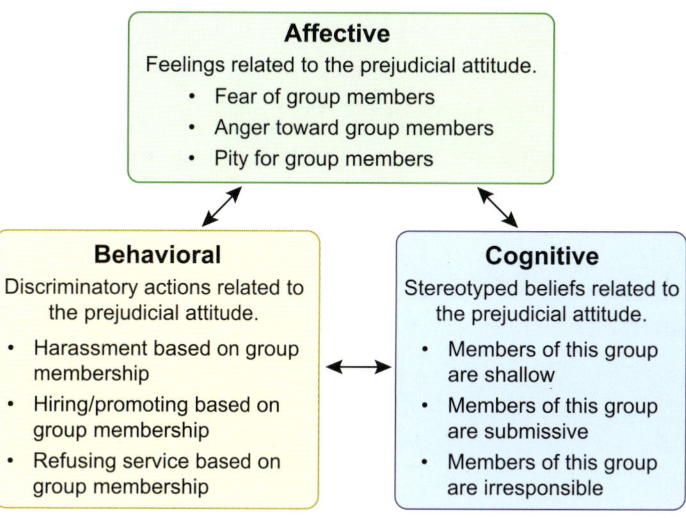

ABC Attitude Components of Prejudice

Despite this, awareness of these stereotypes appears to affect people's performance on tasks related to a given stereotype. In other words, people perform differently when they're told about stereotypes that relate to them or to the task they're doing. This effect is called **stereotype threat** when it negatively affects people's performance and **stereotype boost** when it positively influences performance.

Stereotype threat and stereotype boost can be thought of as self-fulfilling prophecies. **Self-fulfilling prophecies** occur when people act in a way that matches stereotypes related to them, further reinforcing those stereotypes.

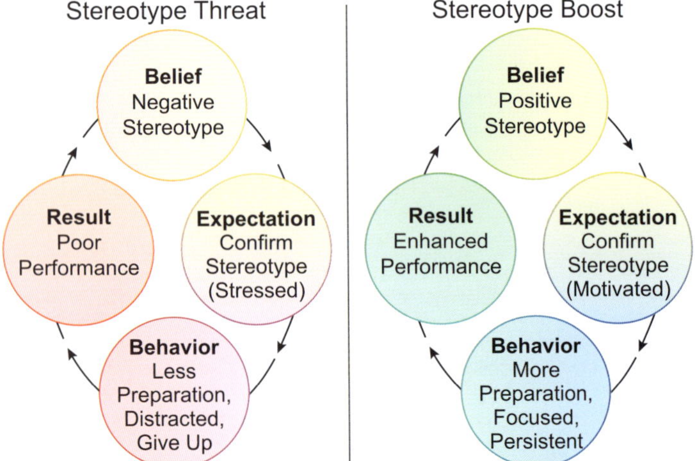

Stereotype Reinforcement via Self-fulfilling Prophecies

Stigma is the strong disapproval of a person based on traits that distinguish them from other people. When a person internalizes stigma about himself, he is said to have **self-stigma**.

Modern research on stigma has focused on the interaction between stigma and the healthcare system. Stigma held by healthcare providers leads to worse health outcomes for patients, and self-stigma can make sick people less likely to get help from physicians and other medical professionals.

A stigma is cognitive, not behavioral. In other words, having stigmatizing beliefs isn't discriminatory since discrimination requires you to actually act on those beliefs. The belief that people with depression shouldn't be trusted to watch children is a stigma—not hiring a babysitter because you know he's depressed is discrimination.

How people look at different cultures can reflect both prejudice and bias. Although there are many ways to do so, two extreme perspectives are ethnocentrism and cultural relativism.

Ethnocentrism is when one analyzes a different culture through the lens of one's own culture. It is thought that ethnocentrism is mainly caused by in-group favoritism, and may have evolved to increase cooperation within a group of people. It is often associated with views that build up one's own culture while tearing another culture down, though ethnocentrism does not necessarily lead to discrimination or negative views of other cultures.

Cultural relativism is when one views another culture from the perspective of people within that culture—in other words, judging another culture based on its own standards. Cultural relativism is standard in social science, and in disciplines like anthropology and sociology it is thought that cultural relativism is a superior way to analyze other cultures.

8.2 Social Structure

Theories of Social Structure

Sociologists tend to study social structure through two main lenses, called microsociology and macrosociology respectively. **Microsociology** focuses on small-scale, face-to-face interactions between people, while **macrosociology** looks at large-scale social structures.

Functionalism, also called **structural functionalism**, is a **macrosociology** theory that views society as a massive structure with parts that work together to keep it functioning stably. It views organizations as mostly static, only making small changes when absolutely necessary.

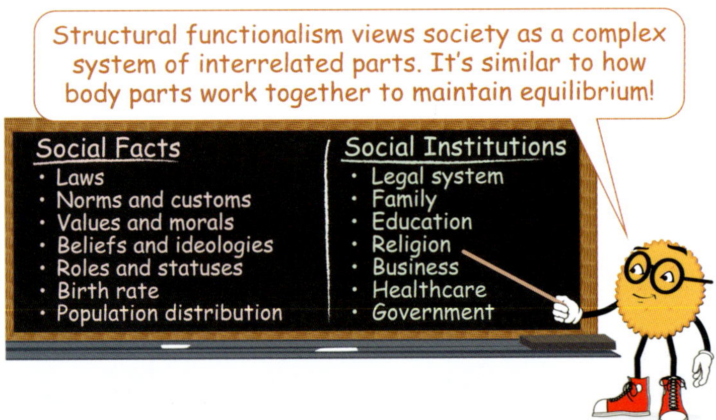

Conflict theory is a **macrosociology** theory that argues that society changes over time due to conflict between groups. If one group wins out, its views become the consensus—if no group prevails, their positions combine to form a compromise between their interests.

Social constructionism is a **macrosociology** theory that argues that some (or all) facts get their meaning not from physical reality but from how people think about them. There are two main types of social constructionism: weak social constructionism and strong social constructionism.

Weak social constructionism concedes that there are **brute facts**, which are pieces of knowledge that do not rely on other facts. These might be explanations of the smallest subatomic particles, be they quarks or something even smaller. Any ideas that require other facts to be true are thought to be socially constructed.

Strong social constructionism argues that all knowledge is socially constructed. In other words, there are no facts, only ideas that are given meaning by people's thoughts and words.

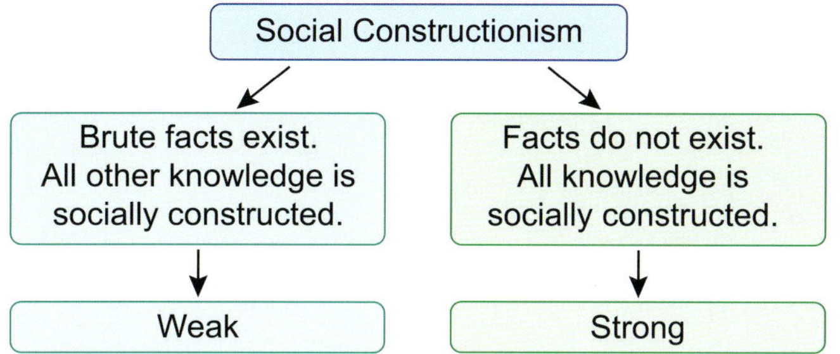

Symbolic interactionism is a **microsociology** theory that focuses on one-on-one interactions between people and on the symbols they use to do so. It focuses on subjective understanding and how that influences people's interactions with each other. Communication, for example, involves responding to symbolic elements and creating meaning based on verbal and non-verbal symbols.

Symbolic Interactionism

Exchange-rational choice is a **microsociology** theory and is a combination of rational choice theory and social exchange theory.

Rational choice theory posits that people run a logical cost-benefit analysis for every action they take. It assumes at least two things: completeness and transitivity. Completeness essentially means that every possible choice they can make can be ranked. In other words, there is no ambiguity in which choice has a better outcome. Transitivity means that if a choice (let's call it choice B) ranks above another choice (choice C) and choice A ranks above choice B, choice A also ranks above choice C.

Social exchange theory holds similar assumptions about how people behave to rational choice theory, but instead focuses on how people interact with each other in social settings. In other words, it argues that many human behaviors are driven by reason, the desire to benefit and not be punished, and that what qualifies as rewards and punishments is different for every person.

Exchange-rational Choice Theory

Feminist theory is a **macrosociology** theory that focuses on studying how gender interacts with society with the ultimate goal of achieving political and social equality between men and women.

Social Institutions

Education is the process of making learning easier, generally through teaching. Aside from learning information that for the most part is forgotten in a few weeks, people also gain knowledge from a "hidden curriculum."

The **hidden curriculum** refers to all the things we learn in school that aren't explicitly taught as part of our education. This includes behaviors that authority figures (e.g., teachers, administrators, etc.) generally want children to learn as well as those they don't—for example, how to sit still and shut up versus how to interrupt class as effectively as possible.

Teachers' expectations have an effect on how students perform in the classroom. In general, their expectations are pretty much in line with students' abilities, though some factors seem to cause an outsize lowering of expectations.

According to functionalists, manifest functions are the intended consequences of social institutions, while latent functions are the unintended consequences. For example, a manifest function of education is teaching grammar and a latent function of education, the hidden curriculum, is learning about fashion.

For a number of complicated historical reasons, schools in the U.S. tend to be segregated to some degree by both race and family income. The primary driver of this trend seems to be the fact that most funding for schools comes from local property taxes, though other elements also contribute. Whereas **educational segregation** refers to the separation itself, **educational stratification** refers to the categorization of students into groups.

Families can be groups of people related by blood or by social relationships like marriage, adoption, or other similar structures. These relationships are all forms of **kinship**.

There are many terms used to classify marriages, including endogamy (marriage within one's group) and exogamy (marriage outside of one's group) as well as polygamy, which is subdivided into polygyny (one husband married to multiple wives) and polyandry (one wife married to many husbands).

There are many different types of family structure, including multigenerational families (grandparents, parents, and kids all in the same house), nuclear families (two parents with at least one child), and single-parent families (one parent and kids at home, the other absent / dead), among many others. In the U.S., multi-generational and nuclear families used to be the most common types—now, single-parent and other non-traditional structures are the norm.

Although divorce rates have skyrocketed since the 1960s, the per capita rate of divorce hit its historic peak in the 1980s before beginning a slow decline, one that continues to the present day.

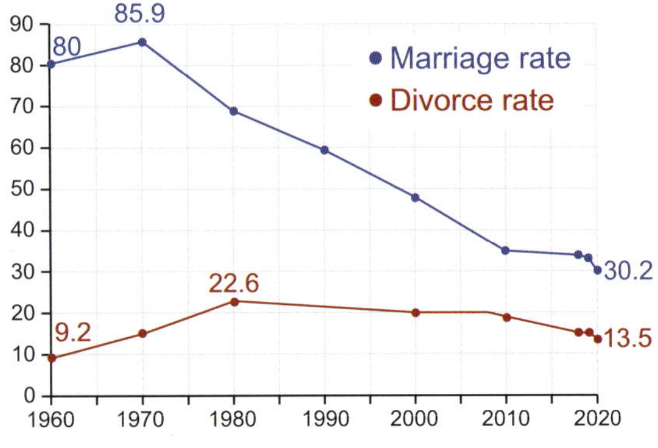

U.S. Marriage and Divorce Rates 1960 – 2020

However, the rate at which people are getting married in the States is also falling. There is a growing class divide among married and divorced people: less than a quarter of people in the bottom third income bracket are in an intact marriage, while nearly two thirds of those in the top third are still in their first marriage.

Violence within the family often constitutes abuse. Most definitions of **abuse** include physical violence, neglect, and mistreating a person verbally, sexually, or really in any way. Abuse is typically categorized as physical, psychological/emotional, and sexual. Abuse and neglect do not have to occur within the family as it also applies to outside caregivers and anyone else who interacts with vulnerable populations, including children, elderly adults, and adults of any age with certain physical or mental conditions.

Physical, emotional, or sexual maltreatment towards children is called **child abuse**, while **child neglect** involves caretakers not meeting a child's basic needs.

Elder abuse is abuse of an older person, usually 60 or 65 years or older. It is extremely common in nursing homes and in the elderly over the age of 80, and is only rarely reported by those experiencing it.

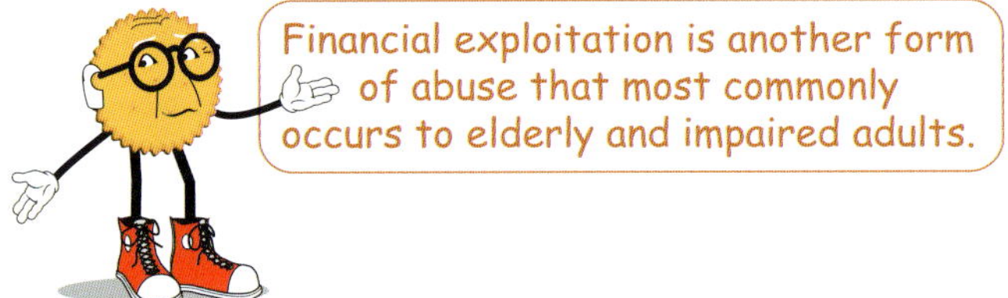

Spousal abuse is where one spouse abuses another. Both men and women are roughly equally likely to commit minor physical violence, while men are overwhelmingly more likely to seriously injure their partners.

Much like religions themselves, there is no universally accepted definition of what constitutes a religion. In general, a **religion** is a set of beliefs or practices that involve belief in the supernatural, in many cases intended to glorify a deity or deities.

Religiosity is a term meaning how religious someone is, whether it be how strongly they identify with religious teachings or how often they engage in religious activities.

Sociologists have historically sorted religious organizations into several different groups: churches, sects, and cults.

A **church** is a religious organization that people enter (usually) by being born into it. They are bureaucratic, inclusive, and compulsory—most people do not choose their own church, but are instead brought up in an already church-affiliated family.

Sects tend to be smaller than churches and are more dependent on people converting to them. Most sects are formed in response to perceived problems with the church from which they originated and with society as a whole. For these reasons, they generally have stricter ethical views and are more radical than churches.

Cults are the most radical religious organizations and espouse views and lifestyles that lie significantly outside of mainstream practices.

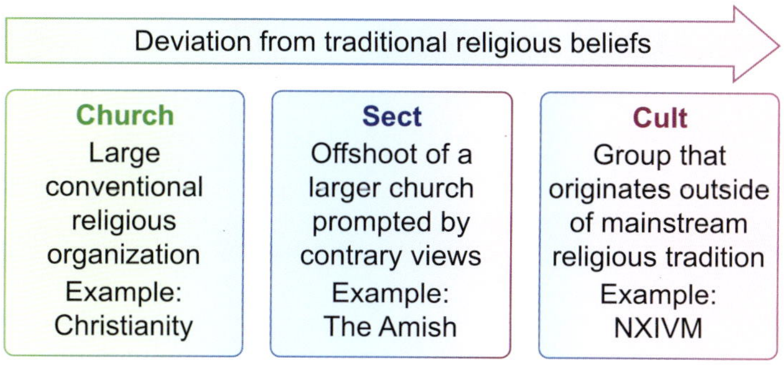

Deviation from traditional religious beliefs
Church
Large conventional religious organization
Example: Christianity
Sect
Offshoot of a larger church prompted by contrary views
Example: The Amish
Cult
Group that originates outside of mainstream religious tradition
Example: NXIVM

Religions have had to face constant pressure to adapt to cultural change, and the modern era has brought dramatic shifts in how people live.

Modernization is when a society undergoes a transition to become more like countries in Western Europe, as well as the United States, Canada, Australia, and some other nations. For reasons that are not entirely clear, this process is closely tied to **secularization**, where people identify less with religious values and institutions and more with their nonreligious counterparts.

Fundamentalism is where a religious group seeks to return to a past standard of belief and conduct, drawing distinctions between those in the fundamentalist group and those outside of it.

Government and Economy

Modern societies place power and authority in the hands of the government. This means that instead of leaving the maintenance of law and order to private citizens, certain people are employed to help keep society running smoothly.

There are many different types of governments. Some of the most common in the world today are **democracies**, where many government employees are elected by their citizens, **autocracies**, where governmental power and authority are in the hands of one person, and **oligarchies**, in which a small group of people holds political power.

Who Has Power (Makes the Rules)?
No One
One Person
Elite Few
Everyone
Anarchy
Autocracy
(Monarchy and Dictatorship)
Oligarchy
Democracy

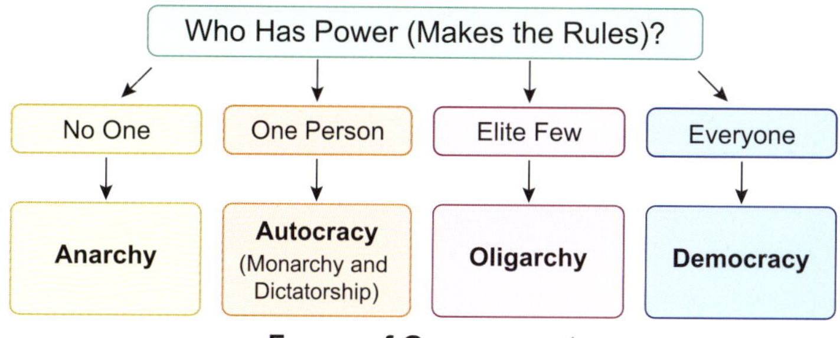

Forms of Government

In many ways, governments control the kind of economic system that a country uses.

Capitalism is an economic system based on private (that is, people that don't work for the government) ownership of the means of production (e.g., businesses and other organizations that make goods and offer services).

Socialism is an economic system that practices social ownership of the means of production. This means that

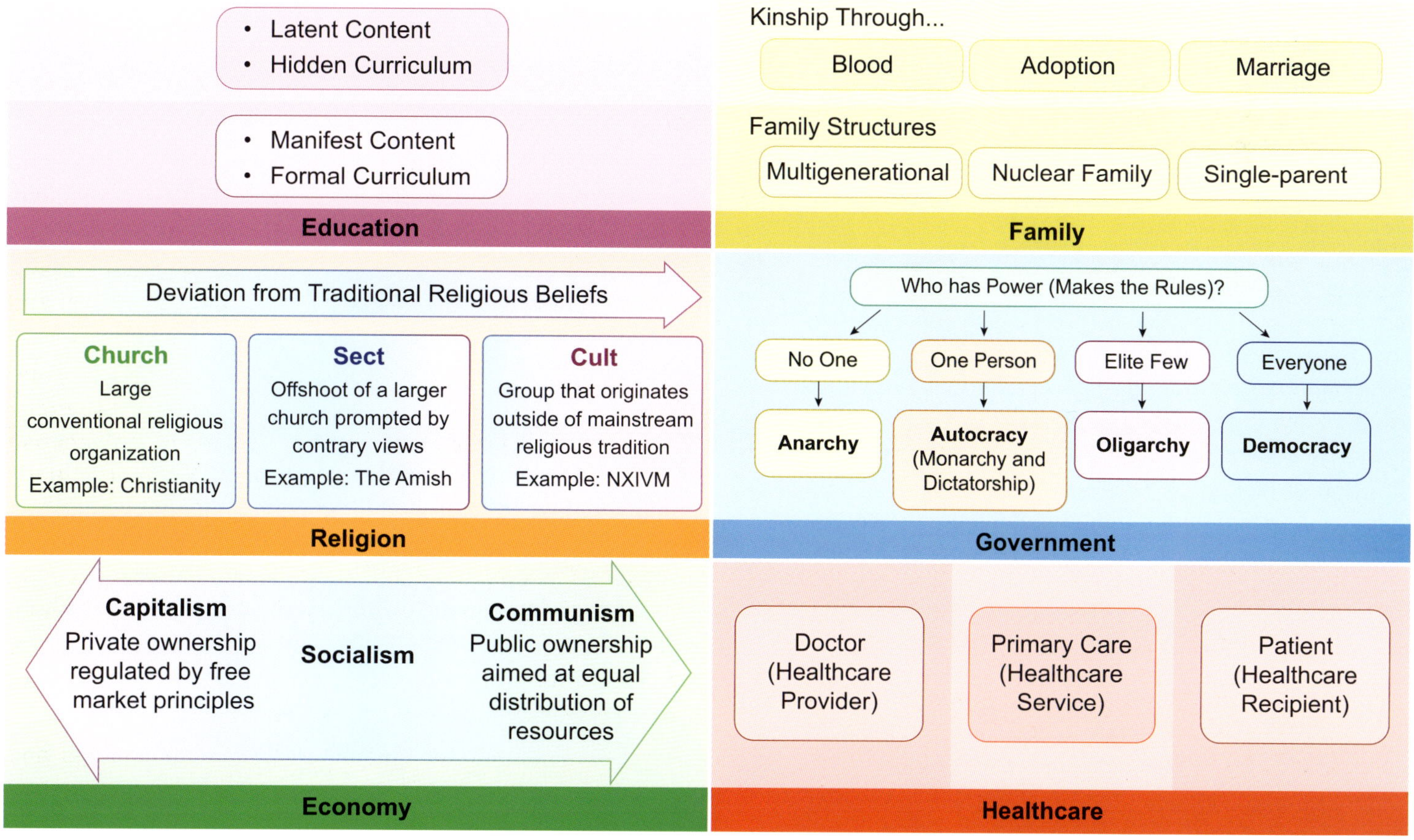

Latent Content
Hidden Curriculum
Manifest Content
Formal Curriculum
Education
Kinship Through...
Blood
Adoption
Marriage
Family Structures
Multigenerational
Nuclear Family
Single-parent
Family
Deviation from Traditional Religious Beliefs
Church
Large conventional religious organization
Example: Christianity
Sect
Offshoot of a larger church prompted by contrary views
Example: The Amish
Cult
Group that originates outside of mainstream religious tradition
Example: NXIVM
Religion
Who has Power (Makes the Rules)?
No One
One Person
Elite Few
Everyone
Anarchy
Autocracy
(Monarchy and Dictatorship)
Oligarchy
Democracy
Government
Capitalism
Private ownership regulated by free market principles
Socialism
Communism
Public ownership aimed at equal distribution of resources
Economy
Doctor
(Healthcare Provider)
Primary Care
(Healthcare Service)
Patient
(Healthcare Recipient)
Healthcare

instead of private individuals, the government controls the production of goods and services. Individuals can still own personal property and assets.

Finally, **communism** is an extreme form of socialism that aims to establish the collective ownership of all property.

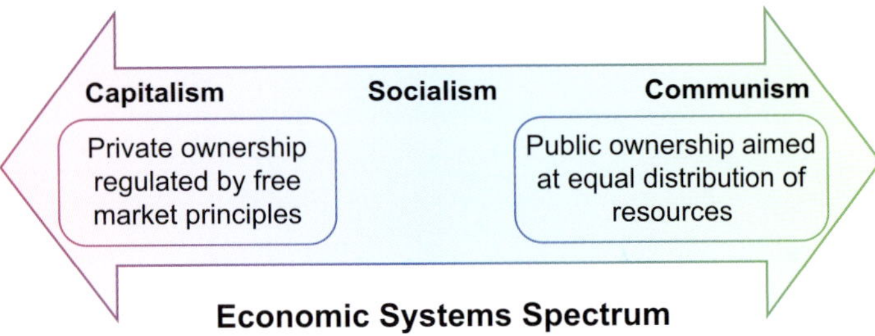

Economic Systems Spectrum

Different economic systems look at the concept of division of labor differently. **Division of labor** refers to splitting work into different smaller jobs to allow people to specialize in a given task.

Humans have been dividing labor for tens of thousands of years. Modern economies are extremely efficient, which is due in no small part to increasing levels of specialization. However, some scholars argue that as the more people specialize, the less connected they feel to their work.

Health and Medicine

Medicalization happens when parts of life shift from being considered general problems to medical problems. This process is how every medical diagnosis came about, but on occasion it goes too far, leading to both overdiagnosis and overmedication.

The **sick role** is the societal role that people take on when they're sick. This includes the ability to deviate from social norms, such as the expectation to work and contribute to society, as well as the expectation that the sick person tries his best to get better.

The **delivery of healthcare** refers to the systems through which a society provides health-related services, including private care and public health. It is a topic of constant controversy in the U.S. because Americans spend more money on healthcare per person (and overall) than any other country and yet health outcomes in the States are by and large no better than in other developed nations. Additionally, different Americans have drastically different levels of access to healthcare, and people belonging to different groups (e.g., racial, sex, income, etc.) also have different average health outcomes.

Doctors are healthcare delivery providers of services like acute care and primary care.

The **illness experience** is the subjective experience a person has while he is ill. Being diagnosed with an illness and getting sick can turn your life upside-down, and some scholars believe that the current medical system does not do enough to try to accommodate how the patient feels about his own illness.

Social epidemiology is a branch of epidemiology (study of where and how common diseases are) that focuses on how social factors affect a person's health.

Culture

Culture is the combination of a set of elements that set a society or community apart from other groups. These elements can be split into two major categories, called material and symbolic culture respectively.

Material culture refers to objects created to serve human interests. Smartphones, pencils, and nuclear weapons are all examples of material culture, while Mount Everest is not.

Symbolic culture is made up of the beliefs, rituals, symbols, values, language, etc. that are found in human societies.

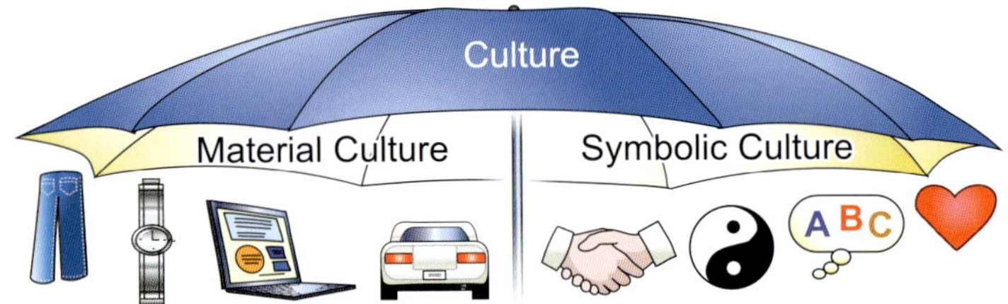

Categories of Culture

High culture can refer to aspects of culture associated with social and political elites or cultural artifacts that are widely recognized by a given culture as being great art. In contrast, **low culture** (or **pop culture)** refers to cultural products that have wide mass appeal.

Mass media is media (tools used to convey information) that reaches a large audience. Sociologists have come up with several theories that seek to explain the influence that mass media have on both individuals and the culture at large, but no dominant theory exists. Some observations that have come from trying to study this are that people are selective in the media they consume, that different types of media tend to communicate information in different ways, and that the effects of mass media are often indirect, among others.

Cultural diffusion happens when elements of culture from one society are transferred from one group to another, while **cultural transmission** is the process by which this occurs.

Culture lag happens when symbolic culture fails to keep up with changes in material culture. For example, in the span of about fifteen years the percentage of Americans that owns a smartphone has gone from 35% to over 85%. However, legislation and regulation is only just starting to catch up with the expanding influence and importance of these devices.

Culture shock can happen when a person is exposed to a culture different from his own—often, it involves a feeling of disorientation, stress, and withdrawal from social situations, though everyone has a slightly different response. It's particularly common and severe in people who move to a different country, though it usually resolves as someone adapts to the new culture.

Assimilation happens when people from a minority ethnic group or a different culture become more like the majority group or dominant culture. Until about the 1960s, assimilation was the explicit end goal for immigrants to the United States.

> Make sure not to confuse this kind of assimilation with Piaget's use of assimilation in his theory of cognitive development.

Over the past few decades, an approach called multiculturalism has come into vogue. **Multiculturalism** has the goal of forming communities of mixed ethnic or cultural heritage that live and interact with each other without sacrificing their own identities.

A **subculture** is a group of people within a culture that sets itself apart from the mainstream culture, but still shares some of the cultural elements of its parent culture.

When subcultures come into serious conflict with the dominant culture, a **counterculture** can form. Most countercultures exist on the periphery of society, but on occasion they can become large and powerful enough to cause cultural shifts—an example of these was the environmentalist movement in the 1960s.

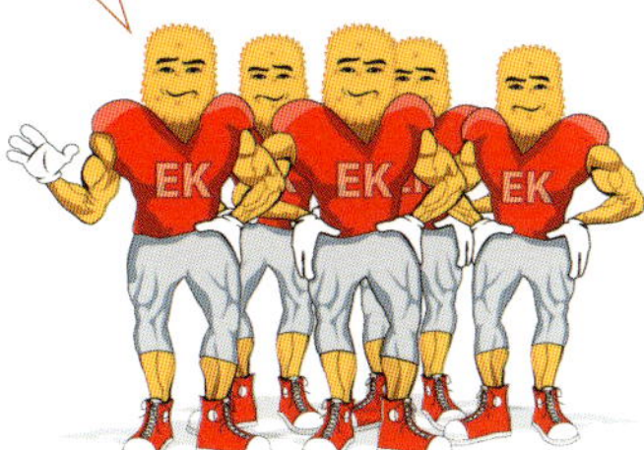

Evolutionary theory can be applied to culture as well as biology. This perspective is called **cultural evolution**, and it looks at how cultures change over time. It argues that beliefs, values, and the cultures that are associated with them compete with other ideas and cultures—the cultures that are most fit for the environment tend to survive, while those that are not die out.

Some aspects of human cultures are found in nearly every known culture. These are called **cultural universals**, and provide evidence that some aspects of human culture may be acted on by "cultural selection," or the mechanism by which cultural traits that make a culture more likely to survive and proliferate emerge and endure. Some of these include the use of language, names of people and objects, gender roles, marriage, magical (i.e., superstitious) thinking, cooking, and several dozen others.

8.3 Demographic Structure of Society

For humans, there are a few things as certain as death and taxes—one of these is aging. **Aging** is the process of getting older and all of the lovely changes that come with it, indeed, any changes in an organism over time. This includes periods of growth and development, such as puberty, as well as **senescence**—the deterioration of the machinery that makes up our bodies.

Growth

Senescence

Most sociologists study aging through a lens called life course theory. **Life course theory** is an approach to studying people's entire lives and the environmental forces that surround them by collecting data about them from birth onward. This data includes biological data, such as their height over time, psychological data, like their likelihood to develop mental disorders, and sociological data, such as the level of education their closest friends attain.

Life course theorists popularized the concept of a **cohort**, or what is more often called a generation. A **generation** is the collection of all people born in a given time period, and while the U.S. Census Bureau only recognizes one of these groups (the Baby Boomers), many other generations have been proposed and have become firmly entrenched in the public consciousness.

The **Lost Generation**: Born 1883-1900. So named because many members of this generation died during World War I.

The **Greatest Generation**: Born 1901-1927. Known for serving in the largest armed conflict in human history, World War II.

The **Silent Generation**: Born 1928-1945. Many grew up during the Great Depression, fought in Korea and Vietnam, and led the Civil Rights movement, among other things.

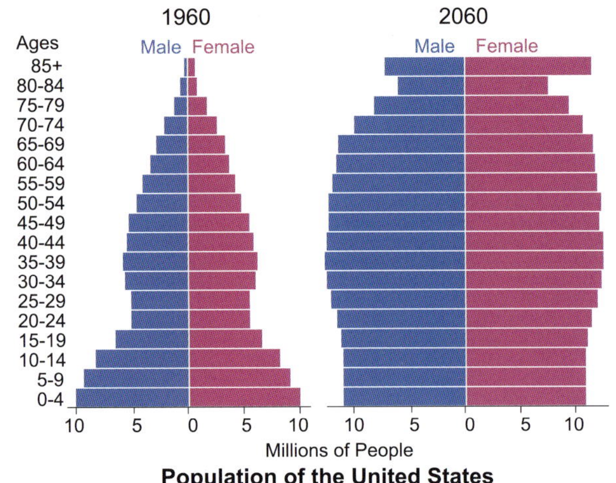

Population of the United States

The **Baby Boomers** (Boomers): Born 1946-1964. Born in the high birthrate era that followed WWII, fought in or protested against Vietnam, and known for their strong work ethic.

Generation X (Gen X): Born 1965-1980. Popularly characterized as "slackers," they have gained a reputation over time as being independent, resilient, and self-sufficient, sometimes even referred to as the "Latchkey Generation" due to higher rates of working parents.

Generation Y (Gen Y): Born 1981-1996. More often called "Millennials," they are commonly portrayed as deeply engaged with technology, as well as being optimistic, pragmatic, and altruistic.

Generation Z (Gen Z): Born 1997-2012. Also known as "Zoomers," many have had internet access since birth, and are often depicted as risk-averse, well-behaved, and concerned with educational performance and their career prospects.

Generation Alpha (Gen Alpha): Born 2013-2025. The most technologically immersed since birth, members of this generation are still children, and thus, defining characteristics have yet to be fully understood.

By 2060, the youngest living Baby Boomers will be approaching 100 years old. This large generation is a major influence on the U.S. aging population.

Sociologists have come up with nearly a dozen other theories of aging.

1. Disengagement theory
2. Activity theory
3. Continuity theory
4. Modernization theory
5. Age stratification theory

Disengagement theory says that older people experience both a physical and social loss of function later in life that leads them to withdraw from society. Although this disengagement is natural and unavoidable, it can also lead to people being marginalized in old age.

Activity theory argues that disengagement from society is not only unnecessary, but harmful. Instead, it focuses on the activities that older people are a part of, and stresses that social involvement is key to prevent the negative effects of aging.

Continuity theory states that older people tend to keep up the activities they were a part of earlier in life, and argues that maintaining the same patterns of activity and social circles helps stave off the negative psychological effects of aging.

Modernization theory posits that modernization is an inevitable process that traditional societies will go through as they adopt modern practices. In doing so, older people are at risk of being left behind by both technological and social change, creating an environment conducive to ageism (discrimination based on age).

Age stratification theory puts forth the idea that society puts pressure on people to behave a certain way depending on how old they are. Different societies exert different influences on the elderly, with some effectively

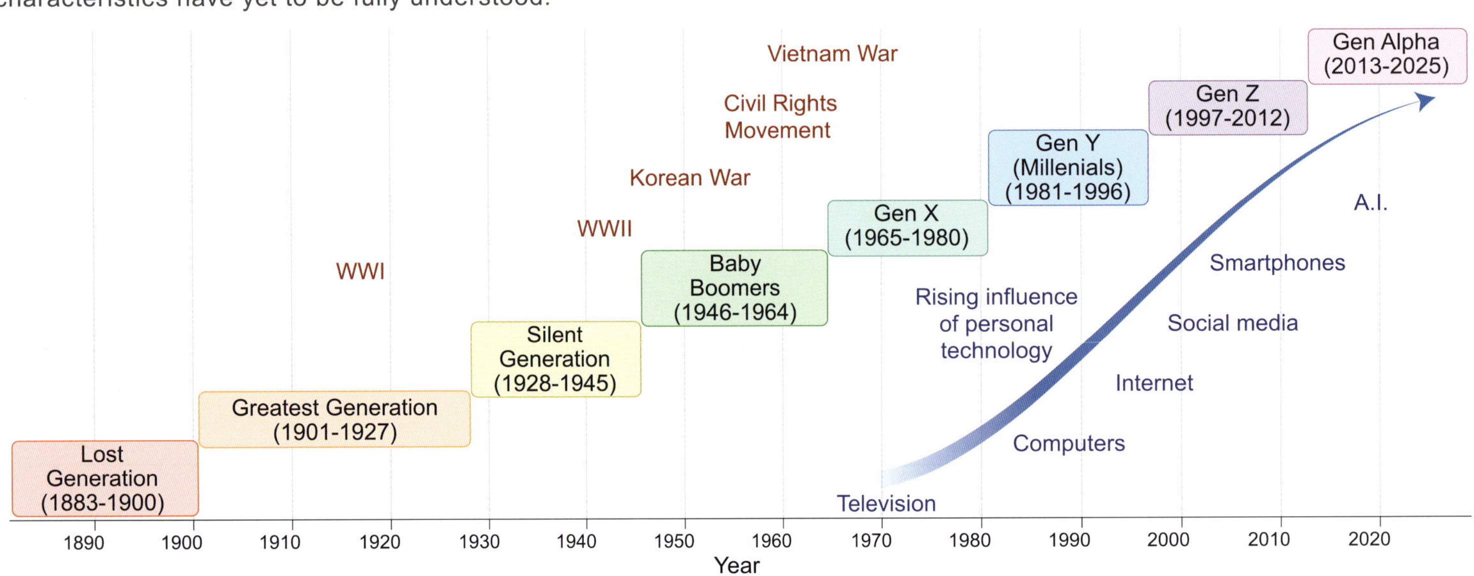

Generational Cohorts with Examples of Influential Events

excluding the elderly from politics, while others expect older people to make use of welfare programs and other government services.

The aging population is due to many factors, including lowered fertility rates and lengthened life expectancy.

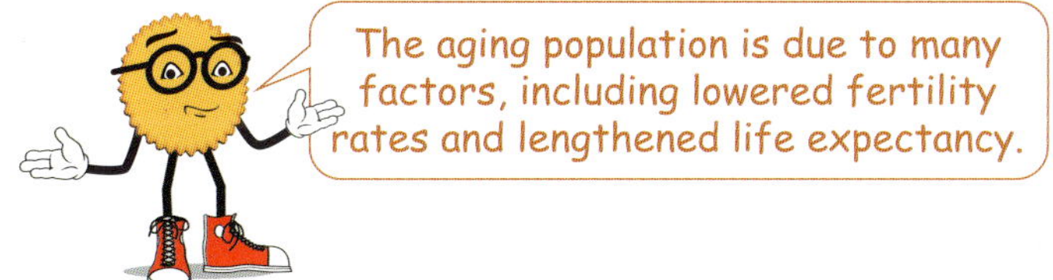

The populations of Western Europe, North America, and Japan (as well as most other nations, though to a lesser extent) are aging. This trend will have far-reaching consequences, including increased demand for health care, the slowdown or reversal of economic growth, and desire for technologies to slow or reverse senescence.

Sex and Gender

Sex is the trait that dictates whether a person is male or female. It is a biological distinction, and in humans is genetically determined.

Gender refers to the spectrum of masculinity and femininity more broadly, and encompasses psychological, behavioral, social, and cultural aspects of being a man or woman.

This distinction between sex and gender was first introduced no earlier than 1945, though defining sex and gender differently entered the academic mainstream in the 50s.

Intersex people are individuals born with chromosomal patterns, external genitalia, or sex organs that do not fit well into binary conceptions of sex as male and female. The prevalence of intersex people is estimated to be about 0.018%.

Many social scientists today consider gender to be mostly socially constructed. This has two main implications: first, people take up beliefs, norms, and attitudes about gender from the people around them, and second, gender is assigned to people based on sex (usually at birth), not something they are born with.

Gender segregation can mean different things in different contexts. One meaning is the tendency of children to separate into same-sex peer groups—this shows up at around three years of age. The other is the observation that people who work in female-dominated occupations tend to receive lower pay and worse opportunities for promotion than those who do not.

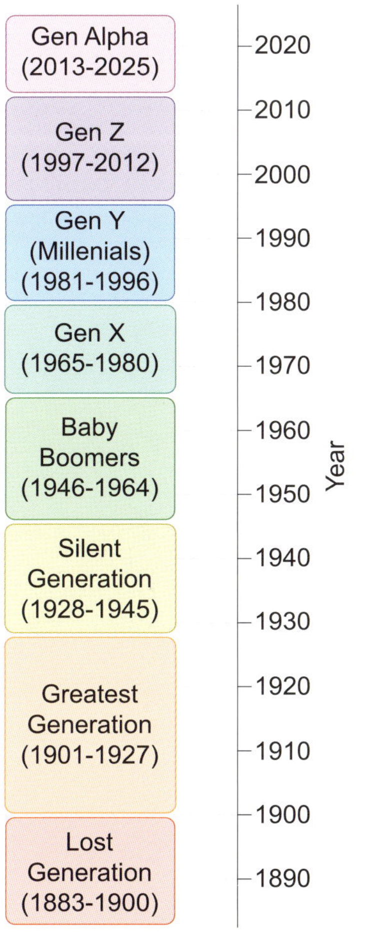

Gen Alpha (2013-2025)
Gen Z (1997-2012)
Gen Y (Millenials) (1981-1996)
Gen X (1965-1980)
Baby Boomers (1946-1964)
Silent Generation (1928-1945)
Greatest Generation (1901-1927)
Lost Generation (1883-1900)
2020
2010
2000
1990
1980
1970
1960
1950
1940
1930
1920
1910
1900
1890
Year

Generational Cohorts
Collection of people born in a specific time period

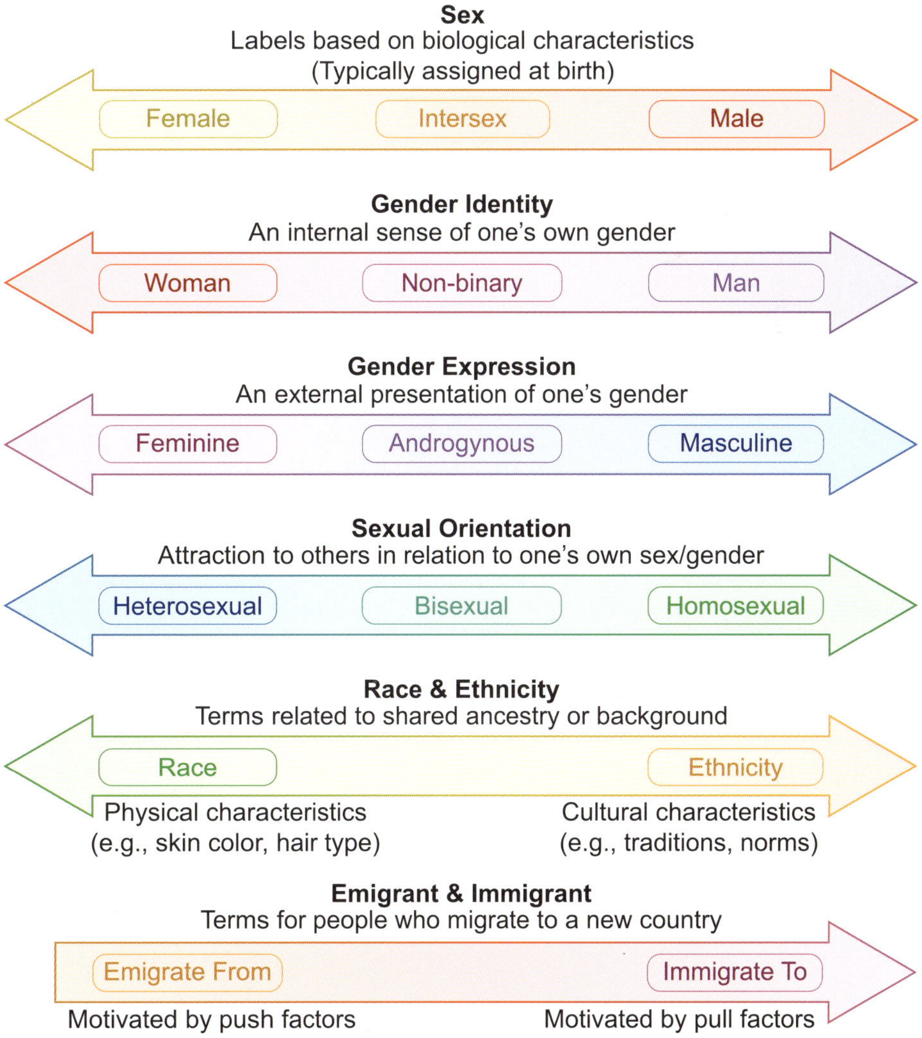

Sex
Labels based on biological characteristics
(Typically assigned at birth)
Female
Intersex
Male
Gender Identity
An internal sense of one's own gender
Woman
Non-binary
Man
Gender Expression
An external presentation of one's gender
Feminine
Androgynous
Masculine
Sexual Orientation
Attraction to others in relation to one's own sex/gender
Heterosexual
Bisexual
Homosexual
Race & Ethnicity
Terms related to shared ancestry or background
Race
Ethnicity
Physical characteristics
(e.g., skin color, hair type)
Cultural characteristics
(e.g., traditions, norms)
Emigrant & Immigrant
Terms for people who migrate to a new country
Emigrate From
Immigrate To
Motivated by push factors
Motivated by pull factors

Race and Ethnicity

Race is a term used to sort people into groups based on their physical appearance or social characteristics. Who falls into which racial group changes over time within a given society and tends to be different in different cultures, indicating that race is socially defined.

Ethnicity is similar to race, and their definitions overlap in many ways. While racial definitions tend to focus on physical characteristics, ethnicity is more concerned with traditions, language, religion, and other cultural aspects, though heritage still factors into ethnic identity.

Race and ethnicity can be similar or different. For example, someone who identifies with the racial category of Asian, may view their ethnicity as Korean, Italian, Latino, etc.

The physical traits of humans vary gradually, with groups that are geographically closer to one another being similar to those that are further apart, and their genes follow the same pattern—this phenomenon is called **clinal variation**. Furthermore, genetic studies have been used to sort people into relatively discrete racial groups, but these studies tend to use populations separated by vast geographic differences. Even when intermediate populations (that are closer to each other) are included, distinct groups show up—however, they do not map on to American racial classifications—people of Spanish and of Portuguese descent, for example, can be split into two genetically different groups.

However, the vast majority (about 85%) of genetic variation is found within populations. When compared to other mammalian species, humans show a low level of genetic variation overall, prompting geneticists to reject popular notions of racial categories.

Racialization happens when racial identities are ascribed to people in a given group, regardless of whether they themselves consider themselves to have that racial identity. This process can have effects on education, incarceration, labor, and other core parts of life—when people are associated with a racial identity, any stereotypes that come with that identity are applied to them. This effectively limits what roles they can play in society.

Racial formation is a theory that states that race is socially constructed and that the meanings of different racial categories rely on social and political factors. It also argues that race is a fundamentally unstable social category and is in constant flux—take for example the way that public perception of race changed after the Civil Rights movement. This theory also argues that political movements that secure racial reforms tend to only bring people on the same side of the issue together, and do not eliminate racial issues.

Immigration

Immigration to the United States has historically come in waves, the most recent of which being from Mexico and other Latin American countries, though the number of people entering the U.S. from Mexico probably peaked around 2010. Since then, the leading countries of origin for immigrants have been China, India, and Mexico.

Immigrants to the U.S. face a number of challenges, including but not limited to finding work, acclimating to new laws and cultural norms, and unequal treatment of them and their families by natives. However, most immigrants assimilate successfully within 20 years of arriving in the States. The rate at which they assimilate seems to be affected by their country of origin.

Emigration (exit) refers to moving away from a country and immigration (in) refers to moving to a new country.

Why do people emigrate from their home countries? A commonly-used theory breaks down reasons for migration into push and pull factors.

Push factors are things that "push" people from one country to another. They tend to be unpleasant, like poverty, war, famine, discrimination, and religious intolerance.

Pull factors are factors that "pull" people towards a particular country. They are generally things like better economic opportunities, good medical care, as well as lower crime and family ties.

Push and Pull Factors

Sexual Orientation

Most people are **heterosexual**, meaning they are sexually attracted to members of the opposite sex. Others are **homosexual**, meaning they are sexually attracted to members of their own sex. Still others are **bisexual**, meaning they are attracted to both men and women. In Western nations, about 90% of men and women state that they are exclusively heterosexual, about 8% say that they are bisexual to some degree, and about 2% report that they are completely homosexual.

A person's sexual orientation is thought to be determined by genetic, hormonal, and environmental factors. Some specific genes and chromosomal regions have been found that are associated with homosexual behavior in both sexes, but scientific understanding of how sexual orientation might be inherited is still extremely limited. Both the levels of sex hormones a fetus is exposed to and the maternal immune response to the fetus during development seem to be related to the child's eventual sexual orientation. It's anyone's guess as to what other environmental factors shape sexual orientation.

Demographic Shifts and Social Change

Malthusian theory assumes two things: first, our ability to grow the food supply for a population is linear, and second, that populations naturally follow a pattern of exponential growth. It concludes that past a certain point, we will lose the ability to support our population, leading to a rapid population decline (i.e., a famine).

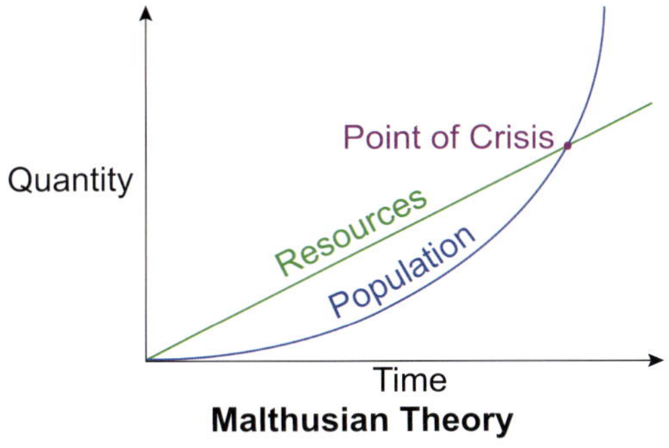

Malthusian Theory

This theory is certainly logically appealing, since we can't just assume that population growth will naturally slow or that technological innovation will save us from ourselves. However, a model concerning population growth called the demographic transition model poses serious challenges to Malthusian concerns.

The **demographic transition model** has five stages, creatively called stage 1 through stage 5.

In **stage 1**, both birth rates and mortality are high. As a result, there is little to no population growth over time. Most societies across the world remained in this stage for thousands of years, but almost all societies today have moved out of it.

In **stage 2**, mortality falls while birth rates remain high. This happens because the health of the population improves, leading to reduced infant mortality, but fertility is still high. This stage tends to create extended family structures, with most families having many children that survive to adulthood.

In **stage 3**, mortality remains low and birth rates fall. A number of reasons have been proposed for why birth rates fall during this stage, including parents adapting to high standards of living and choosing to delay or give up having children, economic changes make having children less financially viable, and women becoming more educated and entering the workforce.

In **stage 4**, mortality stays low and birth rates reach a low. Population growth slows to a standstill or reverses, and many societies that reach this stage implement programs to promote fertility or encourage immigration to try to prevent population decline.

What happens in **stage 5** is not yet clear, as people in the most developed countries are living through it right now. Although fertility rates in these nations showed a slight upward trend about a decade ago, it has since reversed and continued declining in many countries. In the U.S., for example, the fertility rate hit an all-time low in 2021.

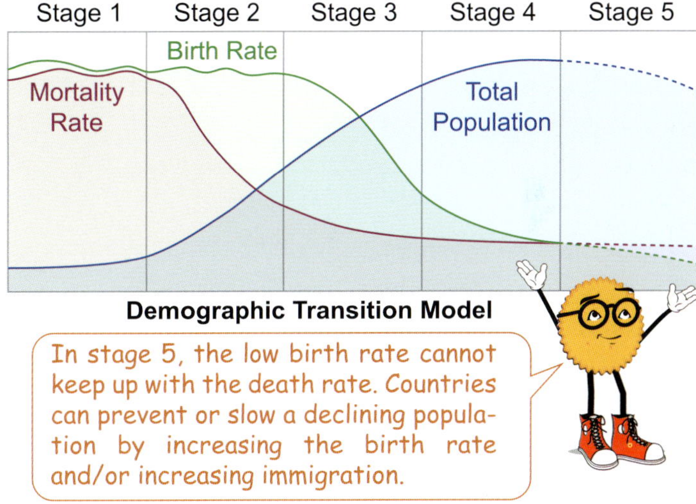

Demographic Transition Model

In stage 5, the low birth rate cannot keep up with the death rate. Countries can prevent or slow a declining population by increasing the birth rate and/or increasing immigration.

The United Nations both track the current global population and project what it will be at various points in the future. Current estimates predict that the number of people on Earth will peak in about seventy years, around 2090.

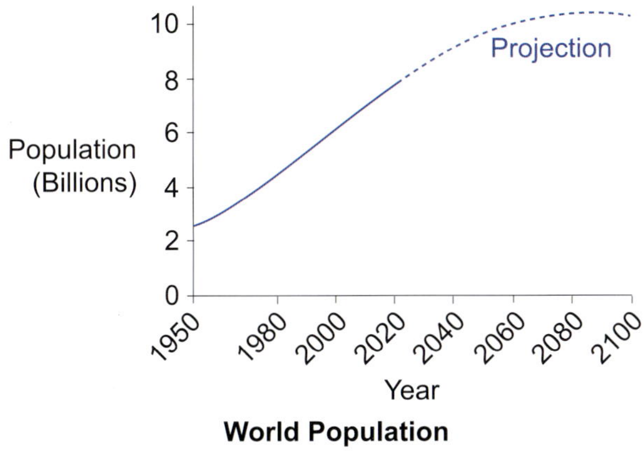

World Population

Population pyramids are a way of visualizing the age distribution of men and women in a given population. The following chart is a composite of population periods from different decades.

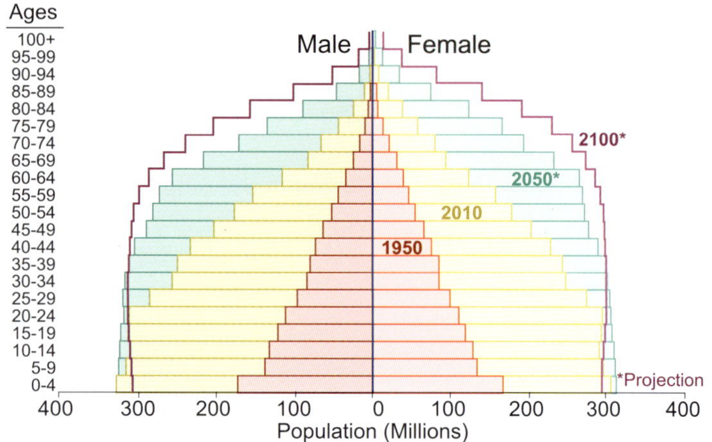

Demography of the World Population

This might look complicated to interpret, but it's not as bad as it looks. To start, look at the pyramid for 1950—it's the innermost region colored in red. The red bar at the bottom that corresponds with age 0-4, represents the number of people in the population aged 4 or under in 1950, with the number of males on the left and females on the right. As you can see, the population distribution becomes increasingly less pyramid-like as time goes on, which reflects the increasingly aging population.

We talked above about fertility and mortality rates—if you're wondering what those are, you're in the right place. The **crude birth rate** (also called **natality**) is the number of children born per year per thousand people in a population. The **mortality rate** (or **death rate**) is the number of people that die per year per thousand people in a population.

The **total fertility rate** (**TFR**) for a population is the average number of kids a woman is predicted to have in her lifetime. It's calculated by adding up the **age-specific fertility rates (ASFRs)**, which are the number of kids women at specific ages are projected to have, for the population in question.

The global TFR has been declining for decades, and will probably drop below the replacement rate (the TFR that maintains the current population) sometime in the next eighty years.

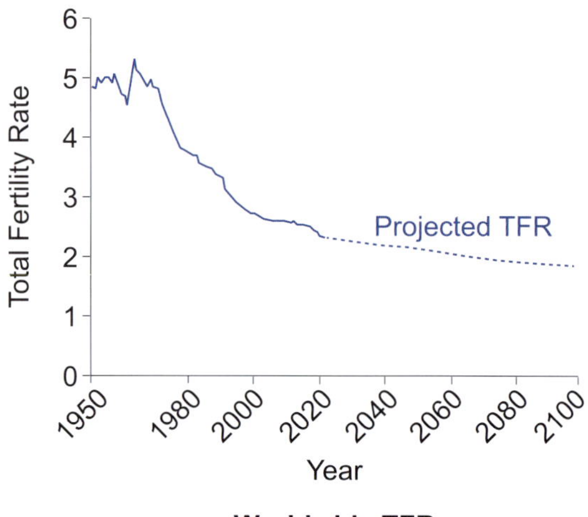

Worldwide TFR

It isn't yet clear how mortality rates will change over that same time period, but it is likely that it will drop as well as developing countries become richer.

Social Movements

Social movements are organized efforts by a significant number of people to enact change that affects everyone (reformative or revolutionary social movements) or change that is limited to specific individuals (alternative or redemptive social movements). Social movements can also be classified as progressive (aimed at enacting a new change) or regressive (aimed at resisting or undoing change).

Target of Change	Scope of Change: Partial (Specific)	Scope of Change: Total (Broad)
Individuals (Specific)	**Alternative Social Movements** (Change an aspect of an individual)	**Redemptive Social Movements** (Fundamentally change an individual)
Everyone (Broad)	**Reformative Social Movements** (Change an aspect of society)	**Revolutionary Social Movements** (Fundamentally change society)

Types of Social Movements

Social movements can be difficult to classify. Alcoholics Anonymous, for example, could be considered an alternative movement because it targets a specific behavior (not drinking) or a redemptive movement due to its fundamental impact on a person's life. In general, self-help falls under alternative and religion falls under redemptive.

Social movements require strategies and tactics in order to create change. A **strategy** is an overall plan for achieving the aim of the movement and a **tactic** is the specific action taken. For example, a strategy might be to change the current law and a tactic to do so might be lobbying.

There are a few theories that have been used to explain how these movements work.

1. Relative deprivation theory
2. Resource mobilization theory
3. Political process theory
4. New social movement theory

Relative deprivation theory argues that people join social movements because they feel like they're worse off than people they are exposed to and that joining a movement will make their lives better. In this theory, relative means compared to others, not an objective or absolute measurement. Basically, people feel discontent and motivated to participate in a social movement because they view themselves as disadvantaged relative to others.

Resource mobilization theory says that people are only able to join social movements and effect change because they have the resources and motivation to do so. It also assumes that people join these movements for rational reasons, and calculate the costs and benefits of participating in them.

Upward Comparison and Relative Deprivation

Political process theory posits that three things are necessary for social movements to form: insurgent consciousness, where people feel that they are living in an unjust system, organizational strength, which is basically the same thing that resource mobilization theory says makes social movements possible, and political opportunities, such as a weakness in the current political system.

New social movement theory puts forth two main claims: first, that the economic transition that many developed countries have gone through away from manufacturing and towards a service-based economy has caused many modern social movements, and second, that these movements are fundamentally different from the movements that came before them.

How do social movements develop? First, they emerge due to some aspect of society that a group of people feel needs to be changed. Then, they coalesce, generally in response to an event or set of events, and enter the public eye. Then, they bureaucratize, gaining many of the characteristics of organizations, such as hierarchy, explicit rules, and division of labor. From this point, many things can happen—the movement can succeed and accomplish its goals, it can fail, it can be suppressed and forced into obscurity, it can be co-opted by other movements and organizations, or it can go mainstream. The eventual outcome of all these possibilities is the decline of the social movement.

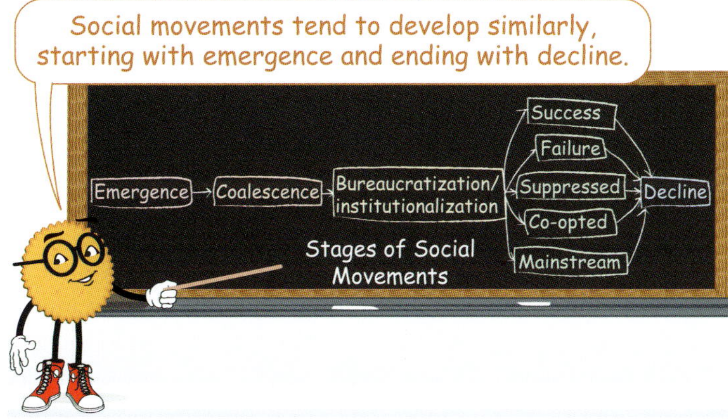

Globalization

Globalization is the integration of smaller groups of people into a worldwide network of ideas. Although globalization has been going on throughout human history, recent economic and technological developments have accelerated it to a blistering pace.

One main driver of globalization is communication technology. The internet alone has made it possible for vast numbers of people to be able to communicate nearly instantaneously. Despite its recent invention, the internet has become extremely widely available—in 1990, about one half of one percent of the world had access to it. Now, over half of the people on earth are online.

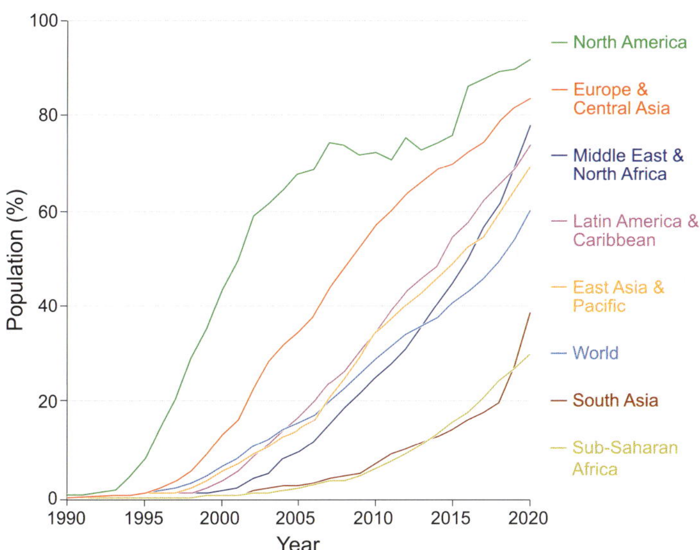

Share of the Population Using the Internet

Globalization also drives economic growth. In the decades after 1980, countries that encouraged international trade and close connections with other nations saw their economies grow as much as 5% per year, while those that did not performed much worse, at best growing 3% yearly, though average growth rates were much lower. This economic growth has dramatically reduced poverty globally, and in most countries that globalized income inequality has also fallen substantially.

Although the vast majority of economists believe that globalization is a positive force for economic growth, others argue that globalization carries significant drawbacks. Their arguments vary, but some common claims are that it is incompatible with nationalism, that it contributes to environmental degradation, and that it leads to a rise in tension between ethnic groups. Perceived inequalities related to globalization can cause social changes, including setting the stage for civil unrest or even terrorism.

Sociologists look at globalization using several different theories. The first of these that we'll look at is **world-systems theory**, which breaks up the world into three types of nation, called core nations, periphery nations, and semi-periphery nations.

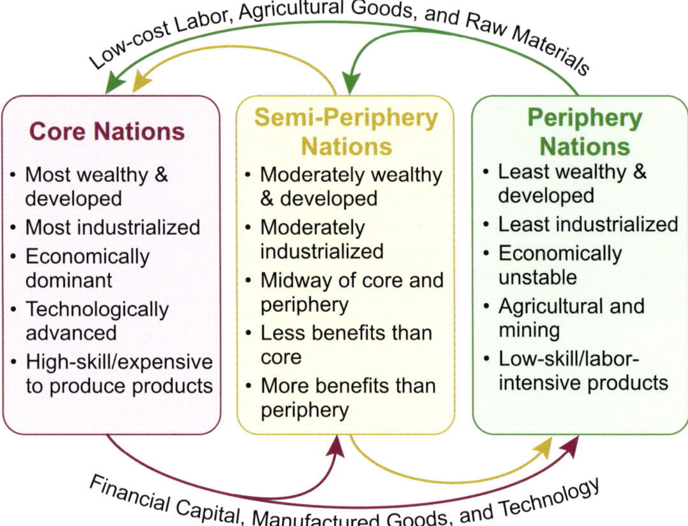

World-systems Theory

Core nations are economically, technologically, and militarily powerful, and can exercise a great deal of influence on non-core nations. **Periphery nations** are comparatively less developed, and are extensively influenced by both core nations directly and by transnational corporations. **Semi-periphery nations** are somewhere in between the two main groups, and strive to join the core states and seek to avoid becoming part of the periphery.World-systems theory essentially views the global system in terms of this economic hierarchy and its resulting trade patterns.

Dependency theory is also built on the idea of core and periphery nations. Like world-systems theory, it argues that core countries suck resources out of peripheral ones, which causes already poor regions to become impoverished, while rich areas become richer. Unlike world-systems theory, it does not recognize any benefits to the periphery nations. Its claims have been complicated by the explosive growth of India and many Asian economies over the past thirty years, as well as the reduction in global poverty seen over the same period.

Dependency theory views core countries as exploitative, while modernization theory views them as aiding growth.

Modernization theory can also be applied to globalization. This perspective states that all nations will follow similar paths in development, and that globalization will help developing nations modernize faster. World-systems theory and dependency theory emerged as critiques of modernization theory.

Urbanization

Urbanization happens when people from rural areas move to cities. Although it has been happening for thousands of years, the number of people migrating from the countryside to urban areas has increased exponentially over the past 200 years.

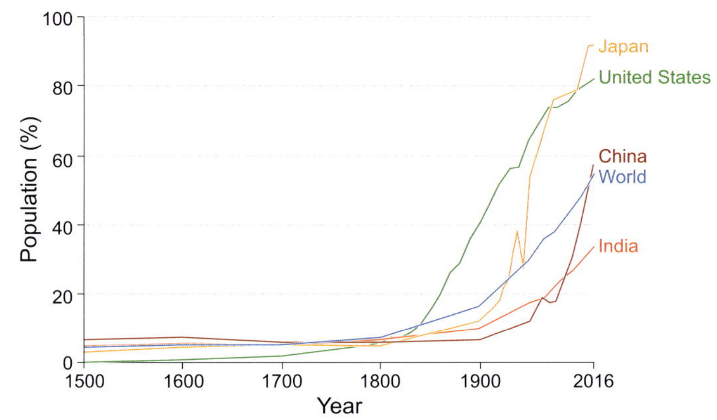

Urbanization Trends

Historically, **industrialization** has led to the growth of cities. Workers moved from villages into cities to take work at newly-constructed factories, often bringing their extended families with them. These families increasingly took jobs in the growing cities, and as farming became less economically viable in comparison to industrial work, more and more people migrated, causing cities to grow extremely quickly, a phenomenon aptly named **urban growth**.

During the 20th century, many people in some highly developed nations began to move out of urban centers and into **suburbs**, leading to a decline in inner city populations and the rise of **urban sprawl**, where land that was previously undeveloped starts to become used for housing and business. This in turn has led to an increased use of cars and drives up the cost of road infrastructure and transport more generally. Due to people leaving the cities, **suburbanization** leads to **urban decline**.

In recent decades, the high demand for suburban living has driven the cost of land down in many inner cities. This land is then bought and improved, attracting wealthy people who want an urban lifestyle in a safe, conveniently located area. Simultaneously, many cities have been undergoing **deindustrialization**, where manufacturing and heavy industry decline due to economic competition from service-based industries. This has also led to a mass exit of families from city centers, further driving down the price of urban land.

This process of urban land being improved and new residents moving in is called **gentrification**. While it generally makes the area better off economically and reduces crime rates, it also tends to displace the people already living there, as rent prices become too high for them to afford. The movement of people back into city centers as they become nicer to live in is called **urban renewal**.

The population of rural areas in the U.S. peaked in the 1940s and 50s, and has been generally declining ever since. There was a short stretch of **rural rebound**, where many areas began to see growth due to people migrating there, but it was short-lived—today, most rural areas continue to lose population as young people leave to find work in nearby cities. The term counterurbanization is sometimes used to describe the process of moving from urban to rural areas.

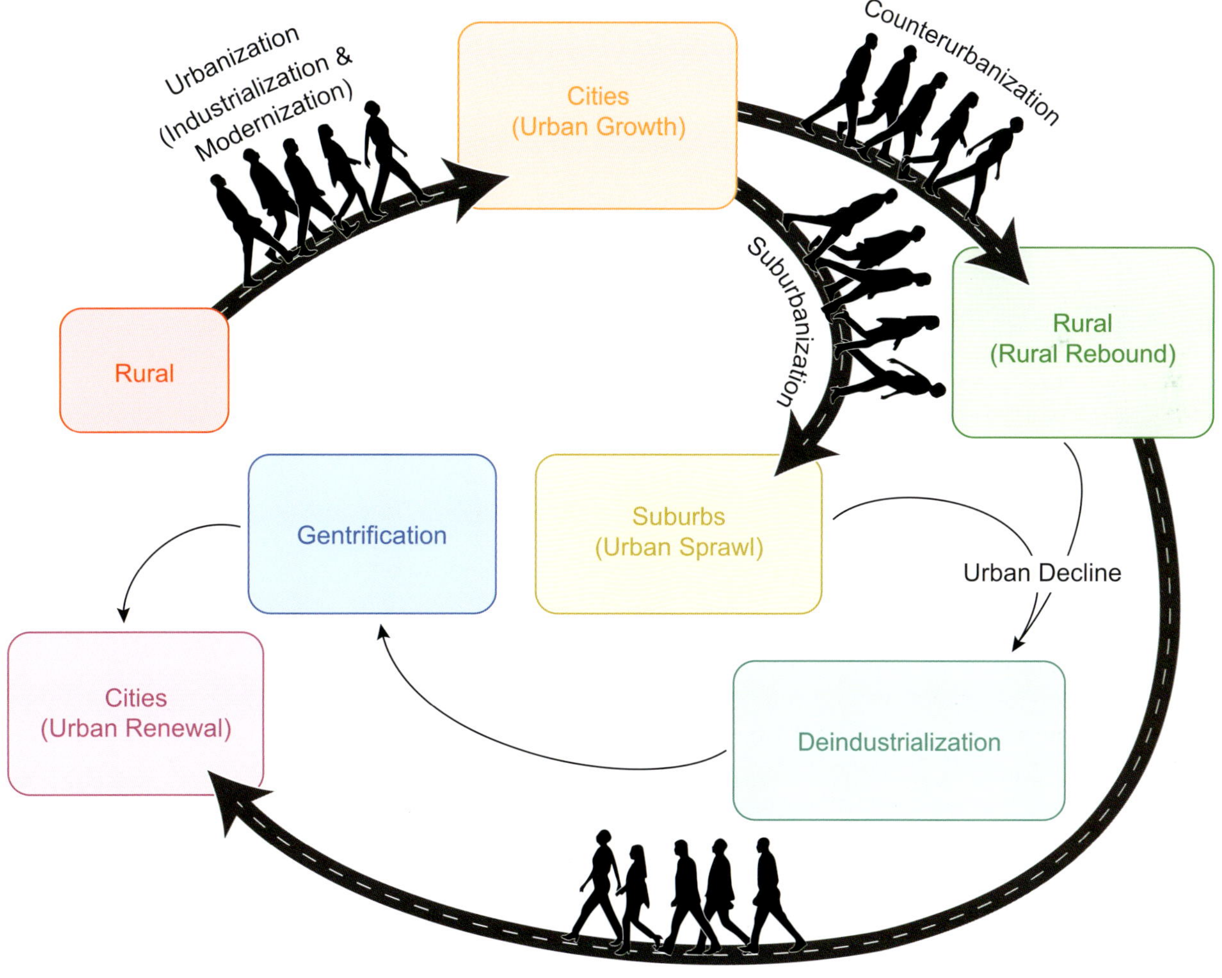

PSY

Social Interactions and Social Disparity

9

9.1 Elements of Social Interaction

Social status is a person's social position relative to the society around him. This status is a combination of all his smaller, more specific statuses, such as his status as a father, a physician, a citizen, and so on. These smaller statuses come with both rights and responsibilities and can be either achieved by or ascribed to an individual.

An **achieved status** is a status that is acquired through individual effort and competition with other people. In other words, it has to be earned. These statuses are much less common than ascribed statuses.

An **ascribed status** is a status that a person gets because of the way he is born. Differences between people who will eventually be granted this status, including those in their temperament or ability, do not matter. Ascribed statuses far outnumber achieved statuses in all social systems.

Unlike achieved status, ascribed status is based on involuntary factors, like sex, age, and inherited wealth.

A particularly important status can be called a **master status**. Master statuses tend to override other statuses, and can be either achieved or ascribed.

When someone puts the rights and responsibilities that come with a status into practice, he is performing a **role**.

Role conflict occurs when a person has trouble carrying out two or more roles because they conflict with each other. For example, working parents may find that both their performance at work suffers due to the effort of raising kids

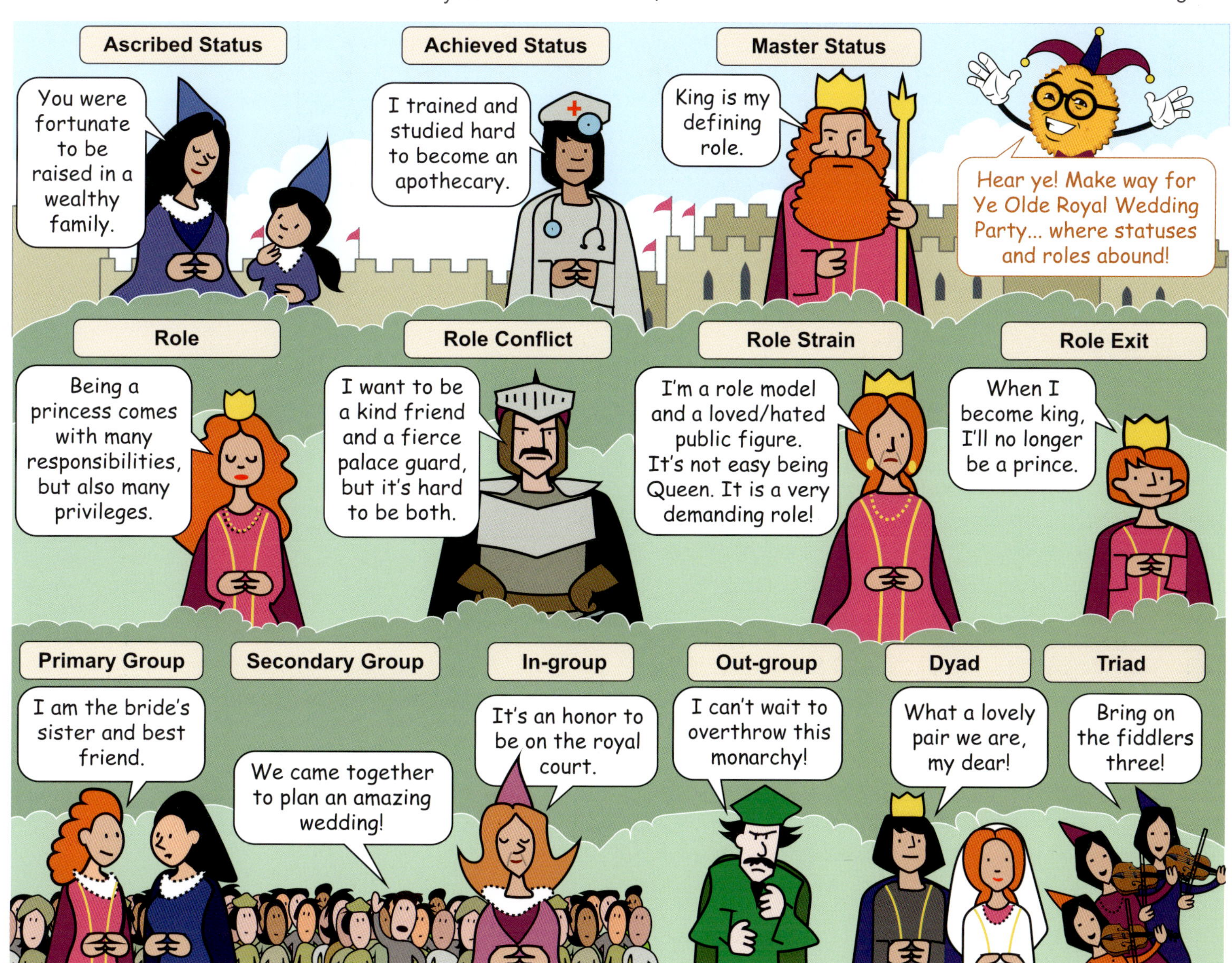

and that they can't take care of their kids as much as they'd like because of professional obligations.

Role strain is when people have difficulty performing the various obligations that come with a certain role. For medical students, these might be keeping up with lectures, studying for the STEP exams, exercising regularly, doing daily flashcards, and remembering to eat every once in a while. They might reduce this strain by minimizing interruptions, giving up nonessential roles, or delegating the tasks they need to do for other roles to different people.

Role exit happens when someone gives up a role that was previously central to his identity and takes on a new role that takes the previous role into account. For instance, a student graduating from college and going to medical school is exiting his old role as a college student and picking up the new role of medical student.

In social science, two's not company—it's a group. In general, a **group** is made of two or more people that interact with each other on a regular basis within a group structure where people have defined roles, expectations, and status.

Primary groups are usually small and are marked by close, personal, and long-lasting relationships among their members. They tend to be extremely important to the people in them, though people tend to only be in a small number of them at a time.

Secondary groups are larger, more impersonal, and easier to enter and leave than primary groups. Groups at work, volunteer organizations, and religious groups are all examples of secondary groups.

An **in-group** is a group with which a person identifies, while an **out-group** is a group with which he does not identify.

Dyads are groups of only two people, while **triads** are groups of three people. Dyads tend to be less stable than triads since they are more intimate, increasing the amount of damage any change of heart or disagreement can have to the group.

Social networks are structures formed by the social relationships between a given group of people. They aren't physical constructs, but are nevertheless important for understanding a wide range of phenomena. In medicine, analyzing social networks can be used to predict people's risk to start smoking, develop obesity, get an STD, and many other health outcomes.

Social Networks

Modern societies are dominated by **formal organizations**. There are three types of formal organizations.

1. Normative organizations
2. Coercive organizations
3. Utilitarian organizations

Normative organizations (a.k.a. voluntary organizations) are formed due to the shared interests of their members, and benefit people in them in intangible ways. Chess clubs, the American Legion, and student councils are all examples of normative organizations.

Coercive organizations are groups that people need to be forced into joining.. Some examples are prison and psychiatric hospitals.

Utilitarian organizations are centered around achieving material rewards for their members. For example, graduating from medical school gives people a medical degree, and a hospital or private practice is formed to make money.

	Normative Organizations	Coercive Organizations	Utilitarian Organizations
Membership	Voluntary (As Desired)	Involuntary (Forced)	Voluntary (Contractual)
Benefit	Intangible (Moral, Interest)	Corrective (Rehabilitation)	Tangible (Money, Status)
Example	Doctors Without Borders	Prison	Universities

Formal Organizations

Over time, pretty much every formal organization tries its best to become a **bureaucracy**. An ideal (one that serves as a model for other bureaucracies, not necessarily one that everyone agrees is best) bureaucracy has four main attributes.

1. Hierarchy
2. Division of labor
3. Impersonality
4. Explicit rules

A **hierarchy** is a structure where some people are in charge of other people. If you have a boss or you are the boss, you're in a hierarchical organization.

A **division of labor** means that different people in the organization do different things. In an emergency room, for example, EMTs take patients from an ambulance to a room, medical students try to get medical histories from said patients, and ER physicians do their best to stop said medical students from killing anyone.

Impersonality is the removal of personal feelings from a professional setting. It's the attribute of organizations that requires physicians to provide treatment for someone who injured himself while breaking into a house or for a person you suspect to be abusing his spouse.

Explicit rules are written, standardized, and generally have formal punishments for breaking them. In the medical field, these are normally outlined in contracts with the hospital, clinic, or university that you're working for.

Hierarchy	Impersonality
Division Of Labor	Explicit Rules

Attributes of an Ideal Bureaucracy

Some scholars have argued that bureaucracies (and every organization that starts as a democracy) follow a trend called the **iron law of oligarchy**. This "law" states that as time goes on, organizations tend to become less democratic and more oligarchic, meaning that the organization's power is concentrated in the hands of fewer and fewer people.

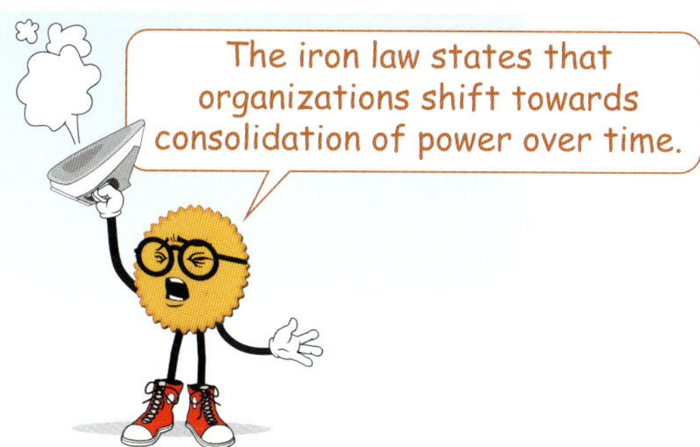

Another proposed trend in organizational structure is called **McDonaldization**. If you've ever driven through a small town and seen the bizarre, slightly depressing combination of boarded-up shops on Main Street and a hodgepodge of fast food (and other chain) stores, you were looking at the results of McDonaldization.

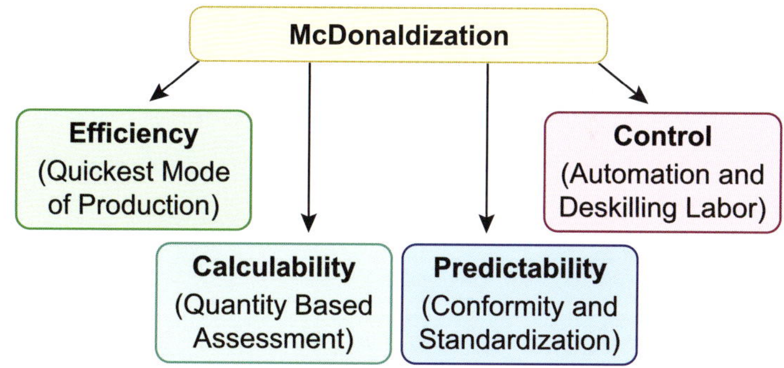

Principles of McDonaldization

	Normative Organizations	Coercive Organizations	Utilitarian Organizations
Membership	Voluntary (As Desired)	Involuntary (Forced)	Voluntary (Contractual)
Benefit	Intangible (Moral, Interest)	Corrective (Rehabilitation)	Tangible (Money, Status)
Example	Doctors Without Borders	Prison	Universities

Formal Organizations

Hierarchy	**Impersonality**
Division of Labor	**Explicit Rules**

Attributes of an Ideal Bureaucracy

McDonaldization

Efficiency (Quickest Mode of Production)

Calculability (Quantity Based Assessment)

Predictability (Conformity and Standardization)

Control (Automation and Deskilling Labor)

Principles of McDonaldization

Time

Democratic (Shared Power)

Oligarchic (Consolidated Power)

Iron Law of Oligarchy

Trends in Bureaucracies Over Time

In more general terms, McDonaldization is a name for the observation that more and more organizations are run according to the principles that made McDonald's successful. These are, in no particular order, efficiency, calculability, predictability, and control.

9.2 Self-Presentation and Interacting with Others

Detecting Emotion

Most people are able to intuitively understand how other people are feeling based on their facial expressions, the tone of their voice, body language, and other factors. Not everyone is equally good at this, though. Differences have been found between men and women, people from different cultures, and people with various mental disorders.

Children are typically good at identifying facial expressions of anger, but have a harder time with emotions like surprise.

In general, women tend to be better than men at detecting emotion in subtle facial expressions. They also tend to be superior at picking out emotions when the expression is at the limit of what can be consciously processed, such as when faces are flashed on a screen for less than a second. Men and women seem to be equally good at identifying more obvious expressions of emotion.

People from different cultures detect emotions in different ways. On the whole, people from East Asian cultures tend to focus on the eyes when determining which emotion a person's face is displaying, while Westerners are more likely to look at the whole face to make a determination. Additionally, people across a broad range of cultures change how they look at others' faces depending on the social context of an interaction.

People with certain mental disorders, such as autism spectrum disorder and schizophrenia, detect emotion differently than people without these disorders. It is currently believed that people with autism develop alternative methods of determining what emotion a face conveys, improving their performance on these measures to match that of people without autism. People with schizophrenia, on the other hand, show more extensive deficits in emotion recognition, and men with the disorder seem to be affected worse than women are.

Presentation of Self

If you've ever seen (or read) Shakespeare's *As You Like It*, you might be familiar with one of Jacques' now-legendary monologues, known best by its opening line, "all the world's a stage." Sociologist Erving Goffman took this speech about as literally as he could and created **dramaturgy**, a sociological perspective that tries to explain how people present themselves to others using metaphors derived from the theater.

Dramaturgy splits people's actions into **stages** (like one in a theater, not stages in a process). The **front-stage self** refers to how people behave when they know they're being watched by others, while the **back-stage self** refers to people's actions when they are no longer performing for others—that is, when they know that nobody's watching.

Front-stage Self

Back-stage Self

Dramaturgical Approach

People spend a lot of time and energy controlling how they come across to other people—dramaturgy calls this **impression management**. In general, the front stage is where people put the most effort towards impression management, since they have an audience to critique their every action. The back stage, where the audience is not allowed to go, is a place where actors can rest and recuperate. There they can act how they please, and usually spend time refining their routines for the next time they go to the front stage.

Verbal and Nonverbal Communication

We rely on both verbal and nonverbal communication to transmit information to other people. Although researchers don't universally agree on what constitutes verbal and nonverbal communication, for our purposes we're going to consider verbal communication the transfer of information from one person to another using words, while nonverbal communication is any method of communication that doesn't use words.

Verbal vs. Nonverbal Communication

Some scientists have tried to quantify the relative importance of both types of communication, coming up with figures from 66% to 93% for the amount of meaning carried by nonverbal communication with the remainder being attributed to verbal communication. For our purposes, these percentages aren't terribly important. Instead, it is important to recognize that both types of communication are important.

Verbal and nonverbal communication work in conjunction with each other. The two types of communication can conflict with one another, leading to confusion, or they can complement each other—imagine someone nodding and saying, "yes," versus someone nodding and saying, "no." Nonverbal communication is the starting point for face-to-face communication—verbal communication works to clarify meaning that can't be captured using purely nonverbal communication.

Animal Signals and Communication

Unless you find yourself in a Disney movie, or perhaps in a particularly bizarre dream, non-human animals can't talk. However, they are still able to communicate with each other and with animals from other species. To do so, they use practically every tool available to them, from simple visual signals to complex patterns of sound.

There are dozens of different modalities that animals use for communication, but for the MCAT it's most important to understand the types that most animals (including humans) share. These include: visual, auditory, somatosensory, and olfactory/gustatory signals.

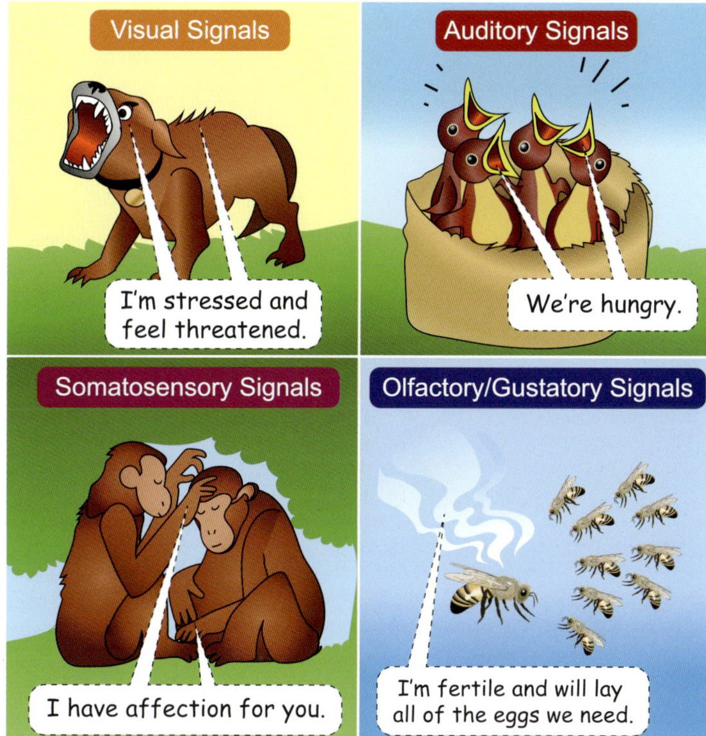

Animal Signals and Communication

Visual signals include gestures, postures, facial expressions, color changes, and anything else that can be visually identified by other organisms.

Auditory signals range from vocalizations to stridulation (rubbing body parts together), but all involve making noise for the purpose of communicating.

Somatosensory signals are touches, and can include grooming, huddling, mating, and other related behaviors.

Olfactory/gustatory signals are smells and tastes, and fall under the broader umbrella of chemical signals.

Like humans, non-human animals communicate to change the behavior of other animals. Some animals even perform **autocommunication**, or communication with oneself to get information—bats do this through echolocation, while electric fish accomplish this with electrolocation.

9.3 Social Behavior

Attraction refers to the feeling that leads people to form relationships with others. These relationships can be platonic or romantic, and both types of relationships are founded on similar psychological principles.

One of the strongest predictors of whether people will become friends or romantic partners is **proximity**. Although physical distance is an important factor in evaluating proximity, even more important is **functional distance**, or the likelihood of two people coming into contact in some way. This means that people who frequently write letters to each other or are in constant contact on social media can be said to be in close proximity, while next-door neighbors who never meet aren't in close proximity.

Most researchers think that the reason we tend to like people in close proximity to us is due mainly to the **mere exposure effect**—that is, we prefer objects, people, ideas, etc. that we are more familiar with over those that are unfamiliar to us.

Mere Exposure Effect

Other factors that help explain why proximity is a good predictor of the likelihood that two people will get to know each other are predictability (though too much can be boring), low costs—you don't have to give much up to stay in contact with this person, and an expectation of continued interaction. If you can't easily avoid coming into contact with someone, such as at work or school, you'll tend to try harder to see his good sides and downplay things you don't like about him.

Similarity is another important factor in predicting whether two people will form a relationship. How people look (physical characteristics like attractiveness and ethnicity), what they believe, how they act, and their social status all seem to be factors that people use to compare themselves to potential friends or romantic partners.

For better or worse, **physical attraction** seems to be the most important predictor of whether or not people will enter and maintain romantic relationships. Other factors, like social status and personality, are by no means useless predictors, but pale in comparison to physical beauty.

Although many aspects of physical attraction vary somewhat across cultures, what it means to be beautiful is surprisingly similar around the world. Physical characteristics that are nearly universally considered attractive for men to have are the combination of broad shoulders, a narrow waist, tall height, a muscular body, and a generally "masculine" face. Women's beauty, in comparison, comes from wide hips, firm breasts, a narrow waist, and a neotenous (young-looking), "feminine" face.

Both men and women are generally considered attractive if they have a normal to slightly-below normal BMI, a flat abdomen, and symmetrical faces and bodies. Additionally, "average" faces, which are composite pictures of faces generated by using thousands of pictures of people, are consistently rated as more attractive than any random face from the set of images used to generate them.

Aggression is behavior intended to cause harm. It can be direct or indirect, physical or verbal, and is thought to be influenced by several factors, including biological, psychological, and cultural factors.

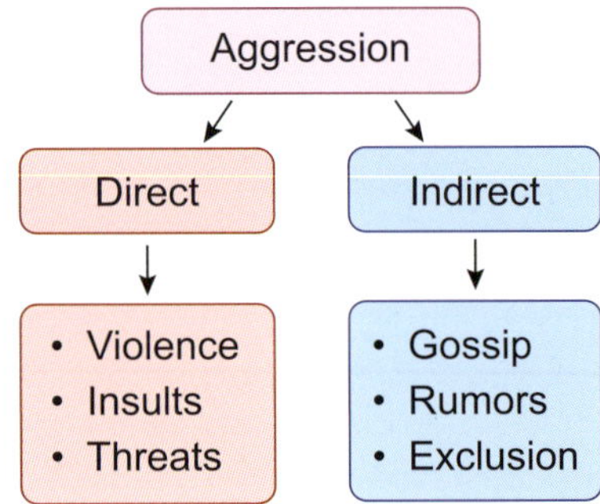

Direct vs. Indirect Aggression

Biological factors that impact aggression include a person's sex and genetic makeup. On average, men are more aggressive than women are. This includes both physical and verbal aggression, though men and women tend to express verbal aggression in different ways, with men being more direct (e.g., open insults) and women being more indirect (e.g., gossip / rumor spreading). It is thought that these differences come primarily from different average levels of **testosterone** between men and women, though cultural expectations of how men and women are supposed to act probably influence aggression too.

As with most traits in humans, aggression is influenced by both genetics and the environment. Although individual genes that make people more or less likely to be aggressive have not been identified, twin studies have consistently shown that aggression is a heritable trait.

One of the oldest psychological explanations for aggression is the **frustration-aggression hypothesis**. This hypothesis states that people display aggression when they are prevented from accomplishing a goal. This aggression can be directed at the source or can be displaced onto someone else.

Related to the frustration-aggression hypothesis is the **relative deprivation hypothesis**, which argues that people are more likely to become aggressive, hold prejudiced views, and discriminate against others when they believe they have been deprived of something they rightly deserve.

Another proposed psychological theory to explain aggression is **behavioral modeling**. Most closely associated with Albert Bandura and his Bobo Doll experiment, this theory argues that people learn aggressive behaviors from other people and use their actions as a model for how they should act. So, if a kid sees his parents yelling at each other during an argument, he might learn that yelling is appropriate when you disagree with someone else.

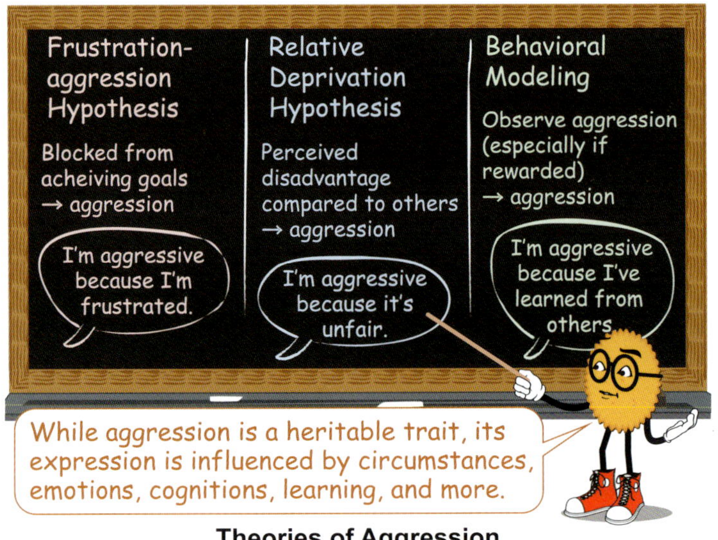

Theories of Aggression

Cultural differences can also change how people express aggression. For example, Americans from the South tend to be more likely to respond with aggression to insults or accidental physical contact (e.g., bumping into someone) than Northerners. When people are asked what circumstances might justify different types of aggression, there seems to be cross-cultural agreement about when physical aggression is appropriate. However, people from different cultures disagree over the use of verbal aggression, suggesting that verbal aggression might be more heavily influenced by culture than physical aggression.

Attachment refers to a close bond between two people, usually between a parent and child. Attachment theory, originally developed by Mary Ainsworth and John Bowlby, says the relationships between kids and their parents can be sorted into different types of attachment, called **attachment patterns**.

Bowlby came up with attachment theory in response to a set of experiments performed by Harry Harlow that were designed to test why children became attached to their mothers. To do so, he took infant Rhesus monkeys away from their mothers shortly after their birth and raised them in a lab with two types of artificial mother. The first of these, the wire mother, provided the babies with food but with no physical comfort. The second, the cloth mother, offered no food, but was soft and looked more monkey-like than its metal counterpart. When the monkeys were scared to see which mother they would run to, they overwhelmingly chose the cloth mother. This suggested that the little ones had a stronger attachment to the cloth mother than to the wire mother.

Mary Ainsworth also used experiments to investigate attachment—however, she tested human children instead of Rhesus monkeys and was consequently nicer to her test subjects. Using a setup called the **strange situation procedure**, which involved eight episodes in which the baby is with their mom and/or the experimenter (stranger) or alone. Based on the baby's reactions, she identified three distinct attachment patterns: secure attachment, anxious-ambivalent attachment, and avoidant attachment.

Harlow's Experiment

Babies who show **secure attachment** use their mother a bit like a home base while playing, venturing out on their own but returning to her when they've had enough. When they're separated from their mothers they become clearly upset, but they are quickly calmed when she comes back.

Anxious-ambivalent attachment is marked by a baby being anxious even in the presence of his mother, completely breaking down when she leaves, all while not being particularly happy when she returns.

Infants showing **avoidant attachment** don't seek much contact with their mothers at all, and aren't generally upset when she leaves or happy when she returns.

	Secure	Anxious-Ambivalent	Avoidant
Reaction to Mom Separation	Mild Distress	Intense Distress	Indifference
Reaction to Mom Returning	Happy/Soothed	Upset/Clingy	Ignore/Reject
Reaction to the Stranger	Explore/Interest	Avoid/Fear	Indifference
Comfort by Mom/Stranger	Both (Prefers Mom)	Mom Only	Both (Equally)
Schema (Working Model)	I am safe	I am scared	I am alone
Caregiver Behavior	Consistent Care	Inconsistent Care	Unavailable Care

Attachment Patterns

How mothers treat their children when they're infants seems to influence which attachment style the kid in question will form. Specifically, mothers who are sensitive to their children's needs are more likely to have securely attached children than mothers who are less sensitive.

Attachment patterns are pretty stable over time. Securely attached children tend to have higher self esteem, have fewer problems with aggression, and show better cognitive development throughout adolescence. Adults who were securely attached as children also are more likely to have fulfilling romantic relationships, to be less accepting of casual sex, and to be more comfortable with their own sexuality.

How parents treat their children matters throughout their development, not just during the first few years of life. Parents' strategies towards child rearing are called **parenting styles**. There are four main parenting styles.

1. Authoritative
2. Permissive
3. Authoritarian
4. Neglectful

Authoritative parents are demanding and responsive—in other words, they have high expectations of their children's behavior, but are forgiving, foster dialogue with their kids, and encourage their children to develop independence. Children raised by authoritative parents have been shown in some studies to be more successful than children raised by parents using other parenting styles.

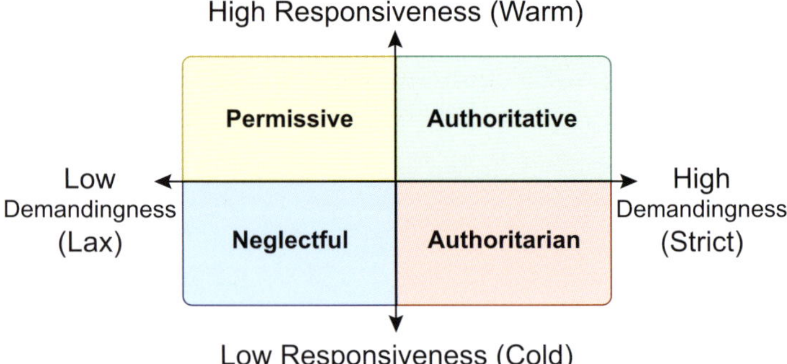

Permissive parents have few expectations for their children, but are still deeply involved in their kids' lives. As such, children of these parents tend to feel nurtured and accepted, but because their parents don't require them to develop self-control, they seem to be more likely to engage in risky, dangerous, or aggressive behaviors.

Authoritarian parents are strict, but do not adequately respond to their children's needs. This can result in kids becoming adults who are conformist, obedient (or rebellious!), and unhappy.

Neglectful parents have little or no expectations for their children, and do so because they are not involved in their children's lives. Kids raised by neglectful parents are more likely to feel lonely, sad, and become involved in abusive relationships or engage in risky behavior.

Altruism is behavior intended to help others that has no immediately obvious benefit and a clear cost to the person performing it.

Evolutionary biologists have long been perplexed by altruism—some perspectives from these thinkers will be covered in more detail later. Psychologists don't widely agree about whether true altruism exists, mainly because

	Secure	Anxious-ambivalent	Avoidant
Reaction to mom separation	Mild distress	Intense distress	Indifference
Reaction to mom returning	Happy/soothed	Upset/clingy	Ignore/reject
Reaction to the stranger	Explore/interest	Avoid/fear	Indifference
Comfort by mom/stranger	Both (prefers mom)	Mom only	Both (equally)
Schema (working model)	I am safe	I am scared	I am alone
Caregiver behavior	Consistent care	Inconsistent care	Unavailable care
Example	Mom is my safe base and my needs are usually met.	I have to exaggerate my needs to ensure they are met.	I have to rely on myself to get my needs met.

Attachment Patterns

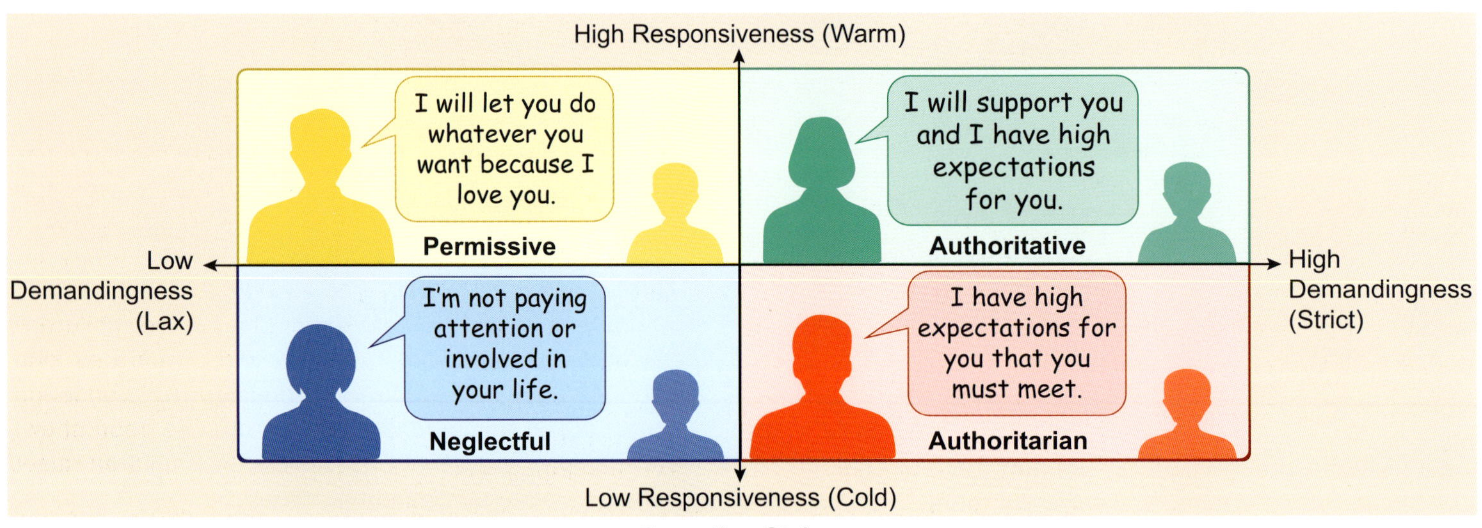

Parenting Styles

it's not clear whether people actually benefit from altruistic acts or not.

The **empathy-altruism hypothesis** states that people are intrinsically motivated to be altruistic because of their capacity for empathy. In other words, people help others due to genuine concern for their well-being, and are not necessarily motivated by a reward. **Social exchange theory**, on the other hand, argues that people only act altruistically when they think they're going to benefit from doing so (and that what they gain is greater than what they give up in the process). This perspective views altruism as a fundamentally selfish act.

Most psychological studies of altruism, including ones that look at people's volunteerism, acts of kindness, and general support of the people around them, find that altruistic acts improve the health and well-being of the people that perform them.

Social support is where a person gives something, be it time, money, or a shoulder to cry on, to another person with the intent of making their life better. There are four main types of social support.

1. Tangible support
2. Emotional support
3. Informational support
4. Companionship support

Social Support

Tangible support is support in the form of material goods or services. **Emotional support** is help in the form of concern, love, trust, and other related ways. **Informational support** is aid in the form of guidance or other useful information. Finally, **companionship support** is support that gives people a sense of belonging to a social group.

People who feel like they have good social support are more likely to enjoy better physical and mental health than people who report low levels of social support. Men and women tend to use their social support networks differently, with women tending to seek emotional support more often than men do (both sexes rely on support networks to the same extent for the other types of social support). People from Western cultures are more likely to lean on support networks and to expect more from said networks than those from Asian cultures.

Biological Explanations of Social Behavior in Animals

Foraging is how animals search for food in their surroundings. Both genetics and learning influence foraging behaviors, and the extent to which either factor contributes depends on the animal in question. There are two types of foraging: solitary and group foraging.

Solitary foraging is when animals hunt for food on their own. Most species of bee are solitary foragers, and seldom if ever search for food with their conspecifics.

Group foraging is where animals hunt for food in a group. Compared to solitary foraging, group foraging carries the drawback of potentially leading to conflict within a group over limited food resources. However, animals that forage in groups can catch prey that is risky or impossible to catch on their own, which might outweigh the cost of splitting a quarry among multiple hunters.

Solitary Foraging **Group Foraging**

There are three main strategies that animals use to find mates (reproductive partners).

1. Assortative mating
2. Disassortative mating
3. Random mating

Assortative mating describes a mating pattern where animals choose mates that are more similar to them than would be expected with random mating. Humans tend to pick partners that are like them both genetically and socially. In other words, spouses are more likely to be genetically similar than if they were chosen at random, and the same goes for their social statuses.

Disassortative mating is where animals choose mates that are more different to themselves than if they chose mates at random. Although this mate choosing style doesn't seem to heavily influence human mating, it has been shown that humans prefer mates that have different genes than they do for specific traits. For example, people tend to like the smell of partners that have different MHC complex genes from them.

Random mating (a.k.a. panmixia) is a strategy where animals choose mates at random. Although random mating is one of the assumptions required for Hardy-Weinberg equilibrium , random mating only shows up in a handful of species.

Of these three types of mating, humans fall squarely into the camp of assortative mating. That is, people tend to choose partners that are like themselves instead of people that are different from them. Biologists think that this happens because assortative mating increases humans' inclusive fitness.

Inclusive fitness is a measure of evolutionary fitness that takes into account how many offspring an organism supports, regardless of whether or not those offspring are direct descendants of that organism. Mating with humans that are genetically similar to yourself means that even if you aren't particularly successful from an evolutionary standpoint (i.e., you have low personal fitness), your family members are more likely to pass on genes similar to your own.

Game theory is the study of how rational people play games with clear rules. When applied to evolution, it's called **evolutionary game theory** and examines how genes can cause game strategies to change over time.

The details of how evolutionary game theory works are considerably more complicated than required for the MCAT. However, it would be good to know that it's been used to model altruism, human morality, and private property, among other things.

Now's a good time to look at altruism again, this time through an evolutionary lens. Evolutionary biologists have proposed a few different mechanisms that might drive the development of altruistic behavior.

1. Kin selection
2. Reciprocal altruism
3. Costly signaling

Kin selection is a form of inclusive fitness in which an organism favors the survival of its relatives over all else, including its own safety and reproductive success. In humans, this means that people tend to treat their relatives nicer than strangers, and their children better than anyone else.

Reciprocal altruism is where people are kind to others with the expectation that the person they help will reciprocate. This hope can be for direct compensation, such as when a wealthy donor gives money to a medical school with the expectation that they will someday name a building after him. It can also be for indirect reciprocity, like boosting a person's reputation in general.

Costly signaling is when an organism uses signals to communicate that they have resources. In humans, this often manifests as altruism—for example, the more money someone has, the more he can donate without seriously compromising his standard of living. Among other things, hunting, art, and long courtship times have been proposed as examples of costly signaling.

Evolutionary Theories of Altruism

Discrimination

Discrimination is the behavioral component of **prejudice**. This means that instead of including prejudicial feelings or thoughts, discrimination refers to prejudicial actions.

Discrimination carried out by a single person is called **individual discrimination**, while discrimination carried out by an organization is called **institutional discrimination**.

As with many things in life, power, prestige, and class can make it easier for someone to discriminate against another person and get away with it relatively unscathed.

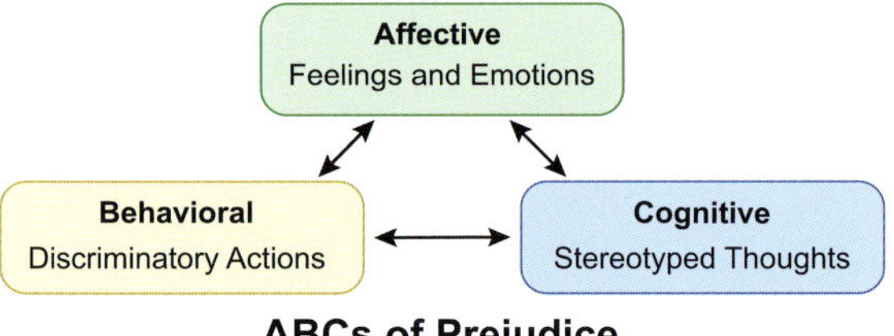

ABCs of Prejudice

9.4 Social Inequality

Social inequality is the unequal distribution of opportunities or treatment of individuals within a society based on various demographic categories, such as age, race, and gender.

Social inequality can exist on the global, national, or local level. **Global inequalities** are evident in the disparities between regions and nations in gross national product, natural resources, access to healthcare, and types or amounts of work available, among other things.

Spatial inequality describes how geography impacts unequal access to resources. For instance, some poor areas (labeled by the U.S. Department of Agriculture as **food deserts**) lack convenient access to grocery stores. Spatial inequality influences health by affecting access to healthcare providers, diagnostic equipment, and options for treatment.

Where someone lives affects their access to jobs, healthcare, and other resources.

On a local scale, separation of demographic groups into different neighborhoods is referred to as **residential segregation**. Location affects access to transportation, quality of education, availability of goods, health hazards, and levels of crime or feelings of personal safety. In U.S. cities, residential segregation often involves race and/or income level.

Residential Segregation

People who live in segregated areas may feel that they are excluded from society. This occurs in a process called **social exclusion** and can be due to a number of factors—for example, many people in segregated areas have reduced access to resources like good schools, healthcare, and employment. Additionally, segregation can cause people to perceive that they are cut off from mainstream culture, further contributing to feelings of exclusion.

Social isolation occurs when a person does not have frequent, meaningful interactions with other people. It commonly leads to loneliness, which in turn may lead to an increased risk of cardiovascular disease, high blood pressure and cholesterol, and obesity, among other conditions. Common treatments for chronic loneliness include cognitive behavioral therapy (CBT), physical exercise, and antidepressants.

Both segregation and social isolation can make people feel socially excluded.

The degree to which a neighborhood is violent or safe affects everyone who lives in it. For example, kids that live in violent neighborhoods tend to perform worse in school, older adults in unsafe neighborhoods have worse health outcomes than those in safe neighborhoods, and neighborhood violence increases the rate of depression in adults that live in them. There is some evidence that cleaning dilapidated neighborhoods up helps reduce the crime rate, though many other possible interventions have yet to be studied.

Environmental justice is the fair treatment and meaningful involvement of all people regardless of race, or income, with respect to the development, implementation, and enforcement of environmental laws, regulations, and policies. More simply stated, environmental justice asserts that lawmakers should consider the welfare of all people when creating laws that affect the environment. One important aspect of environmental justice is evaluating and addressing inequities related to location and exposure to health risks.

9.5 Social Class

Social stratification is the separation of society into groups according to similarities in social standing. **Social standing** involves 3 key aspects.

1. **Status**—the relative prestige, authority, and privilege of a person or group
2. **Power**—influence and control over others
3. **Social class**—associated with socioeconomic status (SES), which is defined by one's **income** (assets earned), **wealth** (assets already owned), education, and occupation

Status is how an individual ranks or is perceived to rank in the hierarchy of his social group. It is related to his reputation and his prestige. **Prestige** refers to the degree of respect afforded to an individual due to rank, reputation, and authority. In the United States, prestige is often connected to wealth and occupation.

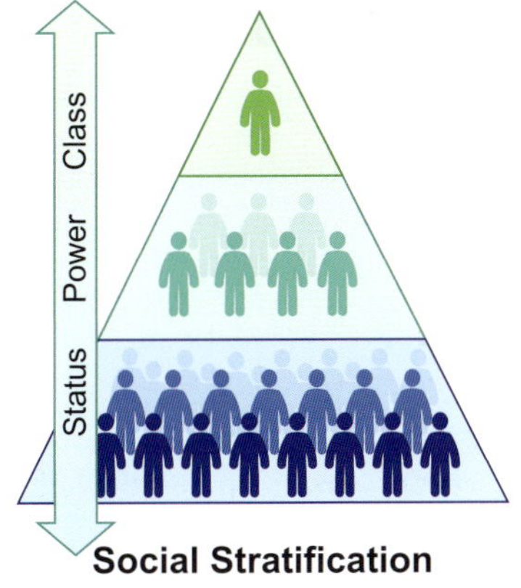

Social Stratification

Power is divided into two categories.

1. **Authority** (lawful use of power)
2. **Coercion** (unlawful use of power)

There are three types of authority.

1. **Traditional authority** (involving power that is inherited)
2. **Legal-rational authority** (based on laws)

3. **Charismatic authority** (based on one's identity and traits)

Social Standing
Status
Prestige
Power
Authority
Coercion
Traditional
Legal-rational
Charismatic
Social Class
SES/Wealth
Education/ Occupation
Demographics
Social standing is based on three key components: status, power, and social class.

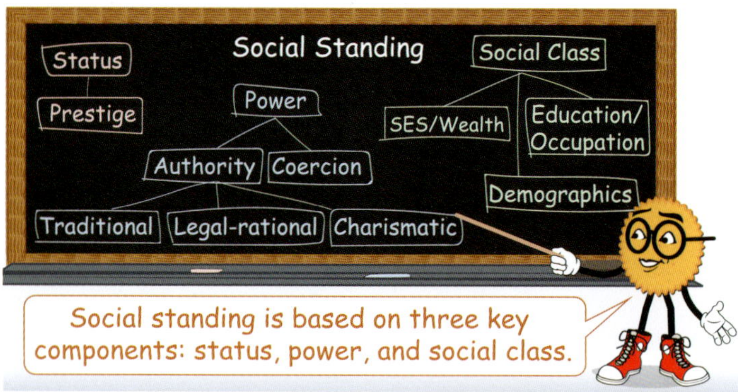

The AAMC adheres to a uniquely American definition of **social class**, relying on economic rather than social factors, yet using class to emphasize social disparities between demographic groups. For the AAMC, an individual qualifies for a social class through either his economic or demographic position. As such, the AAMC may view wealthy minorities as being in a lower social class than one might expect, while explaining differences in outcomes between different groups through social factors instead of economic ones.

Classes are loosely divided into upper, middle, and lower classes. The **upper class** consists of the wealthy and, in some cases, those born into prominent or once-wealthy families. Members of the upper class are more likely to receive greater educational opportunities, work in high-paying careers, and have greater influence in cultural and political affairs.

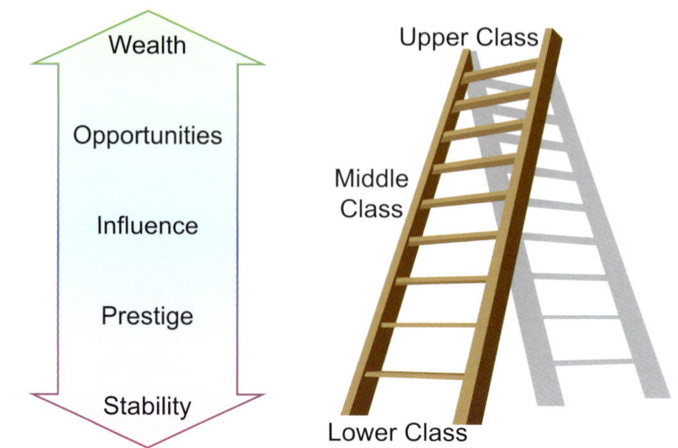

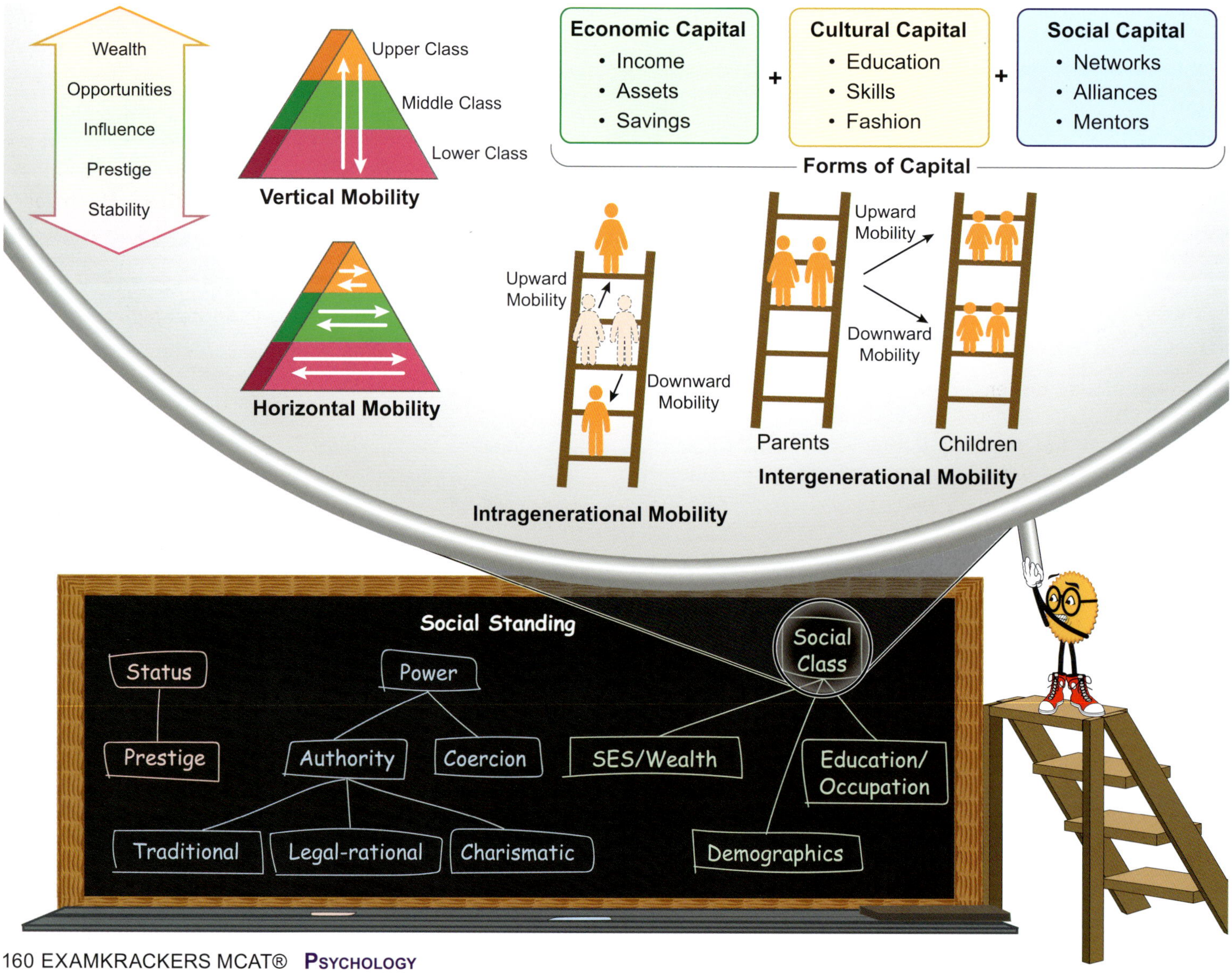

Wealth
Opportunities
Influence
Prestige
Stability
Upper Class
Middle Class
Lower Class

Wealth
Opportunities
Influence
Prestige
Stability
Upper Class
Middle Class
Lower Class
Vertical Mobility
Horizontal Mobility
Economic Capital
• Income
• Assets
• Savings
+
Cultural Capital
• Education
• Skills
• Fashion
+
Social Capital
• Networks
• Alliances
• Mentors
Forms of Capital
Upward Mobility
Downward Mobility
Intragenerational Mobility
Upward Mobility
Downward Mobility
Parents
Children
Intergenerational Mobility
Social Standing
Status
Prestige
Power
Authority
Coercion
Traditional
Legal-rational
Charismatic
Social Class
SES/Wealth
Education/ Occupation
Demographics

The **middle class** describes financially stable individuals, but those with less wealth than the upper class. Middle class has been redefined so many times that it is a nearly meaningless term. In the U.S., college degrees and post-graduate degrees are common among the middle class. In the U.S., it has become common for members of the middle class to receive some type of government assistance. Members of the middle class are often active in the local public school system and local government.

The **lower class** is characterized by economic hardship or uncertainty. Members of the lower class include lower-paid wage workers, the unemployed or underemployed, and the homeless. Members of the lower class rely heavily on government assistance. They may be less aware of the opportunities available to them that lead to improved economic status, or they may lack the encouragement from family members to pursue such opportunities.

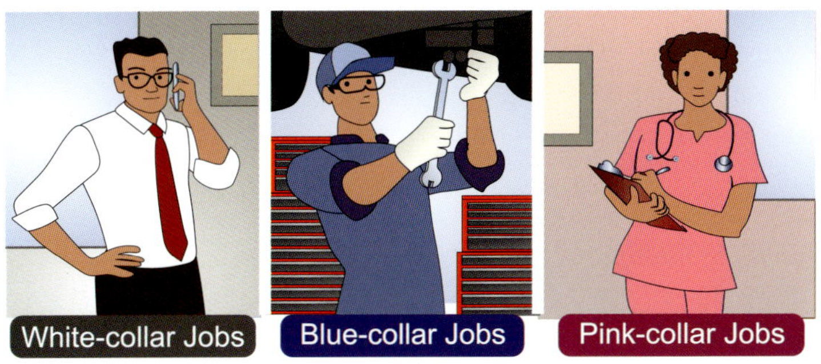

White-collar work describes professional, administrative, or managerial jobs. **Blue-collar jobs** are occupations requiring skilled or unskilled manual labor. **Pink-collar jobs** are those jobs that were once considered women's work, such as nurses, teachers, secretaries, etc., and tend to be lower paying than other jobs.

9.6 Patterns of Social Mobility

Unlike a class system, which likely includes fluidity to move between classes, a **caste system** strictly defines the hierarchy of society. Position is inherited, and movement or marriage between castes is prohibited. In a class system, it may be possible for individuals of all classes to move up or down class hierarchy.

The extent to which movement in a class system is possible is known as **upward and downward mobility.** Movement upward may be achieved through education, marriage, and career or financial success. Movement downward may be the result of unemployment or underemployment, reduced household income due to divorce, lack of education, or health issues.

Mobility can also be described as vertical or horizontal. Mobility can also be described as vertical or horizontal. **Vertical movement** involves movement into another class (upward and downward). **Horizontal movement** involves movement within the same class, such as doing the same job for another company. The U.S. has a highly mobile social system compared to many other countries, but opportunities for upward mobility have remained mostly the same since the 1970s.

Vertical movement is shifting up or down to a new class, whereas horizontal movement takes place within the same class.

Someone with **privilege** has advantages of power and opportunity over those who lack the same privilege. Privilege may result from perception, custom, or law.

Power	**Prestige**	**Privilege**
• Influence	• Reputation	• Benefits
• Control	• Respect	• Advantages

Three P's of Social Status

In some societies, race may be connected with privilege. Because a minority, by definition, has fewer members, its members may be perceived by society as different from the norm. If the difference is perceived negatively, a general prejudice may form, and members not in the minority may enjoy opportunities not enjoyed by members of the minority. This is known as **racial privilege**. Note that the negative perception of the minority may come to be held by even the members of the minority themselves. The reverse may happen as well, where prejudice directed against the majority groups may arise. Members of minority groups, especially those with inclinations towards racial activism, are especially likely to hold anti-majority prejudicial views. Similarly, members of minority groups can integrate prejudices against other minority groups.

Racial privilege can become ingrained into a society by custom in spite of law. For instance, in the old South, "separate but equal" legislation segregating Black people rarely resulted in equal conditions, yet it was widely accepted as ethical. In another example of racial privilege by custom, currently in the U.S. the commonplace suggestion that a member of the majority is an inappropriate candidate for certain positions of power and prestige based at least partially upon race. Racial privilege may be codified by law, such as slavery in the early U.S. and affirmative action in the modern U.S. Such racial privilege is said to be institutionalized.

People don't just have one social identity, but many. Social scientists tend to focus on an extremely limited number of demographic categories, chiefly race, gender, SES, in their research—this is due in part to the predictive importance of these classifications, as well as the convenience of collecting data pertinent to these groups and ideological commitments to the centrality of these demographic groupings in particular. A person's place in society extends far beyond these demographic groupings—indeed, there is a near-infinite number of characteristics a person can have that affects him socially. On top of this, these characteristics interact with each other, sometimes in extremely unpredictable ways. These two elements form the foundation of **intersectionality**.

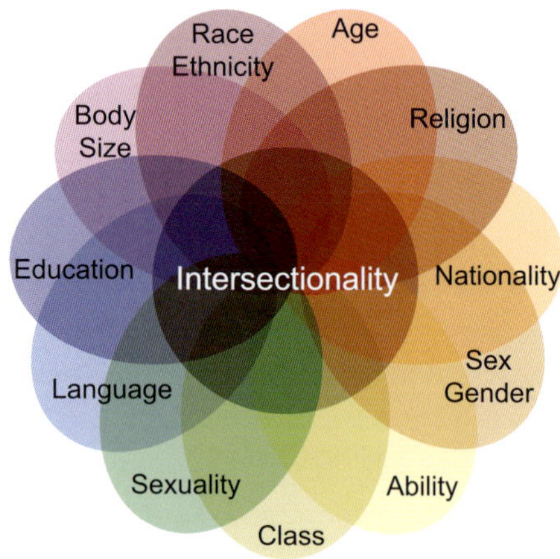

The validity of intersectionality as a concept is undeniably real. A person born with prodigal musical ability might go on to become a famous violinist due to his immense inborn talent. The same person, were he born without functional hands, would probably not be able to do so. However, intersectional theorists, and by extension the general public with even a passing interest in intersectionality, have the tendency to hyperfocus on the demographic categories of race, gender, and sexual orientation. While there is nothing inherently wrong with investigating how these categories interact with each other to shape people's lives, hyperfocusing on any set of characteristics runs the risk of oversimplifying the diversity of human traits and how they combine to produce different outcomes for the people that exhibit them.

Sometimes immigrant families moving to the U.S. may lack formal education, professional skills, or mastery of the English language. However, their children or grandchildren may become physicians, lawyers, and senators through greater access to resources gained over one or more generations and move into a higher class. Movement within the class system that takes place in a single generation is called **intragenerational mobility**. Movement requiring more than one generation is called **intergenerational mobility**.

> *Intra means within, while inter means between. So intragenerational mobility happens within one generation and intergenerational mobility happens between two or more generations.*

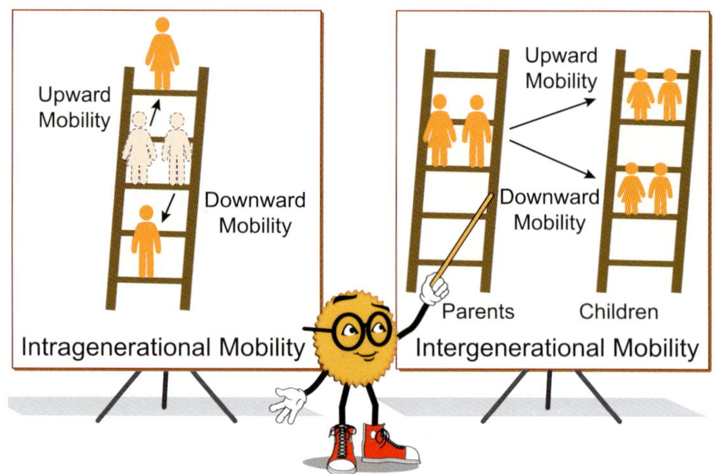

Although no other country in the world offers more opportunity to all its citizens, America is not a pure **meritocracy** (a society in which advancement is based solely on merit). For example, the law in America provides for an individual to have some influence over the distribution of his wealth after his death. In other words, wealth—**economic capital**—can be passed down from parents to children, creating greater opportunity for the recipients of generational wealth. Additionally, there are complicated social systems that both hamstring people who are already performing highly and that prevent people from achieving their full potential—some examples of these are affirmative action programs and widely held prejudices based on race or gender.

Cultural capital, as well, is a happenstance of birth. Cultural capital is the set of non-monetary and non-social network factors that contribute to upward social mobility. Examples of cultural capital include dress, accent, vernacular, manners, education, cultural knowledge, and intellectual pursuits. Different cultures value and nurture cultural capital to different degrees, creating unequal advantages for upward mobility for their children.

Social capital is another non-monetary factor contributing to upward mobility. Social capital refers to an individual's social networks and connections that confer an advantage in social mobility. The essence of social capital is that "who you know" matters.

Inherited economic, cultural, and social capitals contribute to the maintenance of a stratified society. The transmission of social inequality from one generation to the next is known as **social reproduction**.

Economic Capital
- Income
- Assets
- Savings

+

Cultural Capital
- Education
- Skills
- Fashion

+

Social Capital
- Networks
- Alliances
- Mentors

Forms of Capital

Social Reproduction

Of course, some inequality in and of itself is not only inevitable, but can be a positive attribute of a society. Accomplishment of any kind is generally rewarded, perhaps by financial gain (economic capital), academic credentials (cultural capital), or new connections (social capital). These rewards serve as motivation for continued productive behavior.

Perhaps more importantly, the essence of any economy depends upon inequality; one person wants what another person has, resulting in trade. When no one is perceived to possess something desirable to another, there is little motivation to work or to trade, which makes it difficult for an economy to function.

Equality, then, is often conflated with fairness, but this all depends on what is meant by equality. Fundamentally, fairness is equality of opportunity, not equality of outcome. Some individuals, therefore, differentiate equality from equity. Equality refers to giving everyone the same opportunities and access to resources, while equity refers to recognizing differences in circumstances and allocating opportunities and resources based on those differences, with the goal of reaching an equal outcome.

9.7 Poverty

Poverty can be detrimental to health. **Poverty** is insufficiency of material goods, monetary wealth, and access to resources. In many less affluent nations, poverty is more widespread. Even though the U.S. is one of the most prosperous nations in the world, poverty still exists within it. Those in poverty have fewer options compared to those with greater financial resources. People in poverty are subject to **social exclusion**, as they are often excluded involuntarily from opportunities available to others.

Poverty can be divided into two categories: absolute poverty and relative poverty. **Absolute poverty** describes the lack of essential resources such as food, shelter, clothing, and hygiene. Every definition of **relative poverty** is different, but it is generally defined as some income above the official poverty line but less than the median income in a given country. Poverty is often a temporary condition. Poverty that persists is called **long-term poverty**.

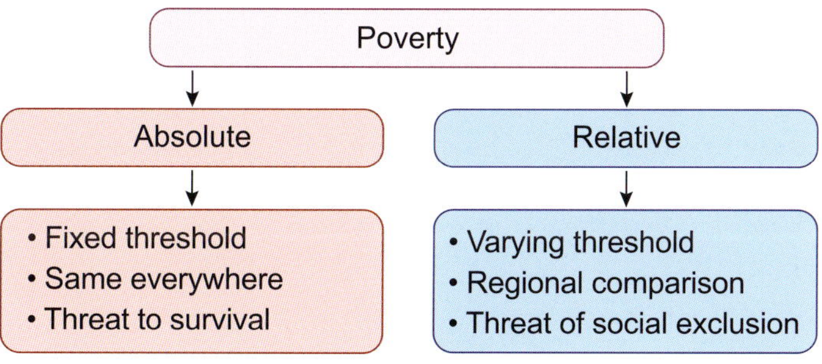

Categories of Poverty

Social theorist **Karl Marx** argued that poverty and class inequality could be remedied through violent political struggle. Marx argued that for this to happen the lower class must first come to understand itself as a class – a group with shared needs and interests. Marx called this collective self-awareness a **class consciousness**. According to Marx, in the absence of this class consciousness, the lower class would be divided by differences and would not act as a class. When the working-class desires material goods or approves of political ideologies and institutions other than communism, Marxists call this **false consciousness**. Marx never used the term—instead, it was introduced by his colleague Freidrich Engels.

9.8 Health and Healthcare Disparities

Health and healthcare disparity refers to differences in health and healthcare that occur between groups of people. Though due in large part to income disparity, these differences can occur according to demographic categories such as age, race, gender, class, and sexual orientation and can affect the prevalence and prognosis of disease.

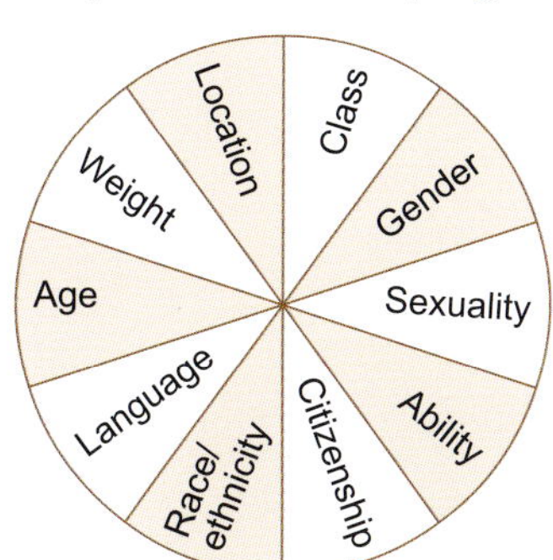

Sources of Healthcare Disparity

In the United States, health disparities between racial groups are well-documented. For example, Black Americans are significantly more likely to die from cancer than White Americans, and at least some of this difference is due to differential access to healthcare between Blacks and Whites.

Much like race, class has a significant impact on health and health care access. The notion that socioeconomic status can influence health is called the **socioeconomic gradient in health**. People with higher socioeconomic status often have better overall health due to a variety of factors, including differences in exposure to environmental hazards, stress, amount of leisure time, quality of diet, and behaviors associated with positive health outcomes.

Social epidemiology considers how social factors affect the health of a population. Health outcomes often correlate with race, class, gender, and age. For example, mortality differs between the sexes. In most countries, women tend to live longer than men. This disparity in lifespan is often attributed to hormones and physiology as well as the prevalence of men's participation in high risk behaviors. In countries where women have lower social status than men or where there is a high incidence of mortality from childbirth, the sex gap in lifespan decreases.

The problem of differences in health between demographic categories is compounded by disparities in quality of healthcare. Those of high socioeconomic status are often able to afford more specialized healthcare than lower socioeconomic status individuals, who are often uninsured or underinsured. These differences have more subtle manifestations as well. In some communities, women are less likely to seek out health treatment because they are not allowed to see male physicians or travel to a clinic on their own.

The individual needs of each patient must be considered in order to provide equitable and sufficient healthcare. When a patient only speaks Spanish and an exam or explanation of results is conducted in English, the patient's understanding will suffer. To improve care, a Spanish-speaking physician or translator is necessary. Healthcare providers with an understanding of gender, class, and racial disparities in health and healthcare and a sensitivity to differences in lifestyle and culture are better able to address health problems and find health solutions that fit individual patients.

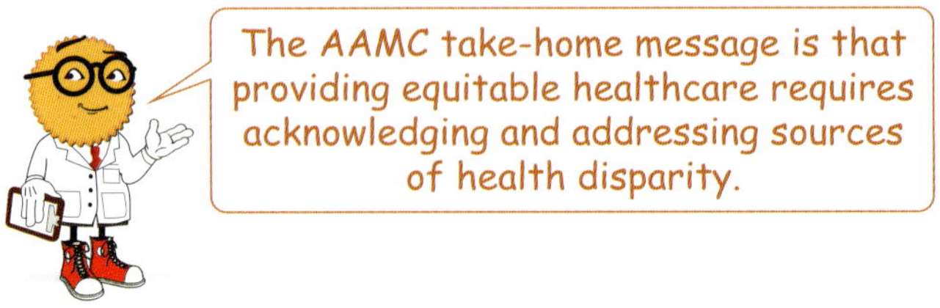

The AAMC take-home message is that providing equitable healthcare requires acknowledging and addressing sources of health disparity.

Disadvantaged social groups have access to fewer resources, resulting in decreased health and wellbeing. Socioeconomic status matters for health.

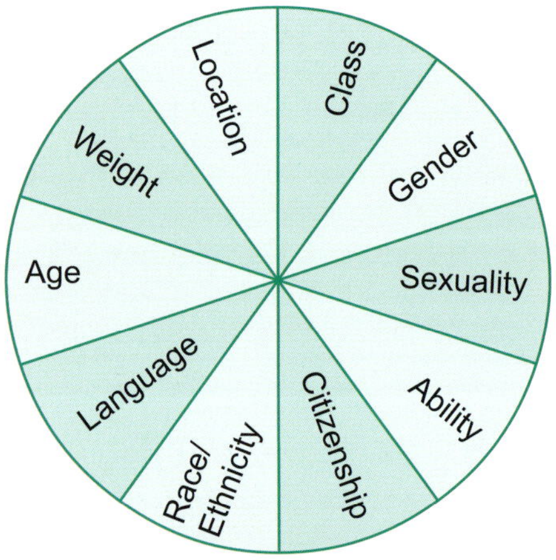

Sources of Healthcare Disparity

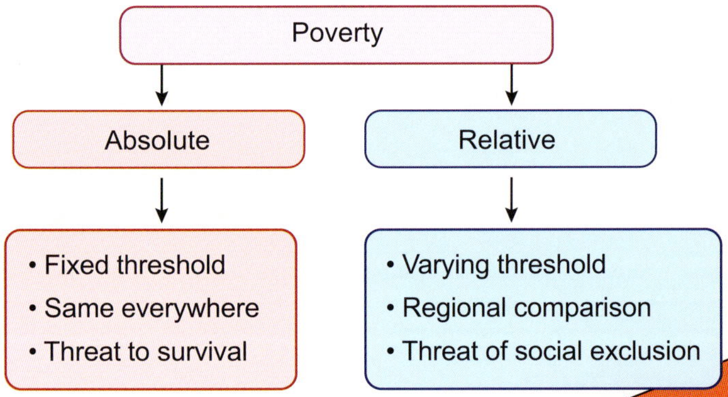

Categories of Poverty

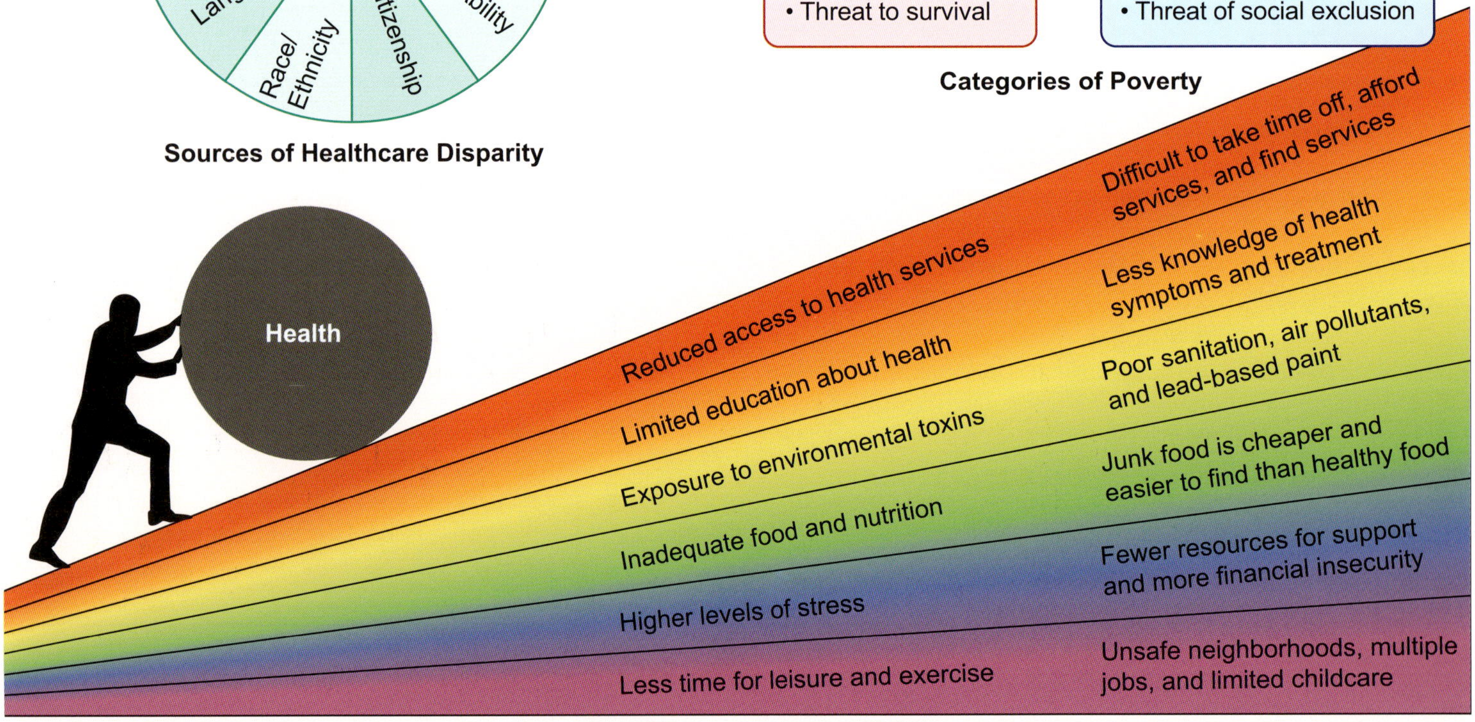

Socioeconomic Gradient in Health

Index

Symbols

A

B

C

D

E

F

G

H

I

J

K

L

M

N

O

P

R

S

T

U

V

W

Y

Z

About the Authors

Michael Muzinich, a medical student from the Midwest, combines his background in science with a passion for language learning, holding degrees in both Biology and Japanese. His academic interests include psychoanalytic theory, behavioral genetics, and psychopharmacology, reflecting a keen interest in the psychological underpinnings of health. An Examkrackers affiliate since 2020, Michael has utilized his diverse knowledge base to both excel in his own studies and to contribute to the learning of others. He sincerely hopes that readers find this book edifying and useful on their paths to becoming physicians.

Ashleigh Louis, PhD, LMFT is a licensed psychologist and marriage and family therapist with over 10,000 hours of applied clinical experience in school-based and private practice settings. Her clinical specialties include anxiety and stress management, attention-deficit/hyperactivity disorder, chronic illness and pain conditions, and relational skills. In addition to clinical work, Ashleigh has taught 13 different undergraduate and graduate psychology courses across over 75 course sections, including biopsychology, psychopharmacology, health psychology, abnormal psychology, and personality psychology. She is also a published research and academic author in the fields of health psychology and behavioral disorders. Ashleigh recently celebrated her one-year anniversary of working with Examkrackers and is excited to continue supporting students in learning behavioral science for the MCAT.